BEAUDUIN

A PROPHET VINDICATED

To

OR   TB

MWC

and

JQ

BEAUDUIN

A PROPHET
VINDICATED

Sonya A. Quitslund

NEWMAN PRESS

NEW YORK   PARAMUS, N.J.   TORONTO

ACKNOWLEDGMENT

Much of the material that appears in Chapter 4 was first published in an article in *The Journal of Ecumenical Studies*, Vol. 8, No. 2 (1971), pp. 255-258. The material in Chapter 13 first appeared in great part in *Nouvelle Revue Théologique* 91 (1969), pp. 1073-1096.

Book and jacket design by Paula Wiener

Library of Congress
Catalog Card Number: 72-86594

ISBN 0-8091-0168-8

Published by Newman Press
Editorial Office: 1865 Broadway, N.Y., N.Y. 10023
Business Office: 400 Sette Drive, Paramus, N.J. 07652

Printed and bound in the
United States of America

Contents

Foreword

In 1958 my Paulist superiors sent me to Europe with a glorious freedom and generous trust to sniff and sift out the gentle breezes of continental Church renewal in wide-ranging pastoral theology and practice. I was surprised to uncover a small common market in which prophetic Christians shared their strengths and weaknesses, well knew each other in person and in writing. By obvious osmosis, each felt in his own special concern the influence of others. Already in those immediate pre-Vatican II years, the biblical and patristic "back-to-the-sources" trend, the liturgical, ecumenical, and missionary movements, social action revitalization, shared responsibility between clergy and laity, monastic rethinking and family life concerns, catechetical updating—all these growing movements were beginning to be evaluated, integrated, orientated. In a positive use of the phrase, the small, happy cloud of the II Vatican, small as a child's hand, was seen in Europe's tired skies.

Over the past decade, the flesh-and-blood instigators of renewal became "in names" on these American shores. But a few precursors are still not known except to a few eye-straining experts. Such a man is Dom Lambert Beauduin, O.S.B. (1873–1960). As liturgist and ecumenist, he never caught the well-paying U.S. lecture circuit. He contributed to specialized French and Belgian journals. His only book found an American publisher, and that was in 1926.

But many of the Vatican II giants from Belgium, France, Germany, Holland, and Italy, were admittedly standing on Beauduin's shoulders. For example, among those who helped shape the ecumenical dimension of the council, Beauduin's name was heard often on the lips of Augustus Bea, Jan Willebrands and Jozef Suenens, Gustave Thils, Charles Moeller, Ives Congar, Emmanuel Lanne, Roger Aubert and C. J. Dumont. Above all, an aging Pope John admitted that already in 1926 it was Beauduin who indicated to him "the way to be followed to foster the unity of the Church." For those who bet on long-shots, a few years before Pius XII had passed away Beauduin openly predicted his successor correctly. Furthermore, during their frequent private evenings together in Paris, when the future pope was nuntio to France, the two of them fantacized about the need and possibility of another ecumenical council. Beauduin died in 1960 with the memories of his Roncalli chats and the happy fulfillment of Pope John on Peter's chair and of the Vatican Council in full-swing preparation.

Beauduin, in Congar's description, was "the personification of Christian realism, nourished on the monastic tradition and the living liturgy." Yet—or consequently!—his life was filled with ecclesial pain. He was manipulated and misunderstood, for a long time exiled from public Church streams. But during those long, harrowing years the Benedictine knew that seeds were confided to the earth and ripening there. This stubborn Belgian had the profound patience of the prophetic sower who knows that "something will spring up." And so it did.

We all are now feeling, in John Tracy Ellis's phrase, the "curse of present-ism." We nostalgically hunger for an understanding of where we bewildered but hope-filled Catholics of the 1970's come from. To help fill in those gaps, we are grateful for Sonya Quitslund's labor of love, her careful research into the life of one of many vindicated prophets.

Thomas F. Stransky, C.S.P.
President, Paulist Fathers

Preface

There have already been two rather different works published about Lambert Beauduin, the great churchman whose ideas so marked Vatican II. Louis Bouyer, who intended his book to be only a first sketch, focused on the personality of the man, picturing him in the midst of numerous friendships. Another work, a condensed fifty-page booklet by Maieul Cappuyns extracted from *La Revue d'Histoire Ecclesiastique* of Louvain, contains biographical details from many documents, but unfortunately is limited by a certain polemic. The wealth of the available material and the richness of Beauduin's life have enabled biographers to bring out something new each time. So it is opportune that the life and thought of this man be known outside the frontiers of Europe, for his stature is bound to increase.

We must therefore be grateful to Sonya Quitslund for having undertaken this new life of Beauduin for American readers. Her contribution is twofold: Not only has she tirelessly sought out and translated documents from private archives, she has also made the first synthesis of Beauduin's theology. And she has not been afraid to present his ideas against the background of his extremely active life—which, because of his originality, lends itself to digressions which tend to reinforce his story and which outlines his qualities with greater clarity. The enormous mass of details gathered by Dr. Quitslund through conversations with those who knew Beauduin make this a valuable collection of facts which otherwise would have been lost to history.

Without a doubt, there is still more to be said. Beauduin was an extraordinarily prolific correspondent; many of his letters have not yet been uncovered. With each discovery we can add new lines to the portrait of the man who marked the life of the Church in so many ways in the first half of the 20th century. The results of his work can be seen particularly in Vatican Council II which he sensed from afar by a prophetic charism, and which fulfilled most of his aspirations, if not all of them. Today the fruits of his efforts can be discerned in nearly every movement which has marked the Church in this century.

The three most important doctrinal advances of Vatican II, at least regarding the inner life of the Church, were in the areas of liturgy, ecumenism, and ecclesiology. Over a period of fifty years, as he slowly matured, Beauduin had anticipated each of these developments. Interestingly enough, he went through the same stages that the Fathers of Vatican II went through in four short years. The Fathers addressed themselves first to liturgical renewal. Then they took up ecumenism, turning away from the classical (or traditional) positions which Catholics have maintained for centuries regarding non-Catholics. The final parallel between the Fathers of the Council and the work of Beauduin can be seen in the definition of the episcopacy, restoring some equilibrium to what Vatican I had left unfinished and unbalanced. Thus Beauduin was one of the great forerunners of Vatican II in its three key areas.

I am sure that in the next ten or fifteen years still more works will appear about this great pioneer. It is no small thing to have contributed so painstakingly to the ultimate synthesis of Beauduin's life and thought.

Olivier Rousseau
Monastery of Chevetogne

Introductory Note

In this era of social involvement, liturgical renewal, and interfaith cooperation, one of the most influential leaders in the Church movements of the first half of the 20th Century remains an unfamiliar figure to much of the American Catholic world. Inspired by the directives of Popes Leo XIII, Pius X, and Pius XI, Lambert Beauduin helped spread the reform movements which swept through the Church in recent years and which received such a signal impetus from Vatican II. Who is this man and what did he do? How relevant are his ideas today? These are some of the questions the following pages will try to answer.

The legend on the cross over his grave best captures the motivating forces in the life of this pioneer and prophet: *Monachus Presbyter Vir Ecclesiae* (Monk, Priest, Man of the Church). Behind these four words lies the story of a life filled with the excitement one expects to find in fiction, but a life that too often reflected the anguish and struggle of a society and a Church to come of age.

Interesting as his life may be, Beauduin's thought constitutes an equally rewarding chapter. Thus this study combines a reflective interpretation of both aspects, the first attempt at such a synthesis. Few people succeed in living their beliefs as fully as Beauduin. His action flowed from deep inner convictions, and it is particularly the prophetic dimension of his life which warrants a wider publicity to his work. He recognized that the problem of disunion had to be faced honestly and humbly, and approached comprehensively. Extremely sensitive to how deeply engrained the spiritual tradition of any given religious community becomes, and the valid and valuable role it played in an individual's personal relationship with his God, Beauduin could not see conversion as the only way or even as a generally acceptable means to union. To uproot an individual spiritually in order to achieve some global conformity was no solution to the religious crisis. For this reason he advocated group reunion—an idea officially countenanced only since Vatican II's *Decree on Ecumenism*, which made it quite clear that conversion is not ecumenism. The price Beauduin was willing to pay rather than dilute this central insight of his life, makes him a truly admirable figure.

Any theological synthesis of his thought is no easy task if one seeks an honest presentation. Most of his writings date from his earlier years and include no major theological work. As he grew older, he became increasingly reticent about expressing himself in print. Although it is possible that censures had dampened his enthusiasm, there is no indication of it. He certainly had become more convinced that a genuine theological contribution had to be the fruit of much contemplation. Talking or thinking about a truth almost invariably gave him new insights, but it was not always easy to capture them and to express them verbally, even in conversation with his close friends.

It is therefore difficult to write about the theological development of a man when some of his richest thought is to be found chiefly in letters to friends and in his unedited notes. The author is totally dependent on what others are willing to share. Already some invaluable collections of letters have been lost; others, because of their confidential nature cannot be used.

To judge Beauduin by his printed words alone, however, would leave the reader with a very incomplete picture. There is rarely room for humor in scholarly journals, nor is there place for human emotions. Interviews with those who knew him and letters to his close friends give rare insights into his inner being. Beauduin was not one to talk about his feelings, but the hints he has left behind suggest a tremendous gentleness, yet a powerful strength and masculinity, in his love. The great happiness a simple sign of friendship or avowal of loyalty gave him remains an eloquent proof of his humanness, and of the fact that, underneath a debonair exterior that laughed in the face of adversity, there was a man very much in need of others. He spoke again and again of the bond that united his friends to him, in love, and that bond was, of course, Christ.

In an age which populates its literature with Christ figures and suffering servants, Beauduin could certainly take his place, and he is no creation of fiction. But the venerable monk would undoubtedly feel extremely ill at ease. In an age which glorifies man but extends a rather shallow comfort to him in his anguish, Beauduin somehow is out of place. Throughout his life he consistently shrank from the limelight. He gloried not in man whose finitude was only too evident to him, but in a God made man. His only goal was eternity *in sinu Patris* (in the bosom of the Father). Such a man, with such a blend of action and contemplation, of humanism and Christian faith, can certainly be relevant in this our age.

If anything of the spirit of this *vir ecclesiae* comes through in the following pages, it is the result of contacts over a six-year period with those who knew Beauduin and graciously shared with me their memories of him, his letters, and even notes taken during his lectures and retreats. While they may not always be in exact agreement over precise details, one fact is indisputable: their obvious veneration of this priest and monk—whether it be one of his own monks, or a nun who listened to words he calmly resumed in a cellar after an air-raid interrupted a conference in the chapel, or a child he prepared for First Communion, or a novice he had spoken to on the eve of his first vows. On each and every one he has left an indelible mark, something that even thirty, forty, or fifty years has not been able to erase.

Those who have helped make this book a reality are too numerous to list. The reader will meet some of them in the pages to follow. But it would be unpardonable to pass over in silence the gracious hospitality of the Monks of Chevetogne whose thoughtful anticipation of my needs and whose willingness to be of service not only created an atmosphere highly conducive to study but greatly facilitated my research. I am particularly indebted to Olivier Rousseau and Thomas Becquet, two of Beauduin's closest and oldest associates, without whose assistance this work would have been impossible. The hours they spent reading and rereading the manuscript in its various stages, searching their personal files and memories for helpful details are beyond calculation. In addition, two "strangers" to Beauduin have immensely strengthened the book by their constructive criticisms for which I am most grateful. Each brought a very valuable expertise to the task: Msgr. Martin W. Christopher, and my editor, Mr. Don Brophy. Nor must the dedication of Miss Debbi Bloom pass unnoticed. She typed the final draft and somehow managed to make the deadline without losing her enthusiasm for Beauduin. Finally, I would like to express my appreciation to the George Washington University whose several grants greatly aided my research and made the publication of this book a possibility.

The Feast of the Resurrection
1972

Chronology

1873   Octave Beauduin born Aug. 5 near Liege.

1897   Ordained April 25. Takes teaching position at Saint-Trond minor seminary.

1899   Joins the *Aumôniers du Travail* (Labor Chaplains).

1900   Assistant pastor at Morlanwelz.

1903   Leo XIII dies. Giuseppe Sarto elected Pius X.

1906   Beauduin leaves Labor Chaplains. Enters Benedictine monastery of Mont César, taking the name of Lambert.

1907   Modernism condemned by Pius X.

1909   Beauduin gives talk on liturgy at the National Congress of Catholic Works in September at Malines. *Liturgical Life* first published at Mont César in November.

1910   First liturgical day held at Mont César. *Liturgical Questions* founded, with Beauduin as editor.

1912   Beauduin's plans for a liturgical institute collapse for lack of support.

1914   Publishes *La Piété de L'Eglise*. War begins. Germans destroy parts of Louvain. Beauduin serves as Mercier's special messenger to Belgian bishops. Pius X dies. Giacomo Della Chiesa elected Benedict XV.

1915   Beauduin in hiding from Germans. Involved in Belgian underground disguised as Oscar Fraipont, a wine merchant. Escapes to England where he meets some leading Anglican ecumenists.

1919 Beauduin named sub prior of Mont César.

1921 Appointed professor of fundamental theology at Sant' Anselmo in Rome. Begins to familiarize himself with Oriental church. Malines Conversations begin in Belgium under the patronage of Mercier.

1922 Benedict XV dies. Achille Ratti elected Pius XI.

1923 Second and third Malines Conversations held.

1924 Pius XI issues *Equidem Verba*, encouraging Benedictines to begin ecumenical monastic foundations.

1925 Beauduin meets Angelo Roncalli in Rome. Foundation of Amay is approved in January. Beauduin visits Ruthenia in the spring. His Proposal read at fourth Malines Conversation in May. Brussels Unity Week held in September. Amay site selected in October. Foundation made in December, with Beauduin as prior.

1926 *Irénikon* is founded. Amay novitiate begins. Fifth and last Malines Conversation is held.

1928 Pius XI issues *Mortalium Animos* censuring ecumenical efforts of the day. Beauduin offers to resign as prior of Amay in July; resignation accepted in December.

1929 Beauduin visits Rome, Eastern Europe, and Middle East.

1930 Visits Greece (Mount Athos) and returns to Amay. Identified by Cardinal van Roey as author of the Malines Proposal. Ordered to leave Amay. Moves to Tancrémount.

1931 Ordered to Rome for trial Jan. 15–30. Returns to Tancrémount. Ordered to Paris in June. Accepts exile in July. Moves to Strasbourg in November.

1932 Named to position in Royal Library in Belgium, but forced to decline. Ordered to En Calcat for two years in March.

1933 Appointment as professor at Institut Catholique in Paris is vetoed by Rome.

1934 Leaves En Calcat in April. Chaplain at Cormeilles-en-Parisis near Paris.

1939 Begins twelve-year stay as chaplain at Chatou. Foundation of Amay moves to Chevetogne. Pius XI dies. Eugenio Pacelli elected Pius XII.

1943 Beauduin collaborates in the founding of the Pastoral and Liturgical Center (CPL).

1945 Renews friendship with Roncalli, the new nuncio to Paris. Involved in pastor-monk project.

1946 Participant in Catholic-Lutheran talks which begin in April, and in Catholic-Orthodox meetings in July.

1951   Returns from exile to Chevetogne.

1955   Writes prophetic view of the Church.

1957   Announces Roncalli will be the next pope. Predicts announcement of a council. In Venice, Roncalli acknowledges his ecumenical debt to Beauduin.

1958   Pius XII dies. Roncalli elected pope.

1959   Vatican II announced. 50th anniversary of the Belgian Liturgical Movement.

1960   Beauduin dies Jan. 11.

1

First Years as a Priest

The staggering developments and rapid transitions that have marked the twentieth century are mirrored in the activities of Lambert Beauduin as liturgist, theologian and ecumenist. Paradoxically his ecclesiastical censure in 1932 which appeared to signal the tragic end of a brilliant career simply provided him with yet another opportunity to serve the Church. We can begin to appreciate the significance of the man and his contributions only when we realize the drama that went on behind the scenes, marked as it was with the maneuvers and intrigues so frequently associated with the human element of the Church. Beauduin's life represents a particularly appropriate commentary on the true nature of Christian and priestly life, especially for those concerned about the widespread unrest within the Church today.

Beauduin understood his priesthood as a consecration to the service of others for the unique purpose of bringing Christ to them. In retrospect, his striking accomplishments are best viewed in the light of his growing appreciation of the meaning of the priestly ministry which expanded with each new experience. Initially convinced that he had something to give to people (social apostolate), he soon discovered that he had something to share (liturgy). The recognition that others had something to give to him (ecumenism) represented the culmination of his world-oriented spiritual evolution. Only through a truly ecumenical love does one begin to be Christian: without a doubt this is the fundamental insight of his life, and as Cardinal Suenens remarked, it is "his heresy." [1] His subsequent experiences deepened these insights into a harmonious and unified spirituality.

In an age seeking to know itself, an age filled with identity crises in every sector, Beauduin's life is a fitting example of one who sought self-knowledge and found it in other people. Through the eyes of others he was able to view not only himself with great objectivity, but all that he held most dear in his ecclesially-oriented life. It is perhaps for this reason that so much of what he taught has since been vindicated by history—thus giving him a truly prophetic stature today.

Early Life in Belgium

Primarily a family of landed proprietors, the Beauduins had been established in the Hesbaye region near Liège in Belgium since the sixteenth century. They were known for their liberal spirit and political activity, and also for their profoundly Christian principles, an increasingly rare combination in a country where by 1879 liberals in the government had succeeded in dropping religion in the primary schools and passing other laws contrary to the spirit of the Church. By the late nineteenth century, only Jean-Joseph Beauduin, the chief magistrate of Rosoux-lès-Waremme, remained on the family estate. His brothers had left the land to launch at Tirlemont a particularly successful sugar refinery which soon had outlets in Italy, Romania and Bulgaria. It was to play an unusual role during World War I in the life of one of their future nephews.

Although Jean-Joseph Beauduin was a gentle man, deeply attached to Church and family traditions, he was no conformist. His outspokenness in matters of principle, particularly his opposition to clerical involvement in politics, brought him into conflict with his pastor. Such differences, however, did not interfere with his strong loyalty to the Church or his being first in the pews along with his children to assist at Mass. His wife Lucie Lavigne's inexhaustible reserve of sympathy, gentleness, and patience provided a needed balance for the quasi-militant influence of her husband.[2] Together they tried their best to instill Christian virtues in their seven sons and one daughter, and to pass on the heritage of their faith.

On August 5, 1873 they welcomed their fifth child and fourth son, Octave. His early life was disappointingly ordinary. He exhibited the normal round of activities and boyish pranks one might expect from the middle child. While no one event has been remembered or cited as instrumental in his decision to be a priest, the healthy piety of the home may well have influenced his vocation. Every evening his father assembled the family, including the domestics, for the recitation of the rosary. The boys themselves often indulged in an activity common enough among Catholic children—playacting the Mass. The musician of the group would install himself on the top of a wardrobe in the playroom, which represented the choir loft and organ. From this prominence he sang at the top of his voice the alleluias and hymns, providing instrumental interludes of trumpets and other instruments. As for Octave (later known as Lambert), he used to climb up on a trunk for his pulpit and improvise, imitating the pastor's homiletic style.[3]

A strong physical resemblance existed among the boys which stayed with them into adult life and which they in turn passed on to their sons. They were of average height, stocky and broad-shouldered, but an extraordinary laughter was perhaps their most characteristic feature. Once heard, its unforgettable combination of sounds could be recognized in an instant as the laughter of a Beauduin.

A scarcity of details veils Beauduin's school days, for he was never one to confide in others. His decision to enter the minor seminary of Saint-Trond seems to have been accepted without question. While reminiscences of several classmates from the seminary have been preserved, there was apparently nothing in the intelligent and hardworking student to suggest his future greatness.[4] Only one departure from the norm is recalled. Instead of going immediately to the major seminary at Liège after the completion of his studies at Saint-Trond, Beauduin interrupted his career with a very brief exposure to monasticism. The smell of cheese, however, in the Trappist monastery proved unbearable.[5] The letters during his last years at the seminary give no sign of anything extraordinary. Beauduin appeared to be the typical seminarian with typical reactions: attuned to the new social questions of his day, ready to voice his opinions on his professors, an imagination easily fired with rumors of some seminary intrigue.[6]

Ordained on April 25, 1897, his first years as a priest were equally uneventful. He returned to Saint-Trond where he supervised the students and taught, but there is no record of what he taught. A photo from the period shows him with curly hair, which he quickly lost. By 1906 he was partially bald.

His father died while Beauduin was still a young man, but his influence was unmistakably present in the young priest's attachment to tradition and to a vigorous freedom of action.[7] Piety and politics in one form or another would be essential ingredients in his diet for the rest of his life. He thrived on the challenge of risk and adventure, often enough offering his spirit of detachment and love of fantasy as his only defenses.

Although his work often kept him far from his family in the years ahead, he preserved a strong attachment for it and for his numerous nephews and nieces. For his mother, however, he reserved a very special affection. Her death in 1927 was a hard blow to a man who carefully hid his deepest emotions from others. She incarnated for him a host of precious memories from a very happy past of shared family joys.[8] While she yet lived, he delighted in his visits home amusing his nieces and nephews no end by his imaginative pranks and love of fun.

On certain holidays his mother used to make large quantities of waffles and exquisite tarts, placing them in a corner nook protected by a locked iron grill. Beauduin arrived on such an occasion and contemplated the delicacies with the coveteousness typical of the younger generation. Then with a sudden stroke of genius, he took a broom handle and firmly attached a fork on its end. One by one he carefully extracted the pastries through the grill for his greedy accomplices. For days his mother puzzled about the mysterious disappearance of her treats.[9]

First Major Apostolate

Leo XIII's encyclical *Rerum Novarum* (1891) appeared about the time Beauduin entered the seminary. The local ordinary, Bishop Victor Doutreloux, gave it a warm and decisive welcome in his pastoral letter of February 14, 1894. The ideas of the pontiff and bishop were new and disturbing to some people. For others they appeared to be an official blessing and recognition of a work by then well underway. Under Doutreloux's initiative, Liège had sponsored congresses on social issues in 1887, 1888, and 1890 which attracted international interest and participation. The moving force behind these congresses was Canon Antoine Pottier who had founded a school of Christian Democrats at Liège.[10] His defense of the rights of workers in 1890 and his insistence that social Catholicism must emancipate itself from paternalism were principles reiterated by *Rerum Novarum*. Opponents of these ideas, however, failed to appreciate his enthusiastic endorsement of the papal document. They claimed that its demands were idealistic and not intended for Belgium. Should this program of social reform be followed, they warned, it would undoubtedly ruin industry and the country as well.[11]

Conservative reactions highly critical of innovations such as labor unions soon surfaced, and the progressive ideas of Louvain and the Christian Democrats were denounced by many as revolutionary. However the primary concern of these social pioneers was to combat the dechristianization of workers, already widespread in the Flemish and Walloon industrial areas, by giving them a mature awareness of their responsibilities and of their needs.[12] For this reason Canon Pottier could not help but praise the bishop's letter, since it augured well for a proposed experiment, the *Congrégation des Aumôniers du Travail* (Labor Chaplains).[13] The idea for such a group dedicated to propagating the faith among workers had been first suggested by an industrialist at the congress of 1887.

This fraternity of priests, conceived late in 1894 and officially begun on March 25, 1895, offered an apostolate based on direct contact between priest and worker. Tastefully furnished hostels for workers temporarily separated from their families provided not only the luxury of one bed per man, but even nutritious meals served by uniformed waiters. Here the priests shared meals with the workers and entered into their conversations and games. In a Christian ambiance, the chaplains hoped that these men would learn to live and to think in a Christian way. Apparently the atmosphere was highly conducive to this end, for within a short time the men began to rediscover their self-respect. External signs appeared first as profanity decreased, cleanliness increased, and habits of dress improved.

No spiritual strings were attached to living in the hostel, but once
the external change occurred, an interior transformation soon followed. While most hostels could only accommodate two or three
hundred at most, the recreation room often served up to one thousand men a day who dropped in for a snack, a game of cards or just
to talk. In addition to looking after the hostel, the chaplains also
familiarized themselves with the jobs, needs and problems of the
workers. It was a very demanding mission that eventually would
suffer from a too rapid expansion and insufficient financial security,
as well as from a number of projects that went bankrupt.

The legacy of a compassionate nature and a sensitivity to the
abuse of men's rights made Beauduin a particularly apt pupil for
the ideas of Canon Pottier who had been his professor of moral
theology. It was no great surprise then that in 1899 Beauduin presented himself as a candidate for the Labor Chaplains, just two years
after his ordination. Unimpressed by the ferment among the intellectuals of the day, soon to be condemned as Modernism (1907),
Beauduin felt an increasing desire to minister to the needs of the
people, particularly the dechristianized masses of the working class.

By 1899 the movement was well established, boasting a total of
eight houses in four dioceses.[14] Within a few months Beauduin
demonstrated his own energy and ability. On his initiative a whole
complex of buildings was constructed at Montegnée, near Seraing
(the cradle of the group), to provide housing for workers. This
complex still exists.[15] While further details about specific activities
are lacking, one can safely assume that he spent his seven years as a
chaplain totally committed to the needs of the workers, counseling
and consoling, teaching and preaching, and in every way showing
that delicacy toward human needs, however small, which so marked
him later on. But undoubtedly he very soon began to experience the
malaise running through the community. Of its twenty-three members in 1901, thirteen eventually left, a rather high mortality rate.
This crisis would last from 1901–1912. By 1906, the year Beauduin
left the community, the Labor Chaplains had lost the support of most
of their patrons through financial losses and political stands. At first
they had vacillated between the two major political parties, and then,
under urging from on high, threw their support to the very party
rejected by the workers, losing, for a time at least, even the confidence of the workers.[16]

These troubled years were not without their value in the formation of Beauduin and in the change of direction he would soon give his life. Documentation is all but non-existent, yet certain clues can be gleaned from Pire's *History of the Labor Chaplains.*

By 1900 many parishes began their own social action programs. The ensuing competition for volunteers hurt the chaplains, since the loss of free labor made the cost of their programs increasingly expensive at a time when they could ill afford it.

In 1900 Beauduin was appointed as assistant pastor at Morlanwelz, a position he held for one year. Perhaps this was the beginning of his disillusionment. In 1896, the pastor had invited the chaplains to set up a center in his parish and to create a number of money-making schemes such as bakeries and cooperatives to support the hostels. Unfortunately, although he "gave" the property to the chaplains, he insisted on administering the project.[17] Beauduin's short stay may have been due to the difficulty of the situation. This experience seems to have marked a turning point for him.

At this very period—February 1901, to be precise—Beauduin had his first contact with a future disciple, Olivier Rousseau, then just three years old. Rousseau's father, an extremely active figure in social reform and founder of the first Labor Office in Belgium (at Mons), had died suddenly, leaving a young widow and four young children. Beauduin went to the funeral to express his sympathy personally. Years later he recounted the scene to Rousseau.

Beauduin's industry and earnestness continued to impress his superiors. In the summer of the same year he was appointed secretary of the council during the community's first general chapter. The following year he was chosen to report on its activities during a congress in Liège. The tenor of his paper clearly reveals that by 1902 he had backed off from a career of sheer social activism in favor of a more evangelical ministry. Voicing his concern about the true nature of a priestly vocation, he said: "One is a priest to give the truth and divine grace to people through the liturgical rites, preaching, the celebration of feasts, and retreats." [18]

Although he agreed that no opportunity should be neglected to bring people in contact with Christ, he later would be highly critical of the subsequent priest worker movement in France because it also failed to promote the liturgical dimension of the priest. Having stated forthrightly that the priest belonged to no class, he insisted that such a man be exclusively dedicated to the ministry of God. Hence the priestly role in social issues is less to excite the worker than to preach to the employer.[19] He found it incredible that some people offered theological arguments in favor of a priest putting aside priestly duties to engage in purely human tasks. He reacted strongly against such proposals. While not denying the fact that a priest can and must encourage lay efforts for the Christianization of everything human, Beauduin nevertheless maintained that it must be done primarily by announcing Christ and by taking him to man.[20]

Other circumstances further threatened the continued existence of the chaplains. With the deaths of Doutreloux (1901) and Leo XIII (1903), those who had perhaps restrained their criticism of the chaplains now voiced their dissatisfaction in increasingly strident tones. They were unwilling to accept the chaplains as a legitimate form of Catholic social action. As a direct consequence, Canon Pottier's influence declined.[21] This was not surprising since Leo himself, alarmed by some of the abusive interpretations of *Rerum Novarum*, had deliberately chosen Martin Rutten as Doutreloux's successor.[22] The new bishop of Liège did not share Pottier's views, and he supported an increasingly radical reaction against the worker movement. Even before episcopal directives forced the Labor Chaplains to abandon their original activities, however, a member at the closing session of the second general chapter suggested that they relinquish their large undertakings and concentrate on hidden, modest works of organization and religious propaganda.[23]

From being a priestly ministry to the needs of the worker, many of them migrants, the congregation was soon transformed into a professional, technical, teaching group. By 1907 they had been effectively removed from any direct contact with the workers. The various worker enterprises they had encouraged were put into the hands of a committee of Catholic employers.[24]

Beauduin, convinced that his vocation as priest was not in economic involvement or in professional teaching of a technical sort, but rather in preaching, felt there was no viable alternative left within the congregation. He therefore resigned in 1906 and for a time remained undecided as to his next step. Of one thing he was certain—that Christ should be known and loved for himself and not for what he could do for people. But the words of St. Paul rang like a challenge to him: "Woe to me if I do not preach." Only one problem remained:

how was he to prepare, to come by the necessary interior, spiritual and doctrinal growth necessary in order to bear immediate and direct witness to the Word? His first thought was of the Dominicans, the Order of Preachers, but a professor at Louvain whose opinion Beauduin valued highly opposed the idea, quite possibly because he feared their political and social conservatism would be incompatible with the liberal Beauduin spirit.

Shortly after his arrival at Louvain in 1904, Canon Jacques Laminne [25] discovered the relatively new Benedictine monastery of Mont César, founded in 1899 by Robert de Kerchove (1846–1942) and some other monks from Maredsous. The Benedictine sense of the tradition of the Church and taste for solid theological study impressed him immediately. Knowing Beauduin as he did, Canon Laminne felt that this was the ideal place for him. One thing was certain: in his present state of mind Beauduin did not want to have anything to do with social action, and the Benedictines were unsullied by such works. Thus, on July 1, 1906, Beauduin entered Mont César, and in the fall of that year, at the age of thirty-three, became a Benedictine novice. On October 5 of the following year he made his monastic profession as Dom Lambert. Lambert was the patron saint of Liège, the diocese of his ordination.

Mont César

Entering the monastery as a formed priest with experience and ideas of his own, Beauduin could hardly be described as an average postulant. His outspoken, even critical attitude of the lack of some of his favorite pious practices did not go unnoticed. He was shocked that First Fridays were not solemnized, and that exposition of the Blessed Sacrament, nocturnal adoration and Benediction were almost unheard-of devotions. His frank concern failed to arouse any active response. It was not long, however, before the Benedictine spirit of docility (the willingness to learn from those more experienced in monastic life) and the influence of the prior, Columba Marmion (1858–1923), brought about a radical change of direction in the new postulant's spirituality. Marmion, an Irish priest who entered Maredsous in 1886, stands as one of the great contemplatives and spiritual directors of modern times. His works have been translated into many languages and remain spiritual classics for their solid doctrinal and scriptural inspiration.[26] The fact that Beauduin and Marmion lived in the same monastery and had so much in common spiritually and liturgically has led to much speculation about the relationship. Some have tried to attribute Beauduin's monastic and liturgical vocations to the Irish monk.[27] There is no denying that Marmion's theology and personality exerted a strong influence on him—so much so that many have expressed regrets that Beauduin did not pay him greater tribute than evidenced in his rather terse description of the man: he was more a theologian than a liturgist, but a complete theologian captivated by the Christian cult.[28]

On one point there was total agreement between the two—their deep love for the Divine Office. In fact this turned into a kind of unconscious rivalry, since Marmion had always been first in choir for Matins until Beauduin arrived.[29] But this enthusiasm is traceable to several sources, including his reading of Guéranger on liturgical prayer and the lectures by the master of novices (B. Destrée) on the chapters of the rule consecrated to the chanting of the Office. The psalms, prayer itself—everything was seen from a new perspective. Nor was this a passing attraction for Beauduin; it formed an integral part of his spirituality for the rest of his life. Even in his last years he would awaken his nurse in the middle of the night to see if it was time to get ready for his confrères to carry him to the chapel.

The radical transformation of Beauduin's spirituality did not occur overnight. It was more than a year aborning. The monastic routine gradually weaned him from his dependence on the piety of his youth, but his insight into the beauty of a liturgically-oriented spirituality hit him like a thunderbolt and eventually ignited the Belgian liturgical movement. The impact of this discovery is best related by Beauduin himself, describing what had been his spiritual outlook prior to coming to Mont César.

I am going to explain first what the Mass should be for the priest and the Christian; I will then tell what it was for me. . . . You'll excuse my frankness: but the missal was for me a closed and sealed book. And this ignorance extended not only to the variable parts . . . but even to the unchanging parts and principally to the canon. . . . Even the great and perfect acts of worship, the principal end of the Mass, of participation in the sacrifice by partaking of the victim, of the union with one's brothers in communion with the body of the lord, the spiritual offering of our good acts . . . in short, none of the great realities that the eucharistic liturgy constantly puts into act, not one dominated my eucharistic piety. . . . Visits to the Blessed Sacrament had a more vital role in my piety than the act of sacrifice itself.

What is true of the missal is also true of the breviary and of the liturgical cycle. I have no memory of having recited my breviary with understanding and love; the psalms, the readings, the prayers were without resonance in my soul. The liturgical acts properly speaking were for me a formality of worship that had no appreciable influence on the direction of my piety. The same is true of the yearly retreats: meditation, examen, recollection alone mattered—a whole spirituality on the border of the liturgy and separated by an air-tight partition.[30]

Such a frank admission of the meaninglessness, indeed the emptiness, of those moments of each day when he performed his priestly functions may be due to overstatement, but they cannot be without basis in fact. In the same article he went into the reasons behind this void which can be ultimately reduced to one: nothing in his spirituality was liturgically-oriented. Since his mind had not been initiated into an understanding and appreciation of the liturgy, it is no wonder that, even as a priest and with all his priestly formation, he failed to draw nourishment from the liturgical prayer of the Church.

. . . I have kept two memories of meditation and spiritual reading from this period:

(1) Never did I make them in liturgical books; my library contained neither missal, nor ritual, nor pontifical, nor ceremonial of bishops, nor martyrologies, nor commentaries on these; all these books in which circulates the traditional interior life of the Church were for me obscure books. Never had I meditated on the psalms, the pontifical of ordination, etc. Moreover, four historical lectures on this last subject by Msgr. Battifol made me understand the priestly dignity better than many pious retreat sermons.

(2) No methodical and continued plan for meditation; the quite subjective plan of the author of the manual regulated the entire continuity of my daily meditations. A caprice, a best seller, an unexpected circumstance brought about a change of book and put me on a completely new diet; the spirit of continuity was infallibly lacking.

And while I gamboled thus by every path, I was totally unaware of
the annual path of spiritual renewal traced by the Church with an
infinite solicitude in her liturgical cycle.

. . . I hardly discerned between new practices and old sacramentals,
blessings of the Church, ancient devotions in harmony with the liturgical seasons. Lent instituted by the Church as a time of penance
and retreat, ember days, vigils of great feasts, the place of fasting in
Christian asceticism, the joys of the paschal season, the celebration
of the great octaves of the cycle, all of that had no part in my life.[31]

As his understanding and love of monasticism increased, Beauduin
was inevitably drawn to the sources of Christian spirituality, the
heritage of centuries of Christian life and worship preserved in the
official documents of the Church: Scripture, liturgical books, writings
of the Fathers, conciliar documents. But above all, the liturgy as
"the primary and indispensable source of the Christian spirit" [32] was
to be at the heart of his spirituality.

Of these four sources one could wish that he had made greater
use of Scripture. In 1897 all limitations on having and reading approved translations of the Bible had been set aside, and a Biblical
Commission was formed in 1902 by Leo XIII to foster biblical
studies. Yet the climate of the period created by the rationalists and
the Modernist crisis soon brought all scholarly work in Catholic
circles under strict supervision.[33] While Beauduin's writings are rich
in biblical citations, they reflect little of contemporary exegetical
insights. Prudence and the ecclesiastical censor dictated great caution
in this area. Nevertheless, he read and meditated on Scripture daily
until his death, and he even recommended making this practice the
matter of a vow for priests. His appreciation of these sources is
further reflected in the library of Chevetogne, the monastery he
later founded. Because no expense was spared to get the very best,
it possesses irreplaceable treasures in liturgy, patrology and conciliar
documents, as well as various commentaries on Scripture.

Immediately following his monastic profession, Beauduin was assigned to teach De Ecclesia, the standard course on the Church. But
he was totally unprepared for such a task. It would have been logical
to turn to some accepted treatise or manual, but the textbooks of the
day left much to be desired, as did the whole area of ecclesiology.
On the urging of his good friend Canon Laminne to go back to the

sources, Beauduin developed his course around the teachings of the Fathers and the councils, especially Vatican I which had prepared a schema on the Church.[34] The course focused on the idea of the Church as the mystical body of Christ and Christ as the head of this body.[35] This decision ultimately led to a lifelong "campaign" for the resumption of Vatican I so that the nature of the Church could be defined. The sources disclosed much of interest, including the historically-conditioned nature of supposedly sacrosanct structures. The ideas that Beauduin would soon advocate may be seen as a remote preparation for the definition of collegiality, the office of the bishop, and the role of the layman in the Church.

Beauduin's research into the nature of the Church inevitably led to some critical reflections on monasticism itself and an intensive investigation of its origins. His discoveries soon justified the misgivings he was beginning to experience with the Beuronic version of monastic life at Mont César. It combined both romantic and militaristic features foreign to the primitive rule which impinged upon its original spirit of freedom and moderation. The spiritual creativity encouraged by St. Benedict had by and large been forgotten. Instead, a potentially suffocating atmosphere, tainted with an overly large legalistic mentality and rigid fidelity to the past threatened the very vitality of the institution. Perhaps part of the problem stemmed from the fact that their constitutions contained principles found in those that Guéranger had made for the nuns of St. Cecile of Solesmes.

Monasticism

To appreciate Beauduin's eventual contribution to monasticism and his frank criticism of it in his early years as a monk, some consideration must be taken of Benedictine life at the turn of the century. Mont César was an outgrowth of nineteenth-century romanticism and the monastic liturgical renewal inaugurated by Prosper Guéranger (died 1875) who founded the French congregation of Solesmes in 1833. But Mont César did not owe its immediate origin to Solesmes.[36] At the urgings of Princess Catherine of Hohenzollern, Maur and Placide Wolter refounded Beuron. Captivated during a prolonged stay at Solesmes by its spirit and liturgy, they brought Guéranger's interpretation of Benedictine spirituality to their monastery in 1863. Mont César would be an outgrowth of Beuron.

Guéranger had a valid, yet limited view of monasticism influenced by romanticism and its love for the medieval period, a fascination with the gothic and the sages. The chief fault of this approach lay in the decision to base renewal on restoring the splendor of the ancient edifices—the very state in which monasticism had died, suffocated in its own wealth. Guéranger and his followers overlooked the primitive emphasis on work and poverty, the creative element that had originally produced monasticism.[37] This failure to give the evangelical dimension its rightful primacy was at the heart of Beauduin's critique.

Monasticism as lived at Solesmes with all its historical weaknesses was not improved by the German transplantation. To its romantic aspects were added the influences of the young Tuebingen school and a military-like rigidity which did not always favor growth and development. This valid yet limited and historically-conditioned monastic spirit came to Maredsous in 1872. There it flourished so well that in 1899 Robert de Kerchove with several other monks went to Louvain where they began the monastery of Mont César.[38]

In spite of its good points, "Beuronism" was somehow deficient. It too lacked the flexibility of the primitive rule. It had never quite reached the original sources, and what had been uncovered had atrophied into a formalistic and legalistic version of the past. The saintly Abbot de Kerchove stressed silence, dedication to worship, segregation from the world, penance, poverty, obedience, etc. Although he had a profound appreciation of the true value of monastic life, he tended to insist too much on external observances, such as keeping one's hands under the scapular, wearing the capuchon, withdrawing into corners to speak, and punctilious rubricism, not to mention the cult of the abbot! In their discovery of older traditions, the monks had failed to go beyond to the underlying principles, apparently confusing exact observance of externals with fidelity to the past.

Beauduin saw through all the superficialities. He began to dream of a revitalized monasticism which would incorporate the crucial qualities of fidelity to the past as well as to the present in order to be faithful to the future, to the dynamism of the Church. He already had found a willing collaborator and property for a proposed monastery when war broke out in 1914.[39] His contacts with English monasteries during the war would only strengthen his conviction

FIRST YEARS AS A PRIEST

that a more humanizing form of life was not only possible but imperative. So it was that once again his sensitivity to the human dimension, his social awareness, began to reassert itself, both in terms of the monks themselves and in terms of the broader Christian community beyond the confines of the cloister. Monasticism could not be conceived of as an escape from responsibility to and for the total Church. As Rousseau later observed:

> It was with difficulty that Beauduin saw the life of a monk of the twentieth century other than somehow engaged in dialogue. The world today was—he knew it better than anyone else—too deprived of spiritual resources for anyone to give up all contact with it when he is in the service of God. If to others, entering the monastery before any experience and in the ardor of their initial donation and renunciation of the world, the monastic ideal revealed itself differently, for him the awareness of belonging to the Church and to his age made him seek a combination of his love of the cloister with his apostolic zeal, for he felt that in a dechristianized world, the influence [of the monastery] must make itself felt, starting with prayer more than just with a simple presence.[40]

Rather than openly rebel against the institution, Beauduin simply spoke his mind, yet paradoxically remained an outstanding example of monastic regularity and fidelity, excelling in docility and obedience. Still, he suffered from the romantic tinges, the decorum imposed by custom. The practice of exemption and the episcopal insignias and pomp surrounding the abbot falsified the intended sense of spiritual paternity and conferred a quasi-sacramental infallibility on the abbot which, to Beauduin's mind, was a theological error apt to induce a false mystique of obedience. These things, some of them minor in themselves, hindered human relations and affected the sincerity in superior-subject relationships which consequently kept human qualities from developing in a truly family atmosphere.[41] The remedy he would propose, at first discreetly, then openly and constantly, inevitably compromised him with some of his religious superiors. He insisted that the dependence of monastic authority on episcopal authority be recognized and that every monk be engaged in the direct service of the Church, according to each one's capacity.

Religious realism and proper respect of human dignity mattered much more to him than outmoded customs. Because the basic rights conferred and confirmed by baptism were common to superior and subject alike, he never hesitated to challenge pointless traditions when appropriate. He received a measure of toleration, for his previous involvement with the Labor Chaplains had somehow set him apart from the rest of the community. Certain members of the community, however, felt his horizons too broad and therefore dangerous. Still his regularity was irreproachable, and most agreed that it would just be a question of time before he would outgrow his "social" mania. But the condition only worsened.

In less than two years, he would put into effect the first of a series of revolutionary ideas. Some of the monks had perhaps become convinced; others may have been just a little tired of hearing the old refrain of Beauduin's:

What a shame that the liturgy remains the endowment of an elite; we are aristocrats of the liturgy; everyone should be able to nourish himself from it, even the simplest people: we must democratize the liturgy.[42]

Beauduin's initial insight that monasticism would have its true impact on a dechristianized world through the prayer of the liturgy was soon followed by another. One day during the community Mass he suddenly realized that it is in the eucharistic celebration that the Church takes flesh. His former students still recall the "explosion" that occurred in the class immediately following as Beauduin rushed in and announced with great gusto: "I've just realized that the liturgy is the center of the piety of the Church!" This principle enunciated with such clarity was the result of the slow maturation of previous ideas such as the democratization of the liturgy. But what had once been one idea among many now became the central preoccupation of his life. The liturgy was no longer just a beautiful expression of piety, so beautiful that its treasures should be opened up to the faithful; it was *the piety of the Church*,[43] the very dynamo of ecclesial vitality. The opportune moment to solicit support for popularizing these notions soon arrived, and out of the liturgical movement that resulted Beauduin drew some of his finest insights into Christian spirituality.

2

The Belgian
Liturgical Movement

Today Catholics find it as hard to feel completely at home with a description of popular piety at the turn of the century as with an album of nineteenth-century relatives. It is difficult to bridge the gap. The majority of modern Catholics have been raised in a Mass-centered spirituality, and while their elders may miss the "old time religion," one wonders how many would really be content with just the "old time religion" of their fathers.

Most are aware, no doubt, that Pius X promoted frequent and even daily communion. But few realize that his famous decree of 1905 failed to stress that communion is an integral part of the liturgy. Part of Beauduin's liturgical campaign would be to make communion the high point of the Mass—a battle effectively won only in recent times. Prior to 1905 and actually since medieval days, yearly communion was not only customary, it was seen as the norm, although a movement for frequent communion gained attention in Belgium, France, and, to a lesser degree, Bohemia in the thirteenth and fourteenth centuries. Christmas, Easter and Pentecost had become so firmly established as suitable times for reception of the sacrament that in many places, unless there were nuns in the congregation, no provision for regular distribution existed for the rest of the year. Even religious were lucky if allowed to receive two or three times a week. To seek greater frequency was more likely interpreted as a sign of pride than as sincere devotion.

Popular eucharistic piety had to seek its outlet elsewhere and found it in adoration of the consecrated host. A devout gaze at the moment of elevation, time spent during exposition of the Blessed Sacrament or attendance at Benediction of the Blessed Sacrament compensated for the inaccessibility of the eucharistic Lord. These were cherished moments of spiritual communion. Even in monasteries, more pomp and solemnity surrounded Benediction than the community Mass. When their Lord was hidden within the tabernacle, the pious could then multiply their visits to the "divine prisoner of love" and even spend whole hours or nights in worshipful silence.

Participation in the Mass on the whole was non-existent. It was a clerical performance to be observed by the laity. The content of the liturgy was so little esteemed as appropriate spiritual food for the laity that as late as 1900 translations of the Roman missal were still officially forbidden, although some had been made with at least local approval in the nineteenth century, such as those by Guéranger and Gerard van Caloen (1853–1932), a monk of Maredsous.[1] Women were even more excluded than men from "active participation." They could not sing in parish choirs, and their only sense of sharing meaningfully in the worship came from contributing men and boys to the service of God, plus perhaps some of their lace work or their services cleaning the sanctuary and decorating the altars.

But Catholics at the turn of the century were a pious, if sometimes superstitious, lot. Their lives were filled with a host of devotions to name days and baptismal saints, to Mary, to the holy angels, to various physical aspects of Christ—his sacred heart, five wounds, precious blood—and to the Infant of Prague. They did what they could to fill the void created by an a-liturgical liturgy. They dutifully assisted at Vespers (if it had not been abandoned by the clergy in favor of Benediction), processions, missions, days of recollection, and seasonal devotions such as the Way of the Cross; they prayed their rosaries, lit candles, made novenas, and snatched at each passing spiritual fad in their hunger for spiritual riches.

The laity were not alone in this quest. Many of the clergy saw the liturgy more as a performance than a prayer. If they too sought their nourishment elsewhere, it is no wonder that the laity remained ignorant of the treasures contained in the liturgy. There were, however, some perceptive spirits abroad, even among the laity.

Godefroid Kurth, a noted historian, spoke at the International Eucharistic Congress held in Brussels in 1898 on behalf of the liturgy:

> Open up [to the faithful] by teaching them the sense of the liturgical ceremonies in which they must not assist as simple spectators, and the people who have unlearned the way of the Church will return to it, drawn by its natural attraction; worship will be for them what it was for our ancestors: the source of all their emotions and joys.[2]

Again in 1902 at the Eucharistic Congress of Namur he reiterated his pleas, but those concerned with the loss of faith in Belgium were more prone to point the accusing finger at materialism or rationalism. The Church, and therefore all her practices and customs, was of divine origin and hence could not be reformed, or so thought these loyal sons of Trent.

The year 1905 brought radical eucharistic changes, but in their wake new abuses crept in, particularly in boarding schools with their inflexible schedules. Pious practices such as morning prayers written by the foundress and thanksgiving after Mass had to be maintained at any cost. Since daily communion was to be encouraged, a solution was found that left "traditions" untouched. As soon as prayers were over, the Mass began, and several priests immediately started to distribute communion to the assembled students. Thus were morning prayers and thanksgiving after Mass preserved intact; classes began on schedule and the pope was obeyed. Some dioceses actually forbade the distribution of communion during Mass because priests objected to the disruption of their recollection. In such cases, the laity could then receive either before or after Mass.

The goal and fundamental theme of the Belgian liturgical movement in 1909 was to restore Christian spirituality, and the means proposed was the restoration of the parochial High Mass on Sunday, with full participation. Beauduin refrained from any attempt to confuse liturgical renewal with liturgical reformation, either by going back to more ancient rites and usages or by trying new and un-precendented experiments, although he remained quite open to the possibility of future change. However he structured his movement on the principle that the liturgy belonged to the Church; hence he took it as she offered it and urged that it be known, understood, and carried out *as it was*—that is, as it was meant to be. The Belgian movement consequently never got lost in archeologism or wandered off into innovations of doubtful value. Perhaps the true reason for his astonishing success is that he revitalized the sense of the word "ecclesiastical." [3]

The drama behind the official beginning of this movement was not without its humorous moments. We pass over in silence some of Beauduin's liturgical ancestors who, while they shared his basic insights, apparently lacked his dynamism and dogged determination to popularize their ideas. That Haquin places the first beginnings of the movement in 1882, and Beauduin discovered the liturgy only in the course of his novitiate during 1906–07, suggests it was not too widely known or esteemed. The earliest hint we have that something liturgical was brewing in the back of his head came on February 2, 1909 when he invited some students to an informal discussion of the liturgy. They showed great enthusiasm for a little liturgical pamphlet edited by Desclée which a student (F. Mercenier, O.S.B., 1885–1965, later a monk of Amay) had taken to Beauduin earlier in January. At that time Mercenier proposed that something comparable with the Mass texts added be produced for the laity.[4] The hand-picked group soon began to meet on a regular basis.

The Liturgical Movement

A quick sketch of the launching of the Belgian liturgical movement might leave one with the impression that its success was due to pure chance. In September 1909, the National Congress of Catholic Works (*Congrès national des Oeuvres catholiques*) was held in Malines under the patronage of Cardinal Désiré-Joseph Mercier. Although Beauduin did present a paper on the liturgy, some remarks by the historian Godefroid Kurth made a much greater impression. At the close of the Congress, his suggestions pertaining to the liturgy were incorporated into resolutions and enthusiastically passed. In November of the same year, Mont César began the monthly publication of *Liturgical Life* in both a French and a Flemish edition. The following June a liturgical day was held at Mont César. Over two hundred fifty people were present and Cardinal Mercier spoke.

Because of the success of this project and *Liturgical Life* (subscriptions rapidly reached the impressive total of seventy thousand and Mont César was forced to announce in the public press that no more subscriptions could be accepted for 1910), two new creations saw the light of day. *Liturgical Questions* (*Questions Liturgiques*), a monthly destined for the clergy, sought to form them liturgically and keep them abreast of developments in the field. It also appeared in two editions. The Flemish numbers were published by the monks of Affligem under the same inspiration as the French version but not necessarily with the same articles. As a means to make the liturgy better appreciated on the popular level, liturgical weeks were also proposed. The first was for French-speaking Belgians, August 22–26, 1910. Only the lack of proper accommodations dimmed the enthusiasm of a few, for Beauduin installed the participants in the cells of the monks of Mont César and his confrères had to shift for themselves for the duration of the week. Several days later the Flemish counterpart began (August 29–September 2). It suffered from a lack of prominent speakers and poor attendance. Despite these various setbacks, these "weeks" became annual affairs until the outbreak of World War I. In 1912 the Liturgical Library (*Bibliothèque Liturgique*) began to appear which published the *Ritual for the Faithful, Liturgy for the Dead, Sunday Missal* (*Rituel des Fidèles, Liturgie des Defunts Missel Dominical*).

An outline of this kind naturally overlooks all the detailed planning and even scheming that went on behind the scenes prior to the opening of the National Congress. In its brevity it fails to answer some very basic questions: How was Beauduin chosen to present a paper? Who chose the topic? How could a magazine be developed, worked out and published in little over one month with such amazing success?

It seems important to look more closely at Beauduin's "method," a technique he used to the end of his life. Convinced that people rarely take the projects of simple monks seriously, he invariably looked for a "front" man in any major undertaking. In the case of the liturgy, to obtain maximum publicity for his ideas, he availed himself of a text of Pius X, the patronage of Cardinal Mercier, and

the services of Godefroid Kurth. Pius X's words served as the
crucial catalyst. On November 22, 1903 the pope had published
a *motu proprio* urging the restoration of Gregorian chant. One day
while leafing through the text a key phrase had caught Beauduin's
eye: "Active participation in the sacred mysteries and the public
and solemn prayer of the Church is the primary and indispensable
source of the Christian spirit." Beauduin never tired of expounding
just what the Holy Father meant by this active participation. The
unique thing about his exegesis of papal documents is that in this
case—there would be others later on—his interpretation took hold.
It is highly questionable that Pius X really envisaged all Beauduin
did with that now famous phrase, but his explanation certainly was
not contrary to the principles for which the great and saintly pontiff
stood.

Many incomplete versions of how Beauduin managed to get his
name on the speakers' list for the Congress have been given. That
Mercier had invited him was clear. Beauduin admitted this in 1959
when questioned about his campaign for the liturgy at the Congress
in 1909:

> *Question:* What was the determining element that pushed you to
> campaign for the liturgy at the Congress in 1909—was it your course
> *De Ecclesia?*
>
> *Answer:* The determining element . . . was first Cardinal Mercier
> who wanted a paper on this question and next my course *De
> Ecclesia.*[5]

In actual fact Mercier asked Abbot Hildebrand de Hemptinne,
abbot of Maredsous, for someone to give a paper on the liturgy at
the Congress. The abbot suggested E. E. Vandeur (1875–1968),
author of *La Sainte Messe, Notes Sur la Liturgie* (who later became
prior of Mont César when Marmion became abbot of Maredsous
in 1909). When Beauduin's students heard this, they immediately
expressed their dismay, for Vandeur could not begin to compare
with Beauduin's impressive and vivid style of delivery. Finally, persuaded by their enthusiasm, Abbot de Hemptinne asked Abbot de
Kerchove for permission to assign the task to Beauduin. Word came
to the latter while in the midst of preaching a retreat to some nuns
near Charleroi. Delighted with this unexpected opportunity, he was

immediately bothered by the fact that neither did he know the cardinal nor did the cardinal know him. For this reason he introduced himself as *un inconnu* in a letter which can leave the impression that he literally but discreetly proposed himself and the idea.[6] Thus began a friendship which lasted until the cardinal's death.

As the date of the Congress neared, Beauduin experienced two major disappointments. The first was the lack of appreciation for the ideas in his paper evinced by a fellow Benedictine who was president of the sub-section under which liturgy was placed. Beauduin's dismay was shared by his fellow liturgists whose enthusiasm had been steadily growing over the summer months. The second cloud on the horizon was created by the insignificance of the actual place reserved for his paper and the outcome of his attempts to change it. He recounts the details himself in his message to the 50th anniversary celebration of the liturgical movement in 1959:

Its [the liturgical movement's] first steps in life were hesitant; we first had to win a spot in the sun. I made several attempts in vain: I first tried to get the paper on the liturgy listed in the doctrinal section. . . . A categoric refusal from the president of this section who regarded the paper like a Cinderella of the fairy tale. A second move—the section on morality—underwent the same fate. The third, at the section on piety, was even more badly received: they considered the liturgy as a whimsical kind of piety that could not have any place in spirituality! Finally, on the advice of an architect, I was able to find a spot in the section on art where it [the liturgy] cut a strange figure.[7]

The section was actually called "Literary, Artistic, and Scientific works." Someone had the kindness to create a sub-section, naming it "Liturgy and Religious Music." [8]

One can well imagine the frustration that this chain of events caused Beauduin. Failure to obtain a suitable place for the liturgy by direct means forced him to resort to some behind-the-scenes maneuvering. In the light of his past efforts on behalf of the liturgy, Kurth was the logical choice to give liturgy a more prominent place. Moreover, he was scheduled for one of the main addresses at the opening general session. Beauduin lost no time in contacting the historian, whose enthusiastic cooperation considerably encouraged the monk, although neither could have anticipated what an impression Kurth would make. It is not hard to imagine the sense of triumph they shared when the local newspaper saw fit to print this excerpt from the opening speech:

> The Church also teaches us the language we must use in speaking to God; it is in the liturgy that the magnificence of the divine Word is found. The liturgy is the supreme summit of poetry and thought. It speaks to God of the needs and infinite misery of men. If there is one thing that explains the desertion of a number of our churches by many Christians, it is certainly the insufficiency of the prayers which are substituted for the ancient, beautiful, and traditional liturgy. On the day when the holy missal will stop being for many an unintelligible book, on the day when all will find again the key to what the priest says to God at the altar, a great number of those who have deserted the temples will return to them.[9]

There is no doubt as to the real author of Kurth's moving words. Even the journalist who wrote the article for *Patriote* made allusion to Beauduin's probable authorship. Kurth's thoughts and Beauduin's paper are almost identical.

The impact of the address can best be measured by the fact that the subsequent resolutions were drawn up not by a Congress solely concerned with religious affairs but by one dealing with the political, social and economic problems, as well as the over-all needs of the Belgian people. Lest the originality of the Congress be exaggerated, it is only fair to note that the resolutions passed were the same as those with which Beauduin ended his paper.[10] The essence of these formal statements can be reduced to two points:

1. To spread the use of the missal as a book of piety and to popularize at least the whole text of each Sunday Mass and Vespers by translating it into the language of the people.
2. To make piety more liturgical: this included such things as the restoration of Compline as night prayers, of the parish High Mass, of liturgical customs in the home, as well as suggestions about music and chant (including that choir members make an annual retreat at a center of liturgical life, like Mont César or Maredsous).

One can well imagine Beauduin's satisfaction over such an unexpected turn of events. But the proposals of many congresses often remain dead letters. Such was not to be their fate in this case, since extensive preparations for the implementation of these very points had already been carried out.

Instrumental as Mercier and Kurth had been to the success of Beauduin's project, the groundwork was done with care early in the spring of 1909, long before a paper at the Congress became a reality. His first attempts to win his superior's support were not very successful. A fellow enthusiast decided to try a different (and apparently more effective) tack by dropping a medal of St. Benedict into the abbot's mail box. As the story goes, the abbot spent a sleepless night and in the morning informed Beauduin that he had changed his mind about the liturgical idea.[11] But Beauduin's vision went far beyond the walls of his monastery—to the Benedictine congregation and from there to the whole Church.

The archives of Beuron have preserved proof of the comprehensive nature of his preparations. In a formal proposal addressed to the arch-abbot entitled *De Promovenda Sacra Liturgia* (On Promoting the Sacred Liturgy), Beauduin modestly suggested that Benedictines charge themselves with a threefold apostolate.[12] They should first study the liturgy in depth in order to bring about a renewal of their own spiritual life. This in turn would necessarily and quite naturally create a liturgical apostolate for them through which they would share their discovery with the diocesan clergy and the faithful. Beauduin's insistence on the necessity of initiating the diocesan clergy into a deeper understanding of the liturgy so that they in turn can communicate this understanding to the laity represents his major contribution to the Benedictine liturgical vocation.

Encouraged by his superiors' tacit approval of what he proposed, Beauduin began preparations for *Liturgical Life* in earnest. Assuming that if the people knew what the priests were saying at Mass their participation in the liturgical life of the Church would be that much more fruitful, he started work on booklets containing the texts of the Sunday Masses.[13] They were subsequently complemented by *Liturgical Life: Monthly Supplement* which explained the liturgy, offered some brief doctrinal formation and served as a type of public forum in which people aired their views, reactions, and objections to the liturgy and things liturgical. Already in the preparation of his first issue, Beauduin showed how progressive his ideas were: he sent out one hundred samples to members of the hierarchy, clergy and laity with a questionnaire asking for their reaction. Of the seventy-five that were returned, all but three or four approved of the experiment.[14] The vast majority were very enthusiastic. Again in 1912 when he was perfecting his Sunday missal, he once more consulted the parish clergy.

In these first days of the movement, Beauduin often worked non-stop through the night, fortified only by a pot of black coffee that one of the brethren used to bring to him. In order to accomplish more, he used a dictaphone supplied by his publisher. This explains the spontaneity of some of his early articles, reflecting the give and take of an oral conversation rather than the polished prose of a writer. As the movement progressed, it became even harder to get articles from him. He had to be pushed, pursued by the editors and the printer.[15] The production and mailing of these booklets was demanding not only on Beauduin but on everyone. Once underway, almost all the youth in the monastery were mobilized, even to the point of occasionally interrupting class schedules in order to meet deadlines.

Convinced of the central role to be played by the clergy in any liturgical renewal, Beauduin sent a second proposal to Beuron in 1910. Although his abbot agreed that a special school of formation would be the answer, the arch-abbot did not. But this did not discourage Beauduin. He worked out several elaborate yet extremely realistic plans, hoping that through such a school the clergy would learn the full extent of their pastoral responsibility and so be able to lead the laity into a more active and intelligent participation in the sacred mysteries. In view of the sad state of affairs in matters liturgical at the turn of the century, it is no surprise that his several attempts in 1910 and 1912 to set up a model school met with defeat.[16] (Only after World War II did Mont César start a liturgical school. At the same time Sant' Anselmo and the Institut Catholique at Paris began liturgical institutes on the university level, although the first liturgical institute as such opened in 1947 at Trier.)

In the 1912 plan for a liturgical school, Beauduin was scheduled to teach the general history of liturgy and notions of Oriental liturgy. The school came close to being realized, but the abbots posed reservations about the adequacy and preparation of the professors.[17] Concerned with quality, not quantity, Beauduin provided for a selective student body, composed of monks, priests, and clerics, and possibly even laymen "rich and without any special occupation." [18] His precautions and foresight are particularly instructive in view of the liturgical situation today. Most of the tensions and reactions touched off by the post-Vatican II efforts at renewal can be traced to an insufficiently prepared people *and* clergy.

Beauduin's special knack for understanding the diocesan clergy's liturgical problems contributed to the success of *Liturgical Questions* and the very popular "Letters to the Editor" section. Some of the letters verge on the incredible. Beauduin actually admitted to having authored a few of the better ones, signing them in a style reminiscent of "Dear Abby" letters—e.g., "a pastor absorbed by the care of souls" or "a chaplain in the clutches of uncomprehending nuns." [19] In short, Beauduin was always ready to clarify or to defend disputed questions, even if he had to raise the issue himself. If people accused the leaders of the movement of being immature and impetuous (and they did), Beauduin was only too ready to agree that some were probably guilty of these charges. But he would then continue with the deliberateness of a surgeon about to make an incision and point out his opponents' lack of logic or weak theology in dealing with the real issues. This invariably led to a charge that his adversaries had completely misunderstood the purpose of the movement.

Organized opposition soon appeared, with private piety versus liturgical piety surfacing as the real issue.[20] Beauduin simply reaffirmed the frequently reiterated principle of *Liturgical Questions:* the liturgical movement is not a question of substituting an anonymous religiosity for personal, conscious activity.[21]

A typical example of the deep concern aroused by this periodical is reflected in the following letter from a priest in Carthage:

I return the number of *Liturgical Questions* which you kindly sent to me. It is impossible to subscribe to the review. Let me tell you in all frankness how much your articles which attack the devotions approved by the Church, and especially meditation made according to the method of St. Ignatius, harm the cause you support and are of a nature to do immense harm to the clergy. The results of these attacks will be deplorable for a great number.

For us, formed in the spiritual life according to the method of St. Ignatius, we regard this book of spiritual exercises as our true treasure.

You attack definitively every religious order founded in the last three centuries, all of which have methods analogous to that of St. Ignatius. Their rules, however, are approved by the infallible authority. Meditation is rigorously prescribed for them, and all these orders regard it as the fundamental exercise of their religious life. According to you they are all wrong and the Church with them. For my part I bitterly deplore these attacks. My pain is truly great to hear you tell us with perfect assurance: you have taken the wrong path.

Be monks as in the days of St. Benedict and the world will again become perfect. Forgive me, Mr. Director, I am a poor unknown, with no authority. I only wanted to tell you my pain and fears.[22]

It was in 1913, however, that the battle royal broke out over Maurice Festugière's book *The Catholic Liturgy: An Attempted Synthesis* (*La Liturgie Catholique, essai de synthèse*). The Benedictine author accused contemporary spirituality of being responsible for the growing indifference on the part of Catholics to the Church and her liturgy. Furthermore, he blamed "modern piety" of being little more than a systematic organizing of a religious individualism which is neither Catholic nor Christian. Although direct attack such as employed by Festugière had never been Beauduin's technique, he nevertheless was very pleased with the book and gave it a rave review.[23] The Jesuits in particular felt that their latest contribution to the spiritual life, the apostleship of prayer, was being held up for ridicule. They therefore chose one of the editors of their most outstanding review, *Etudes*, to vindicate their honor. Fr. J. J. Navatel came forth with a severe criticism of the liturgical renewal, which he labeled a "Benedictine innovation." [24] His generalizations and over-simplifications left him wide open to attack. However, rather than resorting to more polemic, Beauduin disarmed all by the naiveté of his simple confession of what the discovery of the liturgy meant to him.[25] Then, unable to resist the temptation, he added the finishing touch by publishing an article in praise of Fr. Cros, S.J., who forty years earlier had led a campaign in favor of frequent communion which had just been recalled in *Etudes!*

That this opposition came from within the Church, primarily from the clergy, those who should be most in tune with the Church, was hard for Beauduin to accept. His only defense was to turn to the Church and to quote her teaching. What was the liturgy after all? It was the method authentically instituted by the Church to assimilate souls to Jesus, which meant assimilation to his mystery, his body, the communion of saints.[26] Unshakable in his convictions, he once more reminded his critics that the Holy Father had said that the surest way to preserve people from religious indifference is to give them an active role in the exercise of worship.[27]

Beauduin's magistral answer to the whole issue was *Liturgy: The Life of the Church* (*La Piété de L'Eglise*).[28] While he carefully abstained from direct involvement in the on-going debate, the title alone left no doubts as to where he stood. Rich in thought and human psychology, even today after more than fifty years the book continues to make not only interesting but fruitful reading, although some of its boldest affirmations may appear rather tame if not banal. The theological principles that inspired his thought are clearly presented, as well as his concern for a worshiping, hierarchical, social community. The table of contents gives a bird's-eye view.

Within five years the liturgical movement was an accepted fact, due in no small part to the indefatigable efforts of Beauduin and his colleagues at Mont César. The cooperation of his superiors ultimately benefited both the movement and Benedictine monasticism. Firmly established on a solid base of operations, in an atmosphere of study and research where the initial insights of its founders and disciples could be nourished and deepened, the movement seemed destined to contribute much. Mont César in particular now possessed a vital apostolate, shared to a certain extent with some of the other Belgian monasteries, a work with apparently endless possibilities of influence on and service to the entire Church. Thus the "democratization of the liturgy" and the "popularization" of a truly Christian spirituality filled many with great optimism. But in the midst of the creativity and enthusiasm fostered by the movement, storm clouds had already begun to form within the monastery itself. The object of this resentment was not the movement but the founder. Personal hostilities, however, and other equally disturbing factors soon became secondary with the outbreak of World War I and the consequent struggle for survival. Only with the restoration of peace would circumstances once again bring matters to a crisis point, the subject of a later chapter.

The Contribution of Beauduin

In presenting Beauduin's contribution to the liturgy, there has been no intention of suggesting that he was the Belgian liturgical movement. Many had gone before him and prepared the way. His major contribution was to have put into the hands of the people and their pastors what had been the private domain of a few specialists. Under his deft guidance the liturgical movement became solidly grounded in theology when it very easily could have degenerated into an activity solely concerned with keeping people busy during Mass. In a very real sense he brought theology to the laity through the liturgy, especially through its insights into the Trinity, the incarnation and the mystery of the Church.

His failure to convince everyone about the urgency of each point of his program did not mean that his breadth of vision went unnoticed. On the occasion of the fiftieth anniversary of the liturgical movement, Pope John XXIII, writing through the intermediary of Cardinal Domenico Tardini to Cardinal Joseph-Ernest van Roey, Archbishop of Malines, first acknowledged his awareness of Beauduin's over-all contribution. Then toward the end of the letter he underlined what he considered to be a very important aspect of this work: the liturgical formation of the clergy, a project that never really got beyond the planning stage in the dimensions desired by Beauduin but which was realized at least partially in his liturgical retreats and later in the sessions of the Pastoral Center in Paris (*Centre de Pastorale Liturgique*) during his exile.[30]

It is now half a century since Rev. Fr. Dom Lambert Beauduin—whose untiring zeal and persevering efforts the Sovereign Pontiff is pleased to recall today—attracted the attention of the members of the Congress of Malines to the importance of a liturgical life for Christians and thus was made, with the blessing of the eminent figure of your predecessor, Cardinal Mercier, the promoter of a movement whose intentions aimed first at the spread of the text of the Missal among the faithful and an ever more intense liturgical formation of the clergy.

There is, however, an important aspect that His Holiness wishes to underline in the development of this movement: It is the work in common of the two clergies according to the directives of the hierarchy, since that was also in its beginnings at the Congress of Malines.[31]

If we were to attempt to summarize Beauduin's contribution, in addition to the specific points already mentioned by the pope's letter, we would call attention to his prolific pen in the first years of the movement. It is impossible to estimate how many priestly attitudes, even lives, were changed because of his writings, not to mention the carry-over into the lives of the laity. In general these writings fall into two broad categories: speculative and practical. The speculative articles deal with the fundamental principles of the liturgical movement, the liturgy itself, and the Mass in particular, as well as dimensions of Christian spirituality. Other articles discuss the practical implementation of these ideas. Nowhere do we find a trace of provincialism. His vision always encompassed the whole Church. Often enough this meant that he turned to the traditions of the Christian East in order to throw light on Western developments. Such scholarly competence was not always appreciated, since even Eastern Catholics were regarded with suspicion by many in the West at this time.

Beauduin tried to make even his theological writings practical and relevant to contemporary problems. Frequently he accentuated the theme of fraternal solidarity, for he considered an ever deeper collective participation in the divine cult as the most ideal and efficacious way to preserve and to develop true brotherhood.[32] Such discussions often raised the rather delicate issue of obedience. Beauduin abhorred "blind obedience" which too easily encouraged inaction and irresponsibility in the name of virtue. The tendency of many to stress the norm of liturgical prayer as that prayer established by the Church here and now made him particularly uneasy. Such people, including his former prior and prefect of clerics, Marmion, insisted that when prayer deviated from this norm it was no longer liturgical—hence, the necessity of perfect submission to ecclesiastical authority.[33] While agreeing in essence with this, Beauduin nevertheless realized that it could easily become an excuse for senseless conformity. Obedience for the liturgist had to mean a sensitivity to authentic tradition (rather than to varying historical aspects) viewed in the light of current custom. In the last analysis, it was the spiritual vitality of the Church that mattered, much more than any man-made law. The dynamic nature of the Church obviously had precedence over the latter.

Beauduin's theological contribution in these first years of liturgical productivity are notable in several respects. The liturgy was his primary guide and so he avoided the dangers of eclecticism. Whether he was examining the eucharist or the Trinity, he drew his conclusions from the texts of the liturgy itself, and this was most unusual in his day. Two works stand out from this period: *Liturgy: The Life of the Church*, and his "Liturgical Manual" (*Essai de manuel fondamental de liturgie*), an unfinished series of articles containing his most extensive and comprehensive theologizing on such topics as the Trinity, the incarnate Word, the Mass, and the Church as the new humanity introduced sacramentally and mystically into the life of the Trinity.

The particularly significant aspect (among others) in this work was his emphasis on the risen Christ, the unique priest who here and now accomplishes our liturgy. This stress on the resurrection was a forerunner of what was to become a familiar motif in contemporary theology. But the uniqueness of his eucharistic theology must also be recognized. In both works we encounter the centrality of the sacrifice of the Mass in Christian life and the mission of the hierarchy in helping man realize his union with God. Until the sacrificial and hierarchical dimensions of the Mass take on their vital meaning, he insisted, the liturgy will fail to take on its true significance. To appreciate the uniqueness of his insights, which sound rather commonplace today, we must remember that his articles preceded the appearance of Maurice de la Taille's *Mysterium Fidei* or Marius Lepin's *Idea of the Sacrifice of the Mass* as well as Abbot Anscar Vonier's revival of the Thomistic idea of sacramental sacrifice.[34]

The introduction to and the chronological bibliography of Beauduin's works at the end of the book give an excellent idea of the topics he treated in these first years of the liturgical movement. Those we single out not only show him at his best, but also, perhaps, at his idealistic worst.

In 1909–1910, writing in *Liturgical Life*, he returned constantly to the theme of the communal nature of the liturgy. Its loss in the Western Church is traced to the lack of concelebration and the nature of private Masses. Before long he raised the question of restoring the role of the deacon. But the vital importance of the parish was really his favorite theme, so much so that he devoted a series of articles to this topic in *Liturgical Questions*. The matter of communion during Mass was also raised for the first time, but not the last. This had, of course, been the very point of van Caloen's proposals in 1883.[35]

The appearance of *Liturgical Questions* in 1910 gave Beauduin a more substantial platform from which to address his public. A major series of articles dealt with the temporal cycle, providing a wealth of homiletic material to guide the earnest priest into the mind of the Church so that he in turn could help his congregation to a more fruitful celebration of the particular liturgical season. To emphasize the importance of homilies, Beauduin pointed out their prominent role in the first centuries. So thoroughly was the liturgy preached that one can even reconstruct the canon from the homilies of that period. Beauduin also argued for the elevation of Wednesdays and Fridays to the rank of major ferials and suggested that all saints of a given order could be celebrated on the founder's feast day, thus reducing the sanctoral cycle in favor of the temporal cycle.

Beauduin also tried in 1910–1911, but without success, to persuade the Belgian bishops to insist that the temporal cycle be celebrated at least on Sundays. One of his liturgical "converts" in France, Msgr. Raoul Harscouet, director of the major seminary of Saint-Brieuc and later Bishop of Chartres, obtained permission to celebrate the Lenten ferials, vigils, and ember days in his seminary.[36] But most Catholics remained ignorant of the beauty and riches of the liturgy of the temporal cycle until relatively recent times.

A second group of articles examined the eucharistic cult and related devotions. Beauduin opposed exposition during Mass because it detracted from the sacrificial action. Still other articles discussed features of church architecture—the cross, altar, vestments, holy water fonts, etc. Another urgent concern was to keep the readers informed of current or pending liturgical developments. This might include a commentary on a recent papal document or an analysis of proposed liturgical reform, giving historical background to support the action. The conscientious priest could then inform and prepare his people for anything from calendar reform to new Mass texts or even the possibility of concelebration.

A series guaranteed to bring a wry smile to the face of most parish priests was devoted to a proposed two-year course of instruction for altar boys. Beauduin favored centrally located schools where the boys could study the essentials of worship: history, music, art, and archeology, as well as the religious and doctrinal values of these subjects. The emphasis during the second year would be on liturgical rites and books. But at the same time, he pointed out that servers should recite the Gloria, Creed, Sanctus, and Agnus Dei with the priest. Moreover, he noted that the server had the canonical right to read the epistle.

His more prophetic dimension was represented in his proposal that the eucharistic fast be eased so that more could participate fully in the Sunday High Mass, as well as out of consideration for the needs of workers, those who must travel a distance, and priests who say late Masses. He suggested that two or three hours constituted an adequate fast. (The editors received a letter asking that this article not be published. It was considered too dangerous.)

Sensitive to the problems associated with introducing dialogue Mass, Beauduin nevertheless urged pastors to inaugurate it, reminding them simply that under no circumstances were they to allow the people to say the Our Father with the priests. The three-year cycle of readings in the Jewish liturgy also caught his eye, although he did not initiate action to adopt it.

If he occasionally comes across as being a trifle legalistic (at least by some modern standards), Beauduin's intention was constant and consistent: to enrich the parish priest so that he could help his people to grow, to distinguish pious folk traditions from essentials, and above all to enter more intelligently into the prayer of the Church. He was particularly hard on those clergy who watered down the parish life to suit the lowest common denominator instead of trying to challenge all to a higher spirituality, and he was very keen on rehabilitating the liturgical role of the bishop of the diocese.

Pius XII's *Mystici Corporis* (1943) and *Mediator Dei* (1947) and Vatican II's *Constitution on the Sacred Liturgy* (1963) would never have come to be had it not been for the constant and enlightened efforts of men like Beauduin to mold and support the work begun by Pius X in his *Divino Afflatu* (1911) which announced the reform of the breviary, and *Abhinc Duos Annos* (1913), primarily concerned with the restoration of the true spirit which originally animated the liturgy. The challenge for the Christian as well as for the liturgist is to harmonize obedience with the demands of truth. For the true nature of the liturgy to be made manifest and relevant to each age, a knowledge of what liturgy meant in the past and an active fidelity to this knowledge are indispensable.

The role of liturgy and monasticism in the formation and development of a solid Christian spirituality proved to be the most far-reaching insight of these years. It would provide the foundation on which Beauduin constructed his future projects. Liturgy, the permanent center of his entire life, alone touched the whole man. It challenged his mind to sound the theological riches enshrined in the official prayers of the Church and then, in responding to the intellectual invitation, to open himself to the transforming presence of the Holy Spirit who acted through the sacred rites.

To revitalize the liturgy, however, was a task that transcended the capabilities of a simple monk. Belgium represented but one small corner of the universal Church, yet in her small way she mirrored the needs of the entire body of Christ. Thus, almost from the moment of its inception, Beauduin viewed the liturgical movement as an integral part of an even more pressing need: the obligation of the Church to face the twentieth century with a clearly defined philosophy of life attuned to the needs of the age. The validity of such a philosophy presupposed that the Church would know who she is.

It was from this perspective that Beauduin faced the challenges and crises of the immediately ensuing years—namely, World War I. Unforeseen experiences during these years deepened his convictions and opened new horizons, bringing unexpected breadth and depth to his understanding of the nature of the Church and his responsibility as a member. Under the impact of events, certain intuitions and dreams—for some time vaguely persistent but obscured by the press of liturgical activities—clamored with increasing success for his attention. Eventually a radically new orientation for this priest-worker-turned-liturgist brought him into close personal contact with some of the leading figures in ecclesiastical circles. The war years thus provided a *hiatus* and a turning point which prepared the way for these new directions.

3

World War I
and the Postwar Period

In August, shortly after war had broken out in the Balkans, the mighty German military machine swept into Belgium, brutally putting down what resistence the stunned people could muster. The outright violation of the neutrality of this small, defenseless country, innocent of any provocation, shocked the entire world. For centuries the pleasant rolling countryside of Belgium had offered invaders easy access to the rest of Europe, but this did not mean that the outwardly placid citizenry had no fighting spirit. They were realists. The more aggressive citizens, who were dissatisfied with pursuing a personal policy of survival, went underground to make the occupation as costly and as unpleasant as possible for the Germans. Admirable as such courage was, it nevertheless cost dearly.

The occupation forces knew from the start that they were not welcome. This naturally put them on their guard. The atmosphere quickly became heavy with distrust, suspicion, and outright hatred. Tragedy lurked at every corner. An equivocal act could call forth a fusillade of bullets. Hundreds fell in this manner—ninety-one in one town. In Louvain, 176 persons, including infants at the breast, the aged and sick, were either shot or burned in the first months of occupation. Sad testimonies to the fear and anger of the invaders exist everywhere today: small plaques placed on buildings giving the name, sometimes the age, and the date of one of these victims.

If not shot on the spot, people were arrested, often for no apparent reason, and regardless of age or sex were subjected to all sorts of indignities and physical abuse. In one city alone, 3,100 civilians were taken off to prison shortly after the Germans arrived. The elderly frequently were most severely affected, both physically and psychologically. Upon their release from even a short imprisonment, many returned to their families broken in spirit and went to an early grave.

Material damages only augmented the anguish of this nation. Some villages were all but destroyed. Out of 380 homes, 130 were left in one town; in another only 11 out of 200 dwellings remained. The sack of Louvain (August 25-29) left buildings destroyed in the city and its suburbs. But its most tragic loss from a material and cultural point of view was the university library. The intellectual fruits of five hundred years went up in smoke. In general the Germans showed little discrimination in their initial onslaught; even the cathedral at Malines was bombed.

The fact of bloody reprisals and the possibility of yet more aged many in those first weeks of occupation. It was as though they had lost all desire to live. But this was precisely the tactic of the oc-cupier: to break the spirit of the people and then to offer them the "peaceful" co-existence of collaboration. The "prudent" succumbed to the temptation. The patriots arbitrarily refused any compromise on principle. The invasion brought about a radical modification in everyone's life, including that of the monks. But it opened what was to be perhaps the most unusual chapter in Beauduin's life.[1] Courting danger with apparent delight, he discovered unlimited pos-sibilities for the deployment of his imagination and new vistas of service to his fellow men.

These adventures throw light on certain facets of his psychological makeup which will make the accounts of his comportment in later ecclesiastical battles over conflicting ideologies more credible. We are dealing not with a plaster-of-paris saint who gazes on the turmoil of life from the safety of his niche in the wall, but a man who never let himself be mastered by events because his roots were so firmly planted in the realities of life. Thoroughly convinced that "in him we live and move and have our being," Beauduin kept everything in perspective. Life, death, success, failure—like the great apostle, he was ready to risk all in the service of the body of Christ.

The glamor of his escapades must not distract us from his source of inspiration or from the contribution they made, whether directly or indirectly, to his spiritual and theological growth.

The highlights of the war years included the special missions assigned him by Cardinal Mercier, his dedication to country and countrymen, his discovery of the theology of Theodore de Régnon, and his first serious contacts with the English. The post-war years witnessed a brief but informative Roman career which would introduce him into the ecumenical circles of the day and a chance meeting with Msgr. Angelo Roncalli (later John XXIII) which blossomed into a lifelong friendship.

Espionage Activities

When news of the approaching soldiers reached Mont César, the abbot quickly evacuated the community and left Beauduin as caretaker. Upon their arrival the Germans interrogated and frisked the solitary monk. A more thorough search was then performed in the refectory. After unceremoniously stripping him and having found nothing subversive on him, they let Beauduin get dressed before formally presenting him to his new "community"—the soldiers and their commanding officer, Lieutenant Rheinbrecht.[2] Situated as it was on a prominence overlooking Louvain, the august citadel of Mont César proved ideal for the German headquarters.

Beauduin was made responsible for the new governor's safety, and soon Rheinbrecht was confiding in the monk as to a spiritual father and friend.

Unfortunately Rheinbrecht's stay was cut short by orders to the front lines. Mortally wounded in the battle of the Marne, he nevertheless sent a last message to Beauduin from his deathbed—a most eloquent sign of their genuine friendship.

Called away on August 20 to the conclave that elected Benedict XV, Cardinal Mercier had anxiously followed reports of atrocities in his homeland. Upon his return several weeks after the invasion, things had quieted down almost to normal, but he found many of his flock without Mass because their priests were dead or in detention camps. Before long he summoned Beauduin to perform the extremely delicate task of visiting those towns and villages particularly ravaged by the Germans.

As patriot and pastor, the cardinal was very much aware of the particular threat created by the presence of German troops. That a neutral country had been invaded and occupied in violation of all international agreements was only one facet of the problem. An abrupt change of policy in October on the part of General Moritz von Bissing, the "supreme authority" of the occupation forces, provided an even greater cause for concern. In an attempt to win over the people, the Germans had suddenly become very pro-clergy and pro-Church. Mercier quickly realized the insidious nature of this new tactic. Cooperation with the military would gain the Church protection but it would also be a silent acceptance of the injustices committed, an act of collaboration. Mercier decided to make a stand and to break any bridges before they were built, but he needed help.

Initially he planned to write a pastoral letter on the current crisis as a Christian message from the entire Belgian hierarchy. Such a testimony of solidarity would, he felt, encourage the faithful in these troubled times. Confronted with an all but hopeless political and military position, however, his response was conceived in far bolder terms than the situation seemed to warrant. Mercier clearly believed that the letter should be a strong, unified protest against the injustices of the invasion and the occupation of a neutral country. In order to carry out his idea of a joint pastoral, the other bishops had to be contacted without arousing the suspicion of the German authorities. Mercier proposed this potentially dangerous mission to Beauduin, asking him to visit the bishops of Tournai, Namur and Liège. After explaining the plan to them, the monk was to try to enlist their cooperation.

Before sending him off, the cardinal read the text of the proposed pastoral. Beauduin instantly sensed that something was wrong with it. After a moment's hesitation, and without mincing words, although astonished at his own boldness, he told Mercier quite bluntly that as the Primate of Belgium he could not write such a letter. In the first place, the Germans would not understand language which was clothed in the terminology of ecclesiastical diplomacy. Beauduin's unsolicited advice was: "Your Eminence, without unnecessary provocation, you should call a spade a spade." [3] He then went on to criticize a lengthy section of praise on the tradition of Catholic government:

Your Eminence, you cannot come down from your episcopal chair to campaign for a party. It is not the Catholic party that should benefit from your words, but the whole people. You cannot speak to them in the name of a political party, but only in the name of the Gospel.[4]

Mercier immediately recognized the wisdom of these remarks. Tearing up the original, he turned to Beauduin and said: "You are right; we will rewrite the letter together." [5]

Any sense of triumph over this unexpected entry into national politics was soon extinguished. The three Belgian bishops listened patiently to his presentation, asked time for reflection, and within twenty-four hours gave their reasons for rejecting it. Bishop Charles-Gustave Walravens of Tournai had been caught in the midst of his pastoral visitations when the invasion occurred. Arrested, imprisoned, and badly treated, he had returned broken in body and spirit and died a short time later (January 1915). In the light of his personal experience he hesitated to sign because of the inflammatory language of the letter, but he proved a most gracious host. He invited Beauduin to a roast chicken dinner and personally picked the best bourgogne from his wine cellar.[6] When Bishop Heylen of Namur greeted Beauduin he was visibly shaken, since the German governor of Namur was in the adjoining room. After a hushed exchange he told Beauduin to come back later. In the end he too opted for prudent silence and called the proposed pastoral a veritable declaration of war. The last on the list was Bishop Rutten of Liège whose earlier intervention in the affairs of the Labor Chaplains had contributed to Beauduin's disenchantment with the group. In a voice trembling with indignation as he recalled the cruelty and injustices his people had just suffered, Bishop Rutten expressed dissatisfaction with the wording of the document, claiming that it said too much and too little. Nevertheless, he was willing to endorse it if everyone else agreed.

Unfortunately the reservations of the bishops were not exactly unwarranted. In his enthusiasm and optimism, Beauduin had failed to take into consideration the objections that could be raised against the text in the name of prudence. Dismayed, he headed back to Malines, not knowing how he would be able to face the cardinal, for the original letter might well have been acceptable to the other bishops. Vainly hoping that the Flemish envoy to Gand and Bruges would have met with greater success, Beauduin realized that he alone was responsible for the miscarriage of Mercier's plan.[7]

As Beauduin entered the cardinal's office, Mercier instantly read the signs of defeat on his friend's face. To spare him further pain, Mercier told him of the negative results in Gand and Bruges. Moreover, he added, he was not the least surprised at the fate of his proposal. After questioning Beauduin carefully as to the reactions of the bishops, Mercier retired for some reflection and prayer. Strangely enough, the eventual pastoral *Patriotism and Endurance* lost nothing of the substance of the Mercier-Beauduin version. The seminarian who typed the final draft was familiar with Beauduin's handwriting and recognized it on the rough copy.[8]

On December 24, 1914 the finished product was secretly delivered by the seminarians of Malines to every rectory in the diocese.[9] Although news of the letter had leaked out and the Germans were on the alert, they failed to stop it. Priests in other dioceses who managed to obtain copies read the letter as a pastoral from their own bishops. Reprisals were not slow in coming. Copies were confiscated and people intimidated. At the cardinal's request, the center of diffusion was moved to Mont César, presumably the last place the Germans would suspect. A university professor donated 100,000 francs to the cause. In three weeks the new printing of 50,000 copies was exhausted. Boxes and cartons for shipping purposes were supplied by the Beauduin family refineries. Thus, under the camouflage of sugar, the letter that reanimated the courage of the Belgians found its way into every village and hamlet and soon was read and praised by freedom-loving men everywhere.

Somehow the German police found out about the cardinal's attempts to obtain the endorsement of the other bishops. The pastoral, however, clearly implied that although he would have liked to invite his colleagues, he was forced to sign it alone (the unspoken explanation for this sad state of affairs being, of course, police interference). The Germans therefore tried to pressure the cardinal into a retraction and an open admission that the bishops had in fact refused to sign the document. Failing to intimidate him, they tried politics. Although they convinced Msgr. Emmanuel de Sarzana, the chargé d'affaires to the papal nuncio (then at the Hague), that it was his moral responsibility to rectify the matter, de Sarzana failed to make any headway. Mercier realized, as the inexperienced chargé d'affaires did not, that any retraction on his part would be exploited beyond imagining by the Germans. Furthermore, he justified his refusal on the grounds that he had never personally approached any of the bishops. Had he been able to, he was convinced that he would have been able to persuade them of the necessity of the pastoral.

Mercier's tenacity in the face of these threats earned him the admiration not only of his countrymen but even of the Germans. In 1918, when the defeated governor general prepared to leave Belgium, he made a detour to the episcopal residence at Malines to pay homage to the man who had won the moral victory in the war.[10] The cardinal's philosophy in this regard is best expressed in the words he once spoke about those who become afraid and run away from responsibilities: "They want to avoid making a mistake; their very existence is one." [11] For his forthright stand, he became an international figure, a symbol of courage. After the war, as he traveled in the United States receiving honor and acclaim for his famous letter, he wrote these words to Beauduin on a postcard: "It is you who should be here"—a fitting tribute both to the cardinal and to his former envoy.

For the time being, Beauduin continued to live at the monastery, indulging in underground activities on the side. Our earliest written description of him dates from this period. Young Olivier Rousseau, contemplating a monastic vocation, decided to visit Mont César during Easter vacation. In his diary he captured the experience of his first encounter with the great liturgist Beauduin:

> The guestmaster, who knew that I had relatives who were friends of Beauduin (Beauduin came to the burial of my father in 1901), presented me to him after dinner. I was rather astonished to discover such a jovial and democratic behavior. In reading his articles I had formed a much more austere and grave image, a sort of cutting Jesuit, restrained and distant. I had no idea that this man of arguments and doctrine could exist in the skin of a joyful monk with a noisy and exhilarating laugh. The works of Beauduin that I had read (notably his *Liturgy: The Life of the Church*) had a single trait, and I had found therein an expression so adequate of my own temperament that I believe I owe them my Benedictine vocation.[12]

For various reasons, although they soon became "brothers" in religion, they saw little of each other. In 1919, however, Beauduin would become sub-prior and the need for discretion ended.

Cardinal Mercier made his retreat at Mont César in 1915, ending on the vigil of the Ascension. In honor of the occasion, the abbot decided that all must be present for Vespers and refused Beauduin's request to be excused for some extracurricular activities. Because he was to have presided at a clandestine gathering in town, he hastily tried to find a substitute to chair the meeting for him. Willem van der Elst, a young diocesan priest whom the cardinal had first introduced to Beauduin a few months earlier, readily agreed. Since the appearance of the pastoral, van der Elst had been quite active in the underground press. Beauduin quickly filled him in on the purpose and arrangements for that evening.

The festive atmosphere in the monastery was soon shattered. Vespers had hardly ended when word came that the espionage meeting had been broken up by the Germans and that Beauduin's life was in danger. Only through Mercier's intervention was van der Elst's death sentence reduced to a term of imprisonment. Concerned for Beauduin's safety, the cardinal took him to Malines. Thus began a new life of adventure and travel for a monk who was becoming too well known, and for the wrong reasons.

Inasmuch as his priestly work had kept him in the public eye, Beauduin was a relatively well-known figure. To protect both himself and those who knew him, he now resorted to a series of disguises. His first project was to grow a beard. After an extensive search failed to turn up any trace of the wanted man, the fugitive went back to Mont César for a brief visit. He then withdrew to "Emmaus," a hotel near Maredret, a Benedictine convent. The nuns were duly edified by the bearded gentleman who assisted at Mass daily, but one day as he devoutly raised his head to receive Communion he was greeted by an astonished look of recognition. The celebrant was a monk from Maredsous and one of his former students at Louvain. To protect all concerned, Beauduin quietly disappeared.

Not content with a life of retirement and research made advisable because of notoriety, Beauduin soon became actively involved in helping people to cross the border, especially young men eager to enlist in the Belgian army which had its headquarters in England. Normally this took place under cover of darkness by floating with the current down the Meuse in the vicinity of Maastricht where Belgium, Holland, and Germany come together. So successful was this method that the Germans eventually put a high tension wire on the Belgian side to discourage further defections. For the sake of variety, Beauduin once chartered a local street car, loaded it with young men, and in broad daylight, under the astonished eyes of the Germans, sent them careening across the border. Later when circumstances made it expedient to live abroad, he devised from his retreat in Holland an ingenious method for continuing this little apostolate. With the connivance of the doorkeeper at Mont César and cards for ordering missals, he managed to get additional young men across the frontier.[13] The unobtrusiveness of this arrangement was revealed by the abbot's astonishment when, at the end of the war, the doorkeeper received a medal for his contribution to the resistance.

Fortified with a new identification card provided by one of his brothers, Beauduin now crossed the border frequently and with impunity. His new disguise as Oscar Fraipont,[14] a wine merchant specializing in altar wines, gave him a valid excuse to visit his priest friends. With his striking moustache (which replaced the beard), soft felt hat and stylish pince-nez, he cut quite a figure. On one occasion he inadvertently left his briefcase filled with compromising papers at a ticket window. Preferring to risk his life rather than that of others, he nonchalantly got back in line to retrieve it. A German officer, however, had noticed the briefcase and already taken charge of it. When Beauduin asked for it, the officer returned it with a few words to spark the Belgian's appreciation for the honesty and good order of the Germans. But his adventures did not always have such happy endings.

One evening after hiding men in the woods for the trip down the Meuse, Beauduin went to a nearby rectory. Although he pretended to go to bed, he had sensed the approach of the Germans and hid in the cabbage patch instead. His premonition was soon verified. The Germans came, searched the house and left. Returning prematurely, Beauduin was subsequently caught in the wine cellar where he had fled precipitously when the Germans decided to double-check. Both he and his unfortunate host were taken to headquarters.[15] It was June 25, 1915.[16]

Beauduin had no doubts as to the outcome. His kind of fame had definite drawbacks. However the Germans, conscientious about military regularity, particularly when notorious spies were involved, wanted to give him due process. Fortunately a tribunal was already in session so that he would be spared the torture of an endless wait.

Another prisoner was already waiting to be called. The officers who were to judge him took time out to come for a look at the famous O. Fraipont before installing themselves in an improvised tribunal across the corridor.

The first prisoner was summoned; his escort never returned. As the interrogation seemed to be prolonged interminably, one of the two remaining guards left to investigate and failed to return. Finally the sole remaining guard fell asleep. Beauduin could not resist the temptation. He turned to his companion and nodded toward the unguarded door. The latter refused to budge, so Beauduin cautiously got up, tiptoed across the creaking floor boards and, with a certain amount of trepidation, went downstairs. His casual smile and hearty greeting of "Ich bin frei!" (I'm free!) caught the sentry off-guard, and he automatically responded with a cordial "Ach! Schön!" (Wonderful!)

The bold fugitive maintained perfect composure until he turned the corner; then he frantically started looking for a hiding place. Spotting a group of coopers, he slipped into their midst, picked up a hammer and started to work on a barrel. The foreman soon expelled the intruder. After similar fruitless attempts to find cover, Beauduin spotted a church. His sense of relief lasted but a moment. Scarcely had he crossed the threshold when to his consternation he realized that the building had been converted into an officers' mess. A less inspiring edifice ultimately provided a place of refuge—the public latrine, where for the time being he was safe, even from bloodhounds. His meditations were soon interrupted by a discreet knock. One of the sympathetic coopers informed Beauduin that they would help him escape in the evening with the aid of their group pass. At the appropriate moment, with the help of some borrowed clothes, he successfully eluded his captors. That night he slept under a bench after having dined on a few grains of corn found in an empty wagon.

Early the next morning a railroad employee led him to the station master, one of his former students from St. Trond, who locked him up in a freight car. After properly sealing it he attached it to a passenger train headed for Campine. At each stop Beauduin could hear the Germans searching the passengers cars. Then there was an unscheduled stop in the middle of a pine forest and Beauduin's car was detached. At first he had no idea where he was. Once he had his bearings, however, he headed for the home of a priest friend. As luck would have it, he soon saw three priests coming toward him. One was the very friend in question. Beauduin recognized all three but passed them unnoticed because of his clothes. As soon as he was behind them he shouted out: "So that's the way it is now! One no longer greets his old professor?" They abruptly turned about. Their amazement was indescribable at seeing the very subject of their morning conversation. With amusement they informed him that the Germans were so convinced they were dealing with a dangerous spy that his value had skyrocketed to a breathtaking 100,000 francs.

To preserve such a notorious member of the clan proved quite a challenge to the Beauduin family. The escapee's brother Lucien suddenly decided to ship some sugar to Holland. Among other things a boat had to be purchased, and such preparations could not be made overnight. But this caused no great inconvenience to Beauduin; he simply assumed another disguise. Fortified with new identification papers which included a medical certificate stating that he should be kept in seclusion because of emotional instability, he soon adapted to his new home—St. Elizabeth's Hospital located at Uccle, a suburb of Brussels. The two weeks' wait while his brother prepared to export him was extremely important in Beauduin's theological formation. Among other works, he devoured de Régnon's work on the Trinity: *Etudes de Théologie Positive Sur le Dogme de la Trinité*. In later years he often referred to this enforced retreat as one of the happiest periods of his monastic life.

What were some of de Régnon's ideas that so impressed the captive? Undoubtedly it was not only the breadth of his patristic knowledge but also his original and lively comparisons, his fresh style and his ability to stimulate thought. This very ambitious four-volume undertaking emphasized the Greek Fathers.[17]

An important part of de Régnon's contribution to the theological development of Beauduin no doubt lay in his insistence on viewing the Greek Fathers apart from the trinitarian controversies, from Photius and the *filioque*. One thing is quite clear: De Régnon's presentation of Greek trinitarian theology was consonant with the theological vision that Beauduin drew from the Roman liturgy.

Certainly the importance of the Trinity in his thought is definitely attributable to insights gained at this time. One might even wonder

whether de Régnon's theological method of refusing to isolate a
writer from the comprehensive whole is reflected in Beauduin's
approach to ecumenism and his eventual rejection of any attempt
to separate the Anglican, Orthodox, or Protestant question from the
broader problem of unity. Such thoughts however were undoubtedly
far from his mind as he waited to make good his escape.

Finally, hidden in a case of sugar and carefully packed between
powdered sugar and molasses, he successfully crossed the frontier
between Belgium and Holland. Much of the next few years was
to be spent in the British Isles. His fame had gone before him,
however, so apparently he was called upon to do some counter-
espionage work for the British Intelligence Service in Holland, working with the famous Lieutenant Marcel (Fr. Vincent de Moor, later
professor at the Institut Catholique of Paris). The two worked
briefly on *Libre Belgique*, an underground publication which survived the war to become one of Belgium's leading newspapers. The
exact nature of their other activities remained a closely guarded
secret, unknown even to Beauduin's closest friends. When not engaged in some such official capacity, he divided his time between
England and Ireland, and the last few months of the war were
spent in Rome.[18]

In Ireland he encountered several of his former students while
teaching theology at Edermine,[19] a temporary priory established by
Abbot Marmion for the young monks of Maredsous. Parts of England also became familiar to him. One of his first contacts with
Anglicanism was in the person of Rev. G. K. A. Bell, the recently
appointed chaplain to Randall Davidson, the Archbishop of Canterbury. Bell, the future Bishop of Chichester, was to be one of the
pioneers in the ecumenical movement, and as secretary to the archbishop would follow the Malines Conversations with great interest.

One of the most incredible coincidences imaginable occurred during Beauduin's first summer in England. He decided to go to London—whether on business or for pleasure is not known. Arriving
late in the evening he found to his dismay that all the hotels were
booked solid. In desperation he asked a clerk if he could not please
find him a bed. After checking the register carefully, he noticed
one room still vacant, with a double bed, although reserved by a
French clergyman. Beauduin begged him so successfully for half
of the bed that the clerk finally let him have his way, supposing

no doubt that because of the lateness of the hour the other party was not coming. Beauduin found the room and with a sigh of triumph crawled into bed. In the middle of the night, someone tried to rouse him—physically and verbally. He presumed that it was the priest who had reserved the room, so rather than lose his half of the bed, he played possum. Imagine if you can the scene the following morning. In an attempt to make up for the rudeness of his intrusion, Beauduin introduced himself: "Dom Lambert Beauduin, monk of Mont César, director of *Liturgical Questions*." The other party, startled, looked at him as though he were a ghost or worse and replied: "Fr. Navatel, *Societatis Jesu*, editor of *Etudes*." He was the very Jesuit who had waged such a bitter attack against Beauduin and the liturgical movement shortly before the war.[20]

Peace and Its Aftermath

The signing of the armistice ended Beauduin's patriotic activities in the resistance and opened a new period of searching in his life. The liturgical movement, the center of heated polemic on the eve of World War I, had weathered the storm. It was an established entity now on the Belgian scene, but it had taken a new turn in his absence which displeased Beauduin considerably. The liturgical publications and training sessions still functioned, but the new blood that had assumed leadership saw the movement less and less as the restoration of the ancient piety of the Church. They wanted to integrate it into modern spirituality. In short they sought to adapt the liturgy rather than to adapt themselves to it. What is more, they even favored the vernacular. This was too much for Beauduin who had conceived the movement as a preservative force to restore full meaning and significance to the gestures, texts, and chants of the ancient tradition.[21] Unable to support the new ideas, it was inevitable that he should turn his energies elsewhere.

Moreover, upon his return to Mont César in 1919, Beauduin found it exceedingly difficult to readjust to the routine, especially after his more liberal existence abroad. This plus internal problems within the monastery created an unpleasant if not stifling atmosphere. Times had changed and monasticism had not, at least not at Mont César.

Beauduin was now forty-six, at the prime of his life. Though of small stature, he was massive, not fat (he lacked the protruding stomach so often associated in cartoons with the middle-aged monk) but solid. His head was particularly impressive, large, strong, with solid jaws (his associates recall that he often cracked nuts with his teeth). His bright blue eyes were full of life and spirit. By disposition a happy man, he was almost always smiling and his distinctive laugh remained full, sincere, and communicative, yet a certain look from him could make a man's words stick in his throat.

His varied activities as a labor chaplain, professor, liturgist, and patriot had made the speaker's podium familiar to him. When he spoke in public he leaned toward his audience and seemed to form his ideas with his hands and offer them to his listeners. His talks were admirable. In simple, direct language and avoiding all erudite words, he divulged tremendous ideas that could set one's mind and heart on fire, because Beauduin himself was fired by the same realities. The perfect teacher, he came across with great conviction, flattering the audience (as though they already knew what he was himself just discovering), making them smile or laugh by his remarks and jokes, and invariably winning them all.

In private he treated everyone as a friend. One left his presence convinced that the exchange had been truly on a personal, even confidential level, such as normally exists only between close friends. Beauduin loved men. Although he was not always the best judge of character (as subsequent events will reveal), his natural inclination was to reach out to everyone who crossed his path and to embrace each with a crushing bear hug—literally and figuratively.[22]

The combination of such a personality plus his very real accomplishments perhaps explain why in September of the year 1919 he was sent as a delegate to the meeting of Belgian Benedictines which led to their separation from the Beuron congregation. Then on October 30 he was named sub-prior of Mont César. Not one to waste time, he soon tried to use his position on the monastery council to modify a few things, especially the infantile treatment imposed on adult men by the Constitutions. But it was useless. His was a voice crying out in the wilderness. The council was not so easily moved as a class or public audience. Beauduin was treading on thin ice; the Constitutions were seemingly sacred and inviolable. Even the proposed revisions at the moment of the formation of the new Congregation of Belgian Benedictines only heightened the tensions from which he longed to be liberated. The changes adopted failed to alter in any substantive way the more objectionable aspects already mentioned in Chapter 1. Consequently, Beauduin longed increasingly for something new, a non-exempt form of monasticism that would promote a more human and therefore more Christian way of life, combining the best in the ancient tradition with a permanent openness to the changing needs of the modern world.

Meanwhile, now that Beauduin had achieved status within the monastic hierarchy, he had become accessible to his "inferiors." Rousseau had been patiently biding his time since that chance encounter in 1915. Now began their real friendship with a series of theological conversations on points which deeply interested the young cleric: the mystical body of Christ, the Church, the hierarchy, the sacrifice of the Mass, etc. As Rousseau later observed:

> I enormously appreciated the remarkable depth of Beauduin's view and his genial theological perception. He is, without a doubt, the man the most convinced and penetrated with the mystery of the Church that I have ever encountered.[23]

Suddenly it looked as though his dream would be fulfilled. In 1920 the Bishop of Liège indicated his willingness to sponsor a new type of monastic foundation in which the monk, although bound by a rule, would still be at the service of the diocese in a pastoral capacity.[24] Beauduin himself had been considering something similar, as well as a piece of property in Tancrémont which had been placed at his disposal and was located between Liège and Verviers.[25]

A visit by the Metropolitan of Lvov, Andrew Szepticky, opened up new and fascinating possibilities. He introduced an ecumenical dimension and suggested that the East could reteach to the West the imperishable values of the Eastern liturgical tradition and the ideal of monastic life.[26] That same fall, Beauduin also preached the annual retreat at Mont César (September 12–19) in which he expounded his monastic dream and further alarmed a number of brethren. His version of Benedictine spirituality had become overwhelmingly non-Benedictine in their eyes with its emphasis on the social dimensions of human relations.

The abbot was not opposed to Beauduin's new interest in a monastic experiment. He had great confidence in him and realized that Mercier had given tacit approval to such a project. However he had sensed a growing opposition from within the monastery to the person and ideas of Beauduin. These circumstances left him unsure as to what action to take. Fortunately, at the crucial moment, an unexpected solution presented itself in the form of a periodic request by Abbot Primate Fidelis von Stotzingen (d. 1947) for the loan of a competent professor to teach at the international Benedictine College at Rome, Sant' Anselmo. For once the abbot responded without a moment's hesitation and recommended Beauduin as professor of fundamental theology.

In the spring, however, Beauduin became seriously ill with phlebitis. Although he recovered, it left its mark on him and would eventually immobilize him.[27] As he prepared to leave for Rome in October 1921 to begin his new tasks, he was much more concerned about reports of his friend Rousseau's health. They met quite by chance as Beauduin stepped across the threshold of Sant' Anselmo. He had only one thought: to do everything possible to hasten the recovery of the young student. He immediately made inquiries about possible convalescent homes in the countryside. Within a day and a half he found a suitable home in Frascati, drove Rousseau there and continued his visits until the young monk was pronounced cured.

Meanwhile Beauduin plunged into his academic responsibilities with great relish. To his earlier enthusiasm for the liturgy he now added a growing interest in union and the Orient. Soon a circle of disciples eager for his ideas had formed. The subsequent indiscretions on the part of a few, too caught up in the romantic element involved, led to a certain discontent among the abbots who feared losing their men to some Oriental fantasy.

Profiting from his experience at Mont César where he had first gone to the sources to enhance his course on the Church, Beauduin did the same at Rome, for the textbook situation had not changed. He supplemented his outline with the rich tradition of the past—the biblical and patristic teachings on the nature of the Church which had in great part been lost sight of by the theologians since Trent.[28] His new interests inevitably led to even deeper insights into the mystery of the Church and an appreciation of the historical complexity caused by schisms.

The texts suggested for fundamental theology were particularly alarming. Filled with numerous errors about the Orthodox and their theology, their approach was deplorably negative and responsible in large part for the general deterioration of the subject matter into little more than a course of apologetics. Beauduin vehemently opposed the idea of supporting one's own faith by misrepresenting the belief of others. He therefore took advantage of the many resources in Rome, especially the libraries of the Pontifical Oriental Institute and the Greek College. The former had been founded by Benedict XV who felt that objective study and scientific research would play a big role in promoting reunion.[29] The latter was the oldest and most important of the Oriental colleges for priests serving Italian Greeks and Christians in the Near East.[30] Little by little through these contacts, Beauduin discovered the ecclesiology of the Eastern Churches.

Ostensibly he had been sent to Rome to teach. In reality it had been a fortuitous leave of absence from Mont César which would give him the relative independence necessary to draw up some workable plan for a new experiment in monasticism. The years in Rome were thus years of almost feverish activity, meeting people, discussing projects, and trying to learn the maximum in the short time at his disposal. Nevertheless, his professional duties were not neglected. Nor had he lost interest in the liturgical movement. He continued to produce five to ten articles yearly for the periodical he had founded.

Some of the issues he raised in the articles from these years sound strangely modern to us: the value of the offertory procession and the ascetical value of the laity's involvement in the liturgy at this moment of the Mass, as well as the kiss of peace, which Beauduin preferred at the offertory. He also pointed out that the prayers after low Mass really did not belong there. In the light of his own goals in 1909, he reminded his readers that in 529 the Council of Vaison had passed five liturgical canons, including one for clerical schools and another on the duty of priests to preach. Both dialogue Masses and concelebration were the subject matter of several articles. The question of evening Mass was also considered and the subordinateness of the hour of Mass to the eucharistic fast. Beauduin concluded that the discipline of the fast need not be immutable. In a piece on the devotion to the Sacred Heart, Beauduin pointed out that the "twelve promises" to Margaret Mary were unknown before 1882. An American compiled them from the saint's works and letters.

Another interesting article examined the question of obedience to Rome and decried those who run to Rome for a decision every time a problem arises. Such action makes scientific work and knowledge useless, and even has dangerous social consequences in the Church. In 1925, the focus of his writings changed from liturgy to the monastic experiment and then to ecumenical issues.

The World in Transition

From 1914 to 1925, one new horizon after another in dizzying succession opened up before Beauduin. Interruptions, far from being impediments, proved providential. The variety of wartime experiences put him in contact with men of all walks of life and of all faiths, deepening his understanding of the mystery of the Church. The periods of enforced inactivity which dispensed him from many of his monastic obligations led him to a more vital appreciation of the real essence of monastic life and enabled him to penetrate more deeply into those areas of theology which particularly attracted him.

At the same time as he was being indelibly marked by the fact of war, the world was undergoing a crisis of faith which increased its awareness of the sin of religious prejudice and the shameful lack of unity among Christians. Thrown as he was into the thick of things, Beauduin could not escape contact with a new awakening which brought the scandal of disunion abruptly into focus. Moreover, political upheavals frequently brought religious problems in their wake, and the Russian revolution in 1917 was no exception to this. It had a direct impact on the orientation of his own monastic experiment and eventually compounded his difficulties later on.

What was to have been a two-year assignment stretched into three, then four, and could have been prolonged indefinitely had not Beauduin insisted on being replaced. But the four years had been well spent. They opened up new dimensions in the development of his understanding of the Church. Introduced to the ecumenical leaders of the day in Rome, Beauduin soon became involved in the nascent attempts at dialogue with the Orthodox and the Anglican worlds.

A chance encounter that occurred under an umbrella at the door to the Greek College, while lacking the drama and humor of the

London hotel room, nevertheless far exceeded the latter in importance. On that rainy afternoon of March 14, 1925, the other party
turned to Beauduin and said, "I've just been named apostolic delegate
to Sofia. I need a secretary." The new appointee was Msgr. Angelo
Roncalli (who had lost his professorial post at the Athenee on a
suspicion of modernism). Beauduin suggested that a colleague, Con-
stantin Bosschaerts—a monk from Afflighem who was looking for
something unusual—might be interested. Roncalli pursued his suggestion. It was through Bosschaerts that he later learned of the
ecumenical projects and methods of Beauduin. In Bulgaria, Roncalli
saw how precisely the ideas of Beauduin corresponded to reality and
put them into practice in his relations with the Orthodox. Several
years later when he returned for a vacation, he went to Amay (1930)
to see Beauduin again and to visit the young monastery. It was the
beginning of a long friendship.[31]

While Beauduin's relations with the Eastern Churches and Orthodoxy have perhaps received more publicity, the Anglican question
was really his "first love." Cardinal Mercier had embarked upon a
rather bold adventure of unofficial dialogue with the Anglicans the
very year Beauduin left for Rome. It was only natural that he
should share the details of these conversations with his friend and even
involve Beauduin—although only indirectly—in them. Unfortunately
this discreet participation in what came to be known as the Malines
Conversations ultimately had seriously damaging effects on Beauduin's career.

4

The Malines Conversations

The episcopal residence of Cardinal Mercier (1851–1926) was the setting chosen for a series of five unofficial "dialogues" carried on by a small group of outstanding scholars between 1921 and 1926. These talks, held in Malines, represented the culmination of more than thirty years of unceasing activity on behalf of unity by two pioneers in this field: an Anglican layman, Charles Lindley Viscount Halifax (1839–1934),[1] and a French Lazarist, Fr. Fernand Portal (1855–1926).[2] While Lord Halifax's pro-Roman views were shared by a significant minority, he certainly could not be considered representative of the Anglican community as a whole. But even those Anglicans who differed with him nevertheless respected his personal qualities, including his deep piety and utter sincerity.

Beauduin, although never present for the conversations, became involved through his friend Mercier. The strong disapproval that his contribution aroused in English Catholic and then in Roman circles led to the subsequent prohibition of any further contact on his part with the Anglicans. This action severely limited the sphere of his activities. Nevertheless the Malines Conversations remain a milestone in his life, for his ecumenical perspective and key insights into the nature of the local church date from this collaboration with Mercier.

In 1966 on the occasion of the 40th anniversary of the conversations, Cardinal Leo Suenens made the pertinent material that had been preserved in the Malines archives accessible to scholars. The documents disclosed hitherto unknown facts and provided new insights into the difficulties encountered by this ecumenical experiment of the 1920's.[3] The world of scholarship owes a debt of gratitude to Suenens. While the equally significant Roman archives have yet to be officially declared open for research, there is evidence that some scholarly investigation is underway. Further details are also to be found in the recently released papers of Randall Davidson (1848–1930; Archbishop of Canterbury from 1903–1928) preserved at Lambeth Palace.

Pre-history of the Conversation

The story behind the Malines Conversations goes back almost a century to the Oxford Movement. Begun in 1830 by Newman, Pusey, and other leading Anglicans, supporters of the movement wanted to work toward unity with other Christians but were divided over which way to turn. Some looked to Orthodoxy, others to Rome. The first generation had been disappointed by Rome's condemnation of the Association for the Promotion of the Unity of Christendom in 1864,[4] though many continued to be interested in and to work for Anglo-Roman unity.[5]

Lord Halifax was the president of the English Church Union for fifty years (1868–1918), an organization dedicated to the defense and maintenance of Catholic principles in the Church of England. In the winter of 1889–1890, he made the acquaintance of Fr. Portal at Funchal (Madeira). The discovery of their mutual concern for unity quickly blossomed into a deep and lasting friendship. After incessantly pressing Lord Halifax during the next two years to make the Anglican Church known in France through a series of articles, Portal decided to take the initiative. He realized that the general policy of Leo XIII was favorable to unity and so sought to draw public attention to this vital issue.[6]

A small pamphlet entitled *Anglican Orders* thus appeared in 1893. Although sympathetic in his presentation, the author, Ferdinand Dalbus,[7] nevertheless came to a negative conclusion, contending that the validity of holy orders depended on questions of fact, not faith. He especially questioned the intention of those who used the Edwardian Ordinal. But the pamphlet in no way reflected his personal

views; he simply wanted to draw attention to the problem rather than
to make any definitive statement. For this reason he deliberately chose
defective arguments. Both he and Halifax favored corporate reunion; their goal therefore was not primarily the recognition of
orders.

This bold challenge to open debate aroused the immediate interest
of a number of Catholic theologians, including the noted Church
historians Louis Duchesne and Auguste Boudinhon (also a great
canonist), as well as Pietro Gasparri, then professor at the Institut
Catholique and future member of the commission of inquiry regarding the validity of Anglican orders in 1896. (Under Benedict XV
and Pius XI he would be Secretary of State and again become involved in the Anglican question.) Msgr. Duchesne, the first to respond
publicly, was particularly dissatisfied with Dalbus' work and took up
his pen to insist on the validity of Anglican orders, deftly demolishing
Dalbus' chief arguments. Soon all reunion debates centered around
this topic.

Leo XIII, realizing the possibilities that recognition of the Anglican priesthood might bring, summoned Portal to Rome in September
of 1894. The latter tried to obtain a direct papal invitation to the
Anglicans for mutual discussions with Catholic theologians. In the
early part of 1895, Leo XIII granted two more audiences to Halifax
and Portal [8] for the express purpose of discussing the possibility of
friendly conversations rather than immediate and official papal action.
Halifax's efforts to stress the positive side and to see recognition as a
solution to over three hundred years of separation were undoubtedly
overly optimistic, but they were counterbalanced by the efforts of
Cardinal Herbert-Alfred Vaughan to promote single conversions
and by the latter's blunt imputations about Anglican motives in this
matter. His lobby was ably represented by the aging pope's protégé,
Raffaele Merry del Val (1865–1930).

Many within Catholic circles had serious doubts about the ultimate
possibility of corporate reunion. Yet the hopes of some and the fears
of others continued to rise. The declaration of *Apostolicae Curae* [9]
in 1896 that Anglican orders were "absolutely null and utterly void"
brought public debate to an abrupt halt. The theologians made their
traditional "submission," and suddenly Anglican orders seemed a
dead issue, though the discussion continued. Roman Catholic theologians tried to find and to express adequate grounds for supporting
the bull, while the Anglicans sought grounds to refute it. The Arch-

bishops of Canterbury and York issued a notable reply. (*Saepius officiis*) which contained one of the clearest statements of the Anglican view of the eucharist and of holy orders.

While much could be said about the bull,[10] two remarks will suffice for the moment. First of all, it did mark a definite gain. The old historical objections were abandoned and the focus shifted to the theological significance of the facts. But this latter point remained in dispute and still is the key question even today. The second point is just one of those historical paradoxes: the bull of 1896 said that only a Catholic with insufficient knowledge would have considered holy orders to be an open question because the issue had already been definitively settled by the Holy See; yet both Cardinal Mariano Rampolla and the Holy Father felt that there was sufficient room for doubt to reopen the question in 1894.[11]

A New Possibility

In 1867 the Anglican Community from all over the world began to hold general decennial meetings at Lambeth, the London residence of the Archbishop of Canterbury, for the purpose of examining current problems. From the very first the members placed the question of Christian unity at the top of their agenda. In 1888 they agreed upon what is known as the Lambeth Quadrilateral (Bible, Creeds, Sacraments, Ministry) as the basis for the Anglican approach to unity, a formula which was actually the product of the 1886 Chicago General Convention of the Episcopal Church in the U.S.A.

In 1920 at the Sixth Lambeth Conference, the bishops resumed their discussions of satisfactory conditions for reunion. Their "Appeal to All Christian People," while directed most specifically to the question of Anglican-Presbyterian-Congregationalist reunion, nevertheless applied to all Churches, including Rome if she should respond. (The Conference of 1908 had specifically said that there could be no true reunion without Rome.)

The proposed conditions for reunion centered around Anglican orders, and the Anglican bishops appeared ready to discuss any mutually acceptable regulation in connection with the ministry, including the matter of conditional reordination. The passage in the "Appeal" which referred to the possibility that Anglican ministers should receive some supplemental commissioning undoubtedly applied to Rome and Orthodoxy, since in general Protestants accept the validity of Anglican ministry.[12] These allusions to Rome did not escape the sharp eye of Lord Halifax who had never abandoned his initial dream of reunion.

On January 24, 1921, Cardinal Mercier received a letter from Fr. Portal containing a short account of the efforts made in the 1890's for reunion, especially the idea that he and Halifax had had of discussions in common on points of disagreement, including that of holy orders.[13] Both Leo XIII and his secretary of state Cardinal Mariano Rampolla had favored the idea of a friendly exchange and in 1894 had suggested Brussels as a possible site for the conversations.

What Portal and Halifax did not know at the time was that a month earlier, in December 1920, Mercier, inspired by a similar idea, had addressed a letter to Benedict XV which said in part:

The painful awareness of division . . . arouses at this moment . . . a keen desire for unity. Already in the course of my trip to the United States, I received expressions of this feeling on the part of non-Catholic theologians whom I believe profoundly sincere. One of them urged me to send a delegate to the religious meeting at Geneva. I naturally declined the invitation, saying that Catholics no longer seek unity since they have the certitude of possessing it.

At least, others told us, agree to an encounter; participate in the conference in order to dissipate the prejudices which keep us apart from one another, for our mutual enlightenment. These conferences, I answered, would provoke, I fear, confused debates, which would perhaps contribute more to driving us further apart than to bringing us together.

However, Holy Father, does not charity command us to facilitate access to the true Church of our Lord Jesus Christ for these souls seeking truth and union? And moreover, did not Christ say: *Et alias oves habeo.* . . . [And I have other sheep. . . .]? Your Holiness will perhaps judge some day that a call to non-Catholics, Anglicans, Americans, Russians, Greeks, etc., would be an act worthy of his apostolic zeal. But while waiting, would it not be wise to begin to smooth the paths to unity? I offer myself to make an attempt. After having asked for prayers for a private intention of Your Holiness, I would try to invite to Malines, successively, one or two theologians of each of the dissident Churches, Anglican and Orthodox in particular. I would keep them for several days and put them in contact with a Catholic theologian of sound doctrine and loving heart. In the intimacy of private meetings, with the grace of God, the penetration of souls can be much more profound.[14]

The strange coincidence of these two letters, his and Portal's, was not without its effect on Mercier. He wrote again to Rome but no encouragement came. Finally, in the fall, at the urging of Portal and Halifax, the group was formed. To Lord Halifax were added Walter Frere (1863–1938), superior of the community of the Resurrection and future bishop of Truro, and Armitage Robinson (1858–1933), Dean of Wells. Later Charles Gore (1853–1932), retired Bishop of Oxford, and Dr. Beresford Kidd (1864–1948), a well-known Church historian and warden of Keble College, joined the Anglican contingent. Msgr. Joseph-Ernest van Roey (1874–1961), the "Catholic theologian of sound doctrine and loving heart" of whom Mercier had spoken, joined his cardinal and Fr. Portal to represent the Catholic side. Msgr. Pierre-Henri Batiffol (1861–1929), a Church historian and former rector of the Institut Catholique of Toulouse, and Canon Hippolyte Hemmer (1864–1945), a patrologist, were later included in the group when the need for historical expertise became evident.

The first conversation took place December 6–8, 1921. Mercier had done nothing by way of seeking official authorization, since he felt it to be unnecessary:

> For nothing in the world would I have wanted one of our separated brothers to say that he knocked with confidence at the door of a Roman Catholic bishop and that this Roman Catholic bishop refused to open to him. . . . I would have judged myself guilty had I committed this cowardice.[15]

He therefore saw nothing fundamentally wrong about engaging in dialogue without having explicit papal approbation. The conversations, privately conducted in a spirit of abandon, had no other goal than for the participants to become acquainted with one another on the level of their relationship with God.

Mercier was not, however, so naive as to disregard the fact that there was a certain boldness connected with these conversations. The Holy See should be kept informed, but before he took any step in this direction, Benedict XV died. Called to Rome for the conclave, Mercier spoke to Pius XI about the matter shortly after the latter's election. The secretary of state, Cardinal Gasparri, proved even more interested than the pontiff, due to his prior involvement with the Anglican question under Leo XIII.

In March, Rev. G. K. A. Bell,[16] secretary to the Archbishop of Canterbury, wrote to Fr. Michel d'Herbigny, S.J.[17] who was in charge of relations with separated Christians. Bell requested information on how to establish official contact with Rome as a follow-up on Lambeth's call to reunion. D'Herbigny, apparently aware of Mercier's group, suggested that Bell be directed to Malines. While Gasparri was writing to encourage Mercier in the name of the Holy Father, d'Herbigny informed Mercier that the Holy See would soon ask him to host a meeting between Anglican and Catholic theologians. The cardinal showed no enthusiasm for d'Herbigny's additional suggestion that some Jesuit theologians such as himself be added to the group.[18] Mercier may have written to Gasparri for clarification about this unwelcome intrusion into a private affair because at the end of May he received word that any invitations were entirely at his discretion—and to be issued in his name alone. Since this left the status of the conversations only semi-official, the Archbishop of Canterbury preferred to wait and watch until Rome herself should take some official action. Having failed to obtain an invitation to the conversations, d'Herbigny made an abortive attempt to set up a parallel group. Later, when opposition to the conversations became open, d'Herbigny sided with Mercier's opponents, attempting to discredit both the cardinal and those associated with him, including Beauduin.[19]

Anticipating problems if some official word did not come, Mercier wrote directly to Pius XI and received an almost immediate answer on November 25:

> The Pope authorizes Your Eminence to tell the Anglicans that the Holy See approves and encourages the conversations, and prays with his whole heart that God may bless them.[20]

In the eyes of Mercier the words "the Holy See approves" were particularly encouraging, since it seemed to imply official approbation and not merely the pope's personal endorsement. Without a moment's delay, he transmitted the response to the Archbishops of Canterbury and Westminster as well as to Halifax. Although Cardinal Francis Bourne remained skeptical, he felt that the meetings should be encouraged.[21]

The actual conversations show that there was a certain ambiguity in the minds of some as to the precise nature of the problem at hand. The first conversation centered on dogmatic points, especially those of a sacramental nature, comparing the teachings of Trent with those of the 39 Articles. The second, held in mid-March of 1923 opened a new phase. The Anglicans came with the official approbation of the Archbishops of Canterbury and York, the Catholics with a tacit appoval from Rome. This time their discussions dealt with canonical topics: use of the vernacular, the mode of nominating bishops, and the special place of the Archbishop of Canterbury in the Anglican Church. The latter point, raised in the context of reunion, suggested an analogy with the ancient patriarchates and brought up the notion of the pallium.[22] Halifax, who was responsible for introducing this new orientation, insisted that practical questions rather than theological issues interested the English. This surprised Mercier and displeased the Anglican Archbishop Davidson. The latter felt that administrative problems should be left aside until the participants came to a real understanding and agreement on the fundamental question of the papacy.

That the problem of the papacy might be more fully exposed, the aid of eminent historians, both Anglican and Catholic, was sought for the third conversation. Seen in retrospect this was, according to van Roey, one of the weaknesses of the third and succeeding talks because too great a place was given to historians to the detriment of theologians.[23] Although some points of agreement were reached during the third conversation [24] which took place November 7–8, 1923, the claims of the papacy still needed further discussion.

In the interval between the third and fourth conversations, the Archbishop of Canterbury made a public statement about these encounters which had by now taken on a semi-official status. Nevertheless he respected Mercier's wish that the fact of Roman approval be kept confidential and simply stated that Rome had been informed. This unleashed a certain amount of controversy in English Roman Catholic circles which denied any Roman approval and insisted that Rome never would have bypassed the English hierarchy. The apparent preference to use French and Belgian intermediaries rankled the English and went counter to every conceivable concept of Roman diplomacy.

Mercier felt obliged to explain his participation and the purpose of the meetings, and so in a pastoral letter dated January 18, 1924, he quoted several letters from the pope's secretary of state which supported his action:

> As for the unfriendly observations which might be made against these conferences with the Anglicans, Your Eminence can reply: The Holy Father knows of our conversations with the Anglicans; he has never sent me the slightest word of disapproval, which is for me a tacit encouragement. This answer will silence the too zealous defenders of the faith.[25]

The pastoral, far from quelling opposition, only increased it. Nor did the translation published by *Osservatore Romano* help matters, for it suppressed a key sentence: "It suffices for us to know that our undertaking is in accord with the supreme authority, blessed and encouraged by it." [26]

A letter from Fr. A. Sordet to Mercier, however, reveals some interesting details heretofore unknown.[27] Upon receipt of the pastoral, Sordet shared it with the English Cardinal Bourne, then at Rome. The latter was delighted with it and admitted that he had been tempted to pass through Malines en route to Rome. The next morning, when *Osservatore Romano* published the pastoral minus the important phrase noted above, Bourne took action immediately and sent Sordet to the editor with the purpose of voicing Bourne's personal displeasure and asking for an explanation. The editor, unable to satisfy Sordet, suggested that he go to Msgr. Giuseppe Pizzardo.[28] The latter, after many weak excuses, simply said: "They have stupidly suppressed this sentence," adding that it was naturally out of the question that the mistake be publicly rectified. (Nevertheless, *Corriere d'Italia*, another Roman newspaper, printed the entire pastoral the next day.)

Mercier himself was dismayed by the pontiff's silence. At the moment of *Ecclesiam Dei*,[29] an encyclical on East-West relations, he had tried to obtain some official statement with regard to the Malines venture. The reply came as a great disappointment:

> His Holiness sees in the present case neither the necessity nor the opportuneness for a public statement.[30]

The cardinal's only consolation was to be Pius XI's public approval of ecumenical activities in his consistorial allocation of March 26,

1924, although no explicit reference to the conversations appeared.[31] Nevertheless there was no thought of discontinuing them, and Gasparri in a note reassured the cardinal that the Holy Father's commendation of those engaged with the "separated brethren" in the hopes of bringing them back to the true faith was directed toward the Malines Conversations. It was simply made quite clear that these dialogues were in no way official nor were they to make any pretense of being official.[32]

As interest continued to return to the matter of the papacy and of the pallium, Mercier decided to follow up the idea. In October 1924 he urged his good friend Beauduin to write a paper on the pallium's historical significance and the role it might play in reunion for the Anglicans. The two had discussed the pros and cons in a casual manner during the previous year, and Mercier possessed a letter from Gasparri which reassured him that every possible concession would be made. Moreover, even reunion according to the formula of the Oriental patriarchs was open to consideration.

A striking indication of the interest that this topic aroused at Malines is seen in the following request from one of the most conservative of the Anglican participants. In a memorandum dated Christmas 1924, he sought further clarification of possible terms for reunion.

> As a minor inquiry I want to ask what exactly is required of any Orthodox Group desiring to become Uniats. Is it the requirements formulated at the Council of Florence? Or the "Creed of Pius IV?" Or what? And are these formulas regarded as final and infallible? [33]

The Catholic historian, Msgr. Battifol, centered his reply around a rejection of any literal interpretation of the canon of Vincent de Lérins:

> It is absolutely forbidden to think that the Roman Church could be content with exacting nothing more than the profession of articles of faith which are adapted to the canon of Vincent of Lérins. In the perspective of development, in fact, none of the articles of faith of the ecumenical councils agree strictly with the rule of Vincent.[34]

As we shall see later, the contemporary position on the deposit of faith is somewhat more nuanced, particularly in the light of Vatican II's concept of a "hierarchy of truths." Beauduin, both in his treatment of doctrinal development and possible modes of union, was to anticipate more recent developments in a truly prophetic way.

The Famous Proposal of Beauduin

Since the pallium had been given by Gregory the Great to Augustine, the first Archbishop of Canterbury, in 597, as a sign of his effective jurisdiction over all English bishops, present and future,[35] Beauduin developed the idea that perhaps there was in this instance something similar to the power invested in the Eastern patriarchs. Pursuing this point, he arrived at the conclusion that the Anglican Church should be united to but not absorbed by Rome—in much the same way as some Eastern Catholics had preserved a definite liturgical and disciplinary autonomy while yet being united to Rome. Mercier read this paper as the work of a Roman canonist, without revealing the author's identity, at the fourth conversation held May 19–20, 1925.

Beauduin's Proposal is one of the great ironies of his life. His conclusion—that group reunion rather than individual conversions is the real solution to the problem of disunity—aroused the ire of Catholics in England and touched off adverse criticism on the continent as well. It reawakened the fears and resentments which had been smoldering since 1896, for such a view threatened certain "vested interests." It is therefore small wonder that he subsequently found himself severely compromised by his refusal to renounce this position. Unfortunate as these consequences may have been, the thesis exerted an important and positive influence on the development of Beauduin's ecumenical vocation.

Guilty perhaps of a gross over-simplification, he suggested that a ready-made approach to reconciliation existed, already sanctioned by historical precedent. He centered his argument on the pallium. This symbol of the Good Shepherd, made from wool and worn around a bishop's shoulders, represented the lost sheep and conferred a share in the power of the Supreme Shepherd. From Augustine to Cramner, this sacramental of patriarchal or supra-episcopal power had been given to the Archbishop of Canterbury.

Moreover, in 688 Theodore, an Oriental monk named by Pope

Vitalian to Canterbury, organized England on the model of the Eastern Churches. (This was, in Beauduin's eyes, a clear example from history of the acceptance of this role by Canterbury.) In 1098 at the Council of Bari, Urban II further enhanced Canterbury when he invited Anselm, then the archbishop, to a seat of honor beside him, saying, "Let him be a part of our circle, he who is in some way pope of the other part of the globe." [36] Thus two traditional characteristics of the English Church had been her faithful allegiance to Rome and her semi-autonomous internal organization with the Archbishop of Canterbury as patriarch and primate. An Anglican Church, absorbed or separated from Rome? Either concept was equally inadmissible. The true formula was the Anglican Church *united* to Rome, for until the twelfth century, argued Beauduin, the title of patriarch or primate had real meaning with effective and extended jurisdiction in the West. But did this fact therefore establish sufficient precedent for the solution he proposed?

After reviewing the various papal documents which outline the fundamental policy pursued by Rome vis-à-vis the Eastern Churches, the Proposal suggested a similar stance toward the Anglicans. The principles for this position are found in Leo XIII's *Praeclara Gratulationis* of June 20, 1894, and *Orientalium Dignitas* of November 30, 1894. The latter stated:

> True union between Christians is that which the author of the Church, Jesus Christ, instituted and wanted: it consists in unity of faith and government. Neither we nor our successors will ever suppress anything of your rite, nor the privileges of your patriarchs, nor the ritual customs of each Church. It has been and always will be in the thought and conduct of the Holy See to show itself lavish with concessions in respect of origins and the customs proper to each Church.

Thus, Beauduin insisted, Rome already had a formula of union which is not one of absorption. If any Church by origin, history, and national customs has a right to these concessions, it is the Anglican Church, if the Anglican Church wants to belong to the visible and unique society of Christ, it must "establish this indispensable bond of submission to the universal Church of which the principle of unity is at Rome": it must become not Latin but Roman.[37]

In the letter accompanying the Proposal, Beauduin singled out its chief obstacle—the trend toward increased centralization at Rome which, to his mind, threatened to become excessive.[38] Although enthusiastic over the contents of the paper, Mercier shared his reservations and urged Beauduin to seek official endorsement of the ideas, at least in principle. He proposed that someone like Justinien Seredi, O.S.B. (1884–1945), professor of canon law at Sant' Anselmo, sound out the Holy Father, either directly or through Cardinal Gasparri. Should Beauduin succeed in obtaining papal approval, Mercier would try to get permission for the monk to attend the conversations in May.[39]

Beauduin promptly raised difficulties. Seredi was too Latin to appreciate the idea; he, Beauduin, was on the point of leaving Rome and lacked the necessary time to pursue this. Moreover, keenly aware of the prevailing attitudes in Rome, he suggested that the Proposal be presented by an Anglican in a private capacity and gave details for how this might be carried out.[40]

Apparently they had no further contact until May 12 when Beauduin wrote from Rome to inform Mercier that he would be at his disposition from the 17th to the 21st, just in case the cardinal wanted to consult him during the conversations. There is no record that the cardinal acted on this offer. He presented the paper with only one reservation—Roman approval. Once Rome approved, only a conditional consecration of the primate of Canterbury would be necessary, and he would then conditionally reordain the Anglican bishops.[41] This suggestion, of course, was not above criticism.

Neither of the English hierarchies appreciated an unofficial group deciding how reunion could be accomplished. Neither could claim unanimous interest in, let alone approval of, the suggested means. Beauduin had even gone so far as to suggest the suppression of those sees created in 1851—a grave measure, but not without precedent, since Pius VII had suppressed more than one hundred sees in deference to the French Concordat.[42] The Anglicans on the other hand might have been basically delighted with some of the implications, particularly the obvious attempt to loosen up the rather rigid ecclesiology of Counter-Reformation Rome, but few would have become enthusiastic at the idea of reordination. While the Lambeth Appeal of 1920, sent to the pope and leading members of the Roman hierarchy, had implied that Anglicans would submit to reordination for the sake of unity, the theology behind it remained ambiguous.

There was no ambiguity behind Mercier's suggestion. On the whole, the Anglican clergy had no doubts about the validity of their orders. The fact that a Belgian cardinal had proposed the method without even consulting the principals concerned obviously increased the irritation, especially in the Catholic camp.

Moreover the Catholic participants themselves had strong grounds for complaint. There had been a tacit agreement to submit all theological papers in advance to iron out any possible problems before presenting them at the conversations. Mercier's open admission of his lack of theological expertise only served to make his independence in this instance all the more incomprehensible and open to criticism, although his decision to go ahead had undoubtedly been determined, at least in part, by Gasparri's letter of 1923.[43]

The Proposal contained some over-simplifications of the Anglican situation even from the Roman point of view. It was based on the unexpressed hypothesis of an already existing unity of faith and ignored certain fundamental doctrinal differences. In sketching a plan of reunion similar to that of the Eastern Catholics, the critics argued, the author had failed to take into consideration that nothing in the past or the present permitted the Anglican Church to identify itself with the Orthodox situation.[44] To suggest that reunion depended on a happy solution of the practical order seemed to ignore the existing dogmatic differences, and this impression brought forth sharp rebukes from Cardinal Bourne and his entourage.[45] Even the monk's friends did not find the Proposal beyond reproach. One of them described it as an example of how Beauduin's zeal sometimes led him to minimize the complexity of certain questions and to fail to take into account all the contingencies.[46]

Some objections undoubtedly reflected the product of a narrow, defensive minority consciousness—the memories of long years of persecution and bitter hostility between the established Church and "popish recusants." Fortunately this mentality is slowly dying out.

Evaluation of the Conversations

A brief summary of the conversations shows that they covered a limited amount of ground. The first, December 6–8, 1921, focused on how truth became *de fide* for Roman Catholics, and while removing some points of contention, it nevertheless revealed a clear difference of opinion on the subject of dogmatic definitions themselves. This matter still remains a great obstacle to unity. The sacramental teaching of Trent was also compared with that of the 39 Articles.

The second conversation, held March 14–15, 1923, dealt with canonical topics: use of the vernacular, the mode of nominating bishops, etc., and opened up new possibilities with regard to organization.

The position of Peter in the primitive Church as based on the New Testament was the topic discussed at the third conversation, November 7–8, 1923, although Halifax insisted that he could not accept as final an interpretation of the scriptural texts that failed to take into consideration what the early Fathers of the Church had said. Despite the initial Anglican reticence vis-à-vis the Roman position, a supplementary memorandum clearly stated that without communion with the pope "there is in fact no prospect of a reunited Christendom." [47] Papal supremacy was clearly the most important problem discussed at Malines. Perhaps the resume of the Roman Catholic participants is a fitting commentary on the past and prophetic of the future. Speaking of the papacy they concluded: "It is better not to go back upon the past but to try to forecast the forms which papal activity might take in the future." [48] For them the essence of the papacy lay in its primacy of honor and primacy of responsibility.

At the fourth conversation, May 19–20, 1925, one paper presented the episcopacy and the papacy considered from the theological point of view, and another presented the same subject from the historical point of view. Although in the 1927 synopsis of the conversations there is no mention of Beauduin's trial balloon either in the text or in the appendix of documents submitted, the topic is alluded to as coming up in the course of discussion. Writing in 1934, Beauduin himself claimed that van Roey's paper on papal and episcopal power, by the originality of its solution and its conciliatory effort, far surpassed a certain "anonymous study" on the pallium. [49]

Surprisingly enough, the concept "united not absorbed" cannot be claimed as a uniquely Catholic phenomenon at the meetings. It was also the final point in a memorandum drawn up by Lord Halifax, Dr. Frere, and Dr. Robinson in December 1921 before they had even left for Belgium: "The Uniate discipline is capable of further application: and its precedents suggest future possibilities." [50] The amazement of the Anglican party can well be imagined when Mercier proposed essentially the same idea at the fourth session.

On May 22 a conversation took place between the Archbishop of Canterbury and the Dean of Wells. It is not clear whether the archbishop was referring to the document of 1921 or to another memorandum prepared by the dean and mentioned by Mercier in a letter to Pius XI, dated March 1, 1923. According to Bell's notes, the archbishop said: "It is that signed document which still rankles me a little—about the pallium." The dean felt that the merit of this paper (which may have been Beauduin's) lay in its recognition that the Church of England had a more independent position in the old days than, for example, the Church of France—and in the great position accorded the Archbishop of Canterbury.[51]

Yet another signed document preserved in the Malines archives might well have annoyed the archbishop. Dated May 20, 1925, written by Halifax, approved by Frere and Kidd, and signed by Portal, it stated:

The Church is a living body under the authority of the episcopate, the successors of the apostles; and the Bishop of Rome, as the successor of St. Peter in the Roman see, is the head of the Apostolic College, the center of unity and by divine *providentia* in possession not merely of an honorary primacy, but of an efficient primacy which invests him with a certain *auctoritas* and *solicitudo* in regard to the whole Church.

That authority is not *separata* from that of the episcopate, nor can the authority of the episcopate be rightly exercised if dissociated from that of the head. In virtue of this primacy the head claims to occupy a position in regard to all other bishops which no other bishop claims to occupy in regard to him. The exercise of this claim has historically varied both in regard to time and place, and it does not seem possible to define with precision the respective rights of the Holy See on one side or of the episcopate on the other—the nature of the rights themselves, relating as those rights do to a living organization, not being susceptible of final or logical definition.

If it is asked further, on the negative side, what would be felt in England to be the greatest difficulty in the Roman position, it may be replied that they are two. One: the apprehension of any attempt to govern the Church of England by the Roman Curia, to which England would never consent; the other: the fear of the episcopate being reduced in practice to mere functionaries of the Holy See.[52]

Halifax did his part to keep the issue of union alive in the ensuing months. In a speech in July he insisted: "It has to be remembered that reconciliation with Rome does not imply any denial of the historic claims of Canterbury." This touched off a debate by mail with Fr. Francis Woodlock (who later attacked Beauduin verbally when the monk's association with the Proposal became known). On July 28, Halifax, suggesting that Woodlock did not really understand his point, concluded the exchange, once again reaffirming that reunion "does not imply or involve the absorption of the Church of England with that of Rome but the union of two Churches under the primacy of the successor of St. Peter." [53]

The purpose of this rather disparate documentation is to emphasize that from start to finish many persons were captivated by the idea of a Church united, not absorbed, and that any attempt to toss off Beauduin's paper as a totally naive or irrelevant intrusion into the proceedings of the conversations is simply a distortion of the facts.

With the deaths of Mercier and Portal (January 21 and June 19, 1926), Mercier's successor and collaborator in the conversations, van Roey, realized that these giants were the heart and soul of the venture and had the good sense to call for a fifth and final meeting, October 11–12, 1926, bringing the series to a close. Gore and the Dean of Wells were absent. Those present simply discussed the proposed publication of the papers delivered during the preceding sessions and approved them for publication. But before taking further action, the approval of those absent as well as that of the French and Anglican hierarchies had to be obtained. Msgr. Batiffol opposed publication of the French papers, and the Anglicans were equally unwilling, fearing that the contents would create more problems than they would solve.

Halifax was determined to go ahead with the publication with or without Catholic consent, with or without an introduction by the Archbishop of Canterbury and with or without the signatures of his colleagues. He felt that he owed it to his recently deceased friends, Mercier and Portal, to the cause of reunion, and to himself.[54] The

unjust attacks to which these ecumenical pioneers were being subjected in the press convinced him that public disclosure of what
actually took place was the best possible vindication of their good
names.

Nevertheless, the inclusion of Beauduin's paper on "The Anglican
Church, United Not Absorbed," represented a double breach of
faith, since the participants had unanimously agreed never to publish
this particular contribution. Although the immediate explosion it
caused was seriously injurious to Beauduin, he bore the venerable
Anglican no ill will. In a sympathetic article at the time of Lord
Halifax's death, Beauduin excused the premature nature of the book,
recognizing that its primary purpose had been to avenge the cardinal
whose intentions and acts were under attack. He fully appreciated
that the dominating passion of Halifax's life had been to try by
every means possible to prepare for a reconciliation between Rome
and Canterbury.[55]

In all fairness to Halifax it must be remembered that at this time
he was about ninety years old and had devoted more than sixty
years of his life to the promotion of the Catholic movement in the
Church of England and to the cause of Christian unity. Perhaps
extreme old age and the fact of having been a prophetic (though often unacknowledged) figure gave him a certain liberty of action.
His ever youthful enthusiasm for unity is best expressed in the following letter of September 25, 1928, sent to Beauduin:

I hope to arrive in Brussels on October 9. . . . And if you want
to tell me the day and the hour when it most suits you to see me,
I will come to find you at your place. There are many things which
are important or that are connected with all we most desire on
which I would like to consult you, and on every issue I would
like your opinion. It will be a great pleasure to see you—and to
know that we have met in this life. We miss the cardinal and
Abbé Portal more and more each day.[56]

In the course of the visit to Amay which followed, the old
patriarch summed up the current ecumenical climate with these
words: "Confidence! The future is ours!"[57] This can be appreciated
only when it is remembered that the devastating encyclical *Mortalium*

Animos had come out at the beginning of the year, seemingly banning all Catholic participation in the growing ecumenical movement.

Consequences of Malines

While Mercier still lived, his enemies hesitated to attack him. After all, he was a hero and an international figure. With his death, however, the critics lost all timidity. The appearance of Beauduin's Proposal in Halifax's publication added fuel to their fires. Mercier's successor, Cardinal van Roey, concerned and alarmed at the tenor of the remarks, attempted to silence the critics by the simple announcement of the real author of the controversial proposal. Beauduin's name was thus linked with his little piece of creative research in *Libre Belgique* on February 22, 1930. At that moment the unsuspecting Beauduin was just returning from his Eastern tour.[58]

Upon his arrival he went immediately to ask van Roey for permission to respond publicly to the charge, for he still possessed the letter from Mercier requesting the paper and thanking him for it. He realized that this whole affair was bound to complicate his already shaky standing in certain Roman circles, and he wanted to make it very clear to all concerned that Mercier had presented the paper on his own authority, without seeking an official Roman mandate, although he had thought of such a procedure. Van Roey, perhaps unaware of Beauduin's need to protect himself in a very delicate situation, asked the monk to keep silent, and he promised to help him in the future should the need arise.[59] Beauduin acquiesced against his better judgment and eventually found the price of his loyalty rather high; for van Roey failed to come to his assistance when this involvement became an issue at his trial.[60]

Beauduin's premonition was more than justified. The bitter criticism, at first directed exclusively toward the Malines Conversations and Mercier, soon turned against Beauduin and his work—the bi-ritual community at Amay. The following is a typical example:

A monk with a quite extraordinary gift for not minding his own business . . . having been charged to look eastward [purpose of Amay], Dom Lambert turned his eyes westward and began to busy himself with the history and practices of the Church called Anglican instead of the Churches called Orthodox.[61]

Such publicity further contributed to the difficulties of the fledgling monastery which preached the "heretical doctrine" of group reunion rather than individual conversions: the mortal sin of Malines and hence of Mercier and Beauduin.

That van Roey's well-meaning revelation seriously jeopardized Beauduin's career is further reflected in the sentence he received in his subsequent Roman trial. It imposed a complete severance of any connection with the Anglican question. A touch of humor is evident in his later articles on Malines and the Anglican situation: all were signed as Halifax had signed the Proposal: XXX.[62] Although Beauduin became associated with the Anglicans by a strange combination of circumstances and afterward suffered much because of this involvement, he never lost his love for them. One could almost think that divine providence put the seal of approval on his efforts because during his lengthy Paris exile (1934–1951) he served as chaplain in two convents which had strong links with the English and a definite ecumenical spirit.

In the light of the repercussions of van Roey's action, one may well wonder how Beauduin's role was discovered. Years later in a conversation with his nephew, Edouard Beauduin, the octogenarian recounted the details.[63] During the Holy Year of 1925 van Roey was in Rome and Beauduin gave him an oral message to deliver to Mercier: "Tell the cardinal that the document requested by him will be sent with a little delay." After Halifax's book appeared, van Roey noted the Proposal's similarity with several of Beauduin's articles that summarized the essential contents of the Proposal.[64] Van Roey thus had little difficulty in deducing the true author. Moreover, when the above-mentioned articles first appeared in 1926 they raised such a storm of protest that, at the urging of Bishop Rutten, Beauduin actually published Mercier's letter of thanks for the Proposal,[65] and even went so far as to associate his articles with the "paper" presented at the Malines Conversations. The matter had quickly subsided in 1926–1927, but by 1930–1931 the ecumenical climate had changed radically, at least in Rome.

However, to return to the content of his paper, it is certainly a little hard to agree with his critics that *nothing* in the past or present permits the Anglican Church to identify itself with Orthodoxy. Admittedly the Anglican position is *not* identical with that of Orthodoxy, but at least since the beginning of the seventeenth century there have been Anglicans (Lancelot Andrewes, for example) who thought it was very similar. Read in the ecumenical atmosphere of post-Vatican II days, therefore, the historical weaknesses of the Proposal are perhaps outweighed by its ecclesiological intuitions and Beauduin's frank recognition of the presence and action of the Holy Spirit in a community.

If bitter invective marred the public image of these exchanges, positive reactions were not wanting. Already in 1930, the Lambeth Conference emphasized the possibilities suggested by this early ecumenical experience:

Since the death of Cardinal Mercier, such conversations have been forbidden, and Roman Catholics have, in the encyclical letter *Mortalium Animos* [1928], been prohibited from taking part in any conference on unity. The committee desires to express its conviction of the value of such conversations and conferences carried out in a spirit of loyalty, and it much regrets that by the action of the pope all such meetings have been forbidden, and Roman Catholics have been prohibited from taking part in conferences on Reunion. This regret . . . is shared by many members of the Church of Rome. They regret also that in the encyclical the method of "complete absorption" has been proposed to the exclusion of that suggested in the Conversations, as, for example, in . . . "L'Eglise Anglicaine unie, non absorbée." There are difficulties greater than perhaps were realized in the scheme proposed, but it has the great merit of attempting to recognize to some extent at any rate the autonomy which might be possible in a united Church.[66]

The method pursued at Malines—that of joint theological conferences—is now recognized as *the* method, with the added proviso that there must be total liberty beyond the absolute essentials. From the vantage point of almost fifty years distance, a more positive evaluation now seems appropriate. Five areas of agreement were certainly reached: (1) the primacy of honor of the papacy; (2) the real presence in the reception of the eucharist; (3) the truly sacrificial character of the eucharist—although of a mystical nature; (4) the nature of the episcopacy as of divine law; and (5) the giving of communion under both forms as a matter of discipline rather than dogma. Nevertheless, crucial problems pertaining to each area were not defined because Halifax thought that "it would be advantageous to consider the extent of the rights accorded to Canterbury by the Holy See, rather than the theological question of the extent of papal power."

After almost four hundred years of separation, two religious communions were brought together. The meeting of minds and hearts initiated by the conversations continues today. To speak of the total or partial failure of these dialogues makes no sense. That they became embroiled in public controversy was an unfortunate circumstance beyond the control of the participants who tried to avoid conflict with their respective institutions. And yet, by their patient perseverance, they nevertheless sought to accomplish what they believed to be the invitation of the Holy Spirit. Although Beauduin's Proposal marked an important episode in the development of Roman Catholic thought over the difference between conversionist and unionist views, it was temporarily eclipsed by a serious weakness in the make-up of Malines. The ideas of the participants were unfortunately associated in their day with theologies representative of minority groups, enjoying only a quasi-official recognition (the Anglicans) or a totally unofficial status (the Roman Catholics). Obviously no one was bound to take their conclusions seriously. Yet the very theological obstacles they found insoluable in their capacity as theologians and historians are the same barriers that continue to keep the two Churches apart: essentially the question of orders, the papacy, the tradition of authoritarianism, and dogmatic definitions, In actual fact then they cannot be considered totally unrepresentative.

The lasting merit of Beauduin's Proposal lies in its implicit recognition of the validity of practices and traditions in other Churches, even though they may differ from Roman Catholic usage. Many of these differing customs are quite in harmony with the essentials of the faith and are in no sense deserving of the blanket condemnation they generally received. Beauduin helped to open eyes to the legitimacy of these traditions and to the necessity of Catholics showing a greater readiness to sacrifice non-essentials, even to the extent of giving up episcopal sees.[67]

In the light of the repeated setbacks which Anglo-Roman efforts experienced in the 1890's and the 1920's, the events of the 1960's are truly remarkable. The momentum generated by these pioneers has reached a crucial point. Already the 1970's have witnessed several exciting developments. Will history record the realization of what was so earnestly sought at Malines? Or will it instead see the demise of the ecumenical movement and the beginning of the "post-ecumenical age"? [68]

The year 1970 began and ended with essentially the same ideas as found in the Proposal circulating in official circles. In January, the Anglican-Roman Catholic International Commission, consisting of official representatives to both the Anglican and the Roman Catholic Chuches as a *whole*, released the following:

> No doubt exists in the minds of any of the members that the final aim of our work is the attainment of full organic union between our two Communions.

And this dramatic declaration was followed by an equally revolutionary editorial in *The Tablet* entitled "United Not Absorbed":

> We should be less than Christian if we made it a condition of the future unity that the Church of England would surrender all this [their own tradition of worship and administration] in favor of our modern traditions which are largely continental or Irish in origin. We should be ready to allow the Church of England, indeed the whole worldwide Anglican Communion, to go on existing in a united Church rather as the Catholic Uniate Churches exist today.[69]

Are these words the expression of a naive optimism or the Spirit speaking in our midst? Only time will tell. Certainly the ecumenical significance of the visit of the Archbishop of Canterbury to the Holy Father in 1966 should give pause for reflection. The protocol was worked out to characterize the event as the visit of one Church to another. The climax came, however, when the pope placed his episcopal ring on Archbishop Arthur Michael Ramsey's finger and said: "This is not yet the ring of marriage but of engagement." One does not go to such trouble for a simple layman. It also raises the question of Anglican orders,[70] a question which may be resolved before this book appears.

At the 1971 meeting of the International Commission, it was agreed that the concept of sacrifice is equally present in the Roman and the Anglican understanding of the eucharist. Moreover, the participants placed the problems of orders and of authority on the agenda for the September 1972 meeting as the next logical step to intercommunion. They concluded that substantial agreement on the doctrine of the eucharist had been reached and that should any points of disagreement arise in the future, they could be resolved in terms of the principles established at the 1971 meeting.

Although the American House of Bishops of the Episcopal Church endorsed the report with "gratitude and enthusiasm," neither Rome nor Canterbury has officially and authoritatively ratified the document. But it clearly represents a significant and positive advance over all previous efforts.

Conclusion

Mercier and Beauduin shared a common enthusiasm for the great movements of the century: liturgy and ecumenism. In both areas their names were closely linked. Their mutual involvement in things liturgical is quite evident, but the extent to which their ecumenical interests also coincided may not be so well known.

Although the cardinal died without ever having visited Amay, he was Beauduin's confidant from the very beginning. In the cover letter accompanying the Proposal, the monk devoted much more space to the foundation he was about to make than to his paper. Mentioning that he was sending the plan for the community under separate cover, he expressed his happiness in sharing it with the cardinal and looked forward with eagerness to working once more under his kind patronage.[71]

Almost simultaneously with his involvement in the Malines Conversations, Mercier had become interested in the Eastern question through the influx of Russian émigrés into Belgium following the revolution of 1917. Thus his Eastern awakening in a practical or immediate sense preceded Beauduin's. Moreover, he had known the majestic figure of the Metropolitan Andrew Szepticky since the turn of the century. This latter was to be one of the several personalities who along with Cyril Korolevsky and Michel d'Herbigny would play a role in the foundation of Amay and the orientation that Beauduin was to give his community.

5

Looking Eastward

Beauduin's involvement in the Anglican question during his professorship at Rome was a brief footnote in comparison to the complex
issues he faced with the foundation of his monastic experiment.
Through a series of unforeseen circumstances this venture became
entangled in intrigue which Beauduin naively thought would evaporate once he left the scene. Two men in particular, with opposing
views as to how unity could best be achieved, each tried to win him
over. It is important that these men—Szepticky, the Ruthenian
metropolitan, and d'Herbigny, the Jesuit curialist—along with their
schemes, be clearly understood if one is fully to appreciate the com-
plicated nature of Beauduin's position and the significance of his eventual plan of action. To these two names we add that of Korolevsky, the noted specialist on Eastern Christianity in Rome at that time.

To give some context to the portraits of these figures, consideration first must be given to the nature of the Church as conceived in
the East and the West. This in itself will explain part of the problems
associated with the early unity schemes, since d'Herbigny preached a
doctrine of mass conversion of Russia while Szepticky promoted the
revitalization of the Ruthenian Church (the Russian Church united
with Rome) as *the* means to East-West reunion.

The Nature of the Church

It is presumptuous to try to depict in a few paragraphs the differences between Eastern and Western ecclesiology. Schmemann says that the Church does not exist and cannot be defined apart from the very content of her life.[1] The Fathers at Vatican II tried to describe this content in the *Constitution on the Church*. Unfortunately the sensitivity we see today to the essential mystery of the Church was frequently lacking fifty years ago.

A colonizing mentality prevailed in Rome in the 1920's which revealed the utter ignorance in Eastern affairs of some of those who determined Church policy. The struggle that seemed to center around Roman primacy was symptomatic of a fundamental misunderstanding of Eastern ecclesiology. Two basically different approaches to the nature of the Church were involved. The West tended to posit unity as a fact, seeing local churches as parts of the whole. In the East, the local church was the focal point, and unity between these churches was the ideal. For Rome there was no theological or practical objection to several different bishops and rites in one place because the criterion of unity was not the bishop but the pope. Orthodox ecclesiology, however, insisted on manifest Catholic unity on the local level. Thus divisions among Orthodox constituted a serious blow to their witness to the world.[2] Separation remains a scandal in the West and the East, but it is certainly defined differently. The realization of the ineffectiveness of some structures within the autocephalous churches has led to an ever-growing concern for unity in the Orthodox world, a concern that was yet in its embryonic stage in the 1920's.

Beauduin would therefore propose that his monks familiarize themselves with these East-West differences which Szepticky so aptly summarized:

Catholics see the *extension* of the Church and the members of the faithful; the Orthodox see the *depth* of the Church and the quality of its members. Historical argument will never convince the Orthodox; the exterior, social, quantitative or statistical facts are of little importance to them. . . . Moral theology as a system is almost non-existent; what the Orthodox call moral is practically the same as our ascetical or mystical theology: love of God, prayer, mystical depths of human life, elevation of the soul towards God.[3]

The challenge lay in accepting the value of both views and in resisting the temptation to label one as superior. Having mastered this initial stage, one could then let this appreciation radiate out into the world. But the residue of alienation which had built up over the centuries proved a major obstacle to any type of reconciliation. How much Uniatism and the Latinizing policies it spawned contributed to this estrangement is anybody's guess.[4]

History traces the remote origin of this phenomenon to Innocent III who in the early thirteenth century wanted to unify the Church along Western lines. This obviously was blatantly contrary to the ancient traditions of the East which had lived for a thousand years under a quite different regime. Nevertheless the pope's emissaries tried to reattach directly to Rome those parts of the ancient Eastern Churches with which they entered into relations. This action simply extended, yet modified, what the crusades had begun, replacing Eastern bishoprics, including patriarchates, with Latin ecclesiastical structures. The essential difference to be noted between what the crusades did and what Uniatism was eventually to achieve is this: the crusades abolished the Eastern rite and sees while the Uniate system tried to save them.

The Russian Church

In the ninth century, Byzantine monks laid the foundations for the Russian Church. Its first episcopal see was Kiev, later moved to Vladimir and finally to Moscow under the Metropolitan Peter 1308–26. The Mongolian invasion of 1240 effectively isolated Russia from Europe for several centuries, and subsequent dealings with Europe, particularly with the Roman Church and her representatives, whether official or unofficial (Teutonic Knights of the thirteenth century), did little to foster trust. Although alliances between Russia and the West were sometimes formed, they frequently dealt with the ownership of Catholic Poland. Rome, operating under the illusion that Russia could be gained for reunion, willingly compromised, apparently unaware that Moscow's dream was to be the Third Rome.[5]

In 1441 the Metropolitan Isidore returned from the Council of Florence and announced union with Rome. Three days later he was imprisoned; after some months of confinement in a monastery he was allowed to escape. Meanwhile much correspondence had been exchanged between Moscow and Constantinople in an attempt to understand the rationale behind this union. Finally, dissatisfied with the answers to their questions, the Russians enthroned a new metropolitan, Jonas, in 1448, and then announced their action to Constantinople. Henceforth Russia was independent. Their first patriarch, Job, was consecrated by the ecumenical patriarch of Constantinople in 1589.

The aggressiveness of the Catholics in the Ukraine starting with the fourteenth century did little to establish friendly relations. The inroads made by Lutheran missionaries and the invasion of Russian territory by the Polish, who desecrated Orthodox churches, furthered the alienation between East and West.

The sixteenth century plunged Poland and the Ukraine into a serious religious crisis. Operating on a policy of religious tolerance, the leaders soon found that many resultant quarrels seriously disrupted the peace and threatened national unity. Thus it was that political movements in Poland and the Ukraine led to the acceptance of Trent in 1564, which opened the way to complete Catholic restoration. With the Union of Brest in 1596, the Orthodox Ruthenians of Galicia entered into the Church of Rome. Since Latin theology was already widely known and appreciated in the Ukraine, a marked interest in and openness to things Latin developed,[6] which added to the prestige of the Ruthenians who soon became the most numerous group of Uniates. Szepticky's task would be to try to undo more than three hundred years of steady Latinizing.

The process of Latinization, often described as enforced, was actually a long process which generally occurred through expressed agreement and was accelerated during times of reform. Deprived of contact with the Church from which they had come, these Churches naturally turned to the available models, especially in the reform of the clergy (i.e., they copied Latin seminaries or sent their men to them and imposed celibacy, etc., in order to be more "apostolic"). The Eastern Christians thus united to Rome progressively lost the cultural character of Orthodoxy through their association with a stronger (and Latin) Church.

Toward the end of the nineteenth century, under Leo XIII, a movement to de-Latinize these Churches began. It contained in germ the awareness that they had originally belonged to a structure other than that of the Roman Church which had unduly burdened them with forms and codes utterly foreign to their proper heritage. This, for example, explains the origin of the Melkite Patriarch Maximos IV's demands at Vatican II that a synod of bishops representing the national conferences of bishops be formed. This would, in effect, establish the equivalent of patriarchates in the Western Church.

At the beginning of the twentieth century, the Russian Orthodox Church was the largest and potentially the most powerful of all national Orthodox Churches. The political upheavals of the first decades of the century completely changed the situation. The determined efforts of the Communists to wipe out all traces of the past, and especially of the religious past, led to a westward migration. Unlike the revolutionaries who admired certain materialistic values of the West, these religious refugees had, with few exceptions, a long-standing hostility for things Western, above all for things Latin.

If it is difficult to understand why these émigrés should have had such a deep distrust of the people from whom they were seeking asylum, two facts must be kept in mind: (1) because of a deeply rooted distrust on the part of the Orthodox toward any initiative coming from Rome, they found it difficult to believe that Rome was capable of disinterested action; [7] (2) although they received a sympathetic welcome in the West,[8] they were nevertheless appalled to realize how totally misunderstood were the circumstances that necessitated their voluntary or involuntary exile. Many non-Russians tended to view the Bolshevik revolution simply as a political struggle between the old order and the new. For the Russian émigré, the Western world was already totally secularized, and for a long time he felt ill at ease in this new atmosphere.

The very make-up of those who managed to escape further confounded the issue. For the most part, the refugees arriving in Belgium represented an intellectual elite, hardly in touch with the common people. Grounded as they were in Czarist imperialism, they inevitably gave an idealized image of Russia which tended to put the actual religious situation—so important to those engaged in the work for unity—a little out of focus. Not realizing that Orthodoxy permeated every dimension of the people's life, men like d'Herbigny concluded that Orthodoxy was dying, if not dead. Its survival was due, however, to its popular character, for the Russian Church never depended solely on the clergy but relied heavily on lay involvement.

Cardinal Mercier was truly admirable in the efforts he expended on the behalf of the refugees. He established a foundation to welcome young émigrés, provided them with the necessities of life and helped them to pursue higher studies. One of these, a nobleman, Constantine Lialine, became a Catholic in 1926. Several years later this eminent recruit joined Beauduin at Amay and gave to the monastery's journal *Irénikon* an indisputable pre-eminence in the ecumenically oriented world of scholarship.[9] Much later he began the internationally-known annual ecumenical days at Chevetogne.

Part of Beauduin's mission would be to combat through ecumenical and liturgical principles the ignorance these émigrés encountered in Belgium. In this way he sought to foster a solid basis for fruitful East-West dialogue. He also tried to reassure these Orthodox that at least some persons in the West understood and appreciated their liturgy and tradition. Although a truly Slavonic vocation may be said to have resulted, Beauduin reacted from the very beginning against an ecumenism that was too narrowly conceived. His repeated emphasis on a totally Russian orientation soon led him to disavow his first contacts, or at least the schemes associated with Szepticky and d'Herbigny.

Metropolitan Szepticky

Almost seven feet tall and ascetic in appearance, Metropolitan Andrew Szepticky cut a striking figure. His influence on Beauduin was not limited to the sphere of Christian unity alone. Some credit must also be given to him for Beauduin's focus on the patriarchate in his famous Proposal, as well as for confirming his sense of the importance of the episcopacy and of the local churches, both of which were too universally absorbed by Rome in his day.

Born on August 10, 1865, at Prylbice, Galicia, of a Boyar family which had abandoned both its ancestral religion and Ukrainian nationality to become Latin-rite Poles, Alexander Szepticky overcame parental objections to return to the rite of his ancestors. Finally, after he had obtained his doctoral degree in 1888, they allowed him to enter the Basilians, a Greek Catholic order. It was at this time that he took the name of Andrew, patron of Russia and Ruthenia.[10] Professed in 1892, he became bishop of Stanislavov at the age of thirty-four and two years later, in 1901, Archbishop of Lvov (Leopol) and Metropolitan of Halycz, Galicia,[11] a position he held until his death on November 1, 1944. In his last years disease reduced him to almost complete paralysis and constant pain. In 1945 all his bishops were deported to Russia, and shortly thereafter, in March of 1946, a handful of clergy and laity revoked the 350-year-old Ukrainian union with Rome.

The pastoral side of this man was truly admirable. Each year he devoted two or three months to visiting some of his seven hundred parishes. In this way he got to know each parish personally. During his visitation he preached, heard confessions, and made home visits. His pastorals often anticipated later pronouncements of the Holy See. Some have called him the Ukrainian Mercier because, like the Belgian primate, he did not hesitate to risk Russian or Nazi reprisals in his attempts to speak to his people.

His love of things Ukrainian frequently led him to Venice in search of old Slavonic manuscripts from the fifteenth century for his museum. On these occasions he invariably combined business with the pleasure of a visit with Cardinal Sarto. Shortly after the latter's elevation to the papacy as Pius X, Szepticky made known his rights to the metropolitan see of Kiev, which included a diocese in Russian territory: Kamenets-Podolsk.

One can measure the typical lack of sensitivity toward Orthodoxy so prevalent during this period by Pius X's reply concerning these rights. He agreed to confer patriarchal rights on Szepticky, including the right to nominate and consecrate bishops without asking Roman confirmation (an Eastern privilege officially recognized by Vatican II). Szepticky's new patriarchal see extended from the Ukraine and the Balkan States to Russia—as far as Vladivostock and the Pacific. The cardinal secretary of state, Merry del Val, who was suspicious and puzzled about what was going on, intervened on various occasions. When the metropolitan mentioned this to Pius X, the Holy Father replied, "You have no need to be troubled about Merry del Val; you have to deal with me myself and that is sufficient." A total of seventeen documents, drawn up as canonical safeguards, were authenticated by various cardinals acting as apostolic notaries; Mercier was one of them.[12]

On the strength of this, Szepticky managed to accomplish quite a few firsts. In 1907 he established the first Greek Catholic diocese for Slavs in the United States. In 1912 he did the same for Canada and

Brazil. At the end of World War I he created the Russian Catholic exarchate in response to a strong hope for the return of the Orthodox, undoubtedly the result of his wartime experiences, since in 1914, when the Russians invaded Galicia, he had been arrested, deported to Russia and finally confined in the Orthodox Monastery of the Transfiguration at Souzdal.[13]

Once peace was restored, the metropolitan went abroad, touring England, France, and Belgium in 1921. While in Belgium he renewed his friendship with Mercier and had his first contact with Beauduin. This visit was motivated by a twofold desire: union and reform. In fact, earlier that year he had given a remarkable conference in Rome on this very topic: "Monasticism and Union." [14] It was through a return to the primitive structures and traditions that both projects would be realized.

On the matter of union he insisted that Eastern Catholics, and in particular his Ruthenians, become more Orthodox as a guarantee to Orthodoxy that union did not mean jettisoning an ancient and valid liturgical and cultural heritage. Moreover, he argued, Roman recognition and appreciation of things Orthodox would add a new dimension to Roman spirituality and truly confirm the Church of Rome as catholic or ecumenical in fact as well as in principle. The very terms accepted by the "Uniates" in the past were seen as more injurious than helpful to the healing of the centuries-old breach.

The creation of a favorable atmosphere between Eastern Catholics and the Orthodox—as well as efforts to arouse Western interest in the problem of union—only reflected part of the motivation behind Szepticky's visit to Mont César. Because he believed that monasticism would play a significant role in the restoration of Christian unity, the metropolitan hoped to elicit some concrete collaboration from Western monks. Already in 1906 he had begun a monastic experiment at Sknylov with a group of peasants, constantly encouraging them to an ever greater de-Latinization in the hopes that they would become an influential example of the pure Byzantine-Slavonic rite for the Ukrainians. Drawing his inspiration from the rule of the famous Stoudion monastery at Constantinople, he called his monks "studites."

The original monastery had been destroyed during the war. Reestablished at Uniov, it was then flourishing. Several new foundations had sprung up, including three convents.[15] With the phenomenal growth in vocations, Szepticky realized the need for more educated monks to guarantee the maximum of spiritual formation for these new recruits. Since monasticism was all but non-existent among the Ukrainian Catholics, he had gone to several French, English and Belgian monasteries trying to attract competent volunteers for this work.[16]

The metropolitan's detailed description of his present monks and the future hopes he had for their contribution to the life of the Church fascinated Beauduin. This Ukrainian brand of monasticism incorporated all he wished for in his own project: a lay monasticism,[17] great importance given to manual work, and an ecclesial renaissance nourished in authentic liturgical life. Moreover, those studites attracted to intellectual work were encouraged to study means of approaching the Orthodox.[18] The possibilities it created were even greater than those anticipated in his own plan.

This encounter with Szepticky was not to be Beauduin's last. Although the former was originally interested in obtaining Benedictine help, once he became aware of Beauduin's plan he directed his attentions to him. Relations subsequently established between Amay and the studites continued spasmodically for some time. World War II and the metropolitan's death, however, brought an end to any dreams of joint efforts.

The metropolitan and Beauduin had a common inspiration: a return to authenticity. Both had embraced a monastic vocation only to find modern monasticism lacking and out of touch with ancient traditions and, on occasion, with reality.[19] Both were keenly interested in a renewal: Szepticky had begun his in the Orient; Beauduin was yet to begin his in the Occident—which, rather than being limited to that of an institution within the Church (monasticism), would direct its efforts toward an ecumenical renewal within the whole Church.

Although this difference in orientation eventually led to Beauduin's disenchantment with Szepticky's approach, due credit must be given to the metropolitan for his sincere and tireless efforts in the work of union, even though he never openly directed his appeal for union to the Russians but only to the Ukrainians with whom he lived. One of the few Eastern Catholics in his day who realized and admitted the serious error of Latinization, he sincerely believed that his method was the only solution. His studites were to play a twofold role: first of all they would reaffirm their loyalty to the Eastern heritage and Rome's recognition of the legitimacy of this heritage; secondly, they would reteach to the West the riches of the East—her liturgy, the true monastic ideal, and her entire spiritual and theological legacy, especially as found in the traditions of the Greek Fathers.

Cyril Korolevsky

A Frenchman named Charon was a fascinating figure who gained fame as Cyril Korolevsky (1878–1959). Ordained in the Byzantine rite in 1902, he soon became extremely interested in the Russian question. When he came under Szepticky's jurisdiction in 1909, he was joined to the Russian eparchy of Kamenets-Podolsk, but his desire to work directly with the Slavs was doomed to frustration. Instead he spent most of his life in Rome doing research into the history of the Ruthenian Church for the metropolitan. Here he achieved recognition as one of the most erudite Orientalists of the day.[20] His ten years on the Vatican Library staff (1919–1929) enabled him to give invaluable service to the newly-formed Pontifical Oriental Institute.[21] Because of this familiarity with Eastern affairs, Pius XI had him accompany Eugene Tisserant (1884–1972), the future cardinal-secretary of the Sacred Congregation for the Oriental Church, on a special mission in Eastern Europe. After Korolevsky's second report on Bulgaria, Roncalli, the future Pope John XXIII, was sent there as apostolic visitor.

Although certainly less directly influential in the formation of Beauduin's Oriental vocation,[22] Korolevsky still deserves credit for introducing the Belgian to the pertinent articles in *Revue Bénédictine* describing Leo XIII's dream and the proposals for implementing it suggested by the noted liturgist and ecumenist mentioned earlier, Gerard van Caloen. The pontiff's seemingly prophetic words that Benedictine monasticism was to be the source of reconciliation between East and West could not help but cause tremors of excitement to run through Beauduin. This discovery touched off an "explosion" at his next class, similar to the one that occurred at Mont César over the liturgy, for papal pronouncements had a quasi-sacramental value in his eyes—especially when they supported one of his projects.

Benedict XV's untimely death in 1922, just as the Eastern question was gaining widespread attention for the first time since Leo XIII, caused great consternation in Oriental circles. Would the new pontiff embark on some entirely different apostolate, or would he adopt Benedict's program?

Michel d'Herbigny

From the very beginning of his pontificate, Pius XI showed himself extremely interested in the Eastern question and especially in the Slavonic East. Under papal patronage, the third significant influence in Beauduin's Oriental initiation quickly rose to prominence: Michel d'Herbigny, S.J. (1880–1957). Named president of the Pontifical Oriental Institute in 1922 (also professor of comparative dogma and fundamental theology at the Gregorianum), he became editor of *Orientalia Christiana* in 1923 and a consultor for the Sacred Congregation for the Oriental Church in September 1924. On June 20, 1925, the Pontifical Commission for Russia was created within the Sacred Congregation for the Oriental Church with d'Herbigny as consultor. From 1930–1933 he was also president of this commission.

Having tried to obtain a visa for Russia since 1922, he finally succeeded and made a preliminary visit to Moscow in October 1925 for the French government. He supposedly went to study the state of those Catholic parishes created since Catherine II and prior to 1914.[23] It is clear that his trip helped pave the way for his elevation to the episcopacy. His gratitude to the nuncio Eugenio Pacelli, who consecrated him Titular Bishop of Ilium (without any co-consecrators) in Berlin, March 1926, is reflected in his account of the ensuing mission into the U.S.S.R.[24] At the same time he was named rector of the Pontifical Oriental Institute, retaining his previous offices as president, prefect of studies and editor.[25]

The unmentioned purpose of the Russian trip was to replace bishops who had been executed or deported. The new bishop divided the province of Mogilev into a number of apostolic administrations and secretly consecrated a number of bishops from among the surviving priests. Through indiscretions, the Soviet authorities found out the true nature of his visit, which immediately compromised the position of the newly consecrated bishops. They were soon tracked down and imprisoned, shot or exiled. Only one survived.[26] Ultimately the trip intensified Soviet hostility toward Rome. From this point on d'Herbigny increased his campaign against communism. In 1936, for instance, the head of the Jesuit Secretariat on Atheistic Communism praised Bishop d'Herbigny for his anti-communist conferences in France. (Sometimes he gave as many as seven a day!) [27]

The fall of this powerful figure proved to be even more rapid than his rise. On January 3, 1932 he received a letter from Cardinal Secretary of State Pacelli announcing papal acceptance of his resignation as rector of the Oriental Institute and naming him honorary president. His duties as rector, prefect of studies, editor of *Orientalia Christiana* and consultor of the Sacred Congregation for the Oriental Church were assumed by Fr. Emil Herman on January 6. [28] Thus he would take his devastating action against Beauduin after he himself began to slip from power, although facts surrounding his humiliation only became known in bits and pieces and still are not too clear. Apparently the Polish government played some part in it, but the Jesuit had also taken liberties with the use of the pope's name. In an attempt to get Brémond's place in the French Academy, he had assured members of the left that such action would please the Holy Father. [29]

In 1934 the Pontifical Commission for Russia was reorganized, and neither d'Herbigny nor the Commission appear in any subsequent indices of the *AAS*. Whatever the circumstances may have been, the penalty that d'Herbigny had to pay was not slight. Deprived of his episcopal rank and privileges, his name was never added to the necrology of bishops or mentioned in the *Memorabilia Societatis Jesu*. Even the Pontifical Oriental Institute simply celebrated a mass *pro defuncto sacerdote* (for a deceased priest) and not one *pro defuncto episcopo* (for a deceased bishop). No official explanation of this matter has even been made public. [31]

If his life itself is shrouded in mystery, his relationship with Beauduin was equally enigmatic. In the beginning, however, d'Herbigny did much to aid the neophyte Orientalist. It was he who first informed Pius XI about a monk at Sant' Anselmo who seemed just the person needed to realize the "Oriental dream." [32] Beauduin soon sensed that their dreams had little in common, but he continued to depend on the positions of d'Herbigny and Szepticky because he felt that influential backing for his bold plan was necessary.

This was a fatal mistake. A certain naiveté is only too evident in his belief that once he was far away in Belgium living a life of pure monasticism, the promoters would turn the complete direction of the project over to him. Based on fundamentally opposing principles, their dreams were irreconcilable. Both Szepticky and d'Herbigny were exclusively interested in training monks to be sent into Orthodox lands. In d'Herbigny's case the first action was more precise. He had visions of a sort of mass invasion of Russia, sweeping the Orthodox off their feet and bringing them back to Rome. Nothing could have been further from the vision of Beauduin. Had he realized the pressures and the problems these associations were to cost him, especially those with d'Herbigny, he might have sought support elsewhere. But it was one of his weaknesses to trust people, even if he had doubts about their sincerity.

Conclusion

In the light of all that has transpired ecumenically in the past fifty years it is easy to be critical of the shortcomings of the views of these pioneers, but criticism is not claim to having found *the* solution, or even a better solution.[33] Certainly it is undeniable that today the so-called Uniate Churches pose a unique ecumencial problem. Viewed by the Orthodox as schismatics, these Christians suddenly find their position vis-à-vis Rome precarious and ambiguous to say the very least. As our understanding of the original schism deepens, as the West accepts her share of responsibility for it, and as the concept of "united not absorbed" gains acceptance, Rome is confused and embarrassed by the existence of these Churches. Having encouraged whole communities to separate from their original Churches, a reality unknown in the first fifteen centuries of Church history, the Vatican is now caught on the horns of the dilemma. To tell the Uniates to go back to Orthodoxy is a rather indelicate solution, yet each overture for reunion is sharply hampered by the existence of these same Churches. Vatican II's *Decree on the Eastern Catholic Churches* clearly states the principles of a particular Church: [34] it has its own theology, liturgy and canonical equality. The different rites "are consequently of equal dignity." Rome herself is just one of these particular Churches. But the existence of two particular Churches, each with the same theology, liturgy, and canon law, does not really make sense. Rome's solution to this dilemma is best expressed by the positions taken by two Vatican congregations: the Secretariat for Unity apparently is pro-Orthodox; the Sacred Congregation for the Oriental Church is pro-Uniate.

As the East-West dialogue develops, the West—Rome in particular—has begun to realize that the great fault of Uniatism is that it creates a dissident Church of Orthodoxy. Eastern Catholics are increasingly reflecting in their own actions the conviction that they must look to the East for their models and that they must indeed become more Orthodox if they in fact are to contribute to the catholicity of the Church. Their role, in short, is to live Orthodoxy in Roman Catholicism. Beauduin had similar intuitions fifty years ago, but he was unable to act on them fully due to the strictures placed upon him, as will become evident in the following chapters.

6

The Prehistory of Amay

Beauduin arrived in Rome in 1921 very much caught up with the possibility of a new experiment in monasticism. In the wake of Szepticky's enlightening conference, the dream had begun to take on shape and form, and the direction it would eventually take was greatly influenced by Beauduin's contacts during the next four years. To his amazement, he discovered that something very much akin to his idea had already been proposed. The preliminary speculation done by these spiritual ancestors provided yet another contribution to the practical realization of the project. At the same time the ecumenical climate in which he found himself matured, broadened, and in some instances even radically modified his earlier views on the nature and reality of the Church.

Remote Preparation

In spite of the vitality radiating from some Benedictine monasteries, the fourteenth centenary of St. Benedict's death, commemorated in 1880, had found the Benedictine order as a whole in a state of progressive but very slow renewal. Something needed to be done to accelerate these efforts to restore the order to its former vigor.

Leo XIII evidently shared this concern. During his pontificate he did everything in his power to upgrade the education of the regular clergy. To attack the problem on an international level he proposed a central college at Rome where Benedictines from every country could pursue their theological studies. The story of this papal project will introduce us to some of Beauduin's "spiritual ancestors."

From the start, the reaction of the various abbots was far from enthusiastic.[1] Not only were they reluctant to send their best men in order to have a first-rate faculty, but they were suspicious that the whole project might set a dangerous precedent for future Roman interference. Leo XIII nevertheless went ahead with his plans. A site was chosen on the Aventine Hill, and Hildebrand de Hemptinne, abbot of Maredsous and friend of the pope, was placed in charge. By 1887 the Benedictine College of Sant' Anselmo had become a reality.

The renewal of the Benedictine Order was not, however, the chief reason for the pontiff's very personal interest in establishing the college. Although perhaps not taken too seriously by the Benedictine abbots when they first became aware of it, Leo XIII had far-reaching plans for the Orient, and he expected the future graduates of Sant' Anselmo to play a major role in this undertaking. Having told the abbots that he counted on their support for the Orient, he then addressed several personal letters to high-ranking Benedictines, hinting at some as yet undisclosed project. Cardinal Joseph Dusmet, Archbishop of Cantania (Sicily), was one of the first to whom the Holy Father addressed himself:

> You know how much this [the erection of Sant' Anselmo] means to us. It is connected with several of our projects, especially in view of the good of the Eastern Church.[2]

Several months later, the Benedictine Gerard van Caloen received more explicit details, including the request that he found a monastery for union.[3]

Although van Caloen never realized the foundation of this monastery, he penned a series of articles on ecumenism in *Revue Bénédictine* between 1891–1896, outlining a program similar to the one Beauduin eventually drew up.

> These monks, formed in advance in the liturgy, the language and the customs of the Greeks, will go toward them as brothers, establish themselves there and lead a purely monastic and liturgical life which

the Greeks admire so sincerely. It will not be a question of con-
verting them or of proselytizing. They will limit themsleves to
forming great centers of prayer, of liturgy, and of serious studies.
. . . One can easily imagine what influence such monks and
monasteries will soon have and what a powerful balance they will
bring to the ideas of unity which are beginning to appear in the
Orient. By their life, liturgy, relations, writings and preaching,
these monks will dispel little by little the prejudices which still
exist against the Roman Church. They will win hearts by abstain-
ing from all irritating polemic. Finally, they will make the Greeks
see that the Roman Church does not in the least dream of taking
away from them their rites, customs, and ancient and venerable
traditions, since she will go even to the point of authorizing Latin
monks to adopt them out of love for their separated brothers.[4]

During an audience in 1893 granted to the students of Sant' Anselmo, the Holy Father developed his original inspiration in seeking
the creation of their college:

You know how concerned I am for the reconciliation of the Eastern
Churches. Well, I count on you to help me bring it about. I have
often said to myself: I need Benedictines for this. The Orientals still
have a deep respect for them, because they have remained men of
prayer and of the liturgy, and their origin goes back so many
centuries. Be docile and the pope will be able to make you his
helpers and send you to reconquer the Orient. This thought was
one of the motives that led me to erect the College of Sant'
Anselmo. Among all the orders, only the Benedictines do not
arouse suspicion in the Orient. When the students of Sant' Anselmo
are familiar with the Fathers of the Church and with Saint Basil
and Saint Chrysostom, they will be able to preach in turn in Greece,
at Athens, at Smyrna, anywhere. If I speak of Greece . . . I think
of the whole Orient, even the Far East. The heart of the pope
must embrace the whole universe. Monasteries must rise up everywhere to bring back to the truth those who have strayed. It is
from Sant' Anselmo that I want to see these colonies leave.[5]

All the fundamental points are present: an approach to the East
through monasticism, an appreciation of its liturgy and great Fathers,
and the realization that the East would be best reached through
Greek rather than Latin channels. What then delayed this apostolate

for more than a quarter of a century? The most obvious explanation is that the times were not ready for such ideas.

Leo XIII showed himself a true champion of the East in his appreciation of the sacredness of the Oriental rite: its liturgy, traditions and theology. Through this respect for the valid differences in the various rites he became one of the first to speak out against the "Latinization" of Eastern Christians,[6] until then an almost expected condition imposed upon any separated Church seeking union with Rome.

In 1897 he took another step toward the completion of his Oriental project. Once again he contacted his friend de Hemptinne, this time to accept in the name of the entire Benedictine Order the direction of the Greek College of Saint Athanasius which prepared priests for Greece and the Near East.

Unfortunately the succeeding popes did not carry on this apostolate with the same energy and conviction as Leo XIII. The interests of Pius X (1903–1914) had a more liturgical and pastoral bent. Benedict XV (1914–1922), at first caught up in World War I and its consequent problems in the post-war years, hardly had time to take up the work of Leo XIII on the Oriental problem before his death. That he recognized the need is evident, for in 1917 he had organized the Sacred Congregation for the Oriental Church, separating it from the Propaganda. He also had established the Pontifical Oriental Institute which he entrusted to the Benedictines. Ildephonse Schuster, the abbot of St. Paul-Outside-the-Walls, a noted liturgist and the author of the seven-volume *Liber Sacramentorum*, became its first president. (Subsequently named Archbishop of Milan in 1929, he died in 1954.) The Institute tried to counteract the errors and prejudices current in ecclesiastical textbooks of the day. The curriculum of the latter gave special emphasis to a comparative study of Catholic and Orthodox doctrine. A further unique feature is seen in the Institute's admission policy: lectures were open to both Orthodox and Catholics.

When Pius XI, former nuncio to Poland (1919–1921), ascended the chair of Peter in 1922, he shared Leo XIII's and Benedict XV's interest in the Orient. His pontificate carried out in large part the ideas and movements launched by these pioneers. Although he extended the teaching of Oriental studies to all seminaries, the most immediate need, due to political circumstances, had shifted from

Greece to Russia. Before long the Slavic question would almost totally eclipse the broader and more established concern for the East which, since Leo XIII, had been viewed in essentially Greek terms. This change of direction introduced a new dimension into the ecumenical question. Heretofore it had been a matter of dealing with Churches which had a history of union with Rome in the past— hence a matter of talking about reunion. With the Slavic Church, especially that of Russia, the situation was quite different, since Russia had never recognized the hegemony of Rome, yet had never officially broken with Rome.

Proximate Preparation

The 1920's were turbulent years on the continent. A new age, politically, economically, socially and spiritually, was opening up, throwing East and West into contact with one another as never before. In the area of religion alone, at least three factors contributed to this ferment: World War I, the Bolshevik revolution, and Leo XIII's letter on Anglican orders.

The recent war had brought men of all faiths together. In the face of death they discovered basic common beliefs that quite naturally expressed themselves in common prayer. With the end of hostilities, the crime of separation stood out in greater shamefulness and ugliness. Even prior to the war, Protestant missionaries to India had realized the scandal of preaching Christ and love to non-Christians in an atmosphere of rivalry and disunity. In 1910, at Edinburgh, they took their first decisive step toward union. "Faith and Order," one of the chief cornerstones of the future World Council of Churches, was an eventual outcome of this conference.

The impact of the revolution of 1917 has already been mentioned. It touched off a mass exodus of Orthodox who felt their religion threatened.

Leo XIII's letter on Anglican orders resulted in the redirection of English hopes for reunion from Rome to the Orthodox East. In 1920 the Orthodox attended the Conference of Lambeth, the official gathering of the Anglican hierarchy. With Patriarch Meletios Metaxakis of Alexandria's recognition of the validity of Anglican orders, intercommunion became a possibility. This act was followed in 1921 by the creation of the first Orthodox see at London.

Two other incidents might be mentioned. Beauduin considered

them of great significance in his article on the increased tempo of Anglo-Oriental relations because they concerned official celebrations: in Sweden at Uppsala Cathedral in August 1925, and at Westminster Abbey, June 29, 1925. In the first case the Patriarch of Alexandria was assisted in the solemn liturgy by the Archbishops of Uppsala and Canterbury. In the second, an Anglican bishop was assisted by the Patriarch of Alexandria. For Beauduin, these events literally consecrated the fact of intercommunion, even though it remained a practice reserved for special occasions.[7]

Did the ferment of the 1920's ignite a latent ecumenism in Beauduin, or was his Oriental vocation perhaps a natural outgrowth of the liturgical apostolate? In his earliest writings he showed not only a familiarity with Oriental questions and problems, but also a deep appreciation for the liturgical principles of which the East, unlike the West, never lost sight.

Both the motto of *Liturgical and Parochial Questions* and the theme of a liturgical retreat given by Beauduin in 1913 were *Ut unum sint* (That they may be one).[8] In article after article during the peak of his first liturgical career (1909–1914),[9] he waxed eloquent on the eucharist as the source of our union with Christ and with one another. On the strength of this, one could conclude that Beauduin was already an ecumenist, and the argument could be further supported with quotations from other articles which show a sympathetic understanding of the liturgical insights of non-Roman Churches.[10] Any such reading between the lines, however, is apparently demolished by the following statement:

In October 1921, I arrived at Rome at the College of Sant' Anselmo as professor of fundamental theology. Totally a stranger up until this moment to ecumenical questions, I was as exclusively Latin as one could be—that is to say, the question was for me non-existent. In my suitcases, lecture notes prepared during the vacation were carefully classified: schismatics and heretics in company with Jews and infidels were condemned *en bloc;* the four classic marks of the true Church, neither more nor less, with a luminous evidence hardly left room for good faith, and the axiom "Outside the Church no salvation" suffered no exception. My orthodoxy was irreproachable.[11]

Beauduin's frank disavowal of any ecumenical leanings prior to this period might cause one to wonder whether there was any continuity between his past orientations and the new horizon about to open up for him. Did it represent a complete change of direction or was it just coincidence that his young friend Rousseau, who was studying at Sant' Anselmo, should introduce Beauduin into the circle of Oriental intellectuals and sympathizers? All the evidence indicates an already long existing sensitivity to the contemporary needs of the Church and a serious mind ever in search of new answers to these problems.

Beauduin's flat denial must therefore be taken with the proverbial grain of salt. A typical Liègeois, he excelled in the local brand of humor—a special kind of understatement. Instinctively he tended to shrink from any attempt to put the spotlight on his personal accomplishments or interior motivation. This often led him to indulge in his favorite vice of putting the indiscreet interlocutor off guard with a half-serious reply.

There are other reasons, however, to argue for the existence of at least an embryonic ecumenism in Beauduin at this time. Although he remained very "Roman" to the end of his life, narrow provincialism was foreign to him. From the earliest moments of his priesthood, his one concern had been to go out to the people and minister to their needs. Because of this great love for people and his realistic attitude toward Church structures, he consistently urged change if the latter interfered with the interaction in love willed by Christ. His outspoken attitude toward the "episcopal trappings" of abbots was just one example of this. It is therefore obvious that in 1921, if his primary interest at the moment was not "ecumenism," the idea itself certainly was not foreign to him.

Andrew Szepticky is generally credited with having ignited the ecumenical spark in Beauduin. This awakening may have taken place at Mont César, but it was certainly confirmed at Rome.[12] Beauduin's own description of the birth of his Oriental vocation is quite clear on this point:

He [Szepticky] gave several conferences at the Oriental Institute in 1922–23. I especially recall that of February 1923, delivered in a remarkable French, which for me was decisive.[13]

In addition to these more formal encounters, Beauduin saw the metropolitan frequently in Rome and discussed ecumenical issues with him informally on a number of times between 1921 and 1923.

Occasionally confined to his bed by a sciatic condition, Szepticky received his friends in his bedroom. Carried away with an idea, he would sometimes stand up on his bed to emphasize a point, and all present held their breath for fear that the frail folding cot would collapse.

Almost from the moment of his arrival in Rome, Beauduin frequented the Oriental circle. He recalled some of the leading names in his *Memoirs:*

> At this period, thanks to the influence of Dom Zimmerman,[14] the Greek College had become the rallying place of the principal Orientalists of Rome: Msgr. Papadopoulos, then assessor of the Oriental Congregation, Fr. Cyrile Korolevsky, Fr. Serge Verighine, Dom Placide de Meester, Fr. Delpuch of the White Fathers,[15] consultor since 1917 for the Oriental Congregation, Oriental prelates passing through Rome and especially the Metropolitan of Lvov, Msgr. Szepticky. How many agreeable and constructive hours were spent Sunday afternoons in that old parlor with low arches and thick walls where each had his place, and often again in the course of the week in the delightful intimacy of the study of Dom Cyril Korolevsky.[16]

Differing Views on Unity

Although the Orientalists of the day were agreed on the urgency of restoring unity, two opposed approaches existed. One group favored an organized missionary activity directed to the conversion of a supposedly decadent Orthodoxy; the other supported a reversal of the historical process of Latinization through a systematic de-Latinization. It was this latter view, true in essence although still very partial, which was complemented by the important declarations of Vatican II's *Decree on Ecumenism.*

Each of the men with whom Beauduin was to deal in the preparation of his foundation had his own interpretation of the two approaches. The fact that no two were in complete agreement only added to the monk's difficulties. The influence of Szepticky, a staunch supporter of de-Latinization, was to be for the most part beneficial. Nevertheless, because of the nationalistic overtones involved and an abrupt disenchantment even with de-Latinization, Beauduin soon lost enthusiasm for the metropolitan's work.

Korolevsky's vast knowledge of Oriental affairs made him the best qualified, and the most eager for that matter, to initiate Beauduin into some of the intricacies of the East. In the final planning of the Amay project, however, his role was negligible.

D'Herbigny, the champion of mass conversion, aroused Beauduin's distrust almost from the start. Because of the tremendous amount of authority invested in him, it was obvious that the Jesuit had the power to carry through his plans and would brook no opposition. Once Beauduin became an obstacle to these plans, trouble was bound to erupt.

Mention should also be made of Pius XI. Having been in Poland, he had seen the Russian immigration at first hand and eventually would give his enthusiastic approval to Beauduin's proposed ecumenical effort. Moreover, at least on paper, Amay will appear to be a direct response to the pontiff's request that the Benedictines consider such an undertaking. One may therefore wonder why the Holy Father's name does not figure more prominently in the details that follow. The answer is simple. Those opposed to Beauduin's ideology were far more influential in shaping the sequence of events than the pope himself. Besides, as opposition to ecumenism increased, Pius XI's public support for it waned, and he would follow the same course of action toward Amay and its founder as he had toward Mercier and the Malines Conversations: namely, quiet withdrawal. Consequently, while the pope remained an inspiration for the inception of Amay, in the end he proved to be a disappointment as a friend.

Disappointments

As the end of Beauduin's two-year teaching assignment drew near, he eagerly awaited the expected recall to Belgium. It did not come. Instead his assignment was extended another year. That was not his only disappointment. He had been given permission to visit the Studite monastery of Uniov in Poland, but political intrigues on the part of Szepticky made the trip unfeasible.

While the diplomats were busy remaking the map of Europe at Versailles, Szepticky, patriot that he was, tried to see what he could do to establish an independent Galicia. It must be remarked in passing that as metropolitan he was ex-officio vice-president of the legislative assembly of Galicia and had a seat in the Herrenhaus at Vienna (by birth he was a count). Under the Russian occupation of 1914, he and not the Austrian or Polish civil officials had been made responsible for the good behavior of the citizenry. He was, however, eventually deported, and upon his return in 1917 he was interned by the Poles.

In 1917 the Ukraine became independent, and the metropolitan almost persuaded some influential government officials and Orthodox ecclesiastics to proclaim the union of all Ukrainian Orthodox with the Catholic Church. The communist victory in Russia obliterated that chance. But in 1919 the chief of the young Polish state wanted to reconstitute Poland on the basis of a federal union with the Ukraine and Lithuania. He went to Lvov to see if the Ukrainians were for or against the idea. But the preliminary, unofficial conference with the metropolitan never came off because of police interference.

Szepticky's political ambitions for Galicia were never fully appreciated. Many Poles believed that he was anti-Polish. Poland was Roman Catholic and Szepticky wanted Galicia established as a beacon and haven for Eastern Christianity, a bridge between Orthodox Russia and Catholic Europe. So it was that in the summer of 1923, just as Beauduin was preparing to leave for Poland, news reached him that the metropolitan was in some difficulty with the Polish authorities. After being detained in Vienna for some time and then placed under surveillance in a monastery at Poznan, the metropolitan was finally given his passport and allowed to proceed on his way. But precious time had been lost, forcing Beauduin to change his plans,[17] because it was not until November or December of 1923 that the metropolitan's case was settled.

As weeks passed by, Beauduin's letters betrayed how completely he was caught up in his monastic project. In September he wrote: "I have the impression that great events will take place this year."[18] Months passed, and as the year drew to a close no spectacular event had occurred to confirm his optimistic statement.

In the meantime Beauduin tried to decide on a workable plan for the proposed monastic experiment which would be directed toward the Orient. He saw at least four possibilities. He could go with a group to Lvov, become a Studite, and wait for future developments. Or he might found a monastery in Belgium of the type he planned before coming to Rome and make it a center of preparation for union. A third possibility was to go back to Mont César and establish a group within the community, after the fashion of the Bollandists, which would work for unity. A last idea, and the one around which he eventually developed his community, was less definite in outline. It involved neither founding nor organizing anything definitive, but making a three-year trial effort with some followers and letting the experience guide them.

As Beauduin patiently waited for the propitious moment to arrive for launching his latest project, help came from an unexpected quarter. From his first-hand experience in Poland, Pius XI's general awareness of the extent of the religious upheaval going on in Russia convinced him that the Soviet regime would not last. He consequently took advantage of the 300th anniversary of the martyrdom of St. Josaphat, Archbishop of Polstsk in the Ukraine and a champion of Catholic unity, to attract official attention to his hopes for Russian union with Rome. The resulting encyclical, *Ecclesiam Dei,*[19] outlined a program of union which emphasized the necessity of a holy life and, above all, of love toward the Slavs and other Orientals.[20]

Cardinal Mercier, fully informed about Beauduin's hopes for a monastic experiment, wholeheartedly supported his old friend's plans and agreed to help in any way possible. Beauduin lost no time. At his request Mercier wrote a letter to the pope [21] which in turn led to the pontifical letter *Equidem Verba.*[22] In Beauduin's eyes this document turned his project into a papal imperative. Almost two decades later, he recounted the sequence of events behind the official letter:

Mercier . . . in November 1923 wrote to Pius XI to suggest a Benedictine foundation in view of the reunion of Churches, a copy of which letter he sent me at that time and which I no longer have. It was Fr. d'Herbigny who delivered it to the pope, after giving it that Russian emphasis . . . which it did not have. And then the letter *Equidem Verba* was to have been addressed to me, and I considered this . . . as a "monastic" blunder and suggested that it be sent to the abbot primate. Perhaps that was my greatest mistake. . . . What is important is to disengage the essential: the two great ideas joined together—monasticism and ecumenism—which, well understood, strengthen one another mutually while at the same time they constitute a platform for the ascetic life, intellectual work and apostolic activity. To untangle, I say, this essential from the concrete modalities which have been hesitant and variable in the beginning, and which have finally stabilized themselves—this is what is important.[23]

What Beauduin failed to mention was Mercier's letter of December 11 in which Beauduin's role becomes crystal-clear. The cardinal expressed his hope that he had grasped the goal Beauduin had in mind, and he added quite simply: "If it must be touched up, have the goodness to send it back to me as I did not keep a copy." [24]

Mercier's letter to the pope was not the only force to act as a catalyst on the pontiff. Spurred on by d'Herbigny, Pius XI created the Pontifical Commission for Russia and placed d'Herbigny in charge. As preparations got underway for the first ecumenical conference, scheduled to be held at Stockholm, pressures from different quarters increased, urging Roman participation. The Eternal City was particularly alive with speculation about who might be sent. All these events heightened Beauduin's optimism, but his own project remained uppermost in his mind:

I am happy that you haven't forgot the Orient; you must think of it more than ever. The year will not end, I believe, without something decisive for me and, I hope, for you.[25]

Although 1924 looked promising and Beauduin was busy taking three hours of classes daily at the Oriental Institute as well as teaching at Sant' Anselmo, he nevertheless had certain apprehensions:

I had thought that in the course of this year a Benedictine work for the Near East would have seen the light of day, but I am beginning to despair.[26]

Continuing in the same letter, he noted that the abbot primate's heart was not in it, but he felt that in spite of this the primate would be forced to do something if only to save face, since the pressure was coming from on high.

While Beauduin may have been purposely staying in the background, the following letters indicate that he was by no means uninformed.

I am confident that soon the Holy Father will address a letter to the abbot primate asking him to make an appeal to the whole order in favor of the Russians, with some precise points to be realized right away [the sending of those interested to Rome to prepare]. . . . Starting next October . . . it is going to provoke an orientation in the whole order; the Holy Father wishes it. In his thoughts, the apostolate of the Near East should be the work of his pontificate, and what is more, the monks of the West should be his principal auxiliaries in this work.[27]

We are eagerly awaiting the letter of the Holy Father of which I have seen (just between us) the outline. It is sufficient in order to justify, and to authorize in advance, all the desires of the Oriental apostolate . . . monastic, apostolic, social, etc. It is the *liturgical prayer:* that is, the apostolic work which the Church asks of us, nothing more.[28]

No greater proof of the continuity in Beauduin's vision is needed than the testimony of this letter as to the nature and essence of the new venture on which, he was confident, he would soon embark. In a subsequent note he linked this apostolate with the liturgical prayer of the great High Priest: "That they may be one." Dated May 29, 1924, this letter referred to the document prepared during the previous November which immediately aroused the Holy Father's enthusiastic support. Nevertheless the abbot primate tried to dissuade the pope, especially from the "now" aspect. As Beauduin put it, "he didn't dare plead complete rejection" because this could only have been interpreted as a direct refusal to obey the express wish of the Holy Father. Beauduin ended his letter with a note of triumphant joy:

Come to Rome for October. Our aspirations now are no longer dreams of "anti-stability"; they are the desires commanded by our supreme superior. . . . The unique ascetic principle of the congregation: *ut unum sint:* the mystical body and the triumphant Christ, the great king! [29]

In comparing the project of Beauduin and the papal brief *Equidem Verba*, it appears that the pontiff simply had the former translated into "pontifical Latin" and then signed it. No substantial idea is in any way modified. As mentioned above, Pius XI had intended to address it to Beauduin, but on the latter's insistence he sent it directly to the abbot primate on March 21, 1924. The letter outlining the new monastic apostolate earnestly begged the primate to act promptly on this papal desire to fulfill the prayer of the Lord on the eve of his death: that they may be one.

With the first major hurdle overcome and now safely behind him, Beauduin turned to the immediate preparations. Using the papal brief as an official source and guide, he worked out the details. Each point was carefully weighed and considered. Even the name he chose for the community, *Moines de l'union* (Monks of Unity), had a subtle significance which he explained in a paper sent to Cardinal Mercier:

It is desirable also that the members of this monastic institute take the name of *Monks of Unity* (*Moines de l'union*), purely and simply, without adding on any other special name like Basilians, Benedictines, Cistercians, etc. This is the ancient custom preserved in the Eastern Churches, and it is all the more timely to hold to this so that the new monastery . . . in virtue even of its purpose may be inspired by different points of Eastern monastic tradition.[30]

In spite of the good omens, nothing definitive was accomplished throughout the rest of the year, for only the abbot of Mont César was disposed to take *Equidem Verba* seriously. Then in December an optimistic note to Rousseau mentioned an unexpectedly favorable reply from Belgium. Beauduin might leave Sant' Anselmo by March. He requested only one volunteer from Mont César [31] (some of the abbots apparently feared a mass exodus of their men to the new foundation), and he would try to spring Rousseau from Maredsous. At the same time a rather devastating document was composed by the abbot primate who despaired of delaying the project any longer and systematically condemned Beauduin's work in advance. The letter was addressed to Robert de Kerchove, Beauduin's abbot at Mont César:

As for Rev. Fr. Lambert Beauduin and his projects, allow me . . . to expose to you in all frankness my humble opinion. I beg you, however, to consider my communications as *absolutely confidential* and to see that they never come into other hands.[32]

1. You know, Very Reverend Father, how much I esteem Dom Lambert. He is fundamentally good and pious, capable of great

sacrifices, full of energy and truly has many fine qualities. However, I see in his character three great lacunae.

a. A man with a very sanguine temperament, he has an extremely lively imagination. He becomes enflamed for his "projects"; he only sees in them the favorable sides and loses the possibility of understanding the other considerations. When he begins the realization of a project, he pushes it with a will that knows no obstacles. It is for this reason that he sometimes lacks equilibrium.

b. The violence of his temperament carries him, not unrarely, to rash words, as you indeed remark in your letter. Because he is aflame for the Orient, he sometimes says things that could be interpreted as contempt for the Western Church. Since this activity which he envisages is not carried on at Mont César, he will say that there is not enough activity, life, etc.

c. A man strongly attracted to external activity, he has never completely understood the work of the cell. That is, moreover, often the case with those who were secular priests.

These qualities and lacunae will naturally come to the foreground in his work for Russia. With his energy and his talent for organization and especially because of his ardent love for the Church, he seems uniquely qualified for such an undertaking. Moreover, we must expect an occasional imprudent remark in his words and— if he is not continually controlled—also in his "writings." By the violence of his temperament and the lack of balance, he is less qualified to be superior of a house. And it is to be feared that this house will not have the truly monastic character that the Holy Father asks and which is absolutely necessary for Russia.

2. As for the concrete projects of Dom Lambert, I do not yet dare declare myself, although we have already spoken several times at length about this. I must study them still more in depth. Certainly this project is conceived in a broader manner than the plan outlined by the Holy Father. The Holy Father had limited our task to the apostolate for Russian monasticism. Dom Lambert would like to found a universal work for the union of Churches with the concrete purpose of:

a. preparing souls for this union by the thorough examination of all related matters and by conferences and publications;

b. organizing the "masses" for the necessary work;

c. gathering funds necessary for this work, especially for the "future" foundations of Paleo-Slav (*sic*) monasteries. . . .[33]

Everything taken to consideration, I believe that Dom Lambert will be able to do a truly great good in creating this work and that it will help our particular work very much—that is to say, the creation of a Paleo-Slav monasticism *if you can put at his side some* good fathers who will complement him on a specifically monastic point of view (for example, a good master of novices) and *if you firmly keep the direction and the control of the work in your hands*.[34]

Although the primate admitted that Beauduin was a capable organizer, he had absolutely no confidence in the latter's ability to understand monasticism or to communicate this appreciation to others. This state of affairs made a difficult task even harder, prejudicing some against the foundation from the very start. With absolutely no financial backing from the Benedictines and little encouragement, Beauduin would see the slightest problem or difficulty as indisputable confirmation that he, with all his "faults," was ruining what under more capable direction would have necessarily succeeded. What his adversaries were unwilling to admit was that they opposed the experiment regardless of who directed it, and they denied the obvious fact—even though disinterested parties pointed it out—that every new undertaking has its problems.

On January 6, 1925 the abbot of Mont César officially informed Beauduin that he had the necessary permission to leave Rome at the beginning of March and promised him much latitude in his new venture. Nevertheless Beauduin's letters during 1925 indicate an awareness of trouble brewing. Confident that the work of union was the will of the Holy Father, he believed that it must infallibly triumph. The most imminent trouble, however, appeared to be coming from the Benedictines.

May we now profit from our victory and win the peace as we have won the war. The heroic times are about to begin; I am determined to bear everything.[35]

By autumn, preparations were in full swing for the new foundation. Unaware of the extent of the lack of confidence in him, Beauduin busied himself with the material details of a foundation. He wanted nothing but the best, particularly in the matter of recruits. Well aware that abbots by nature are more apt to give up an undesirable man than a highly qualified one, Beauduin emphasized the necessity of finding men who shared his convictions and had a solid attraction to the work of unity. An expression that became characteristic of him in his conversation and letters was the qualifying phrase "*dans nos idées.*" Anyone, whether consciously or unconsciously, "of our mind" was someone in whom Beauduin immediately took a deep and not totally unselfish interest. The following excerpt is a typical example:

> Canon Paul . . . is making his retreat at Maredsous at this time. . . . Try to see him and to confirm him in grace—Oriental grace. He is completely apt to understand us thoroughly. Speak to him as you would to me.[36]

With Beauduin's departure from Rome and eventual return to Belgium, a new chapter opened in his life. To the entries in his dossier "one involved in social action," "founder of the Belgian liturgical movement," and "professor at Rome," a new title would be added: "founder of a monastic group dedicated to unity."

In developing the possibilities set forth in *Equidem Verba*, Beauduin drew upon the skills and expertise he had acquired with the Labor Chaplains and in his liturgical activities. Both experiences had taught him the value of influential friends and a strong educational program with conferences and publications. (Even the Chaplains had a weekly newspaper, *The Little Worker*, and since it was published at Seraing where Beauduin spent much of his time, it is more than likely he was in some way involved.)

The talents demonstrated in 1909 in his various schemes for the formation of the clergy and laity undoubtedly received its initiation in the programs of the Chaplains who were equally concerned with the formation of the clergy and laity, although more in social issues than in liturgical matters. Now, faced with the immediacy of his foundation, Beauduin selected the least pretentious of the four plans he had been toying with for several years and carefully worked out the goals and purposes he would soon propose to the first Monks of Unity. From the very beginning he looked for strong lay involvement on the spiritual and educational levels as well as on the material level.

7

The Foundation of Amay

The opposition to Beauduin's efforts to found a community dedicated to unity is almost incredible and seldom edifying. Much of what happened between 1924–1931 was certainly foreign to Christ's simple yet outspoken and straightforward manner of dealing with people. We hesitate to dwell on the events and personalities, some of whom are perhaps still living or only recently deceased, but for the sake of history we will include sufficient documentation to suggest some of the unprincipled duplicity, the truly Machiavellian tactics encountered by Beauduin. For the curious and for future historians, the articles (already cited) of the late Maieul Cappuyns, as well as various dossiers available at Chevetogne, will throw further light on the intrigues of the day.

In the admittedly sketchy picture to follow, it will become only too evident that the very structures supposedly erected to help man fulfill God's will all but smothered the fledgling monastery. An objective study of the facts leads to one simple conclusion: the freedom of the Spirit was definitely, if only temporarily, eclipsed by the designs of some men who were perhaps sincere but bound by a narrow view of reality and crippled by a fear that could only find safety in an all-out attempt to destroy the work and the man considered a threat to their plans or to the status quo. The very breadth of Beauduin's ecumenical vision made them gasp. He frightened them, and only his removal could restore their sense of security.

That the community survived is certainly not due to Beauduin alone or even to the perseverance of some of the first members. As Gamaliel said of the apostles' preaching: "If it is of God, nothing can destroy it." Vatican II's endorsement of an ecumenism which stresses understanding and dialogue rather than proselytizing may be seen as an official recognition of the validity of the work of Amay-Chevetogne. But the Council's ecumenism might even take Beauduin's breath away, since it reaches out not just to Catholic, Protestant, Anglican and Orthodox, but to mankind—to all non-Christians no matter what their persuasion; even atheists are people to be understood rather than objects to be converted or avoided.

Preliminary Plans

Beauduin's only solid backing came from his abbot, Robert de Kerchove, although the latter had serious misgivings about the practical side of the foundation. Beauduin tried to reassure him by spelling out his plan in detail. He wanted to begin with a community of five monks (Beauduin, Dirks, Stoelen, Becquet, and perhaps Porron) and some Russian guests. At an estimated cost of 6,000 Belgian francs per person, he projected an annual budget of 60,000 Belgian francs and volunteered to take on the responsibility of raising these funds himself. The abbot therefore felt justified in approving the project, which he did on January 6, 1925. At the same time he informed Beauduin that he was notifying the abbot primate of the decision taken. The primate, however, kept finding one objection after the other. He and Beauduin agreed on just one point: Amay should be a monastery. On all other points they disagreed. A document in the archives of Chevetogne dated January 9, 1925 indicates that he tried to dissuade Beauduin from pursuing the foundation by telling him that he was to be a theologian at the council.[1] On January 20 he expressed his hesitations in the lengthy document to Beauduin's abbot quoted in the last chapter.

February found Beauduin finally released from his professorial duties, but before taking any concrete action on the foundation, he wanted more time for reflection. This seemed the logical moment for his long-desired visit to the Ukraine which had been canceled at the last moment in 1923 when Szepticky had difficulties with the Polish authorities. The trip, though short, proved profitable, for it helped to clarify some of the questions that had arisen.

On April 7 he celebrated the feast of the Annunciation with the Orthodox at the monastery of Potchaiev (April 7 corresponded to March 25 on the Julian calendar which they used). He came away deeply impressed with the piety of the people and with their active participation in the liturgy. Even a taxi driver turned down a cigarette because it would have broken his fast. Beauduin attributed the deep faith he everywhere encountered to the influence of the monks. The experience convinced him more than ever before that monasticism was the point of least resistance for the interpenetration of the Churches.[2] Before returning to Belgium, he also visited the Studites at Uniov.

Upon further reflection, he abandoned his first idea of beginning with a small mixed group of Latins and Studites in Rome, opting for a more modest attempt on Belgian soil with Latins only. He sensed the importance of the contacts already made between Orthodoxy and the Anglicans and thus became only more confirmed in his belief that the problem of unity must be kept in the broadest perspective possible.

Shortly after his return from Galicia (Western Ukraine), Beauduin put his plan for Amay down in writing: *A Monastic Work for the Union of Churches (Une Oeuvre Monastique pour L'Union des Eglises)*.[3] It was little more than a commentary on *Equidem Verba*, but it carefully avoided the exclusively Russian orientation that d'Herbigny had tried to write into the document. After a detailed commentary on the essential points of the plan, we will underline the openness to the whole ecumenical scene that Beauduin carefully wrote into it, an openness reaffirmed during the following year by his confrère Becquet in the latter's *Union of Churches (L'Union des Eglises)*.[4] Having seen the goals and the plan, we shall then examine the reality.

Goals of Amay

In order to capture the *esprit de corps* of the community, it is fitting to probe in some depth this rather unique union of monastic and ecumenical intuitions. In the light of our contemporary mentality, so impatient with anything slower than the instantaneous, it is difficult to appreciate Beauduin's conception. Above all, in view of today's monastic crisis, one may well question that unity could be best achieved through monasticism.

Today in America, after a decade of feverish activity in ecumenical circles, we are still far from a united Church. People have grown tired of waiting for it to happen; many were opposed from the start. In fact, people seem to be growing tired of the very idea of organized Christianity. Increasingly the young turn toward a more free-wheeling, individualistic religious experience where dogmatic problems play no role.

To appreciate the values and goals of Amay we must judge it not in terms of society in the 1970's but of the vastly different and much slower moving religious culture of the 1920's. We must also try to see the situation through the eyes of a monk who believed in the value of prayer and the power of the Spirit. Disunity had not occurred overnight. The phenomenon of spiritual and cultural estrangement had been built up gradually over the centuries. Unity, for Beauduin, would undoubtedly follow a similar pattern, and so he sought merely to lay the foundation stones for what he imagined would be a long-term program. He realized that one does not just discuss and then decree reunion. A long psychological preparation must necessarily precede true union.

This monk also lived in an era when the faithful were still readily influenced by their spiritual leaders. He therefore directed his efforts to the leaders, convinced that unity could never be achieved so long as ignorance and prejudice prevailed, and that proper notions had to filter down to the people through their ministers.

Although Beauduin's acceptance of working through clerical channels may appear to date his insights in a day when the real spiritual leaders of many Christians are no longer found in the ranks of the clergy, Amay nevertheless was considerably more lay-oriented than either of his previous works had been. Perhaps he sensed that laymen were beginning to tire of being just men in a Church. He certainly knew that for some time many had become impatient with their churchmen and had long since despaired of receiving relevant spiritual direction from the pulpit. Beauduin stood at a turning point in history as regards both ecumenism and lay leadership. If today laymen inform themselves and seek to wrench the reins of leadership from hands too often caught up in irrelevancies, one must abstract the real core which still remains of value today for ecumenism.

Equidem Verba had proposed that each Benedictine congregation, or at least each country where there were Benedictines, devote one monastery exclusively to the task of preparing for unity as a prelude to the formation of an Oriental monastic community with its center at Rome. To prepare for both projects, each abbot was invited to send suitable men to Rome to study at the Pontifical Oriental Institute. Beauduin had no illusions about the willingness of the abbots to engage in such a major undertaking. What mattered most to him was the papal approval and the acquiescence of his own abbot. For the sake of history, it was only after World War II that the Benedictine congregations as a whole began to take the proposed program seriously.

In *A Monastic Work* . . . Beauduin described the twofold means for accomplishing the purpose of Amay: (1) an indirect apostolate of prayer, propaganda and study, and (2) a more direct one of hospitality, with temporary sojourns abroad in Oriental monasteries and Oriental foundations.

Beauduin particularly questioned the effectiveness of the community unless each member were thoroughly imbued with a Roman spirit, an Oriental soul, a monastic regime and a Catholic sense. Great stress was therefore placed on loyalty to Rome and familiarity with all the pertinent papal teachings. It is almost as though the founder anticipated future aberrations or charges when he wrote:

> It would be a strange way to serve the interests of union to espouse in any way suspicions and prejudices against the Roman Church or to soften certain points of the more contested doctrines.[5]

Anything less than a loyal and objective exposition of Catholic doctrine was clearly intolerable, for Pius XI had insisted on the importance of exploring theological questions which contributed in any way to separation between East and West. But Beauduin was equally concerned that his monks be fully aware of how much fundamental agreement existed. To give additional weight to this point he quoted from a papal address:

> The work of reconciliation cannot be attempted with any hope of success if, on the one hand, we do not abandon the false way of looking at the question which is ingrained in most people on the subject of the doctrines and institutions of the Oriental Churches,

and if, on the other hand, we do not apply ourselves more attentively to searching out the agreement between the Oriental and Latin Fathers in the one and the same faith.[6]

Beauduin rightly concluded that a thorough investigation of Eastern theology could not but enrich Western theological reflection.

The program of studies expected each member to pursue either his theological studies or some branch of Oriental studies at Rome. The authorities counted on this formation for the development of a truly "Roman spirit." While Beauduin certainly wanted his men to have a Roman spirit and would never cease insisting that they were first of all Latin monks, his original idea had been to send his men wherever their special interests could be best developed. In his own way Beauduin may have tended to exaggerate the Roman dimension in an attempt to dispel the romantic fancies of some men who presented themselves as candidates. But it was the primate and d'Herbigny who insisted on this specific mode of Roman orientation. Moreover, at that time the promise of study at Rome offered an additional enticement, since many students for the priesthood dreamed of just such a privilege.

A second characteristic of the Monks of Unity, their "Oriental soul," presupposed an extremely thorough acquaintance with the whole of Oriental culture: language, history, literature, art, and institutions, as well as the writings of the Fathers.

> The first indispensable work . . . is to enter into close contact with the Oriental world . . . the liturgy and the theology, the whole culture of this people whose civilization is so rich and so different from ours; to make oneself familiar with their feelings, aspirations, hopes, loves and hates, born in the course of this history of sixteen centuries in the soul of these races who forget nothing— this gives one an Oriental soul.[7]

This notion was synonymous with another term more frequently used in his ecumenical writings—that of psychological *rapprochement*, which has been translated simply as reconciliation, although Beauduin certainly never believed that all differences would immediately evaporate. By *rapprochement* he meant a drawing closer together again through a mutual understanding and appreciation of the other, leading to a true spiritual union of minds and hearts.

Rapprochement was the first step to reconciliation. In the light of the two most popular solutions—mass conversion or group reunion—Beauduin showed a marvelous balance and practical realism in the method he proposed to his monks.

The vitality of the Benedictines revealed in the liturgical renewal [8] awakened some to yet another possibility. They saw in monasticism the key to the spiritual compenetration of East and West. Just how it could be brought about, however, was not evident to everyone and led to heated exchanges, especially between Beauduin and his superiors. In contrast to popular Western spirituality, which often had little connection with the liturgy and tended to stray down the by-ways of private devotions and individualism, the Benedictines had preserved a certain sense of balance by the centrality given to the liturgy. Christians in the East also drew their essential nourishment and direction from the great feasts of the Church year. As such, their religious life revolved around the divine liturgy much more than that of their Latin brothers, although they too had their own religious traditions and customs. By its very nature, Benedictine spirituality therefore appeared as a natural and logical means to validate in the eyes of Eastern Christians both an authentic Western appreciation of the liturgy and the liceity of private devotions.

Beauduin differed sharply with high-ranking Benedictines over the issue of imposing by rule certain traditional pious practices. His vehement arguments against such devotions as the rosary, the way of the cross, and visits to the Blessed Sacrament were easily misunderstood as directed at the particular form itself, and this inevitably compounded his problems. He objected to them not because they were wrong in themselves but because their presence in his rule would be diametrically opposed to what he hoped to accomplish, for they could do more to destroy than to reinforce the reawakened yearning for unity. Not only might they give an ambiguous witness to the Orientals as to the relative importance of the liturgy, but they might even be interpreted as a criticism of Eastern spirituality. Moreover, to make them obligatory could hardly be supported by arguments from history or tradition, since most of these "objectionable" practices did not even exist in the days of St. Benedict. They were merely the accretions of later generations and eras.

A further and, at the time, unheard of use of the liturgy was also

envisaged. The monks would be bi-ritual. To facilitate this, Beauduin
wanted a Byzantine chapel side-by-side with a Latin chapel. Visitors
then, whether from East or West, could participate in either or both
liturgies and become acquainted with the unfamiliar one in an authentic setting. This seemingly utopian practice was not as revolutionary as one might think. In the first centuries of the Church it was
not uncommon for a visiting bishop to concelebrate with the local
ordinary in the rite of the place, even though he himself was of a
different rite.[9] The very act witnessed to the unity that existed in
spite of diversity of ritual. Since the Oriental liturgy was the more
ancient of the two and, in actual fact, the inspiration of many facets
of Latin liturgy, it would ultimately be chosen as the official and
unique liturgy for Sunday.

The monks were to be instructed in both rites, but because Beauduin wanted them to be adopted sons of the East, the Eastern rite received special emphasis. Novices were to spend a prolonged period
in the Oriental chapel. In fact, as the founder later explained, a
candidate who was indifferent to the Eastern rite or incapable of
totally mastering both the rite and its language would not be accepted. Those with a special aptitude and desire to pass definitively
to the Oriental chapel would do so, but only with the prior's approval. But the monastery itself was Western, as were its observances, and so it ought to stay. It was not as Oriental monks that
some celebrated the Eastern liturgy, but as monks of Amay.[10]

While the Oriental chapel clearly played an important role in the
work, Beauduin maintained that the Latin chapel was indispensable
for a number of reasons: for recruitment (especially for postulants
who might find a complete severance from their inherited liturgical
practices too hard to bear), for those who understand but cannot
adapt completely to the Eastern rite, and out of respect for the
individual. Beauduin realized one cannot demand that a man change
his rite; one can still be dedicated to the ideals of Amay and stay
in the Latin rite. Finally, the Oriental chapel was above all for visitors
from both East and West.[11]

The work of the monks from the very beginning was most directly
experienced by those who accepted the monastery's offer of hospitality. Originally it was intended primarily for refugees in order to
help them become acquainted with the West and Roman Catholicism.
Clergy and laity, secular and religious, whether in communion with

Rome or not, were to find in the monastery monks familiar with their customs and able to speak their language.

Furthermore, the presence of an Oriental chapel in which the rite would be celebrated with solemnity and devotion would not only provide an act of worship but would also help destroy the myth that Roman Catholics were bent on the Latinization of the entire Church. In such a setting, devoid of all polemic and ulterior motives, Beauduin hoped that fruitful and informed discussions on the differences between East and West would further the work of reconciliation, but such was not necessarily the case. The Orthodox in particular would question the propriety of Latin monks celebrating habitually in a rite not their own, although this did not automatically prevent their frequenting the monastery or collaborating in the work of union.

Another dimension of the direct apostolate concerned an exchange program which would be mutually beneficial to both Eastern and Western monasteries. Beauduin believed that monks from the West, well formed in the ancient monastic traditions, would be able to give new vitality to Eastern monasteries by sharing community life with their Oriental brothers. Additional benefits would undoubtedly come from such an opportunity to absorb the spirit and customs of the East. This practice also had the potential of facilitating friendships between Eastern and Western monks.

Theodore Belpaire (later prior of Amay) was the first monk to take advantage of this possibility. In 1927, at the end of his canonical year of novitiate, he went to the famous Orthodox monasteries of Mount Athos in Greece. Beauduin's stay in the course of his trip to the Orient in 1929–1930 convinced him that in terms of ecumenical collaboration it was pointless to pursue the exchange. He found the monks totally out of touch with and not really interested in the work of unity as he conceived it.

In his original outline, Beauduin argued for a proposed Oriental foundation. He dreamed of a network of Eastern-rite monasteries which would form one congregation with the Monks of Unity. Just as the purpose of Amay was to witness to the value of the Eastern liturgy for the Occidentals, so too would such a monastery in the Orient witness to the value of the Latin liturgy. Ideally this would produce similar apostolates in both East and West, creating a healthy climate of understanding and hastening the moment of recon-

ciliation. All of this remained a rather grandiose dream. Had Beauduin's career not been interrupted by exile, perhaps the provisions
might have been carried out. Given his changed attitudes even by
the end of 1925, however, it seems highly improbable that he would
have ever implemented them even though he made no attempt to
modify them in the second edition of the brochure.

Education, a basic part of the monk's formation in the West,
would be given a similar stress in these new monasteries. Beauduin
insisted that this educational apostolate not be a disguised form of
Latinization but an attempt to restore among the Orientals themselves
their distinctive traditions, customs, and culture.

The founder's lucid explanation of the fourth characteristic of his
community—a Catholic sense—revealed an awareness not too prevalent in the 1920's. He urged his monks to be Latin with the Latins
and Byzantine with the Byzantines, for he realized only too well
that the failure of the Church to bring about unity in the past was
in large measure due to a deficient catholicity:

> The missionaries have often remained too European in the eyes
> of the Orientals, too patriotic, too Latin. Some have kept the inti-
> mate conviction of the intellectual, moral and religious superiority
> of the Western Churches; they have looked on those they sought
> to bring back to union as second-class Christians. They have pre-
> served the rites and ecclesiastical law of the Orientals only as the
> lesser of two evils and have not hidden their desire to see their
> return to unity become a slow Latinization.[12]

The same idea is to be found in these words of Benedict XV
who seemed to echo St. Paul:

> The Church of Christ is neither Latin, nor Greek, nor Slav, but
> she is Catholic; all her sons are equal before her: whether they are
> Latin, Byzantine, Slav, or of any other nation, all have the same
> place before the Apostolic Chair.[13]

Beauduin concluded this section with a reminder of the severe measure taken by Leo XIII against those who engaged in any way in
this Latinization—one fault of which Beauduin was never accused.

For the actual working out of his ecumenical program, Beauduin proposed a fourfold plan. First of all, not only must papal documents expressing the Holy See's love for the East and the importance attached to this work of reconciliation become thoroughly familiar to the monks, but they must also be made known and explained to the public. Second, books and articles on Eastern questions such as ecclesiastical law, liturgy, saints and customs must be published to dispel doubts and prejudices and to arouse a lively interest in and desire for reconciliation. Third, the tremendous contribution of the East in theology, liturgy, spirituality, its saints and its incessant struggles against heresy must be recognized—which in turn would strengthen the nascent sympathy for and confidence in the Oriental Churches. Finally, a permanent organization must be created to take care of the financial needs of the monastery and the development of the proposed apostolate.

The importance of study in such a comprehensive program was even more fundamental than the academic demands already imposed in the matter of developing a "Roman spirit." An additional motivation behind the insistence on scholarly research was the recognition of Orthodoxy's historical situation. Ravaged by centuries of war and subject to persecutions, many of its once famous intellectual centers were either no longer in existence or struggling for survival.[14] Through the careful examination of pre-schism documents in particular, and following the critical methods of scientific research recently developed in the West, the Monks of Unity, by virtue of their hoped-for scholarly competence and excellence, would gain yet another means of influence in the Oriental world.

Evaluation of the Plan for Amay

A careful reading of Beauduin's A Monastic Work . . . and Becquet's Union of Churches leaves a single impression. Beauduin's refusal to conceive ecumenism exclusively in Slavic terms was fundamental to his mission, and his first disciples—Becquet, for example—shared this conviction. Beauduin's involvement in Malines, the fact that the Conversations were a Belgian "affair," and his own personal contacts with Anglicans all certainly contributed to his enthusiasm for things Anglican. But one must look further for a true assessment of his stubbornness in this regard.

If most non-Eastern references scattered through the two above-mentioned works are to the Anglicans, it is only because serious relations already existed between the Anglicans and the Orthodox. In comparison, Protestant ecumenism was still in its infancy and had much less in common with Orthodoxy. To make overtures to the Orthodox and to pretend that the Anglicans did not exist or need not be reckoned with was unrealistic. Beauduin saw this and touched a central nerve when he suggested that to turn away from the actual situation was to run the risk that ecumenism would either be carried on outside of or in opposition to the Roman Catholic Church. Only in the light of this frank evaluation of the ecumenical scene can one begin to enter into what must have been Beauduin's reactions to the chain of events soon to break forth that effectively arrested Catholic ecumenical efforts, at least temporarily.

Few have loved the Church as deeply and staunchly as Beauduin. No one desired unity more ardently than he, yet few realized with such clarity that no scheme, however fine it looked on paper, could bear fruit unless it had some solid source of life to nourish it. He therefore wanted the whole life and activity of his community to be immersed in the mystery of the Church:

> To grasp the work in all its depth and richness, the doctrine of the mystery of the Church, the body of the glorious Christ who alone is able to give to our whole life its essential, ecumenical, universal and Catholic base, this must be placed at the center of our life and activity. This is the essential and daily work of the Monk of Unity: to become thoroughly imbued with this unique doctrine.[15]

Such knowledge presupposed not only intense prayer but also serious study and research. Because of this, Beauduin and his disciples after him have fought with determination to preserve the monastic-ecumenical formula which inspired the foundation of Amay.

It is in "Notes or Amay," written at various times, that Beauduin most adequately described the true implication of this formula:

> The unique goal of Amay is the harmonious and organic fusion of two spiritual realities: *monasticism* which to find all its dynamism must reinvigorate itself at its sources and draw from there all its apostolic vitality and internal fecundity, and *unity*. The work of unity is not just "a work" but an organic compenetration assuring a vital reciprocity between the elements.[16]

Just how is this organic compenetration realized? Herein lies a key point that has remained theory rather than practice. Beauduin wanted to break with the modern identification of priest-monks. He intended that many of his monks would be simply laymen, and that all should be poor—not just because the first monks were lay and because poverty witnessed to the Gospel, but so that communal life might be encouraged. In the founder's eyes, the presence of a good percentage of lay monks would foster an egalitarian spirit, and poverty would make them physically, spiritually, and socially dependent on one another. The truly common life that would result would be an effective source of vitality in their ecumenical work and a convincing sign of unity.

His wish for a community where monasticism as such would be more important than the priesthood reflected definite ecclesial and monastic considerations. Eastern monasticism had begun as a nonclerical movement and remained predominantly lay, whereas in the West it eventually developed a hierarchic structure that sometimes seemed like a caste system. Those with education became priests; those without education generally remained menial servants. In the East the role of the bishop was never eclipsed, while in the West the abbot dressed like a bishop, wearing a pectoral cross, and through the privilege of exemption acted like one, literally putting the local bishop in the background. A lay monastery in the West would serve a dual purpose, providing a sign of respect for the Eastern tradition and at the same time giving witness in the West to a heritage that perhaps needed reconsideration. Many of Amay's first candidates were already ordained, but the action of the primate effectively eliminated, at least for the time being, any chance for lay monasticism to rise in the West. Eventually he succeeded in imposing the Constitutions of Beuron on Amay, which stipulated that no more than one-third of the community could be lay.[17]

Unfortunately for Beauduin, the publicity campaign launched on May 25, 1925 through his little brochure *A Monastic Work . . .* eventually compromised him.[18] Its nuanced exegesis of *Equidem Verba* highlighted the Anglican and Protestant dimension that Beauduin discovered "between the lines." He understood the true spirit of *Equidem Verba* while others preferred to insist on the letter alone. His "unacceptable horizons" are concisely summed up in a letter commenting on an ecumenical session at Louvain to mark the opening of the academic year:

The session at Louvain was a great success. Lord Halifax and Abbé
Portal provoked a veritable enthusiasm, and they especially accentuated that our work for the union of Churches is for the West and
England as well as for the Orient. I especially wanted this affirmation—and I am above all eager through them to join our efforts to a
still greater and more universal Oxford Movement.[19]

Letters such as the above make it quite evident that Beauduin was not
simply inspired with the idea for a monastic experiment. He was on
fire with the dream of Church unity.

Never for the slightest moment did Beauduin think of limiting his
undertaking to the Orthodox, let alone the Russian Orthodox. Reconciliation of Orthodox with Eastern Catholics might be a possible
phase of union, but he could not bring himself to adopt it as the only
or even as the most direct means. The Orthodox problem could not
be understood in isolation, yet there were many in Rome who refused
to view it in its total historical context, a context that concerned not
only the *past* but also the *present*. Rome's error lay in her failure to
understand the significance of the newly developed relationship between the Anglican Church and Orthodoxy. Her only interest was in
Russia, and leading Vatican figures would never tire of insisting that
all energies be expended in that direction alone. Beauduin resisted.
Several reasons explain his breadth of vision: a natural reaction to
limitations inspired more by "vested interests" than the need of the
Church, as well as Christ's plea "that they may be one"— plus, of
course, the papal encouragement that meant so much to him:

> I told the Holy Father that people were complaining about my
> interest in the Anglicans and Protestants. The pope said: Not just
> them; you must be concerned about Mexico too, about the whole
> world.[20]

So caught up was he in the mainstream of ecumenism that in spite
of the many demands the new foundation would make on him, he
also would find time to make plans to send one of his monks
(André de Lilienfeld) to the ecumenical conference at Lausanne in
1927 as a reporter for *Irénikon,* but this ultimately remained an
unrealized dream.

8

That They May Be One

The dream first conceived with clarity during the uncertainties of World War I was about to materialize. The disappointments and delays suddenly faded from memory as Beauduin intensified his activities in the final months of preparations. An elite group of men already formed in the monastic life and with a professed ecumenical vocation eagerly awaited his call to come and their abbots' agreement to release them. To this handpicked few, others would soon flock.

However, Beauduin's energies were not caught up exclusively in the problems related to the foundation. His experience in the liturgical movement had taught him the value of quiet preparations behind the scenes followed by a massive assault through the mass media. So it was that even before the actual site for the monastery had been selected, he was busy capitalizing on the providential publicity that the Malines Conversations created for Christian unity. Nor was he at all timid in drawing the eminent personalities associated with the Malines Conversations into his own projects. In the fall of 1925 he therefore organized a series of ecumenical days: at Brussels, September 21–25, at Liège and Verviers, November 11–15, and at Louvain, November 19. In addition he arranged for conferences in various educational institutions throughout Belgium.

In the course of these ecumenical days, the foundation took shape. The first purchase for the Monks of Unity would be–of all things–

a typewriter, an indispensable tool for yet another project: the review *Irénikon*, which would be making a name for the community even before the novitiate was canonically established.

But ominous signs were not slow to appear. The routine of the new priory (it would only attain the status of monastery much later at Chevetogne) hardly had a chance to become established before a series of events occurred which culminated in a restructuring of the constitutions along Beuronian lines and the exile of the founder.

The Work Begins

The Unity Week Conference at Brussels represented a further turning point in Beauduin's attitude toward the Eastern situation. Szepticky gave a major address on the psychology of union, and Portal spoke twice on the Anglican Church and the question of unity in the nineteenth century. Beauduin himself discussed the Catholic position on unity in the light of Vatican I.[1]

In his presentation he stressed two main points. The first was the unbalanced treatment given by Catholics and non-Catholics alike to the work of Vatican I. Almost without fail they tended to pass over in silence the fact that the bulk of the council's time was taken up discussing a proposed constitution on faith which at least the Orthodox would have found totally acceptable. Secondly, Beauduin observed how many placed a false emphasis on the papacy at the expense of episcopal dignity, which is also of divine origin. In the light of the role of the bishop, Beauduin insisted on the dignity of the diocesan church. In short he concluded that Vatican I, clearly understood, did not compromise the work for unity.

Understandably, considerable emphasis was given to the Orthodox question in the course of this week. Long before the week, Beauduin had arranged for a monk of Mont César, André Stoelen (whom he had known quite well at Louvain and Rome), to spend some time with Szepticky in Lvov. Stoelen's initial contribution to Beauduin's work was a translation of the Byzantine liturgy which he sent in time to be printed for the 1925 Unity Week.

The scheduled talks proceeded smoothly enough until an impromptu speech by a prominent and learned Russian émigré, Count J. M. Perovski, abruptly broke the irenic tone of the gathering.[2] He chose as his title "The Problem of Union from the Orthodox Point of View," although he made it quite clear that the view in question was his own private view and was not to be construed as an official Orthodox statement. Frankly and without malice he then pointed out the harm done by Eastern Catholics in the matter of unity. His claim that the presence of "Uniates" aggravated rather than healed the schism startled many persons. Nor were they very happy with his declaration that the Russian émigrés had a deep fear of being forced to submit to a Latinizing Polonization. One of the local papers, *The Twentieth Century*, saw fit to give this summary of his words in its September 23, 1925 edition:

> For Russians, the Catholic religion always seems linked to Poloniza-tion. However it is not to the Latin Church as such that they direct their hostility. The Eastern Catholic rite provokes among them much greater distrust. There is a nuance that the Russian does not grasp. The rites are those of his Mass, and yet it is not his Mass; there is a suspicion of insincerity which hangs over the Catholic clergy of the Eastern rite. Are not these men renegades? ask some Russians. The exiled Russian still prefers to assist at a Latin Mass rather than at a Mass of the Eastern Catholic rite.

His concluding remarks dealt with some of the practical and doctrinal issues which also divide East and West. But before he had finished, a noticeable change had occurred in the hall. Van Caloen was the first to say a few words to break the cold silence, and then Szepticky added his comments. Finally a Bulgarian Catholic, Fr. Ivan Nikoloff, chaplain at the seminary of St. Basil in Lille, brought the real issue out into the open. This Eastern Catholic priest who later spent some time at Amay sharply criticized Count Perovski for his use of the term "Uniate," considered an insult by Eastern Catholics (and generally intended as such by Poles and Russians in the 1920's). He demanded that his people be called Eastern Catholics united to Rome. This outburst was accompanied by another silence.

It was during one of these silences that Beauduin realized for the first time that to work with the Eastern Catholics (and therefore with Szepticky) would compromise the whole question of unity. From this moment on he sought to dissociate himself progressively from the metropolitan. The exchange and reactions tremendously bothered Beauduin, but there seemed to be no other feasible line of action.

On the final day of the week Mercier and Szepticky addressed the participants. Surprisingly enough, the cardinal only mentioned the Malines Conversations in passing. He preferred to focus his attention on tracing the history of papal interest in the Orthodox East. Urging support for the newest foundation for the work of union in Belgium (Amay), he praised the generous heart and apostolic soul of Beauduin. To help purify the atmosphere troubled by the earlier outburst of polemic (Perovski-Nikoloff), Szepticky stressed the role of love in bringing about unity. He tried to raise the whole question of unity to the level of love. Love unites; hate separates. Each is responsible to foster the growth of love and to dissipate any and every trace of hatred or enmity.

But the Perovski-Nikoloff exchange did not die in the conference room. In the September 25 issue of *Catholic Review of Ideas and Facts (RCIF)*, Msgr. Joseph Schyrgens summed it up in these words, and misunderstanding continued to reign:

Count Perovski took upon himself the thankless role of devil's advocate in the question of union, amassing all the difficulties that a scrupulous Orthodox conscience could pose when confronted with the great plan [of unity].

Perovski, however, found this description unacceptable. His letter to the editor, subsequently published in the October 22 issue, read in part:

The difficulties that I assembled were not suggested to me by my "Orthodox conscience," at least for the most part. I have analyzed the mentality of my compatriots, such that I know it, very often without sharing it in any fashion. I have cited many typical incidents as examples, and without identifying in any way with the mentality that engendered these incidents. It seems strange to me that anyone could have mistaken the sense of my words.

Msgr. Schyrgens was much closer to the truth when he said that my conference was tinged with pessimism. In fact, I think that the difficulties which are opposed to union are, on the Orthodox side, less great than one generally believes. Is to ennumerate them to prove one's hostility? . . .

If I were hostile to union, I would not have written in *20th Century* that it seemed very important to me that we obtain, right from the start, guarantees of freedom of action for Catholicism in liberated Russia from the leaders of the anti-Bolshevist movement. I was prevented from developing this thought in my conference . . . because I had to suppress almost all of my conclusions, for lack of time.

Just as Perovski's well-intentioned efforts were misunderstood by many, so would some of the actions and positions of the new priory. Nevertheless, like the Malines Conversations, Amay was based on the same premises of peace supported by Christian charity, a continuation on a broader and more enduring scale of the very work begun by Halifax, Portal and Mercier in 1921. While Beauduin could sympathize with the missionary zeal of Szepticky or d'Herbigny, he was much more strongly drawn to an apostolate of study, believing that until ideological differences such as those demonstrated at the Unity Week could be worked out, no effective basis for peace, harmony and unity could be constructed.

The Foundation of Amay

With a clearer idea of the nature of the mission he was about to undertake and the means he would use to carry it out, Beauduin turned his mind to more practical matters. Two obstacles needed to be surmounted immediately: the lack of a suitable place to house a community and the necessity of a steady income. Already in December of 1924 he had assured his abbot that no funds would be requested from the monastery. The participating abbots apparently took him at his word. The monks who came to him arrived literally with only the clothing on their backs. His own abbot was only too happy to be relieved of any financial responsibility, since his confidence in Beauduin was not shared by all at Mont César, and a request for funds would have undoubtedly aroused controversy. The expenses that would inevitably be incurred in starting a monastery were only part of his concern. Besides the basic necessities, Beauduin also had to provide sound security for the future in order to assure the realization of the rather extensive educational program he had mapped out for his monks. His brochure *A Monastic Work* . . . was a first appeal to help raise funds.

A suitable site was another major concern. As early as October of 1923 some land had been put at his disposal.[3] This property at Pepinster near the pilgrimage spot of Tancrémont unfortunately lacked suitable buildings. Although it was kept for future expansion, he decided to look elsewhere for something more appropriate and ready for immediate occupancy rather than risk delaying the foundation. Then someone proposed a vacant Carmelite monastery at Amay-sur-Meuse.[4] This miniature-size monastery near Liège had sheltered an expelled community of French Carmelites who had since returned to their country. Its inadequacies did not dampen anyone's fervor, least of all Beauduin's.

The October 1925 choice in favor of Amay accentuated the urgency of the financial problem which the founder had promised to shoulder. Once again his family came to his aid, setting themselves up as a corporation. This enabled Beauduin and a handful of followers to make the foundation a concrete reality in December of the same year.[5] Only in 1931 would the contract come under fire when for other reasons Beauduin was summoned to Rome to answer a series of charges related to the foundation.

The success of a new foundation in capturing the founder's spirit normally depends in great part on the amount of time he devotes to forming its first members. Probably one of the more remarkable things about Amay was the thoroughness with which Beauduin's principles were ingrained, almost in spite of adverse circumstances. In the first place, the primate had no desire to see Beauduin become the first superior. Out of courtesy the latter urged Msgr. Gerard van Caloen, whose articles written some thirty years earlier had inspired Beauduin, to assume the responsibility of forming the new community. When van Caloen refused and no other suitable candidate appeared, Beauduin had no choice but to assume the office, a task he was quite willing to accept.

On September 14, 1926, following an authorization from Rome, the novitiate officially began with five novices. By October the community had grown considerably.[6] On the twentieth of the same month, the novitiate achieved canonical status by a decree of the Sacred Congregation for the Oriental Church, under whose jurisdiction Amay was to be rather than that of the Congregation for Religious. In a letter to his abbot,[7] Beauduin explained why this arrangement was advisable. Amay was not conceived of as a foundation by Mont César, and it involved the Belgian congregation simply to the extent of the temporary loan of some monks for the purpose of establishing a bi-ritual monastery. It therefore seemed logical that the monastery depend on the Sacred Congregation for the Oriental Church, since its proposed mission was to the Oriental world. Such an arrangement automatically relieved Mont César of any financial responsibility even from a canonical point of view.

Beauduin certainly had no idea of a merely temporary involvement. It was foreseen that after a trial period those monks on loan might want to become regular members of the new community. Furthermore, the above status offered definite canonical advantages, removing the monks to a great extent from any contact or dependence on the local general chapters. Very much aware of the opposition existing in the Belgian congregation, Beauduin sought canonical protection from any direct intervention.

From the very beginning novices came from many countries, giving Amay an international flavor.[8] At first Beauduin was thinking in terms of almost simultaneous foundations, and in his eagerness for men he often showed himself a poor judge of human nature as well as of monastic vocations. The inevitable departures and even "defections" among those who presented themselves as candidates would later add to the founder's cares and concerns.

Life at Amay

Monasticism as lived at Amay would have made some abbots blanch. Materially it was very poor. Moreover, many of the Beuronian features that had annoyed the freedom-loving, democratic Beauduin were gone. On one point alone he was intransigent. Everyone must participate in the liturgical offices. No excuse short of being confined to one's bed was acceptable. The daily routine thus remained essentially Benedictine, particularly in the constant stress on prayer, work, and study. But Beauduin took manual labor more seriously than many contemporary Benedictines did. No one, not even the prior, was to be excused from this monastic duty. For this reason Beauduin felt it imperative to set an example for his monks, especially when the more unpleasant tasks arose. Once it was necessary to clean out the sewer. The unbearable stench did not deter him; he proved as vigorous with a spade as with a pen. Frequently he was found scrubbing floors or sweeping the halls. He took special delight in performing before the astonished gaze of visiting dignitaries, for such duties were unimaginable for a monk of his position. On other occasions his guests might be kept waiting because kitchen duties detained him.

This emphasis on manual labor was not a form of theatrics. Amay was a serious attempt at an authentic form of Christian asceticism. The image of idle monks whiling away their time between liturgical functions was an image he never wanted to be associated with his monks. If he caught someone wandering about the corridors after terce, he did not hesitate to stop the monk and ask him what he was up to—because he should have been either working or studying.

There were other equally upsetting innovations at Amay. Sunday, the day of the resurrection, the day of joy, was anticipated Saturday night with talking at the evening meal (as well as on Sunday). Sunday also featured an extra dessert, longer periods of recreation, and time for a walk.

Unlike more traditional monasteries of the period, Beauduin trusted his men and treated them like adults. Furthermore, he expected them to treat each other in the same fashion, but it was something they had to be taught. One of the first to learn this new dimension of freedom was Becquet. Trained in the "old school," he dutifully went to Beauduin to make a report upon his return from a short trip. The prior interrupted him rather abruptly: "I don't need to know all of that; you're big enough to look after yourself."

Life at Amay became what one might call "regular" by the summer of 1926. The community included several Russian émigrés, which made it easier to realize the bi-ritual nature of the monastery. The canonical hours of matins and lauds were chanted by all. For the community Mass they assisted at the Oriental liturgy. Beauduin said his own Mass before the morning offices and so rose earlier than the rest. Becquet generally served his Mass.

After breakfast (Beauduin insisted that the coffee be rather strong to wake everyone up), each went about his assigned task: some form of housework. This was followed by Scripture reading—at least a half hour was of obligation. Beauduin was very strong in his insistence on the importance of Scripture in the formation of monks. He urged his men to use every available scientific resource in this task, including the commentaries of the Fathers and the liturgy's use of the different passages from the Bible. For Beauduin, study was another form of asceticism, especially if it were rigorous, thorough study. Intellectual tasks followed Scripture reading: classes for the novices and students, and study, research and writing for those engaged on the review *Irénikon*. On his own each monk privately recited the little hours (terce, sext, none) at the appropriate hours. Beauduin recognized prime and compline as appendices to lauds and vespers, and so they were recited, not chanted, immediately after the major hours.

Reading at the noon meal brought the community together again and provided possible points of discussion afterward at recreation. The work details which followed were designed to permit the prolonged exchange of ideas. It was recommended, however, that one speak "calmly," a reflection perhaps on the impassioned tenor of some of their recreation exchanges. Current projects and events of the day, especially those concerning the Church, Russia, the East, England and Protestantism, were the most frequent topics to which they turned at these moments.

Toward 3:30 none was to be recited, privately or with another monk. The final work period ended at 6:30 with vespers. After supper and recreation the monks went to the Oriental chapel for compline and matins for the next day (in Latin). This arrangement was modified on Saturday when they would rise at 11:30 P.M. to recite Sunday matins and then go back to bed.

It was customary that all take advantage of a Sunday walk, but during the week only the younger members took a walk on Thursday afternoons, for, as Beauduin pointed out, if laymen had to work on weekdays, so should monks. Once a month they had a whole day off for a real hike. This privilege was optional for the older monks.

Despite the seemingly enlightened regime, Beauduin was not without his discipline problems. A lay brother on loan from another Belgian monastery was particularly difficult. One day Beauduin was heard shouting in his room with great anger at the man. Shortly after this reprimand, another monk had to see the prior. He entered Beauduin's room with some trepidation and to his great astonishment found the prior convulsed with laughter. Sensing that some

explanation was in order, Beauduin composed himself and said simply: "Sometimes you have to act violently with thick skins in order to get through to them."

The double liturgical life (Latin and Eastern) did not please everyone, especially those of Eastern origin or those Westerners who wanted to make themselves "Slavic Souls." This often led to verbal skirmishes as they tried to exert pressure for a completely Eastern orientation. Beauduin's original idea had been simply for Latin monks to enrich themselves through a familiarity with the theological and liturgical treasures of the East and to maintain a Byzantine group in the priory for this express purpose. The Orientalists, however, judged this procedure offensive to the East, putting the liturgy and the Byzantines in the community on display like ants in an ant farm. The friction was eventually solved by dividing the community into two choirs, one Latin, the other Eastern, which celebrated their respective offices and liturgy integrally, with the exception of certain major feasts when all would join in a single celebration—either Latin or Byzantine, depending on the nature of the feast.

The Orientalists also won the day in their request for permission to follow Eastern customs concerning dress. This included a different habit, long hair and a beard. While everyone was expected to be thoroughly initiated into the various rites, it ultimately would be up to the prior to determine who passed to the Eastern rite when the constitutions for the monastery were finally approved on July 24, 1952. With this major exception, brought about by a change in the founder's original concept of the nature of their work, everything else was in common—work, studies, meals, etc.

At first, aided by Franco de Wyels, Beauduin devoted his mornings to the formation of the novices, lecturing on theology and asceticism, and trying to share with them as well as to impart to them his love of the Church. After one year he reluctantly gave up this most important task of formation, since administrative details, conferences, and lectures kept him too busy. But he did his best not to let these responsibilities interfere with his participation in the community life.

On one occasion, obliged to return immediately after a conference, Beauduin found to his dismay that the only available train to Amay was first-class. Since there was no choice, he reluctantly paid his fare, hoping that no one would see him. As luck would have it, another gentleman shared the same compartment with him. Beauduin felt ill at ease. Afraid the stranger might judge monks harshly because of his apparent extravagance, he explained his dilemma. His fellow traveler laughed and admitted that he also was going first-class because there was no other train. Although Beauduin arrived late that night at Amay, true to form he rose with the community, unwilling to make any exceptions for himself.[9]

The Founding of Irénikon

A few months after the monastery opened, in April 1926 to be precise, a review created for the purpose of furthering scholarly competence appeared for the first time. Abbé Portal was in large part responsible for its inception, having persuaded Beauduin and his followers of its necessity. The name itself is not without significance. *Irénikon* comes from the Greek word for peace, and so it accentuated the spirit of their work.[10]

But even the most efficient operations sometimes commit serious oversights. The following letter from Portal to Beauduin illustrates this. Writing shortly before his death he first spoke of his health and then came to the point:

> I am better and happy to write you by my own hand. I must go easily and be prudent. . . . And now, blush up to the top of your eyes. . . . I have not received a single copy of *Irénikon*, not one issue—do you hear me! All the same I still love you.[11]

Another eminent name among the first subscribers, Eugenio Pacelli, the nuncio in Berlin, apparently had no complaints. His interest in the periodical perhaps stemmed from his close association with d'Herbigny whom he had just consecrated bishop. Later on, at the time of Beauduin's trial, Pacelli would appear in a less favorable light.

Under the direction of Becquet the monthly soon achieved international circulation and renown. Published primarily to keep persons who were interested in unity informed on progress in the movement, the staff also hoped to further the cause by encouraging sound scholarship and indirectly to make the work of Amay more widely known. From the very beginning, articles dealt with Protestantism as well as Orthodoxy, a fact which only antagonized those who were not disposed to view the question of unity so widely.

The first issue opened with an explanation of the review's purpose:

In response to Pius XI's call, it is an organ of the movement for reunion, to promote the spiritual reconciliation of minds and hearts that must precede official and juridical reunion.[12]

The editors consequently sought to bring together all persons interested in responding to the pontiff's call in this work. If the liturgy, particularly QLP, was originally directed to an elite, the work of reconciliation was directed to everyone from the very beginning.

The goals of Amay and its founder came under fire from the very start. In view of this Irénikon served a practical purpose, for Beauduin made frequent use of its pages to expound, or have expounded, his doctrine of spiritual reconciliation and to reiterate his stand on conversions. His sincere concern for the complete exposition of doctrinal points and his professed willingness to submit without reserve to ecclesiastical authority failed to convince many critics.[13] His approach was too different. The opponents of Amay failed to realize that one of the first steps toward achieving some kind of doctrinal unity was to establish the state of the question and to fix the sense of the terms involved.[14]

It was therefore no surprise to the monks when Irénikon was threatened with suppression three times by the Roman authorities in its first years. Usually an exchange of telegrams or the intervention of a high-ranking friend staved off disaster. On one occasion Pius XI, in reply to a request for suppression, remarked: "I read this periodical pencil in hand, and I do not see any reason to condemn it." [15] While Beauduin was still prior of Amay, the tempest became such that he himself decided to suppress the review. However, several of his friends dissuaded him from this action and the review continued.[16]

Irénikon became embroiled in some of this controversy through what might be called a monastic indiscretion. Beauduin had made arrangements for the imprimatur of the review which were not at all to the primate's liking. Quite naturally, the former had chosen censors with some sympathy to and understanding of the work of union. Such criteria probably would not have guided the primate if he had had the final say about the matter, and he resented Beauduin's independent spirit. No "good" monk would have gone ahead with such arrangements without first consulting his superior. By way of compromise, Beauduin finally agreed that one censor should be chosen by the abbot of Mont César (who was, after all, his friend). But these early skirmishes spelled trouble ahead.

Today no one denies that *Irénikon* has furthered a truly indispensable element in the program of the Monks of Unity. Through scientific research it has helped Christians to arrive at a common understanding of ecumenical problems, many of which were more semantic than theological in origin.

Beauduin was not exactly prolific during the years 1925–1929. Some of the articles published were simply talks he had given (perhaps over and over again). In general we can say that the ecumenical problem was viewed from one of two angles: liturgical or doctrinal.

From the liturgical side it was especially in the eucharistic cult that he found the greatest differences. Since the Eastern rite was recognized as older than the Latin, he felt that greater consideration should be given in the West to major points of difference—concelebration, the use of the vernacular, the audible consecration, and the reception of both species during Mass and in a standing position, as well as the fact that infants could also receive communion. All these practices were common to the East. Why did the West differ so radically? Why were Benediction, Forty Hours and Low Mass unknown in the East? He also urged his readers to ponder the impact of the absence of a pontifical liturgy at Rome. The East concluded from its absence that legislative and administrative aspects had obliterated the concept of the body of Christ in the Roman Church.

At a 1924 liturgical week, Beauduin had reminded the audience that if religious education does not fortify one's faith, then it is a failure. Faith to be faith must pass into the substance of one's life. When religious education is carried on through the liturgy, it finds the individual already (hopefully) in a religious attitude disposed to receive the gift of faith. In short, he uttered a plea to pastors to utilize those moments entrusted to them for religious education. By way of suggestion, he pointed with admiration to the example of Chrysostom who would announce his topic in advance so that the faithful could read and meditate the appropriate passage beforehand and then reflect further after his homily.

At the Amsterdam Eucharistic Congress of 1925, Beauduin pre-

sented a detailed study of concelebration at Rome, tracing its rise
and fall, and offering historical reasons for its demise.

From the very beginning of Amay, Beauduin had been searching
for a copy of Mansi.[17] He finally located the impressive work at the
Welter firm in Paris, but the price was prohibitive: 45,000 Belgian
francs. The family of Pierre Dumont, a monk of Amay, came to the
rescue, and *Irénikon* could soon boast of its latest gift which arrived
July 28, 1927.[18] Everyone was immediately put to work leafing
through the magnificent collection to see what conciliar support could
be found for Amay's basic principles, and what light the documents
might throw on those points of theology more frequently contested
by the various Churches. Beauduin singled out Franco de Wyels for
a specific assignment which led to a remarkable series of articles on
Vatican Council I and union. It was unfortunately interrupted by his
recall to Afflighem (his original monastery) where he became involved in a foundation for religious women.[19]

Ephemeral as it may have been, Beauduin was also involved in the
formation of a feminine group. He agreed to the idea and entrusted
the task to Stoelen who established the convent near Martelange and
served as chaplain, director and professor for a small community of
five or six women. During 1928 the group moved to a house near the
Amay priory but was disbanded before the middle of the year by
Etcheverry. Stoelen returned shortly thereafter to Mont César and
much later entered the Carthusians at Parkminster.

Beauduin's doctrinal articles from this period focused on papal
infallibility and union, and Mansi provided him with an almost
inexhaustible source of material. In all he devoted three articles to this
specific question alone, for Vatican I's definition had had a shattering
impact on persons desirous of unity, and Beauduin wanted to spread
a more adequate understanding of what the council had really said.
Two points to which he would return with increasing frequency
in the years ahead sound particularly contemporary: his emphasis on
the collegial aspect of the episcopacy and the necessity of decentralization at Rome.

He insisted that the pope is not the first and last word of Roman
Catholic ecclesiology. If the pontiff seemed to monopolize the
Church and to absorb the episcopacy, he was not acting in accord
with the divine nature and origin of the office, nor did Roman tradi-

tion support such a centralizing interpretation of the office. This creeping centralization often as not emanated more from the Curia than the chair of Peter and on more than one occasion brought Beauduin to the end of his patience.

One day, incensed with the Curia's maneuvers, Beauduin gave vent to his feelings. Then fearing that he had said too much and had scandalized his companion, he interrupted their walk. Turning to Rousseau, he looked him straight in the eye and said, "Don't you think that this is how Luther began? The trick is to know how to stop in time!" Then with a resounding burst of laughter, he started walking again.[20] He himself waged an unending verbal war against any distorted concept of infallibility which absorbed the rightful prerogatives of bishops and which fostered an abuse of the virtue of obedience by excess by pre-empting the individual's own sense of responsibility.

One other doctrinal point did receive notice, and because it had become such an integral part of his spiritual make-up we must mention it. What can the West learn from the East? The sense of the resurrection, of paschal joy, of celestial man. How central the resurrection was to Beauduin will be reflected more profoundly in the next chapter, but the following anecdote conveys one aspect of its meaning for him: One day in Rome, walking near Sant' Anselmo, Beauduin and Rousseau came across the Anglican cemetery where Shelley was interred. An inscription which dominated the monumental grillwork caught Beauduin's eye: "Resurrecturis" (To those who will rise). He paused, reflected a moment, and, letting the word escape from his lips, sighed: "It takes the Anglicans to think of that. We would have put a skeleton's head and two shin bones." [21]

Mounting Tension over Amay

An unfortunate chain of events now began to unfold in the story of Amay. Certain circles had become increasingly alarmed by the growing interest in unity, first at Malines, then at Stockholm and finally at Lausanne. Catholics in England, upset by reports of the Malines Conversations, quite naturally voiced their concern and warned against any relaxation in doctrinal positions. Beauduin's "doctrinal development" sounded heretical in their ears. Prominent leaders in

Rome supported equally conservative views and were particularly opposed to any change in attitude toward conversions. Beauduin on the other hand had consistently said that he was not interested in conversions.

As pressures increased from without, Beauduin began to have troubles from within. First the validity of the professions at Amay was questioned. The primate would have liked to suppress the monastery, and this provided a possible excuse. By a decision of the Congregation for the Oriental Church, novices had been allowed to make their novitiate prior to the canonical existence of the house. In response to the primate's request for clarification, Beauduin obtained a formal statement from the Congregation.[22] This storm weathered, Beauduin could then write in August of 1927: "The abbot primate has become aware that Amay is an irreducible force, an impregnable citadel." [23] But the battle had just begun. Although his foresight in insisting that the new community depend directly on the Holy See and be under the Congregation for the Oriental Church proved advantageous, it failed to satisfy the legalistic mentality with which he had to contend.

The first ominous cloud on the horizon appeared in August 1927 when rumors of the decree of canonical erection establishing Amay as a priory *sui juris* reached Beauduin.[24] The terms were harsh. Erection would be granted only on agreement that three conditions be met, the first two being radically opposed to Beauduin's principles: (1) the reintroduction of the Beuronian aspects of monasticism (office to be said in choir, pious practices of obligation, etc.) which Beauduin had successfully eliminated from his constitutions; (2) the redirection of all energies principally if not uniquely to the "return" [25] of Russia to Catholic unity; (3) the agreement to work for the foundation of an Oriental monastery as soon as possible. The first was clearly the work of the primate; the last two were obviously a triumph on the part of d'Herbigny. For the moment, however, these remained rumors. No official word had been received.

The uncertainty of these first months did not dampen Beauduin's zeal. An unexpected achievement, even if only a hint of success, immediately brought forth an enthusiastic reaction:

Tremendous and astonishing news: the general chapter has unanimously decided to propose to the primate that the Greek College be entrusted to the Monks of Unity! . . . I said . . . that the primate's opposition would be insurmountable.[26]

The unanimous decision was not necessarily a tribute to Amay, for the Benedictines had never been overly eager about the college in the first place. History, moreover, would bear out Beauduin's realism regarding the primate.[27]

No one was more stunned than Beauduin when, without any forewarning, Pius XI's encyclical *Mortalium Animos* appeared early in January 1928.[28] Many rejoiced at its forthright, vigorous and trenchant censure of the theological shallowness of Protestant ecumenical efforts. Following as it did on the Protestant ecumenical conferences of Stockholm and Lausanne, it seemed to sound a death knell to all Roman Catholic involvement in ecumenism. Many viewed ecumenism as a possible resurgence of modernism and breathed sighs of relief when the pope stated Rome's position concerning unity and spelled out how true religious unity should be promoted. Misunderstood by many, especially the Russians, some even interpreted it as a direct attack on Amay, if not an outright condemnation. Even an official papal reassurance that it was not directed against the community [29] could not undo the harm already done by this unintentionally bad publicity. It is said that five hundred subscriptions to *Irénikon* were canceled because of the encyclical.

The tensions created by this document forced Beauduin to take up his pen for some more "exegesis." [30] Attempting to interpret the encyclical in a favorable light, he stressed the fact that it treated of principles, not of methods and that in no way did it condemn the methods of Amay. The work of the monks was not to redo doctrinal definitions but to remove the obstacles to love. The article ended with a quotation from Cardinal Mercier: "Union itself will be the work of grace." [31] The Protestant view of the encyclical was not quite so sympathetic. The famous Swedish ecumenist and Archbishop of Uppsala whose vision eventually gave rise to the World Council of Churches, Nathan Soderblom, prophetically stated in 1929: "Church history tells us that when Rome has spoken the case in concluded—*causa finita est*. But in fact, when Rome has spoken, it is far from concluded." [32]

Soon after, some "defections" occurred at Amay, provoked, it seemed, by the unfortunate tone of the encyclical. Three monks announced their intention to become Orthodox. Only one, however, eventually took the step. Moreover, another novice, prematurely converted to Catholicism, returned to his original Church.[33]

These events received undue publicity. Cardinal Bourne, as spokesman for the English hierarchy, took full advantage of the unfortunate circumstance. D'Herbigny, increasingly powerful in Rome, also had cause for complaint; his protégé's absolute lack of enthusiasm for a missionary conquest of Russia provoked the prelate. The primate was just one more figure only too ready to intervene on the side of the opposition. An unexpected opportunity soon presented itself in the person of Beauduin's secretary and financial administrator for the past three years, Walthère Boland, an oblate of Clervaux.

Beauduin wanted to help this son of a stockbroker out of friendship for Boland's in-laws who were worried about their daughter (his wife). The founder let himself be taken in by the man who then abused the confidence placed in him and insisted so much that Beauduin finally entrusted the priory's funds and securities to the senior Boland. These securities eventually became so entangled in Boland's affairs that they were irrecoverable. Beauduin, not Boland, would subsequently be accused of mismanagement of funds by the ecclesiastical authorities. This charge was false on two counts, since at the time of his resignation Beauduin left 75,000 Belgian francs in the bank, and secondly, he knew that he could always count on the generosity of his brothers.

When Boland's competency was finally questioned and he was dismissed, he took a rather spiteful revenge on the community and especially on its founder. He boasted of having sent a report to the apostolic visitor, Abbot Maur Etcheverry,[34] with seventy or eighty charges against Beauduin. He also sent a frenzied denunciation of the community to the abbots of Maredsous and Clervaux. The two abbots forwarded the letter to the primate who immediately sent an apostolic visitor. The latter, far from condemning the community, found nothing irregular. He could not hide his edification at the religious spirit and the strong sense of unity present among the monks which he discovered during his stay, February 9–18, 1928.

What were the specific charges? The original list does not seem to have been preserved, but the burden of the accusations concerned heresy, immorality and mismanagement of funds. As secretary, Boland saw everything that Beauduin wrote, even his rough drafts. Although nothing of Beauduin's was ever censured, he admittedly often toned down or clarified possible ambiguities, inaccuracies, exaggerations, etc., before submitting them to the censor. Other articles, for similar reasons, were left unpublished. Boland copied anything that he considered suspect in the rough drafts and notebooks of Beauduin. On February 21, Beauduin wrote to Dumont: "For six months he's been spying and reporting everything to the abbots of Clervaux and Maredsous."

The charges of immorality apparently are traceable to such incidents as the following: One night, returning from a conference, Beauduin opened the train door window to see where they were. In the process his hat blew away. When he knocked at the priory door, Boland opened it, saw him without his hat, his hair ruffled, and an unusual expression on his face, and he immediately concluded the worst.[35]

Out of loyalty to Boland's in-laws, Beauduin felt that the man should get a second chance, but finally he told Rousseau: "Don't write anything more to Boland. It is he who has spread the most incredible calumnies about all the monks of Amay and has made scandalous reports about them."[36]

Some five or ten years after this episode, on a visit to Becquet at Tancrémont, Beauduin was still ready to forgive and forget. Becquet asked him how on earth he could continue to support and defend Boland after all he had done to him. Beauduin shamed Becquet with his response: "I know, but are we Christians if we do not know how to pardon?" Beauduin continued to display a fatherly weakness toward Boland until his disappearance during World War II.

By the time this was settled, the decree of erection of the previous year had been published. Not at all pleased with the contents, Beauduin decided on a trip to Rome to see if he could work out some compromise with the authorities. In the course of various consultations he politely protested the constant outside interference and harassment that Amay was experiencing, and he even offered to resign should the commission insist on complete Russification, since he had no competency in this field.[37] Then, apparently content with what he had accomplished, he returned to Belgium and announced the results to his monks. Amay was to be an autonomous priory independent of the Belgian congregation, with an abbot to be delegated by the Holy See.

But Beauduin evidently was unwilling to leave well enough alone. In July he wrote a lengthy position paper on Amay and the principles which had inspired it and sent it to the Pontifical Commission for Russia. This turned out to be a tactical blunder on his part. Returning to the issue of an all-Russian orientation, he again reiterated his lack of competency and his opposition in principle to this approach, and he suggested in all simplicity that perhaps his presence was detrimental to the foundation, especially since Rome seemed bent on the Russification of Amay. If such was the case, resignation seemed the only sensible solution. As a successor he suggested Theodore Belpaire, who undoubtedly was the most qualified for a number of reasons, including his obedient, saintly monastic life, his age, his earlier experience, his enthusiasm for things Russian and his stay at Mount Athos (as well as his personal wealth—in 1939 he bought Chevetogne for the community). Nevertheless, for the sake of accuracy, it must be added that Beauduin was well aware that at the time of the conception of Amay a short four years earlier, Roman circles had been unanimous in their conviction that there was only *one* man for the job: Beauduin.

The terse reply from a staff member of the Pontifical Commission for Russia to the above contained neither acceptance nor refusal. Cardinal Luigi Sincero was away for the moment and must be consulted before any decision could be rendered on such a serious matter. Sincero did not return until October. By then, with the monastery erected, Beauduin had all but forgotten his tendered resignation—not that he ever thought it would be accepted. Still, he began to have the distinct feeling that he was being avoided. Meanwhile, Rome was trying to find someone willing to accept the role of delegated abbot of Amay. Beauduin's offer of resignation in July played a decisive role in the resolution of this problem,[38] for few were willing to take on the forceful personality of Beauduin.

The long silence was finally broken by a letter from the Pontifical Commission dated December 12, 1928. His resignation had been accepted.

Afterthoughts

The question of the precise nature of Amay's apostolate, disputed from the earliest days, was not to be definitively settled for several decades. Yet there had never been any doubt in Beauduin's mind as to the real nature of the work for union and its extension. The confusion came from outside interference. Writing to Rousseau in 1927, he clearly outlined the purpose:

> Amay, a monastery *sui juris*, will centralize the work of union, in the first place for Russia, and then (with more discretion at this time) in other regions, but in England without direct opposition to the bishops.[39]

Well aware of the delicate state of affairs in England, he nevertheless felt that any group dedicated to union must be open to the whole world. He later commented on the imposed limitations:

> Did limiting the apostolate to Russia alone narrow the original breadth? No. In the first document, *Equidem Verba*, Pius XI exposes the plan and explicitly says: *Maxime ad ingentes Russiae populos mens nostra nunc amanter se vertit*, and then goes on to trace the main lines of the project. The second key document, the canonical erection of July 31, 1928 states: *Unitatem cum Catholica Ecclesia inter dissidentes, praesertim Russos susciperent*. There exists, therefore, no incompatibility. The Roman specialization furnishes a concrete and realistic field of action and avoids idealistic and speculative conceptions.[40]

As can be seen from the quotations, the documents in no way forbade an openness toward other faiths, although they obviously pointed to Russia as the prime area of concentration.

9

The Near East

The acceptance of the all but forgotten offer of resignation after five months of silence stunned Beauduin. But the conditions of his departure were beyond belief. The letter, dated December 12 and received two days later, "invited" the founder to prepare for his departure within ten days. He suddenly felt very much alone. When the inner turmoil had calmed down, he was able to view the matter with greater detachment. On December 21 he spent several hours at the train station with one of his friends, a young monk of Mont César (Maieul Cappuyns). The abbot visitor Etcheverry arrived later that afternoon to promulgate the changes. In a simple ceremony Beauduin was discharged from his duties and told to leave immediately, without luggage and in secret.

The most he could hope for at this time was that his absence from the scene would help dispel the rising opposition to Amay and to all it represented. He was convinced that he, rather than the experiment, was the real object of hostility. But such thoughts were small comfort to a man ejected so pre-emptorily from his religious family almost on the very eve of Christmas, a feast particularly dear to him. Reluctantly he boarded the train for Liège where he stayed with some English Benedictine oblates for about ten days and visited with his family. His exile, which eventually under various disguises would become an absolute prohibition for any further return to Belgium, had begun.

On January 1, 1929 he met with Becquet at Liège and recounted the most recent events. Becquet had just returned from Ireland where Beauduin had sent him to learn English and to study. Once the younger man had recovered from his initial shock, Beauduin asked: "How would you like to visit the Near East, Egypt, Palestine?" Becquet replied enthusiastically: "I've been dreaming of just that for a whole year!" "Well, get ready for the trip. I will ask Belpaire, your new prior, for permission to take you as my traveling companion. I have been strongly urged to become acquainted with the East. The Oriental Congregation has asked me to make a report. I want you to collect information about persons to see and places to visit and to inform yourself about the conditions there. We will leave in September." [1] With the matter decided, they parted.

Under Belpaire the life at Amay continued much as when Beauduin had been in charge. Despite the conditions attached to the canonical erection, many of the changes (especially some of the Beuronian features) occurred only on paper. For twenty-one years Belpaire would guide the community, caring for its spiritual, intellectual, and financial needs.

Shortly after his meeting with Becquet, Beauduin went to Rome hoping to assess the position Amay held in the eyes of various key figures, as well as to check rumors about his own popularity. The surprise he registered in the following letter to Rousseau is a hint of what he expected to find:

Your letter just arrived, February 1, and I'm answering it immediately. I have been very well received here:

(1) Yesterday I saw the Holy Father in a private audience, a long conversation which lasted thirty-five minutes, on the union of Churches, the necessity of working to prepare for it, patience in difficulties, etc. Three times I gave him an occasion to reproach me: (a) Very Holy Father, I have been touched by your condescension and your paternal generosity in excusing our faults, imprudences, failings, etc. Response: No, no, I only remember your courage and your tenacity, and I have nothing to reproach you for. (b) But Very Holy Father, we have sometimes been imprudent. Response: But, my son, you want me to scold you for something and I only want to demonstrate my complete satisfaction and total sympathy. (c) Afterward, in the course of the conversation, I said: We have had some sad surprises at Amay. Several who

entered have left and returned to Orthodoxy. Response: Yes, I know, but the same thing happens at Rome; but we would never become involved with union if we feared to take the risk.

Continuing with a few more remarks about other related topics discussed, Beauduin summarized his reaction to the Holy Father and then turned to other points of concern:

> I left astounded by what I had encountered. . . . The Oriental Congregation is equally very well disposed, only here the action of the primate . . . is making itself felt more. I received very favorable letters for a trip to the Orient and have been given two years' leave to make contact in depth with the Oriental countries; but I must send reports here. . . . Some want to send me to Bari to study and to prepare a foundation, etc., but I asked to be left free.[2]

After a brief visit to Belgium, Beauduin made final preparations for the first of two projected trips. He stayed in Paris for a while to study with some of the great Orientalists of the day in order to obtain the maximum profit from his first tour through Czechoslovakia, Roumania, Bulgaria, Serbia, Hungary and Austria. Stopovers at such ecumenical centers as Prague, Bucharest and Sofia were put to good use. In Sofia Beauduin renewed his friendship with Roncalli. They spent several days together speaking of the work of union. During his stay in Prague (April), he wrote an article on the need to restore the pontifical liturgy at Rome, an article undoubtedly motivated as much by the recent solution of the "Roman question" as by the criticisms raised by leading Orthodox with whom he was in constant contact. He also did a little research on the famous "Infant of Prague." To his amazement he found the statue in a state of neglect. This devotion, so popular in the West, had apparently fallen upon hard times in its "home town."

He interrupted his travels to return to Belgium where from July 11–30 he met with the bishop of Liège and others. On July 12 he went to Amay, and the monks were overjoyed. A lively discussion on July 13 concerning the purpose and ideal of unity made it seem like old times. From Beauduin's perspective, it consisted of working for reconciliation and union. Again he insisted that the monks of Amay were Latin monks working in the Latin Church for this reconciliation. No proselytizing, nor almsgiving alone, nor anything else that could turn them from this ideal was to be tolerated. When the question of Oriental foundations was raised—a point included in *A Monastic Work* . . .—Beauduin could only see them as a possibility in a very distant future. He had never considered the main purpose of his monks as that of making foundations, although he in no way excluded such action. Obviously, in the face of increased opposition from within and without, he wanted once again to underscore their real mission: psychological and spiritual reconciliation.

Destination Egypt

The excitement of adventure filled the Paris air on September 22 as Beauduin and Becquet finished their last-minute preparations. The last rendezvous that remained on their crowded schedule was with an oblate of Amay (Fr. Long) and François Paris (later Canon Paris, active in Eastern affairs). Before these two friends put the travelers on the train at the Gare de Lyon of Paris, the foursome had a gay time over a glass of wine at a sidewalk café. Beauduin was determined to make the most of the trip, although he realized that its real purpose was to keep him away from his monks. His companions could only marvel at his high spirits. Not one word of bitterness escaped his lips. He laughed at the pompous tributes of the Irish priest and always found a humorous side to Paris' remarks.

The account of this trip [3] is valuable not so much for the details about Beauduin's itinerary as for the very human and even personal picture it gives of the man. The centrality of Christ in his life is indicated by the casual entries noting where Mass was celebrated, the "waste" of half a day of sightseeing time trying to track down hosts for the next day's Mass, and the frequency of his visits to the Holy Sepulchre while in Jerusalem, for with Beauduin the resurrection was *the* dogma. To see how integral and natural these insights were to his daily life is ample justification for what may seem a break in the historical momentum building in the previous chapter.

Beauduin was a tourist but never exclusively so. No day passed without his somehow bringing into the conversation the problem of Christian unity, the historical causes of schisms and the obstacles being preserved before their very eyes by men dedicated to Christ. His willingness—indeed his eagerness—to learn and his eye for detail, as well as his interest in the Jews and Muslims, reflect much more than the monk on holiday. One can only regret that he never published a comprehensive evaluation of his experiences on this trip.

Beauduin had received the privilege of using the Greek corporal, and he and Becquet centered their schedule around the daily liturgy. Normally it was followed by a period of silent thanksgiving. The recitation of the Office rounded out the all-important spiritual side of each day. If they were alone, they would recite it together. Moreover, every night before retiring, this man of fifty-six years knelt simply by his bed to say his evening prayers.

If any complaint could be made about his conduct, it would be registered against him for having repeatedly frustrated his companion's efforts to be of service (Becquet was a good twenty years his junior), for Beauduin repeatedly snatched Becquet's suitcase away from the protesting monk and insisted on taking the worst seats in the cars or trains in which they traveled.

Early on the morning of September 23 they arrived in Marseilles. Beauduin immediately looked for a suitable hotel in order to freshen up so that they could celebrate Mass. Then, after a fleeting visit to the town and the Basilica of Notre Dame de la Garde which seemed to have something Eastern about it, the two sailed at noon on the Lotus. On board they met several White Fathers they would see again later in Jerusalem.

They spent September 24 reading in order to prepare for the visit to Egypt. A seemingly wealthy Egyptian obligingly supplemented their education during meals by filling them in with interesting details on the actual situation of his country. By Wednesday Becquet was sick. The seas were rough and so the two men retired early, around 3 or 4 P.M. The next morning they learned that things had become so critical that an alert to stand by to abandon ship had been posted between 6 and 9 P.M. Concerned about the condition of his companion, Beauduin carried him to the deck for some fresh air, but the seas were still rough, and so they went below deck. Almost automatically their thoughts turned to St. Paul and Acts 27. Nevertheless, the storm did not dampen their enthusiasm for learning more about Egypt—a subject they continued to pursue with their Egyptian acquaintance.

The fatigued travelers docked at Alexandria at 5 P.M. on September

28, safe and sound but six or seven hours late. By the time that the formalities of customs were over and they had arrived at the hotel recommended by their shipmate, night had fallen. They soon discovered that Iorio Palace was much too expensive and that their "friend" worked there. But it was too late to change, and Beauduin found himself doubly amused at supper—by the enterprising employee and by the mustard (it came from Belgium). Before retiring they relaxed for a few moments on their balcony, drinking in the sounds, sights and smells of a strange and fascinating world.

On Sunday after Mass they went to the Greek Orthodox liturgy at St. Sabbas, a church of Constantinian origin and the seat of Patriarch Meletios. They were amicably received and given stalls near the iconostase and the seat of the archimandrite, but they withdrew before communion when they realized that some of the clergy were concerned about their "orthodoxy" and uncertain as to how to proceed.

In the afternoon they made a veritable ecumenical pilgrimage of churches—Catholic, Orthodox, Anglican and Protestant. The Armenian Catholic Church with its statues of the Sacred Heart, Our Lady of Lourdes, and St. Thérèse of Lisieux brought forth sobering remarks from Beauduin on the evils of Latinization.

Mgsr. Alouch, the vicar for the Melkite patriarch, was their first contact with a representative of the Eastern Catholic Church. Beauduin immediately felt at home with him, for he had known some Melkite priests in Rome and found them in complete agreement with some of his most basic ecumenical principles. They spent three days with Mgsr. Alouch, enjoying his hospitality. It was through him that they had their first exposure to religious rivalry in the East. A Franciscan church was located a few steps from the Melkite church. Since most of the Melkites were from the upper classes, the later Masses at the Franciscan church attracted them in great numbers. When Msgr. Alouch scheduled a still later liturgy, trouble broke out. Similar problems existed in the area of education, since the religious schools were run by Latins who, in the eyes of the Melkite leaders, did nothing to help either Melkites or Muslims.

Despite the ugly religious picture that such scenes evoked, the city of Alexandria brought to Beauduin's patristically-oriented mind the idea of trying to revive the ancient school of Alexandria—but along the lines of an international Catholic university. Alouch shared his enthusiasm, and soon they were imagining all that such a center could do for ecumenism—not just Christian ecumenism but a truly universal ecumenism, because the vicar envisaged even Muslim participation.

Another feature that struck Beauduin was the inferior situation of women. With his deep fondness for his own mother, he found it hard to understand how husbands and sons could sit chatting nonchalantly while their women did hard manual labor. He also noticed the complete absence of women on the streets in the evening and found the amorous couples of men and young boys disturbing. Alouch and the others with whom he discussed such cultural mores assured him that these patterns would probably change only very slowly.

In the course of conversations during these and following days, Beauduin often returned to the same idea: that one possible path to unity might be found by strengthening an existing Eastern Church like the Melkite Church. Rome should grant to this Church her prerogatives, her traditional independence and her own spirituality and above all purify her of all Latinisms and form a better instructed clergy. Every trace of Latin influence should be removed.

October 3 dawned, and to Beauduin's dismay he found the Melkites celebrating the feast of St. Thérèse. The explanation that many of the faithful venerated her failed to soothe his sadness at this sign of Latinization. After a two-hour trip they arrived at Cairo, and Beauduin immediately wanted to see the city. Several firsts marked this day. They were quickly trapped by an insistent amateur guide willing to show them the sights for nothing. He took them to a mosque supposedly opened only one day a year— that very day—and decorated with one thousand lamps. This was their introduction to the mosque El Rifaieh. They were deeply impressed both by the majestic beauty of the place and the sight of the faithful praying with outstretched hands. Unfortunately they were not so impressed with their freelance guide. At least Becquet's enjoyment of the moment was marred by serious doubts about their security. The guide next took them behind the mosque to a funeral chapel for important people. The dim light gave an eerie effect to the various objects in the room, but their reveries were rudely broken by the guide's announcement that the tour was over. He asked for his tip, but what they offered was insufficient. True guides turned out to be more economical.

On the next day efforts to visit the desert or the Wadi Natroun became bogged down in a hopeless mess of red tape. Their search for the local Anglican bishop also proved futile, since he was on the continent. But this venture was not a total loss, for they met the Anglican YMCA chaplain, Rev. Richmond, with whom Beauduin immediately felt very much at home. He spent the afternoon sounding him out on his favorite topics, including the Copts, the patriarch, and Anglo-Coptic relations.

On Sunday afternoon Beauduin and Becquet resumed their conversation with Rev. Richmond, whose fifteen years of experience in Egypt and passionate interest in ecumenism provided them with an inexhaustible source of knowledge about the Coptic Church and the power of Protestantism in Egypt. Their interest was particularly aroused by what he had to say of a Coptic group bound together by the desire to rid their Church, both in its clergy and laity, of the shameful ignorance and the spiritual and moral inactivity which prevailed in it, and, above all, of the venality which surrounded promotions in the ecclesiastical circles. Richmond had taken a special interest in this group and already felt that he had infused the beginnings of a new spiritual life, which for him meant personal prayer and adoration, especially before the Blessed Sacrament. He realized that union was a long way off. The lack of a common liturgy provided a major obstacle, which he attempted to remedy by silent prayer in common. He made arrangements for the two to meet the leaders of this group of reformers and for Beauduin to attend an ecumenical soirée with the express purpose of explaining the goals of Amay to representatives of different religious groups.

Having viewed the pyramids from a distance on more than one occasion, the two travelers turned tourist on October 8 and took a train to the pyramids of Ghizeh. From there they went by donkey into the desert to one of the oldest tombs—the Mastaba of Ti. The nearby ruins of the monastery of St. Jeremiah caught their eye. They walked through the impressive remains, fascinated by all they saw, and imagined its past life and activity.

Upon their return to Cairo they set out almost immediately for Heliopolis to meet Gommos Ibrahim Loukas,[4] the clerical force behind the small nucleus of Coptic reformers already mentioned. En route they saw definite signs of the vitality of the Copts in the form of the many newly constructed churches. Gommos Loukas, a man in his forties, impressed them as being truly dedicated to working for the coming of the kingdom. His colleague, a lawyer, seemed more circumspect than the priest in his enthusiasm for Beauduin's work. Before taking their leave, at the suggestion of Richmond the five knelt down in common prayer for unity. Loukas said a prayer in Arabic and made some brief comments which were followed by silence. The two monks were deeply moved by the sincerity of these Christians who were working to improve the situation of their own Churches and to bring them more into line with the spirit of Christ.

On Wednesday, after taking care of some business, they returned to their Anglican friends. Mrs. Richmond, a former missionary in Africa, took them to a hospital run by the Anglican mission. In one courtyard they noticed nearly two hundred men seated and listening with intense attention to someone preaching on the beatitudes. Becquet felt a pang of regret that Catholics were not more visibly in the forefront preaching in the name of Christ, as were these devout Anglicans.

That evening they found themselves in a truly ecumenical atmosphere. Richmond had invited representatives of the Coptic, Armenian, Anglican, Presbyterian, and Methodist Churches to an evening meeting. Among these guests, the rector of the American-Egyptian university impressed Beauduin as really having grasped his point of view. In his turn the rector summarized Beauduin's presentation for those unfamiliar with French and invited the monk to visit the university the next day.

In his informal talk Beauduin had tried to give some idea of the basic purpose of Amay as well as its spirit, means of action and organization, stressing the disinterested nature of the work in which no conversions were to be sought. The Armenian present was in full agreement. He seemed to suggest, in private, that he was closer to the Catholics than were the Copts and other Christians.

The intervention of the young Coptic lawyer, however, revealed how profoundly the Protestant "spiritualist" doctrines had penetrated into this Coptic group. In effect he insisted on knowing whether the monks of Amay performed penances, for he could not conceive of monastic life other than a perpetual exercise of mortification. Beauduin responded that Western practices differed from those of Eastern monasteries. Fast and abstinence were observed, but as for the rest, each monk worked out his spiritual program (penances, etc.) with his spiritual father. The monk's entire life is a sacrifice, a penance. Observance of the rule, the austerity of life, obedience—all continually remind the monk of the precept of Christian mortification. The lawyer failed to appreciate this concept of monasticism. He regretted that Western monks were so little attracted to the penitential aspects and so involved in works. In all, the talk and discussion lasted an hour and a half.

Their visit to the American-Egyptian university, an extremely influential institution in Egypt where there was no comparable state university, helped them to understand the immense advance that Protestants had made over Catholics in what concerned the conversion of Islam to Christianity. The student body was composed of Arabs learning the ways of Europe and America, and future American and English missionaries learning Arabic and studying Islamic institutions and literature. The Christian influence on the students was through individual contacts and collectively through the obligation of daily communal prayer and periodic sermons. Apparently the graduates of this university lost much of their fanaticism, but some Christians objected to this approach because while the Muslim students might lose their former religious ardor, they gained nothing very solid in terms of Christianity. In fact, they often became religiously indifferent, which was considered much worse than remaining ardently Muslim, since indifference rarely leads to conversion. On the other hand, the formation given to the missionaries was certainly more enlightened than anything going on publicly in Catholic circles at the time.

The Jesuit high school was their next stop. They hoped to get some information there about the Wadi Natroun, but nothing practical resulted. The conversation shifted quite naturally to the religious scene. The Jesuit father noted that many wealthy Muslim and Orthodox sent their sons to the Jesuits, and he added with a note of pride that the Jesuits had been instrumental in obtaining the decree which permitted children of Eastern Catholics to make their first communion in the Latin rite. Beauduin could hardly repress his reaction to this kind of Latinization, and he exploded as soon as they left the distinguished Jesuit (who was later named to the Belgian Royal Society of Geography in 1930).

The shortness of their stay in Egypt prevented Beauduin and Becquet from visiting all the places that interested them. Nevertheless, in between the time devoted to their ecumenical education they managed to sandwich in an impressive amount of sightseeing, including visits to churches, a mosque, museums and several archeological sites. As they prepared to leave on October 12, Beauduin could look back over the experiences of the previous days and consider it time well spent. The various contacts and the discoveries of occasional petty feuds and rivalries between Churches served a concrete purpose, accentuating the too often human element in disunion whose bases frequently proved to be much more psychological than theological. It simply reaffirmed his earlier conviction that union could never be decreed; it would have to be a gradual growing together again. A similar experience awaited them in Palestine, their next destination.

Palestine

When they arose on Sunday morning in Palestine, the landscape was still reminiscent of the Egyptian desert, but the dwellings and vegetation were different. At Lydda they changed trains for Jerusalem. The new plantations and orchards were eloquent witnesses of the energetic efforts of the Zionist settlers, offering a striking contrast to their first glimpse of Palestine. At one stop young girls in lovely costumes boarded the train offering fruits and flowers to the travelers. The olive groves were bustling with activity. It was harvest time and people seemed to be everywhere, in the trees and on the ground.

The train slowly wound through the valleys and hills. Suddenly, without warning, they arrived in Jerusalem. It was 9:15 and in the crowd a White Father acquainted with Amay was waiting for them. As he drove them to St. Anne's where they were to stay, the two tried to drink in everything. No sooner had they arrived than Beauduin asked to say Mass. The altar selected was in the crypt of Mary's home, the traditional site of her nativity—a tradition verified by numerous texts inscribed in the nave of the church. After Mass they met the superior, Fr. Antoine Delpuch, an amiable man whose twenty years in the East plus his own talents made him one of the best qualified men in Oriental matters.

Their rooms faced the temple esplanade and a nearby minaret. For the first time since their arrival in the Near East they would hear the call of the muezzin which punctured the early morning stillness at 4 A.M. and was repeated six more times in the course of the day.

In many respects the religious scene was similar to that encountered in Egypt where petty rivalries were a major obstacle to a genuine Christian witness. The effectiveness of Franciscans as guardians of the Holy Land was seriously questioned by all non-Franciscans and even by one friar they met.

Despite the many changes over the past two thousand years, the pilgrims nevertheless felt that they could imagine what the country must have been like in Christ's time, for neither the sky nor the mountains nor the vegetation nor the customs of men and animals had changed.

Fr. Delpuch offered to take them into the city for an imperative first visit to the Holy Sepulchre. It was only as they walked through the streets that they began to discover Jerusalem, a city vibrant with life and history. The panoramas they had caught earlier in the day were about as revealing as a postcard. On their right Fr. Delpuch pointed out a wall under which they had found the sub-foundations of the atrium of the basilica constructed by Constantine to enclose the Holy Sepulchre and Calvary. Some Russian nuns now lived in the building and spent their time in perpetual prayer in honor of these holy mysteries. On entering the church itself they were immediately struck by the "noise" of Christian disunity. The Latins were busily performing their daily procession accompanied by their own chant, while the Greeks in the choir were chanting office and several Coptic priests sang psalms in their nasal tones from the opposite side. One Greek monk stood guard to watch the crowd of pilgrims lest any impropriety be perpetrated. The fact that one had to blot out the signs of pettiness and the mediocre, often competitive attempts to put on some liturgical show was regrettable but did not prevent Beauduin and Becquet from returning several times during their stay in Jerusalem to be more deeply impregnated with the realities associated with this holy place.

On October 14 they visited the apostolic delegate—the future cardinal and assessor of the Sacred Congregation for the Oriental Church, Valerio Valeri. To their astonishment he asked if Cardinal Sincero knew of their trip. Apparently Rome had failed to notify the "authorities." However, Beauduin was prepared; he pulled out his ecclesiastic passport and satisfied the delegate with the legitimacy of his business in the Near East.

A visit to the Syrian major and minor seminaries directed by the Benedictines of Belloc (France) proved most satisfying. Situated on

the Mount of Scandal, the large building offered a magnificent view
of Old Jerusalem. The prior (later abbot) Anselm Chibas-Lassalle
received them with open arms.[5] His tour encouraged the visitors
greatly, for they saw fellow Benedictines treating the Syrian rite with
knowledge and delicacy, inculcating a love for it in the seminarians.

That evening, their discussions with the White Fathers centered
around the rite of concelebration and the *epiclesis*. Should priests
pronounce the words of consecration with the bishop? In being one
with the bishop, do they really celebrate the Mass? Since the bishop
distributed communion, the evidence seemed to favor a negative
answer to the latter question. As will be recalled, Beauduin had already written several articles on this subject and was delighted with
the opportunity to explore in greater depth the differences between
Eastern and Western practice.

On Tuesday they returned to the Holy Sepulchre. The disorder
was incredible. The only entry to the various monasteries attached
to the church was through the church proper, and 10 A.M. proved
to be the hour that provisions were delivered. As a consequence, in
addition to the throng of devout worshipers, one had to contend
with a horde of Arab tradesmen with their baskets of fruits, vege-
tables, etc. Without any hesitation they elbowed their way through
the crowd, stepping over kneeling pilgrims in order to pick the
shortest route possible to their customers' front doors. Beauduin so-
berly observed the scene and then led the way to the tomb where they
read the Gospel of the resurrection together in a subdued tone. They
were left with the distinct impression that the Latins would never
tolerate unity if it meant leaving these sanctuaries to the control of
Eastern Christians. Their conversation with the Latin Patriarch
Luigi Barlassina, an impetuous and authoritarian man, did nothing
to change their impression. They exchanged ideas briefly on a number
of topics, including the recent concordat between Mussolini and the
Vatican, Belgian universities, and vocations for Palestine. (Beauduin
later remarked that he found the very idea of a Latin patriarch in
Jerusalem an unfortunate reminder of the crusades.)

That afternoon they went to the Mount of Olives with two Bene-
dictines, one of them a former student of Beauduin's at Mont César.
The tour included some recent excavations at the grotto where
Christ reputedly prayed frequently and where he lived with his

disciples while at Jerusalem. Perhaps it was at this same spot that Judas betrayed him with a kiss. A Constantinian basilica, the Eleona, had been constructed on the site and was in the process of being excavated. Their last stop was at the mosque of the Ascension to venerate the footprint of Christ, a tradition recounted by such Fathers of the Church as St. Paulinus of Nola and Sulpicius Severus.[6]

October 16 was marked by a visit to the excavations at the Probatic Pool, a marvel of ancient engineering. The nearby biblical museum of St. Anne with its objects classified and explained by scriptural texts brought forth a pedagogical comment from Beauduin. He regretted that no one had ever done something comparable in European universities and seminaries to facilitate the students' understanding of Scripture.

The travelers were unfavorably impressed by what they saw in the new Jewish quarter. The heavy, unsympathetic mixture of all that was modern and European definitely seemed out of place. Shocked by the dress and manner of the girls and women in the streets, they found no comfort in their companions' assurance that they had literally seen nothing in comparison with what they might have seen. The young Zionists from Europe, filled with ideas of conquest and revolution, apparently delighted in flaunting tradition. Mixed in with the older Jews, especially the Karaites or Sephardim, and with Arabs who looked noble (and biblical) in their flowing robes, these recent arrivals were strangely out of place, disturbing the romantic scenario that the travelers had constructed mentally.

On Thursday morning they headed straight for the mosque of Omar, certainly the most sacred of holy places in Jerusalem and jealously coveted by the Jews. Such were the emotions aroused by this historic site (traditionally built over the very stone on which Abraham prepared to sacrifice Isaac) that they ended up spending the entire morning there. It was easy to lose themselves in thought here on the temple plaza where Christ had walked and taught, worked miracles, and disputed with the Pharisees and the doctors of the law. His curse on the city somehow weighed heavy in the place. Perhaps this explained why it was one of the few truly peaceful retreats they had found where one could meditate at length on the reforming action of Christ.

A rendezvous later in the day with Fr. Bonaventure Ubagh, a man

in close touch with the Arab and Jewish worlds, provided further
useful insights. This monk of Montserrat (at one time professor of
Hebrew at Sant' Anselmo) lived in the Jewish quarter, next door to
the chief rabbi, and soon became one of Beauduin's close friends. He
warned them that the political situation was not as calm as people
were generally led to believe. The Muslims were waiting for the
proper moment to invade Palestine and Syria. At their disposal they
had millions of seasoned fighters. He claimed that in any eight days
they could launch an invasion that no military force then in existence
could stop. All that was needed was the declaration of a holy war. It
would be a wholesale massacre.

Ubagh's comments on his stay in the desert with the Bedouins ap-
pealed immensely to Beauduin's taste for adventure. Later, after he
and Becquet had separated, Beauduin actually spent some time in the
desert with the Bedouins, accompanied of course by Ubagh, since
he was totally unfamiliar with Arabic.

Friday dawned with Mass at Gethsemane, near the supposed rock
where Christ's agony occurred. Afterward they went to Mary's
tomb and the Church of the Dormition. From its bell tower they
could see the Cenacle, but since it was in the hands of some reputedly
surly Muslims, they did not visit it. Beauduin had no desire to beg for
the privilege of praying.

Accompanied by Beauduin's former student they wended their way
through narrow and sordid little streets en route to the Wailing Wall.
Due to some recent trouble a group of English soldiers stood guard.
The monks passed the supposed court where Peter denied Christ
and wept. They were stopped as they approached the mosque of
Omar, for on Friday non-Muslims were not permitted in the temple
precincts. From a distance they watched the important dignitaries of
Islam arrive, distinguishable by their colored turbans and fringed
coats.

At 3 o'clock, along with hundreds of other pilgrims, including
Marie Joseph Lagrange the noted biblical scholar (even though he
contested the authenticity of the traditional route), the threesome
took part in the weekly way of the cross conducted by the Franciscans. The procession had to end by 4 o'clock because then the Greeks
had a special office in the Holy Sepulchre. The pilgrims passed up
this service in favor of a visit with Fr. François, O.F.M. and found

the story of his passage from Orthodoxy to Catholicism truly fascinating.

His was a soul opened to truth, he said, for he had neither been forced, nor urged, nor saddened by Catholic actions against Orthodoxy. He held out great hope for eventual unity, particularly in Palestine, if only the Latins would not offer such unflagging resistance. The monks sensed that he repressed his desire to condemn the Franciscan role with difficulty. Four years earlier he had sent letters to Rome from numerous Greeks and Armenians petitioning for reunion. Almost all the bishops of the synod of Jerusalem and the head of the monastery of the Holy Sepulchre were ready for union. The Patriarch of Constantinople even said: "If I were strong and free I would go on foot to Rome to kiss the feet of the pope." "There is not an Orthodox in Palestine or Transjordan who doubts that the Bishop of Rome is the first among bishops," insisted Fr. François.

He singled out the Abyssinians as a people most ready for union, although the reasons given did not exactly flatter their ecumenical spirit. He described them as ignorant but pious and faithful. Even the priests were ignorant and knew less than a child in catechism class. But the Latin patriarch was completely opposed to any idea of working for union, and apparently the Franciscan superiors concurred. For this reason, he felt that his only recourse was to write directly to Rome. Unfortunately the letters of this sincere man remained without response. Beauduin was deeply touched by the friar's account and promised to return often.

After Mass on the Sabbath, they followed the route that Jesus took on Holy Thursday. Beauduin appeared quite moved by it all. He kept remarking how everything corresponded to the Gospel and to the Bible, and he spoke of the humanity of Christ, frequently returning to the current "heresy" then in vogue: a latent monophysitism in many spiritual authors of the day who spoke only of the divinity of Jesus. The sight of the different people gave Beauduin an idea of life in the days of Christ—the children, the women, donkeys, camels, even the fountains where women came to draw water and carry it home on their heads.

As they walked meditatively along, they passed through the valley of the Cedron and Gehenna. Coming to the whited sepulchres of Gospel fame, they stopped briefly at the tombs of Absalom and

Zachary. From this vantage point they saw the gate through which Christ must have passed on Palm Sunday. Nearby were the fountain of Gibon, the pool of Siloam with the stumps of columns of an ancient Christian basilica emerging from the water, and the ramparts of Jebus. In the valley, the house of the lepers and the field of Haceldama with the convent of St. Onuphre caught their eye. Re-entering the city, they found the Orthodox Jews in their long coats and distinctive hats very much in evidence. That afternoon they went to Bethany and descended the twenty-four steep steps into the tomb of Lazarus.

Their visit on Monday to the vicar and members of the family of the reigning Melkite patriarch was another illuminating experience. Mgsr. Athanasius Moghabghab knew who Beauduin was and immediately opened his heart to the monk. It was a matter of the struggle, one might even say war, going on between the Latins and Greek Catholics which led to a serious charge against the Latin patriarch. To support his story, the vicar produced an incriminating document. When the Latin patriarch learned that the Melkite patriarch planned to visit Transjordan, the former hired a man to hinder any activity on the patriarch's part and to see that he would not be well received. Latin priests generally had little respect for the Melkite patriarch, but the emissary was charged to inform them that they were to refuse the use of their churches and even housing to the Greek Catholic clergy (who had nothing to start with). The envoy did his job and returned to claim the rest of his pay, but the Latins refused to pay him more. In revenge he wrote the report which Moghàbghab held in his hands, sending a copy to Rome and to the Melkites in Jerusalem. Although the story is hardly edifying, the authenticity of the events seemed indisputable.

The Latin priests in Palestine managed to ignore most of the sensible legislation which came forth from the Congregation for the Oriental Church. The congregation stated that Eastern Christians who wished to return to an Eastern rite might join the Greek Catholic Church. The Latin clergy paid no attention to this and raised insurmountable obstacles, preferring to keep such Christians in the Latin fold. While the Melkite clergy insisted on certain conditions before they allowed marriages with Orthodox, Latin priests authorized them easily, provided that the parents of the couple did not assist at the ceremony. The Melkites demanded freedom of religion, as well as Catholic education and Catholic baptism for the children. As a result of these quarrels, the Latin clergy preferred the Orthodox over the Melkites; evidently they felt that there was less to fear from their influence. Most Latins also felt that Rome should intervene directly to settle difficulties in the Melkite and Greek episcopacy— in short, that Rome should nominate their bishops and even the patriarch. This would suppress one of the ancient rights of the Eastern Church, and Beauduin found such a proposal unthinkable. (Even in post-Vatican II days this principle continues on occasion to be violated by Rome.)

At 6 A.M. on October 22 they left Jerusalem by car for an excursion through the Judean desert to the area around the Dead Sea. Their first stop was the monastery of St. Euthyme [7] which had even produced some Bedouin bishops. The desert was flat, without vegetation, and marked only by beautiful and imposing ruins.

Coziba, next on the itinerary, was formerly the central house of a Greek Orthodox laura and the traditional site to which Joachim withdrew to await Mary's birth. It could be reached only on foot by climbing down the bank of a narrow gorge. Two or three monks still lived there. One offered them the traditional hospitality and showed them the sights—an old chapel with some ancient mosaics and a little church. In contrast to Coziba, the monastery of the Quarantine and its beautiful church were perched more than nine hundred feet high on a cliff above the fountain of Elijah. It counted some four or five monks in its community. A visit to the Jordan, to the site of Jesus' baptism and then to the Dead Sea rounded out the day's excursion.

On Wednesday, while visiting a Syrian Catholic parish, the conversation turned to recent religious reforms in Turkey. Certain measures in particular raised the ire of Muslims and led them to view the new regime with disfavor. The most unpopular included the removal of the Islamic flag from the mosques and replacing the carpets with chairs or benches. Henceforth there was to be but one imam for every twenty-five thousand Muslims, and he must have a diploma.

While Msgr. Alouch and others in Egypt had implied by their very actions and attitudes that ecumenism must be conceived more broadly than in simply Christian terms, the same idea struggled for conscious expression in Beauduin during his weeks in Palestine. The genuine spirit of prayer that he constantly encountered in Jew and Muslim, whether in the streets or synagogues or mosques, impressed him deeply. Inexperienced and uninformed as he was in their traditions, he listened attentively to explanations and discussions which touched on these matters. In visiting religious sites shared in common, he could not help but detect beneath the sometimes hostile exteriors of pilgrims a deep common faith in the same God. At the church of Abougosh he was struck by the sight of Muslims who came in silence in the evenings to get water for their sick from its miraculous spring.

In the darkness and silence of the Palestinian nights Beauduin surely must have wondered about the future of these three great religious traditions which shared a common father in Abraham and Moses. Would they one day be united? Would religious dialogue between the three ever become a reality? In the light of the Malines Conversations and of Rome's reception of Protestant ecumenism as voiced in *Mortalium Animos*, Beauduin could only try to repress, with sadness, the hopes that certainly surged forth.

Such bold ideas were never officially voiced by Beauduin, but had his own ideal of ecumenism in the Christian context not been so severely challenged, perhaps religious tolerance would have become fashionable sooner and counted him among its leading spokesmen. As it turned out his disciples and followers would fight for it at Vatican II and give the world the *Declaration on Religious Freedom*, the *Declaration on the Relationship of the Church to Non-Christian Religions* and the *Decree on Ecumenism*. In post-Vatican II days they would open dialogues with Jews, Muslims, and other non-Christians and even with atheists.

Good news from Amay ushered in Friday with the announcement of the arrival of the new class of novices. Another significant event to mark the day was the beginning of a long friendship between Beauduin and the Russian Archimandrite Cyprien Kern, later a professor at St. Serge in Paris. He told them of the piety of the Russians living in Jerusalem since 1917, with their weekly vigil at the Holy Sepulchre on Saturday and their edifying fidelity to prayer in general.

Tragedy threatened the next day. The travelers left Jerusalem at 6:15 to go to Deir Dosi, the Palestinian Monte Cassino, where three or four Greek Orthodox monks yet remained. In his article on the Judean desert, Beauduin recounted several anecdotes about the founders of these early monasteries. Theodosius, the founder of Deir Dosi (*c.* 476) turned down any man without a beard. He did not want effeminate looking novices in his monastery. Its church had been constructed so as to serve monks from three different rites. In former times, after celebrating their liturgies of the Word in separate side chapels, they would reunite in the nave of the church for the eucharist. In the light of such an ancient precedent, who could call Amay a radical or dangerous experiment? Beauduin was jubilant at the confirmation of the validity of such experiments in the eyes of tradition.

Before leaving they exchanged their more modern means of transportation for donkeys. At the sight of a lady donkey gamboling among the rocks, Beauduin's beast instinctively started off in pursuit, hurling the unsuspecting monk head-first into the rocks. The fall upset his companions more than Beauduin. Fortunately nothing serious happened. He was more stunned than hurt, and recovered quickly enough.

Mar Saba, about eighteen miles from Jerusalem and founded by St. Sabas in 478, proved a populous monastery with thirty-five monks, whose cells were formerly the caves of recluses, hollowed out in the side of a cliff. The location of these monasteries gave meaning to the traditional greeting of Palestinian monks: "Near what torrent do you live?" This was just one of several almost inaccessible monasteries they visited, most of which were struggling for survival.

On Sunday, Valeri, the apostolic delegate, celebrated Mass in honor of Christ the King. Representatives from all the Latin communities were there, and he spoke with each, prolonging his conversation with the monks from Amay. They then made their last visit to the Holy Sepulchre and bid farewell to some of their friends. That evening Delpuch revealed his part in saving *Irénikon* when it was threatened with suppression. Beauduin thanked him warmly, happy to know the role played by their host.

En route to Nazareth the next day, they passed through Shiloh and Bethel, stopped at Jacob's well, and enjoyed the sights of Mounts Ebal and Gerizim and the great plain of Esdrelon. Upon their arrival at Nazareth they gravitated quite naturally to the Fountain of the Virgin and to the site of the Annunciation. But perhaps the Melkite priest Stephen Zeitoum impressed them most. Apparently he did not know who they were. He spoke with great warmth,

trying to convince them of the importance of the return of the
Orthodox. Beauduin's continual gestures and verbal affirmations of
agreement seemingly went unnoticed. Zeitoum's clarifications of Orthodox theology proved most interesting. He explained their concept
of purgatory, the cult of the dead on the Saturdays of Lent and
Pentecost, and their belief in a temporal hell. He saw the possibility
of conciliations in such doctrinal issues as the processions of the
Holy Spirit, which he felt to be just a question of words, and the
epiclesis which he considered already Catholic in the explanation
given of it. As far as the papacy was concerned, he insisted that the
Orthodox recognized the undeniable power of the pope, if only
because of the weakness of the Greek churches due to political
fragmentation.

The Melkite pastor complained of the lack of help offered to
the Melkite clergy by the Franciscans who, in comparison, lived
in the lap of luxury, often spending money foolishly, at least in
the eyes of their poorer brethren. The two monks did notice a
proliferation of buildings under construction, including a new church
over the supposed workshop of St. Joseph, discovered near the
Church of the Annunciation.

Tuesday was a calm, uneventful day. It began with Mass in the
grotto of the Annunciation and ended with a promenade to the
Fountain of the Virgin. In between they walked through the countryside breathing in the fragrances of the many plants. From time
to time Beauduin shared his biblical reflections on Christ's life in
Galilee with Becquet. They also visited St. Joseph's home, but Beauduin was unimpressed, especially by the predominance of *hic* (here)
on the various signs, as though it were certain beyond the shadow
of a doubt that *here* he lived and *here* he worked.

On Wednesday they took a trip to Mount Carmel, the scene of
Elijah's triumph over the Baalists and the mother church of the
Carmelites. The grotto of Elijah remains a popular pilgrimage spot
for Jews and Muslims. As a special honor, a Carmelite made the
famous statue of the Virgin in their chapel turn around, which Beauduin considered to be in extremely poor taste.

Early on Thursday morning they left Nazareth and drove by way
of Sephoris and Cana to Tiberias. At 1 P.M. they took a boat for
Capharnaum to see the ruins of the city, and especially to visit the
synagogue where one can still see the benches on which the Pharisees
sat.

Friday morning, after Mass, the two parted company. Beauduin felt it necessary to prolong his stay in Palestine and returned to Jerusalem. He advised Becquet to see as many places and meet as many persons as possible on his return trek to Belgium, suggesting stops in north and south Syria, Constantinople and Greece. In Jerusalem Beauduin took up lodgings with the Benedictines of the Mount of Olives. He judged their work with the Syrians and their knowledge of religious affairs in the Near East of value to his own personal information.

With more leisure time now at his disposal, Beauduin wrote an enthusiastic letter to his nephew, Edouard Beauduin, which gives some inkling of the impact that Palestine had made on him. Suddenly he saw the whole mystery of the incarnation and the humanity of Christ in a new light. It was as though he had received a revelation: "We are not Jewish enough and too monophysite: here is my impression from my stay here: A Christ not *man* enough and not *Messiah* enough, it seems to me, is the defect of our Christianity." [8]

Return to Europe

Beauduin's sojourn in the Near East lasted until January 16, 1930. He then headed in the general direction of Belgium. In February he gave a conference at Constantinople.[9] Leading Orthodox figures and the apostolic delegate (his friend Angelo Roncalli whom he had not seen since the previous spring) were among his audience. Once again he reiterated his views on unity, stressing the two chief obstacles to reunion: ignorance of one another and confusion between our understanding of Catholicism and Latinism. By now he clearly realized that Latinization had often been sought by Eastern Catholics as a vehicle for expressing their Catholic spirit and as an antidote against schism, but this did not excuse its continued use. After the conference was over, he shared with Roncalli some of the highlights of his trip, including his insights and impressions from this first visit to the Holy Land.

The last stop on this trip was Greece. He traveled for a while with one of his own monks, Pierre Dumont, and made a rather prolonged stay at Mount Athos. More details on this very important phase of Beauduin's journey are unfortunately not available, since Dumont's untimely death deprived us of our only first-hand source.[10] But Beauduin did confide to friends that the experience convinced him that Eastern monasticism was not the avenue to union. He failed to strike any sympathetic chord or to arouse any interest in an active collaboration in the work of Amay. The stay at Mount Athos also marked Beauduin in another way. He developed sciatic trouble trying to be both a good Eastern monk and a good Western monk. Western monks work during the day—this he did. Eastern monks pray during the night, standing—this he also did.[11]

Weary but considerably enriched spiritually and intellectually from his wanderings, Beauduin arrived in Naples on March 11, 1930, with some concern and even misgivings about his future. Never in his most pessimistic moments, however, could he have imagined what lay ahead for him.

10

Trial and Exile

Although out of sight, Beauduin's presence and spirit continued to pervade Amay through his frequent letters and contacts with his monks in the course of his travels. None of this helped to make 1929 a favorable year for the acceleration of d'Herbigny's plan, despite the latter's intensified efforts. On August 15, 1929 a new theological college opened under the Jesuits, which became known as the Russicum. This offshoot of the Oriental Institute defined Amay's position even more clearly. The new institute would specialize in Oriental theology; Amay, by implication, was henceforth limited to being a center for initiation into the Slavonic rite. New recruits for Amay, however, like Bruno Reynders and Olivier Rousseau, were not the least bit interested in becoming "Russified."

Three projects bearing the earmarks of Beauduin and emanating from Amay kept the founder's presence painfully alive to those who were trying to forget him. All three plans failed: a plan for union with Mont César, the controversial "Conversations by Mail," and a plan for a bulletin of unity literature in *Irénikon*.

The union with Mont César proposed a cooperative ecumenical effort between the two Benedictine houses. An Oriental group at Mont César would work with their confrères at Amay. The Westerners would work under Beauduin. While Gommaire Laporta was really the moving force behind this idea, Beauduin was not opposed to it in principle. It corresponded to his second formula of December 16, 1924, drawn up along the order of the Bollandists, and he was willing to capitalize on every available means to expand Amay's influence. The new abbot, Bernard Capelle, at first favored the idea, but then he abruptly dropped his support when he took stock of the possible consequences should the powerful personality of Beauduin once more have the freedom of spreading his influence within the walls of the monastery. The final outcome of negotiations for the project was a house of studies in Louvain which existed from October 12, 1929 to March 29, 1931.

On May 6, 1929 a circular was sent to about fifteen individuals. Edited by Beauduin, it announced the formation of a closed and private circle of people interested in exchanging by mail discussions, information, etc., on the question of union. He planned to publish letters of interest received from people he had met on his trips to the East and England. Members could be of any denomination, and —as with the source of their inspiration, the Malines Conversations— the project would engage the participants only in a private capacity. No hierarchy was to be involved. Having sent out this feeler, Beauduin bought a mimeograph machine and prepared the first official "correspondence," but the reactions he received to the initial circular were such a disappointment that he never sent out the first number.

The third project was conceived in November 1929 as an extension of *Irénikon*. The bulletin of ecumenical literature would try to keep abreast of all that was happening and being published in Russian, Oriental, Protestant, Anglican and Roman Catholic circles. This plan, as with the other two, aborted before the end of 1929.

Somehow Cardinal Francis Bourne, Archbishop of Westminster, received a copy of the circular on the "Conversations by Mail" and immediately interpreted it as a secret continuation of the Malines Conversations. Supported by the tone and content of *Mortalium Animos*, instant cries of outrage were raised. Bourne sent an official protest in November to Cardinal van Roey at Malines. This reaction seems to have frightened Abbot Capelle. From this point on his support for Beauduin became increasingly feeble, and this at a most crucial time.[1]

But before its founder returned from his trip, Amay received yet another blow. The January 20 decree of Russification declared that the monks of Amay must study the Byzantine rite; all new recruits would eventually pass to this rite.[2] Beauduin, perhaps not fully grasping the situation, wrote to one of his monks:

> It's not a triumph [for d'Herbigny] but a victory [for us]. In practice Amay has nothing to change, except we must study the Oriental rites; that's a good thing.[3]

Nevertheless, despite this unexpected intervention, a measure of calm seemed to have been restored to the priory by the time Beauduin arrived in March. On the other hand, his situation was threatened even more seriously as he came under fire from new and totally unexpected quarters. The papers from the Malines Conversations had just been published.

Beauduin had published a résumé of his proposal for Anglican reunion in *Irénikon* in 1926. When the articles raised a storm of protest, he discreetly identified them with the Malines Conversations and printed Mercier's letter of thanks.[4] But with van Roey's disclosure in the public press of Beauduin's authorship, the whole controversy broke out anew. His choice of words—"Dom Lambert Beauduin, prior of Amay"—immediately implicated Amay. Extremely concerned, Beauduin went to van Roey with a written statement for the press. He argued that Amay had been unfairly implicated on two counts: (1) the Proposal had been written in Rome before the conception of Amay, and (2) Beauduin had Mercier's letters of approval. When van Roey asked the monk not to publish the reply (because it contradicted the cardinal on these two points), Beauduin tore up his text and threw it in the cardinal's wastepaper basket.

On April 6, 1930, the Gordian knot was tied a bit tighter. The Pontifical Commission for Russia, under the presidency of d'Herbigny, gained its independence from the Congregation for the Oriental Church which continued under the direction of Cardinal Sincero. From this point on d'Herbigny's interventions in Amay's affairs multiplied.

Moreover, scarcely had Beauduin resumed community life when once again fears were aroused in Rome, this time over the financing of the house of studies in Louvain. Since the very idea of the house had been suggested by the canonical visitor, Beauduin was now certain that some people had decided to prevent him from having the slightest influence over the religious community he had founded.[5] In October Capelle wrote to Reynders: "Bishop d'Herbigny has expressly excluded Father Lambert from having any responsibility in the community." [6] On October 15 he once again was told to pack his bags and leave. Accompanied by Becquet, he retired to Tancrémont where he managed to commit yet another indiscretion. Writing to some Anglican Benedictines at Nashdom, he signed his letter: "Your brother in St. Benedict." Someone published it in *The Times*. Perhaps this was the last straw. On January 13, 1931, Beauduin was summoned to Rome to answer a series of charges.[7]

A Roman Hearing

Beauduin interpreted the call to Rome simply as an invitation to talk over some indiscretions, but he soon realized how precarious his situation was. Upon his arrival he was subjected to the equivalent of house arrest at the "Confraternité sacerdotale." Those entrusted with his "supervision," however, soon became his faithful friends and most dedicated collaborators during the months ahead.

What he had expected to be a matter of fraternal correction or paternal caution turned out to be a secret ecclesiastical hearing which took place between January 15 and January 30. The president, who, it seems, also served as the prosecutor of the special commission, was none other than Bishop d'Herbigny.

For the uninitiated, the intricacies of Vatican legal procedures can be baffling. In general, secrecy reigns supreme, which serves to obscure the chain of authority and to hinder normal efforts to get at the crucial facts once a judgment has been rendered—usually under the cloak of the pontifical seal. Beauduin's situation will be no exception to the rule.

In attempting to sift out the facts, it appears that the quasi-tribunal which tried Beauduin's case was a special commission whose members were chosen by Pius XI from the Commission for Russia for the express purpose of clarifying certain issues pertaining to Amay and to Beauduin. In addition to d'Herbigny, Giuseppe Pizzardo, the papal undersecretary of extraordinary affairs, and Msgr. Filippo

Giobbe, secretary of the Pontifical Commission for Russia, sat on the commission (with possibly a fourth person who acted as secretary).[8] Despite the good intentions of the pope, the special commission proved to be little more than a clever means to sanction a decision already made before the hearing began. The primate had a single goal in mind: the removal of Beauduin once and for all from Amay, and in d'Herbigny he found a willing partner who carried out, although not without some equivocation, his wishes.

Beauduin's position was doubly precarious, for not only had the Primate already determined in advance to suppress Amay, but in d'Herbigny Beauduin had to deal with a person who was completely unpredictable, and who as *relator perpetuus* was one of the most powerful men in Rome in matters concerning Russia.

For a long time people had noticed strange characteristics in d'Herbigny's behavior, but most passed them off as harmless (although sometimes expensive) eccentricities. Cappuyns recalled several such episodes. The visiting dignitary made a series of long distance calls all over Europe and then said to the young monk: "I am embarrassed about the great number of calls, and I am all the more embarrassed that you certainly do not want me to pay." Cappuyns then accompanied d'Herbigny to the tram stop. Once again the Jesuit astounded Cappuyns when he said: "I don't know where to go. Should I go to see the cardinal [Mercier] or the rector on the Rue des Recollets? [The cardinal lived in Malines, a town some distance from Louvain.] The first car to stop will decide the matter." And so it was that he happily accepted a ride to Malines (for in reality he was hitchhiking, not waiting for the next tram). He considered the whole affair another sign of the guidance of divine providence.[9]

But the privilege of *relator perpetuus*, reserved to a select few, made d'Herbigny an even greater threat. It entitled him to immediate access to the pope, day or night, without any previous request for an audience. In retrospect it seems that ideas and words he attributed to the Holy Father were frequently his own. It is also possible that Pius XI, an equally impetuous man, was already alarmed at the liberties that d'Herbigny was taking with the papal name and was troubled by rumors of the latter's attempts to manipulate Beauduin, which may account for his decision to select the members of the special commission himself.

On Sunday, January 18, only Beauduin was summoned before the commission. He was bound to secrecy and interrogated for two hours on everything, including the "conversations by mail." He thought that he had convinced the members, especially Pizzardo, of the liceity of his actions. After a period of deliberation, the members asked Beauduin to make a report on his conception of Amay and the inconvenience of Russification. Pizzardo and Giobbe, realizing the injustice being done, apparently sided with the accused. They argued that it would be premature to judge a work that had only begun, and they pointed out that some of the charges on which Beauduin was being tried were inevitable incidents in the beginning of any work, especially in a work such as Amay. In the light of their intervention, it looked as though a hasty and/or unfavorable judgment might be avoided.

Elated, Beauduin gave a full report to his superior. This was a mistake. When Capelle heard that Bourne's complaint of November 30 about the "conversations by mail" project had been raised, he decided that he could no longer defend Beauduin. He soon let himself be won over by the opposition—namely, the primate and Célestin Golenvaux, abbot of Maredsous. During the next ten days Capelle repeatedly refused to see Beauduin.

As the days passed, d'Herbigny hounded Beauduin unceasingly, trying to get the monk to change his mind, to see things d'Herbigny's way, and to agree to his Slavic dream. Although Beauduin was under oath not to relate what went on during the trial, he felt no compulsion to keep silent about these "extracurricular" meetings with d'Herbigny, some of which were marked by more erratic behavior on the part of the Jesuit. During one particular nocturnal drive around the Roman countryside, the conversation turned to the future of Amay. D'Herbigny asked for Beauduin's opinion, and he replied in all sincerity that there was only one solution to assure the future of Amay and to preserve the confidence of the community: to give him back his position as prior. D'Herbigny replied with enthusiasm: "All right, if that is the case, I will speak to the pope."

The sequence of events between January 18 and January 30 remain very vague. Beauduin appeared to have won the support of Pizzardo and Giobbe on January 18, and somewhat later even that of d'Herbigny. He had never had the support of the primate and soon lost that of his own abbot. The story is simply told. After the nocturnal drive with d'Herbigny, Beauduin could not repress the

FAMILY PORTRAIT. Octave (later Lambert) Beauduin seated on a footstool (center) in 1879, when he was six years old. With him are his parents, six brothers, a sister, and a German governess.

NEWLY ORDAINED. Beauduin at Liège in 1898, the year after his ordination.

UNDERCOVER AGENT. Disguised as businessman Oscar Fraipont, Beauduin frequently passed through military lines during World War I. Photo taken in The Hague, 1916.

BRUSSELS UNITY WEEK. Taking part in the 1925 meeting between Roman and Eastern Christians were (first row, left to right) Fernand Portal, Joseph Schyrgens, Metropolitan Andrew Szepticki, Cardinal Mercier, Gerard Van Caloen, and Beauduin. In the second row, immediately behind Mercier, is Maurice de la Taille.

FOUNDATION AT AMAY. Beauduin poses with the monks of his monastery in his portrait taken around 1927. In the front row (left to right) are José Perron, Ildephonse Dirks, Beauduin, Franco de Wyels, Thomas Becquet. Walthère Boland, the layman who kept the monastery's books, stands in the back row, third from the right.

The Abbot Primate
Fidelis von Stotzingen

Michel d'Herbigny, S.J.

THE FUTURE POPE. Angelo Roncalli (bottom left), then apostolic delegate to Bulgaria, visits Amay during a vacation in 1930. Next to him is Bernard Capelle. Beauduin, with a beard, is in the third row, far left.

MAN OF LETTERS. Beauduin at his desk at Chevetogne in 1954 or 1955. Although he wrote only one book, he published a great number of articles and carried on a prodigious correspondence of letters.

CHEVETOGNE. The Oriental chapel, southern facade. The monastery Beauduin founded moved from Amay to Chevetogne in 1939.

LAST YEARS. Photograph taken at Chevetogne in October 1957.

desire to share his good news about the Jesuit's change of heart. He went to the Greek College where he found Capelle with several other monks, including at least one from Amay, and announced: "Guess what! D'Herbigny is going to agree that I may once again become prior of Amay!" In the light of what happened several days later, it has been surmised that Capelle immediately informed the primate of this new development and that the latter brought pressure to bear on d'Herbigny. His success could not have been more complete.

On Friday, January 30, the commission met to render its official decision. Had a bomb exploded in their midst, neither Beauduin nor Capelle (who was present) could have been more shocked. They listened with unbelieving ears as d'Herbigny spelled out the terms:

> Here is the will of the Holy Father that I am charged to communicate to you. An equivocation exists that must disappear. Amay is opposed to the conceptions of the Holy See. This name, the spirit it incarnates, the methods it represents, even the place and the thing must disappear. Nothing can remain of Amay.[10]

Those who so desired would be given the option of applying for admission into the apostolate under the direction of the Pontifical Commission for Russia. A new work outside of Belgium would be organized for those willing to submit to the commission. Beauduin's family could liquidate Amay, and Mont César would settle any deficiencies which might result. At 12:30 it was all over. Capelle was as shaken as Beauduin and hastened to tell the stunned monk that he certainly could not expect to return to Mont César. Beauduin later confessed that these words of his abbot were "the greatest moral shock of my life."

Ordinarily in such a hearing as Beauduin's the decision represents the majority vote of the members of the commission. In his case, however, the decision seems to have resulted from the report that d'Herbigny supposedly made to the pope. If he told the commission that it was the pope's decision, the case would be considered closed and there would be no cause for further action. In short, a vote was not necessary, and it appears that Beauduin's fate depended exclusively on d'Herbigny's report to the pope. (If in fact d'Herbigny simply attributed to the pope his own wishes in this matter, it was not the only such instance.)

That the commission only had the appearance of being a tribunal without actually being one is reflected in the fact that no chance for an appeal was offered to Beauduin. Amay had been confided to the Commission for Russia, and as such owed it the same obedience it owed the Holy See—which gave d'Herbigny, president of the commission investigating Beauduin and of the Commission for Russia, absolute authority over Amay, even though major decisions were to be first approved by the pope. D'Herbigny as *relator perpetuus* would certainly have enjoyed in the eyes of his subordinates an unquestionable authority.[11]

The decision of January 30 led to the reappointment of Maur Etcheverry as apostolic visitor with the request that a prompt report on Amay be made. Those willing to work without publicity (i.e., without *Irénikon*) and who would concentrate on study, editing liturgical books, etc., were to be reported to Rome and perhaps recommended for the "new work outside of Belgium." D'Herbigny included these details in a letter to Etcheverry dated January 31. He also spelled out the chief complaints against Beauduin: an abusive extension of the work for union, financial mismanagement, and a wrong view of monastic reform. Beauduin's failure to form men of prayer and his inability to be content with preparing spiritually for the revitalization of Russian monasticism were also singled out. Criticism of the expressions "Union of Church*es*" and "Monks of Unity" also appeared for the first time. The latter had apparently been adopted without proper permission. The essence of Etcheverry's task was to determine how widespread Beauduin's unacceptable notions of unity were and then to do his best to dissipate any such equivocations.

D'Herbigny's unfortunate intervention resulted in part from his failure or unwillingness to understand the Benedictine ideal. Founded on the concept of autonomous monasteries, Benedictine tradition gave great emphasis to communal life and bound the monk to his particular monastery by a vow of stability. Consciously or unconsciously overlooking these fundamental differences in orientation, d'Herbigny expected to treat monks as Jesuits, to shift them about at will and to interfere in their internal affairs when necessary in order to further his own schemes. Beauduin, thinking in Benedictine terms, expected and demanded total freedom of action. The Jesuit, however, could not tolerate the autonomous situation that Beauduin was trying to create at Amay because it threatened to thwart the very purpose for which he had helped Amay exist.

Several days later, when Capelle left, d'Herbigny unexpectedly changed the terms of the decision and proposed new arrangements. Amay need not be sold; it as well as *Irénikon* could continue. He offered Beauduin the job of procurator for Amay in Rome so that he could stay spiritually in touch with his monks. D'Herbigny even held out the hope that Beauduin might return eventually to Belgium. Showering him with flattery, d'Herbigny reassured Beauduin that he was indispensable for the work of union and for Amay. This abrupt about-face is easily explained: d'Herbigny had come to realize that the primate had absolutely no interest in either Beauduin's project or the Jesuit's. He was simply using d'Herbigny to get rid of Beauduin, and d'Herbigny had sided with him in order to bring Beauduin to his senses. Having exhausted the primate's usefulness, d'Herbigny turned once again to Beauduin and tried to exploit his potential, for the monk clearly had an Oriental vocation and a gift for attracting men to that work. If only he could be channeled and controlled, he would be an invaluable asset to d'Herbigny's plans.

Meanwhile Etcheverry left Rome, supposedly informed of these new measures. On February 16 he summarized Rome's will for the monks of Amay. Between January 31 and February 16 he had received another secret document and distributed parts of it (reputedly from the pope) to all at Amay. It stated that all publications, including *Irénikon*, must stop. Various factors lay behind this decision, which seems to have emanated more from the primate and Bourne's fears than from any specific antipathy on d'Herbigny's part. In any case no serious interruption occurred. An exchange of telegrams enabled publication to continue. The monks were also to decide if they wanted to go along with Rome's wishes, return to their former monasteries, or leave.[12] Etcheverry summed up the purpose of Amay in these words:

> The Holy See does not consider the work of Amay as having as its purpose the union of Churches in general. It considers Amay exclusively as destined to form Benedictine monks in order to establish centers of monastic life in Russia.

On February 26, Beauduin wrote to Reynders, then at Louvain: "The primate wants the suppression of Amay purely and simply. . . . As for me, my fate was already decided before my arrival." He continued to believe that d'Herbigny was their greatest defender, but he admitted that Capelle's unwillingness to allow him to return to Mont César had hurt his position with d'Herbigny. Only when Beauduin was finally able to pay a fleeting visit to Amay some months later did the monks learn that their priory had been suppressed and then reestablished, for he had asked Reynders to say nothing about the suppression.

The visit of Etcheverry had particularly tragic results which further depleted the community at Amay. Two monks left spontaneously. Three were urged to return to their former monasteries or to make application for secularization. These decisions were made on their expressed views of unity which were found incompatible with those of the Holy See (i.e., d'Herbigny). Anselm Bolton, Bruno Reynders and Thomas Becquet were also affected by the decree. Bolton presented an especially thorny case since he had made his solemn profession at Amay and had no monastery to which to return. Eventually he was secularized. Becquet's statement, as can be imagined, proved unsatisfactory. Only at the insistence of Mercenier and Rousseau was he given a second opportunity to state his position which Etcheverry corrected in his presence, explaining that it would help his chances to remain a monk of Amay. (For the next eighteen years he lived at Tancrémont where the monks hoped to but never did build a monastery.) Reynders' case was similar to Becquet's, but he had to return to Mont César.[13]

On March 13 Beauduin wrote to Cappuyns: "No connection with Amay; return to Belgium forbidden; can be procurator (financier) of Amay here at Rome or else at En Calcat." (En Calcat was a particularly strict monastery in an isolated setting suitable for receiving difficult cases; Beauduin had known at least since February 26 that the primate wanted him sent there.) Beauduin balked at such high-handed methods. He insisted on his right to come and go freely and to belong to Amay. Moreover, he demanded that the above threat be declared non-existent and that he be informed of the terms of the new statutes for Amay, as well as the status of its members.

On March 25 he went to Assisi for a few days to escape d'Herbigny. At first it looked as though he had won his point, but then Capelle, the primate, and Golenvaux upset everything. Everywhere Beauduin turned, the presence of d'Herbigny was to be found. At this point d'Herbigny was pressing the threat of En Calcat, constantly urging the stubborn monk to reflect on what the Orthodox and the friends and monks of Amay would say if the founder were sent there.[14] Beauduin asked to arrange his future with Capelle, who after all was still his abbot, but d'Herbigny refused, insisting that the abbot as well as the professed at Mont César wanted to have nothing to do with him. His only choice was either to stay in Rome (under d'Herbigny's thumb) or else to go to En Calcat.

But still the issue was not settled. As time dragged on, Beauduin became increasingly aware of the complexity of the situation. Summing it up with a proverb: "The absent are often wrong," he added, "I believe that we ought to practice the policy of presence."[15] In all he endured five months of anguish. Humiliation, suppression, exclusion, exile, reintegration, re-establishment, and collaboration all succeeded each other in dizzying fashion, and all at the hands of a man who by an exploit unique in the annals of the contemporary Church had freed himself from all outside controls.

D'Herbigny's attempts to get Beauduin to accept a Roman job "to save him from the Belgian Congregation" failed. He refused to give in, and despite d'Herbigny's talk of suppressing Amay, the priory continued to exist and *Irénikon* continued to appear. Then suddenly Beauduin was told that he could return to Tancrémont. He arrived toward the end of May, elated and relieved, yet puzzled by the temporary reprieve. One month later, however, he was told to go to Paris. It was not long before he became convinced that some people were still determined to prevent him from having any influence whatsoever on his community. Rousseau, having written to him about a problem, received the following reply:

I will do everything to help you find a solution, but neither can I nor do I want to do anything unless I have a formal order, precise and written from the Reverend Father Prior and countersigned by Abbot Etcheverry. I have just received an unbelievable letter from Fr. Etcheverry for having taken a step in view of rendering service to Amay. Everything is interpreted in a bad sense; I am obliged to take precautions.[16]

The Exile Begins

The Roman reprieve was obviously not taken by Beauduin's enemies as an exoneration from his supposed guilt. Etcheverry apparently thought that it would be better for the time being if Beauduin lived elsewhere. As usual, Beauduin tried to make the best of a bad situation. Soon he was hard at work:

> I am a minute from the metro of the Porte Maillot . . . which transports me in a few minutes to the libraries of the Sorbonne and of the Institut Catholique. I am forcing myself to collect my already distant knowledge on the Church, on theology in general, and on the liturgy and asceticism and to readjust a bit my already rusty instrument.[17]

Before long, however, Beauduin was once again the victim of ecclesiastical double dealing. Toward mid-July Etcheverry came to see him about a small matter of protocol. Beauduin described the sequence of events in a letter to Reynders.[18] He was asked officially to turn over the business affairs of Amay, severing himself definitively from any further administrative involvement. Etcheverry twice reassured Beauduin that once this was done the whole matter would be finished. If ever anything came up, the abbot's intervention alone would suffice and Beauduin could count on him. With no reason to doubt the man's sincerity, Beauduin signed. The next day a further condition was announced: Beauduin must accept a self-imposed exile for several years outside Belgium in some non-central city. The implication behind the automatic exclusion from any ecumenical center was obvious. It meant complete dissociation from ecumenism and from the monks and the work of Amay. Even Capelle was upset because he felt responsible and never intended such a radical solution to the matter. Furthermore, he claimed that Etcheverry had the decree of exile in his pocket when he reassured Beauduin that nothing more would be required of him.

By July 27 it was all over: self-exile or En Calcat. Beauduin chose exile. His young friend Cappuyns was working on his dissertation at the time and was free to go where he pleased. He offered to accompany Beauduin to his place of exile. Strasbourg was chosen. As

Beauduin made his farewells at Mont César, he found time to write to another young friend, outlining his new approach to union and encouraging him to adopt a similar program:

> The best way for you (and for me) is not to work explicitly for union, to speak or write of it, but to follow this program:
>
> (a) to intensify your personal and spiritual life in the sense of the sacerdotal prayer of our Lord—hence, a profoundly ecclesial piety;
> (b) to enliven our theological studies by the apostolic preoccupation of encountering the mentality of our separated brothers and to speak to them in a language that they can understand instead of making them use our categories: the Word was made *flesh!*
> (c) to popularize the Byzantine-Slav intellectual life, literature, art . . . in order to prepare for a psychological *rapprochement.*
>
> This is also my regime since I can no longer speak *ex professo.*[19]

Beauduin and Cappuyns arrived in Strasbourg by mid-November. The latter became ill and had to leave on February 15, but Beauduin would stay on until April. By Christmas, however, Beauduin had grown restless. Then a sudden brainstorm seemed to solve everything, offering both an intellectual challenge *and* an excuse for occasional trips to Belgium. Encouraged by the financial support of the Beauduin family, the Royal Library of Brussels created a bureau of bibliographical documentation of Byzantine and Slavic studies. On January 28, 1932 Beauduin was named its first director and appointed to the post of scientific collaborator.

Meanwhile Amay was experiencing financial difficulties. Given the extremely involved state of affairs created by Boland, Belpaire had addressed a letter to the primate requesting permission for Beauduin's return to help straighten out things. He did this on the very day that Beauduin's new appointment was announced in the press. D'Herbigny reacted immediately through the primate, who on February 8 renewed the original prohibition to enter Belgium.[20]

This action almost instantly compromised Beauduin's new position. Angered at the incessant and senseless harassment, he sent his brothers, who were politically influential in Belgium, to the nuncio to explain that d'Herbigny's measures might provoke a diplomatic incident with the liberal government—something that the Church could hardly afford. This was a tactical blunder on Beauduin's part, for d'Herbigny soon used the incident to involve the papal secretary of state. Beauduin's contacts in the Royal Library, though of brief duration, nevertheless helped deepen his knowledge and understanding of the Orient. His days, however, were clearly numbered.

An Unexpected Letter

On March 30 Beauduin realized just how infuriated d'Herbigny and the primate had become with his innocent little forays across the border and his attempt to make a diplomatic issue out of an ecclesiastical affair. He received a letter from Cardinal Pacelli, the secretary of state, who personally enjoined the monk to resign from his position with the Royal Library and to retire without delay to the austere and isolated abbey of En Calcat at the foot of the Black Mountain in Tarn, a region in southern France. The sentence was for two years.[21] Amay would not be touched, but Beauduin could have no further contact with the community.

On April 11 the primate wrote to de Kerchove, the eighty-six-year-old president of the Belgian Benedictine Congregation. He warned de Kerchove not to be deceived anymore by Beauduin who had failed to tell the apostolic visitor, the Holy See, or even the senior members on the council at Mont César that his family had backed the loan he had made in Holland. De Kerchove ignored the primate and continued to trust Beauduin. He saw nothing irregular in Beauduin's financial arrangements. His only regret was that no one had kept him sufficiently informed so that he could have intervened on Beauduin's behalf. Now it was too late. There was no one to whom Beauduin could appeal. Advised that obedience was the best defense, the heartbroken founder boarded a train for En Calcat on April 22, 1932. Cappuyns, undaunted by the stigma of ecclesiastical censure now associated with Beauduin, accompanied him to the station.

The Roman archives remain closed to scholarly investigation of Beauduin's case. Because of the recognized irregularities at the time of the trial itself, it is tantalizing to spectulate on how much light, if any, the archives will throw on this affair when they are opened to research. Beauduin himself was never much help, although from various remarks and letters the main sequence of events can be traced. In 1958 he commented briefly on the trial:

> D'Herbigny was put on the commission at the insistence of the primate with this message: "No Benedictine mission, they are contemplatives, etc." D'Herbigny said: "I saw the Holy Father who wanted to suppress Amay. . . ." Pizzardo said the whole thing was premature, moved for a report and advised me to wait and see how things would develop. Then d'Herbigny, driving me back in his car, said: "You should be prior of Amay." Three days later the decision came that I was no longer to appear in Belgium.[22]

That the cards were stacked against Beauduin from the beginning is quite evident. He was associated in d'Herbigny's mind with two personal frustrations: the Malines Conversations and the Russian apostolate. D'Herbigny's own loss of power in January may well have triggered his harsh action against Beauduin in February and March.

The En Calcat Exile

Upon his arrival at En Calcat, Beauduin wrote to a close friend confessing that he did not know why or how he got there, or who was really responsible: "I live as much as possible *in sinu Patris* [in the bosom of the Father] which I have done for almost a year." [23] Under the circumstances, the monks could hardly be expected to be outgoing toward him, but their kindness almost immediately overwhelmed him. Soon he felt quite at home in the austere atmosphere of fasts and abstinences which made it seem like a perpetual Lent, long offices with constant risings during the night, no recreation, perpetual silence, abundant manual labor, and the total rejection of all comfort.[24] Harsh as it may seem, the regime actually suited him. He would have liked to impose a more demanding discipline on his own monks but felt that such a matter should be left up to the individual and the guidance of the Spirit. He realized that not every temperament could stand a steady diet of such a life, and that austerity and ecumenism were two separate vocations—both of which he happened to have.

If the life itself was almost entirely to his liking, there were a few things that bothered him liturgically, but soon this was remedied. His fervor did not go unnoticed. Although Capelle wrote to the abbot advising him of Beauduin's powerful personality, Abbot Marie treated him no differently from the others. In fact, within two months he had been so completely won over by Beauduin's regularity, goodness, and pleasant disposition that he asked him to teach a course on the liturgy. The success of this course helped to prepare the obscure monastery for a significant contribution a few years later when the French liturgical movement got underway.[25] It was so successful that a second, on dogma, was soon assigned. The confidence thus placed in him undoubtedly helped to make the injustice of his "criminal" status at least bearable.

The style of life may have agreed with him, but he was tortured by the fear that "they," the anonymous Roman "they" who sent him to En Calcat, would not be content with his exile and silence: "Don't think I am demoralized or eager to leave here. . . . It's what is going to happen in two years that frightens me." [26]

> For several months I have tasted the austere but profound joy of suffering something for an ideal. I only fear one thing—the invitation to sign some propositions, not doctrinal, of course, but disciplinary, on individual conversions, etc. . . . In twenty or thirty years, prelates of every rank will be able to defend the ideas proposed by *Irénikon* without danger.[27]

Further dimensions of his determination to hold firm were reflected in another letter several days later:

> I will never ask Rome for a lessening of my time of confinement. . . . There is an austere sensual pleasure in showing oneself superior to injustice and in disdaining the pardon of iniquitous judges. It is not a very elevated mystique, but it is a very healthy philosophy that the Book of Wisdom does not condemn.[28]

In the meantime, he planned to work on two books, one on the liturgy, the other on asceticism. Unfortunately, nothing ever came of his good intentions. However by the following year he could boast that he was considered a monk of En Calcat; he took his turn as leader of the office, lector, and preacher, and served at table. Moreover, he was allowed to preach a bit in the neighborhood and was overjoyed at the occasional opportunities that were offered for giving conferences on the liturgy.[29]

En Calcat revealed the depth of Beauduin's obedience and humility and the strength of his Christian optimism. At no moment did any expression of bitterness escape from him.

> Don't publish this letter. Whatever happens to me, always say that I am the happiest of men to suffer something for these ideas, so dear to me: the liturgy of the Church and the reconciliation of our separated brothers.[30]

> There are different ways of working for union, and I believe that the most opportune for the moment is to pray and to suffer for it. Also, I am the happiest of men to think that fidelity to this ideal has occasioned me a few inconveniences.[31]

Beauduin's attitude throughout his trials puzzled many persons, as did his attitude toward authority. He believed that Christian obedience was an act of faith: "It is to give to each authority all the respect that is due, without wavering." But the obedience demanded by d'Herbigny was the adoration of an idol. Although obedience was necessay to preserve order within the Church, it flowed from a motive of faith in the reality of the Church, not from faith grounded in the individual commanding. Beauduin obeyed unjust injunctions not because he saw the Word of God behind them but so that order might be maintained, firmly believing that more good would be effected through obedience than through rebellion. Yet this attitude of docility did not prevent him from sharp criticism of abusive displays of authority. Masters were given to us to preserve us from falsifying the sense of the divine Word, not to establish a screen before it. His attitude toward obedience is best summed up by his commentary on Article 1323 of the Code of Canon Law: "In other words, super-obedience is only a formal disobedience of the lawgiver." [32]

An unwavering concern for the good of the Church took priority even over his own good name. While he could say with a wry smile on his face: "We must lose the filthy habit of calling 'Church' even the least bureaucrat appointed by the pope who decides inconsequential matters behind the pope's back," he could still refuse his family's offer to intervene on his behalf. It was, he said "an affair of the Church," and wanted it kept within the Church.[33] But it would be wrong to conclude from that that he was willing to give up without a fight.

Futile Efforts at Defense

The anguish of Beauduin's situation was deepened by the news of two more "defections"—both close personal friends and promising candidates for Amay. One went directly over to Orthodoxy. The other returned to Mont César when Etcheverry disbanded the community of Amay in March 1931 and remained there until February 1934, when he left definitively.[34]

Cut off from his community, Beauduin's hands were tied. He could not advise them in their difficult moments, nor could he help them to understand the Church and to accept what she supposedly had seen fit to do to him. For all but a few intimates, Beauduin had disappeared without leaving any trace. Some ecclesiastics who considered themselves knowledgeable assured everyone that this was the actual case—which naturally implied that he had abandoned not only the priesthood but also the faith.

His brother-in-law Jules Maisin brought the first "official" news of his supposed apostasy. Abbé Jean Mignot had announced Beauduin's entry into Orthodoxy at a dinner where a Belgian monsignor was present, and he in turn passed the news on to Malines. The all-knowing Abbé gave Cardinal August Hlond, the primate of Poland, as his source. Similar rumors were spread by another priest who had an uncle at Westminister. Belpaire soon put the Cardinal of Malines straight on Beauduin's whereabouts. While Beauduin may have been naive about some things, he was fully aware of the faults and weaknesses of the visible Church, and his profession of faith was in no way dependent on these human elements. How painful such talk of his having left the Church was to him is evident in the following letter:

If I ever had such a temptation, it is not the charity and largess of the views of the Catholic clergy that would have held me back. Thanks to God, such folly has never even crossed my mind, although I am far from finding everything perfect in the Church:

centralization to the extreme, unscrupulous prelatism and hyper-Jesuitism are the human flaws of the twentieth-century Church, just as other periods had theirs. But, in these things, the remedy often comes from an excess of the evil.[35]

At about the same time, some other sensational news reached Beauduin: d'Herbigny's fall from power.[36] The monk's reaction was typical, and without malice: "Why don't they send him to En Calcat? We could make observations on eclipses together and verify the laws of falling bodies." [37]

If Beauduin had turned down his family's offers to go directly to the Holy See, it was not because he had no intention of pursuing some sort of defense. Already on the eve of his departure for En Calcat he had assembled a mass of documents which he left with Cappuyns. There were four charges in particular that he felt were unjustified, and he planned to try to clear his name in these areas: (1) an ecumenical activity conceived too broadly, (2) his anti-Beuronian monastic renewal, (3) the anti-canonical aspects of his financial administration, and (4) his acceptance of an official function without seeking Rome's approval.[38]

The first efforts were directed toward the financial matter. Beauduin admittedly liked to operate in secrecy or, to put it in other words, with independence. But Boland had really wreaked havoc with the book-keeping, and since the apostolic visitor did not want to consult Beauduin—the only other person who knew anything about the books—one hopeless mess had resulted. Beauduin argued that he was morally responsible to those who guaranteed Amay's solvency (his family) and not to Rome. If his family had no complaint, then canon law had no cause to complain either. Moreover, at least according to Dumont, the Beauduins never lent any actual money, just their name.

In *A Supplementary Note* (1932), Beauduin explained that he had never mentioned his family by name, but that no one doubted that they were the guarantors of the loan. Moreover, Mont César never dealt directly with his brothers as he had requested but was content with his written promise that the loan was guaranteed. Since his family established a non-profit corporation,[39] Mont César was never involved. The corporation fulfilled its commitments through the original 250,000 franc loan; nothing was left outstanding, and

upon Beauduin's resignation there was a balance of 75,000 francs.
The Dutch loan of 1927–1931 was also in the name of his family, and
so once again it was a private matter.

At Beauduin's urging, this report was sent to Etcheverry on April
8, 1932. The apostolic visitor wanted to get out of the awkward situation which he himself had created. As a consequence he called a
meeting in February 1933 in Paris. Beauduin, along with one of his
brothers and Dumont, was invited. And still the affair was not settled.

The second matter to which Beauduin turned his attention was his
appointment to the Royal Library. His attempts to have his sentence
changed from En Calcat to a mission in the Near East ultimately
failed. He wanted to save face by justifying his resignation from the
Royal Library and his absence from Belgium and from his family. At
first Capelle agreed to the logic, but as usual he hesitated. Finally,
because he had lost confidence in Etcheverry and d'Herbigny, the
abbot wrote directly to Pacelli on July 3, 1932. He expresssed his
fears that the liberal Belgian government might intervene—which
could harm the situation of the Church in Belgium—and suggested
that Beauduin be sent to the Benedictines in Jerusalem. He received
no direct reply.

Meanwhile the Royal Library refused to accept Beauduin's resignation and gave him an extended leave of absence until the "incomprehensible opposition ceased." On September 29, Beauduin wrote to
Dumont that Capelle foresaw more severe Roman measures if
Beauduin could not get his brothers (one of them, Lucien, was a sena-
tor) to persuade the Royal Library to accept Beauduin's resignation. Eventually the resignation was accepted, to Beauduin's great
relief. One thing he did not need was more trouble.

Despite the above failures, Beauduin was sure that he could get a
hearing from Pacelli. He therefore wrote to Cardinal Seredi (the
eminent canon lawyer whom Mercier had wanted him to consult at
the time of the Malines Conversations) for advice. He received no
response for a whole year. All the time Beauduin secretly hoped that
in the end d'Herbigny would come to his defense. He refused at
this time to admit that Pacelli's letter had been sent at d'Herbigny's
request.

On October 18, 1932 d'Herbigny wrote to Dumont: "The case of
Fr. Lambert no longer depends on the Commission in any way. But I
believe his intimate sacrifice will be more fruitful than even his pres-

ence." Only when this was communicated to him did Beauduin realize that d'Herbigny would be no help to him.

Cut off from every conceivable avenue of approach, Beauduin decided to write to the pope. In a letter to Cappuyns and Dumont (November 27) he explained his reasons. This time, if his efforts failed, he would at least have proof in his archives that he had wanted to justify himself and that the opportunity to do so was refused.

With spring, new hope was born. Bishop Harscouet of Chartres, a loyal friend since 1910, went to Rome in April (1933). He wrote from there that d'Herbigny was seemingly well disposed toward the monk and even looking for a job for him in Rome. Pacelli appeared totally ignorant of the whole affair. He had signed the two-year sentence to En Calcat as a matter of routine business, apparently without even being aware of what it was all about.

Seredi finally answered Beauduin's letter of May 27, 1932. He showed a genuine interest in Beauduin's plight and offered a text for the proposed petition. Capelle and Cappuyns, however, when consulted, found it too detailed and obsequious. By December Beauduin had the definitive text ready. It was a simple request to be allowed to present to his superiors the essential information on his conduct that he had never been given the opportunity to offer. Worried about the possible results, Capelle wrote to Beauduin to the effect that the petition would destroy all the fruit of Beauduin's patience during his two years of confinement. For other reasons, the monk decided to delay because Harscouet announced a new trip to Rome in January. February found Beauduin still hesitating, this time because he had received news that his enemies in Rome were just waiting for an excuse to prolong his stay at En Calcat.

New Horizons

As could be expected, Beauduin used his two-year retreat well, taking advantage of the free time to re-examine the vocation to preach that he had chosen in 1906. To any other man in his sixtieth year, En Calcat might have spelled the end, complete defeat. Convinced that he still had a future to prepare for, he returned to the books— his old favorites like de Régnon, Louis Thomassin and Pétau, all the great sources of tradition, and especially Scripture. Away from the incessant demands of a new foundation and from the subtle intrigues of the Roman court, he could meditate uninterruptedly on the sacred texts which then enabled him to live the liturgy more fully than ever before. By law he could have left on March 30, but he preferred to stay for Easter and would only leave on April 4, 1934 with a certain amount of regret. When war broke out in 1940, he would temporarily seek refuge in the same monastery.

During this period his friends had been busy trying to help him in any way possible with his proposed defense, and they were also trying to prepare a dignified niche for his "retirement" once he was free. The terms of his initial exile had proscribed such ecumenical centers as Paris, London, Prague, etc. The prohibition still held good, and as the end of his term neared, his superiors were bothered about how to dispose of him gracefully. They certainly did not want him back in Belgium.

The Bishops of Chartres, Evreux, Versailles, Paris and at least a dozen other dioceses, as well as the Institut Catholique, had very definite plans for him. In April 1933 he wrote to Cappuyns that he was to be secretary general of the liturgical movement in Paris and to give conferences in those dioceses favorable to the idea. The bishops involved hoped to have him released for the fall term of 1933. When this avenue failed, a new approach was taken. They named Beauduin professor of liturgy at the Institut Catholique in December 1933. At the urging of the primate, however, Rome replied *non expedit* (it is not expedient). [40]

Nevertheless, despite the negative tone of the reply, the climate in Rome had changed. No one was particularly proud of the role he had played in trying to destroy a man and his work. D'Herbigny had even come to the point of laying all the blame for Beauduin's exile to En Calcat on the Curia, while Etcheverry continued to saddle d'Herbigny with full responsibility.[41] But now, with d'Herbigny gone, there was less danger of repercussions if a clause of the original sentence was overlooked. The decision to let Beauduin go to Paris therefore proved agreeable to everyone concerned. No one wanted any more trouble (or guilt). Under the circumstances, however, public acknowledgment of the injustice that was done and total reintegration with his community remained utterly unthinkable. Beauduin's exile had just begun. Seventeen additional years still lay ahead of him.

11

The Parisian Exile Begins

Beauduin's first steps as a free man were uncertain. Although he could count some rather influential Frenchmen among his friends, he remained a marked man to be viewed with suspicion, which made his social status anything but enviable. His friends would do what they could for him, but he was largely on his own. How radically two years at En Calcat could affect one's reception soon became painfully evident. When he asked his Benedictine confrères in Paris whether they knew of any chaplaincy openings, they offered no help or encouragement. Their unwillingness to become involved and to recommend him saddened Beauduin but did not discourage him. Possessed of an imposing dignity and a horror of taking himself too seriously, the enterprising Belgian used a little imagination and initiative. He placed an advertisement in *La Croix*, a Parisian daily.[1]

Beauduin's new exile would last seventeen years. As it unfolds we will find him associated with several religious communities, especially the Benedictine nuns of Cormeilles-en-Parisis and the nuns of the Good Savior at Chatou. Despite restrictions on his travel and writing (which were not always obeyed to the letter), Beauduin would keep in touch with his monks at Amay, and after Roncalli's appointment as nuncio to Paris in 1944, the two would renew their long-standing friendship.

Cormeilles-en-Parisis

The advertisement placed in *La Croix* soon produced results which proved most fortuitous. The Olivétan Benedictines at Cormeilles-en-Parisis responded, and their ecumenically-minded mother prioress (a convert from Protestantism) greeted the new chaplain warmly. As far as she was concerned, his prior life was a thing of the past. In the course of the customary tour of the house and chapel she was startled by a deep sigh of contentment followed by a determined; "I'll stay." Without knowing anything about the community, the sight of the altar devoid of any statuary or floral decorations had immediately reassured Beauduin that he had fallen upon a community with a liturgical sense.

The plain altar was only the first of a series of delightful discoveries. He soon found out that Cormeilles was a meeting place for a small group of Protestants and Orthodox, and before long it also became a center for ecumenical retreats. Although given with the consent of the bishop, these retreats were private and rather extraordinary in their day. Only select Catholics, Protestants and Orthodox were invited, and publicity was forbidden.

Banned from any public role in ecumenism, Beauduin nevertheless avidly followed its every development. In 1936, during a visit to London, he commented in a letter to a friend on the high esteem in which the English held Fr. Paul Couturier. (Couturier, the great promoter of the prayer for unity, became an oblate of Amay in 1932 and inspired the beginning of truly ecumenical contacts between French and Swiss Protestants and the Roman Catholic world.) Beauduin's contacts and experiences in London convinced him more than ever before that the English Catholics remained an insurmountable obstacle to reunion, or even to *rapprochement*. On the other hand, he found the dispositions and piety of the Anglicans most consoling. He concluded his observations with the words: "I am in constant and intimate (but private) relations with them, especially Bell, the Bishop of Chichester. We are true friends."

The following year Beauduin rejoiced to see his monks active, although discreetly, in Protestant ecumenical efforts. Belpaire, the prior of Amay, felt that Thomas Becquet needed a vacation and proposed a visit to Oxford. Catholic presence at interconfessional meetings remained, of course, strictly forbidden, but it was by no accident that the visit to Oxford coincided with the meetings of Life and Work.[2]

During his stay Becquet sought out Bishop Bell who was presiding over the conference. In the course of a meal they shared, the bishop mentioned his relations with Beauduin and asked Becquet if it would be possible to arrange for a monk of Amay to speak on the Catholic liturgy at the liturgical week which Bell was organizing for the Anglican clergy of his diocese. Impressed by the work of Beauduin, Bishop Bell was copying the methods that Beauduin had used in 1909 in trying to bring about the fullest penetration of liturgical principles into the worshiping community. Encouraged perhaps by Becquet's favorable reception at Oxford, Belpaire subsequently sent a message to the Edinburgh meeting of Faith and Order which was read and applauded.

Meanwhile, within the convent walls, Beauduin's contacts with the nuns were of the most genial sort. The impression he made is best expressed in the following observation:

> He had a very great kindness toward all, a goodness which made him sense the slightest suffering in others—even when it was not expressed, and he always tried in the measure possible to ease the burden by a word or a gesture which revealed his heart. Very open to everyone, he accepted the most diverse views. He took over the problems of the other and looked for some efficacious assistance, whether material or moral, for the one in need.[3]

Having suffered so intensely himself, his compassion knew no limits. No matter what the suffering, it would find understanding and comfort in him. And this applied not only to humans but even to animals. By some quirk of fate, out of a flock of ducks destined for slaughter, one somehow had eluded the axe. But haunted perhaps by memories of that traumatic day, or lonely for his former playmates the duck gave signs of acute depression. Realizing that the poor duck was on the verge of a nervous breakdown, Beauduin took pity on him and tried to provide him with companionship. Into his busy schedule he managed to sandwich several visits a day to the poor creature. From a squatting position he would try his best to cheer up the little fellow by pointing out the brighter side of what might seem a rather dismal future.

His relations in the animal world were not limited to lonely ducks.

He loved to play with the nuns' big German shepherd Foulax—so much so that one day he was discreetly observed behind a haystack rolling in the grass and wrestling with the dog. And at lambing time when certain operations were performed on the young lambs, Beauduin assisted on every occasion, filled with compassion for the mother and tenderness for the baby. When it was all over he would bless both of them and send them on their way.

The nuns benefited from his stay in more than just a spiritual sense because he attracted a number of leading figures in ecumenical and liturgical circles. For almost five years (from the spring of 1934 to the end of 1938) he served the nuns, impressing them with his deep love for the Church and an apostolic sense which went out to all without exception. He finally resigned when the prior (the future abbot of Bec) [4] of the male Olivétan community moved to Cormeilles, for Beauduin, quickly recognized that the younger man had a greater right to the post. This did not end his contact with the nuns, however, for he gave them occasional conferences and preached their annual retreats in 1940, 1943, 1944, and 1948.

In their first retreat he concluded with these words: "I have told you many things. Forget everything; remember just this one thing: the risen Christ." How central this mystery was to his own spirituality is reflected in an exhortation frequently heard from him: "Have the courage to believe in the risen Christ no matter what the problem."

Notes taken by the nuns during these retreats reveal one striking similarity: the extremely strong emphasis that Beauduin placed on dogma. In 1943 he came right to the point and said: "Piety is not from what one feels but from the great dogmatic truths. They plunge us more deeply into the life of God." In 1940 his accent differed but little: "Our piety should be ecclesial. Ecclesial asceticism is to go to the bosom of the Father in harmony with the divine plan, with the saints, the members of the body."

But his doctrinal approach was not limited to a review of what the Church teaches; it was an exploration and ever deeper penetration into those doctrines which he considered central to the Christian faith, especially the Trinity, the incarnation, the eucharist and the resurrection. His attachment—one might even say his psychological dependence—on the resurrection is reflected in such observations as:

"Heaven and earth will participate in our resurrection. We are in-viscerated [sic] into this created world while the whole of creation is ennobled by the fact that the Word became flesh." [5]

Beauduin's writings from this period include liturgical and ecu-menical articles for magazines of limited circulation put out by the community at Cormeilles. Since restrictions on his writings had also been imposed, some of the articles of an ecumenical nature were at-tributed to someone else or simply signed XXX. Since the magazines made no pretense at being scholarly journals, there was little that was new theologically or liturgically in what Beauduin said. Some pieces were directed specifically to the life of an oblate, while another series of articles entitled "Liturgical Travel Notes" gave some idea of his travels in 1935–1936, the various churches visited and the litur-gical customs observed.[6] For example he attended the consecration of the abbey church of En Calcat in 1935 and bemoaned the ignorance of protocol evident in the prelates present for the event. A High Mass at Westminster Cathedral in London received more favorable comments.

During the 1930's Beauduin regularly enjoyed the hospitality of Claude, Countess of Kinnoull, in Paris. Her godfather, Msgr. Vin-cent de Moor (the famous Lt. Marcel of World War I), had shared many exciting adventures with Beauduin, and the two old "secret agents" loved to reminisce about their past escapades. But their con-versations also turned to more contemporary concerns—the dangers and excesses of the liturgical and the ecumenical movements. The countess, deeply impressed by Beauduin's wisdom, compassionate nature and wonderful sense of humor, painted an oil portrait of him which, on her last visit in 1954 to the aged Beauduin, she gave to the monks of Chevetogne.

With the outbreak of hostilities, these pleasant soirées ended. The rumor that de Moor was wanted by the Germans and the fact of the countess' British citizenship made it imperative that both leave France. Beauduin also left the Paris region for a while and even considered becoming a permanent member of the community at En Calcat. After his departure from Cormeilles, he spent a short time in the region of Berry, which was not without importance for the years ahead.

At Chalivoy he made the acquaintance of some laymen who

would be among his best friends in the last years of his life. In Sancerre he saw Louis Bouyer, the young Calvinist pastor he had met in the spring of 1938 at the rectory of the Lutheran Church of the Trinity.[7] He was also introduced to the aged Archbishop of Bourges who appreciated Beauduin's gifts and encouraged him to preach retreats for priests and seminarians. The venerable pastor's courage in this matter merits commendation, for Beauduin was still viewed with suspicion by many persons (particularly in Rome). The boldness of the archbishop, however, was amply rewarded. From these retreats eventually came an elite group of men who would initiate the liturgical-pastoral movement in France—a movement that leaders in the French hierarchy had tried to get underway since the early 1930's.

A few of his monks saw him regularly. They came to Paris, or they met him on his rare visits to Belgium. Great care had to be taken in arranging these visits, for Belpaire was quite concerned about creating further difficulties with Rome. During these years Beauduin never went to Amay.

Twelve Years at Chatou

Beauduin's next home, from 1939 until his return to his community in 1951, was with the Religious of the Good Savior of Caen (*Bon Saveur de Caen*) who had an orientation quite different from that of the Olivétans. Their house at Chatou was a boarding school, but the community also specialized in mental nursing and teaching the deaf to speak. Their second founder, Father Pierre-François Jamet, who had kept the order together during the French Revolution, had been very much influenced liturgically by his close friend Guéranger. It was quite natural then that he should have instilled in the nuns a profound appreciation of the wonders and beauty of the liturgy, and the passage of more than a century had not dimmed this love. Hence the nuns immediately made Beauduin feel at home, for they already shared his love of the liturgy.

When his arrival was announced, however, the community was not exactly prepared for what they saw. Normally their chaplains had been well past the prime of life; in fact, the previous chaplain had died only three days after his arrival. In 1939, sixty-six was hardly the age of retirement, and Beauduin's dark beard and sparkling blue eyes took them completely by surprise. In the days and months ahead, he continued to amaze them, but even more to impress them. All were edified by the monastic regularity that he tried to maintain while yet keeping his door open at all times to all visitors. The friendly twinkle in his eyes and the warmth of his smile never betrayed the anguish of his exile during the twelve years he spent at Chatou—years which were marked by the German occupation, frequent bombardments, and all the uncertainties and inconveniences of war.

A special intimacy between Beauduin and the community developed under these circumstances. Often air-raid alerts ended with the celebration of Mass at some pre-dawn hour like 4 A.M.,[8] capped with a paternal remark such as: "You have not had much sleep tonight. Why not go back to bed now?"

It was especially through his words that Beauduin made a lasting impression on the community, and his effectiveness was not limited to the religious alone. In his contacts with children he was remarkably successful. During a retreat for sixteen-year-olds he opened a new perspective for them when he said: "You must see God through your little joys, in the flowers. . . ." When children were present at Mass he always gave a short sermon. His lively talks, which often stressed that Christ is not only God but also man, held their attention, for he never spoke more than ten minutes. On one occasion, however, during a confirmation class, he grossly exceeded this time limit. When asked why he had kept them for a full hour, he confessed with a wistful shrug that one little girl seemed so interested and attentive that he just couldn't stop talking. A similar instance occurred with the nuns. One conference was twice interrupted by sirens and finally finished in the cellar.[9] Although he often spoke of the Trinity and of ecumenism, the resurrection theme predominated. An expression often repeated by him at Chatou was: "With my body I shall see God."

One of Beauduin's own novices, Basile Mercier,[10] was among the circle of those close to the venerable exile during the Chatou years. As professor of Armenian and Georgian Christian literature at the Institut Catholique, Mercier saw Beauduin often between 1935 and 1941. Then, after a brief stay in Syria, Mercier joined his former

novicemaster at Chatou and the two men shared the spiritual responsibilities of the house from 1942 to 1951. Beauduin looked after the
needs of the nuns, while Mercier handled those of the students. Together they also enjoyed many meetings with Protestant ministers in
the area.

A layman who considered himself uniquely privileged to have lived
at Chatou with Beauduin from 1947 to 1951 first met him at the
breakfast table toward the end of 1944. Beauduin was in the act of
conscientiously buttering a piece of bread and immediately took a
fatherly interest in the young man who had taken an unpopular
political stand and was being ostracized for his views. Eventually
he found employment with the nuns, and Beauduin offered to share
his own quarters with him. He installed the political fugitive in his
own bedroom and moved to a little nook under the eaves.

The two men were drawn together by a common political loyalty.
When Cardinal Gerlier announced: "Pétain is France; France is
Pétain," Beauduin hung a portrait of the marshal in his parlor. The
fall of the Vichy government changed nothing for Beauduin. The
portrait remained in its place, visible from the street, until his departure in 1951. In light of his strong patriotism in 1914, many of
Beauduin's friends were left puzzled if not upset by the position he
took in the 1940's, although most attributed his poor judgment to the
fact that he was not, after all, a Frenchman.

For four years Beauduin regaled his young friend with an inexhaustible fund of souvenirs from the past, astute observations on
current prelates, and what amounted to an inside view of the Church
in the twentieth century. He knew the Belgian and French episcopa-
cies by heart—the strengths and weaknesses of its members from
Vatican I to the 1940's. His memory was extraordinary. He never
told the same story twice unless requested. He particularly loved to
recall the tragic years of World War I, the departure from Mont
César, the occupation of the monastery by the Germans, the death of
the commandant, the imperial intervention which prevented the burn-
ing of the monastery, his part in the resistance, his condemnation to
death, his escape to Holland, and how he had met Empress Eugenie
in England (she lived near Farnborough, a Benedictine monastery).

But above all he loved to reminisce about a man who had been so
close to him and such an influence in his life: Cardinal Mercier. Rivalry

between religious orders is a long-standing tradition in the Church, and Beauduin, as a Benedictine, felt a certain chauvenistic joy whenever the Jesuits were bested in an ecclesiastical duel. The Jesuits by tradition had been charged with the clergy retreats in Malines. When Mercier became cardinal he announced that henceforth the Benedictines would preach the retreats. (Because of Marmion, his confessor, Mercier had developed a great admiration for Benedictine spirituality.) But the formerly all-powerful Jesuit Fathers were not about to surrender so easily to the Benedictines. They wrote to Rome, and the father general asked the cardinal to reconsider his decision. He replied: "This year I will preach the retreat myself in order to become familiar with all the priests of my diocese." He preferred additional work to bowing before the Jesuit general.

On a more personal level, Beauduin related how Mercier had offered him his office with all the documents it contained, with the understanding that he could take possession of it upon his death. Several months before his death, the cardinal, stretched out on his chaise lounge, reminded Beauduin of the promise, and then added: "I have given you the office, but please allow me to take certain documents." "But Your Eminence," Beauduin replied, "those are exactly the documents which interest me the most." The cardinal did not insist and let the matter drop.[11]

The daily routine at Chatou was quite simple. Beauduin rose early every morning, generally before 6 A.M., and frequently took a cold bath. He began his Mass around 6:15. His young friend occasionally served but usually found 6:15 to be too early for his taste, so one of the nuns usually gave the responses. However by 7:15 he was usually ready to join Beauduin for breakfast. Since he normally listened to the news as he dressed, Beauduin greeted him with: "What's the news?" They would discuss it in great detail and even with eloquence—particularly Beauduin who was partial to politics and who commented on the communiqués from his own vast experience and with sharp common sense.

After breakfast Beauduin retired to his office, clothed in a very ample cloak fashioned by himself out of a blanket and some rope. There he wrote endlessly, answering mail from all over the world. He filled dozens of pages each day with letters or articles. In the afternoon, if he did not have an engagement elsewhere, he spent long

hours in his office again or in the parlor receiving numerou
visitors. A steady stream of Oratorians, Jesuits, Benedictines, Do
minicans, priest-workers and prelates came.

Often Beauduin went to Paris for ecumenical encounters—some
times at the Russian center of St. Serge or to the biblical circle o
Msgr. George Chevrot, pastor of St. Francois Xavier, a favorite
meeting place for Protestant pastors in the area. At other times he
went to a conference or to the classes of his friend Msgr. de Moo
at the Institut Catholique. The train station was less than a mile
away, and since he did not like to be late, he normally left ten minutes too soon, with the result that he regularly arrived as an earlier
train was pulling in. His companions or the station manager would
rush him to catch it, which often meant that he had to run the last
fifty or sixty feet, and he was now in his seventies. Once in the city
he would not hesitate to take a guest to one of the finest restaurants
However, when he was alone, he normally satisfied himself with
two sandwiches and a bottle of beer.[12]

During the same year that Beauduin moved to Chatou (1939), his
monks moved from Amay to Chevetogne. Despite the difficulties
entailed during the war, he nevertheless managed on several occasions
to cross the border and visit the community in its new home. His
boldness and the obvious joy that it gave him to be with the monks led
them to risk new trouble with Rome by inviting the septuagenarian
to come to their study sessions after the war.

As the war drew to a close, however, some great news brought
forth an explosion of happiness from Beauduin. In December 1944
his old friend Roncalli came to Paris as nuncio replacing Valerio
Valeri (whom Beauduin had met in Jerusalem in 1929). Although in
doubt as to what his reception might be after all these years, Beauduin could not pass up the opportunity of seeing him. As he waited
to be announced, Roncalli recognized the familiar voice and shouted
from the top of the stairs: "Lamberto! Venga! Venga!"[13] After a
rib-shattering embrace, the nuncio led him away, pushed him into a
distinguished looking chair (which they later discovered to be the
papal throne, an obligatory decoration in every legation house) and
insisted on hearing all the details of Beauduin's Roman tribulations.
Afterward they amused themselves miming the audience of an
ambassador with the nuncio, with Beauduin playing the nuncio and
Roncalli impersonating the ambassador.

This was only the first of a series of visits. Many of the future visits would be at the express invitation of Roncalli who wanted to consult Beauduin. No matter what the occasion, there was always a great deal of laughter. Although Roncalli was of peasant stock and Beauduin from the landed gentry, the two had much in common. Both were from the country and shared many attitudes, not to mention common physical, personal, and spiritual characteristics. Both were short in height (Roncalli was the shorter of the two), massive in build and with large heads. They were pleasant, optimistic, simple, frank, enterprising, with fertile imaginations for solving difficult cases, and opposed to ceremony, to officials and to formal, affected people. Not only did they enjoy each other immensely, but they also had a deep appreciation for the worth of each other. While some French bishops reportedly wept at the election of Roncalli, regarding him as a fine man but not of papal caliber, Beauduin prophesied while Pius XII was still in good health that Roncalli would be the next pope. That he had so well sized up the man is further indication of the intimacy of their friendship, especially as it blossomed during the Paris years.

There are few word pictures of Beauduin, perhaps because it was impossible to capture his dynamism. One description of his appearance in 1945, however, is worth quoting:

Short of stature, and with broad shoulders, he walked with difficulty, helping himself with a cane and leaning on my arm. His head was of a magnificent shape, enormous, like a lion's; one might have wished it to be covered with a tawny mane which he certainly lacked. The nobility of his forehead bespoke intelligence; a powerful jaw bespoke an aptitude for struggle. His blue eyes were at one moment mischievous, the next filled with kindness. A rumbling voice, broken, rough, uttering words with a certain precision reinforced by his strong Walloon accent and underlined with a shattering laugh, sufficient to make the house shake.[14]

In 1947 the nuns at Chatou, in honor of the fiftieth anniversary of his ordination to the priesthood, invited many of his Paris friends to a small celebration. His faithful supporter Bishop Harscouet came with many others to offer their congratulations and to pay tribute. Even his homeland saw fit to recognize this milestone in his life.

Libre Belgique summed up Beauduin's fifty years of priestly dedi
cation with these words: "Throughout his life Dom Lambert Beau
duin has given a magnificent and profoundly edifying example
of the religious spirit, of humility and forgetfulness of self." [1]

Although some may have wondered why such a capable, energetic
monk was not living with his community and why no more impor
tant post than that of chaplain in a convent was open to him, only
one nun at Chatou knew: the retired superior, Mother Castel. When
Beauduin finally received permission to return to Belgium perma
nently at the age of seventy-eight, the nuns were told why he had
been with them. They could not hide their astonishment, for he had
never mentioned his exile. Yet the years at Chatou were not wasted
He found ample outlets for his vast energies, and his influence soon
extended far beyond the convent walls, reaching into the liturgical
sphere with the initiation of the French liturgical movement. More
over, his love of monasticism, far from wavering, inspired a new
monastic experiment. And, of course, since he had never lost inter
est in ecumenism, he lent his support to numerous ecumenical activi
ties with Protestants and Orthodox.

The Pastoral and Liturgical Center

Archbishop Jean-Claude Fillon, of Bourges (died 1943), was not the
only member of the French hierarchy interested in Beauduin's spiri
tual and liturgical charisma. But it was Raoul Harscouet, Bishop of
Chartres since 1926, who proved to be one of his strongest supporters
and a major catalyst in launching the French liturgical movement.[16]
In 1933 Beauduin had written enthusiastically to Cappuyns: "Bishop
Harscouet and I are organizing a great liturgical action of which
I will be the secretary general at Paris." [17] Although the bishop en
couraged Beauduin in every way, particularly in the matter of cleri
cal retreats, the grandiose dreams of the 1930's did not materialize
overnight. However, the foundations were carefully laid through re
treats which introduced two themes rather unheard of in those days
when the *Spiritual Exercises* of Ignatius dominated the scene:
liturgy and ecumenism.

No complete record of the retreats Beauduin gave has ever been
compiled. Undoubtedly a thorough classification of his unedited
writings in the archives at Chevetogne would give a more accurate

picture. Some of those for which there is a record, however (thanks to notes preserved by retreatants), are La Pierre-qui-Vire (1936), Paray-le-Monial (1938), and Clamart (1937 and 1942). This last retreat made such an impression that Msgr. Chevrot organized periodic follow-up meetings which eventually developed into the *Centre de pastorale liturgique* in 1943—more familiarly known as the CPL.[18] But not all of the priest retreats were diocesan in nature. Some were given at the *Fraternité sacerdotale* in Paris, a rehabilitation center for "fallen" priests directed by a Canadian community whose house at Rome had offered Beauduin shelter at the time of his trial. The retreatants were priests who met Beauduin's qualifications —who were "of our mind." In addition, he frequently gave retreats at Thieulin, in the diocese of Chartres.[19]

In the notes from which Beauduin preached some of these retreats, one author frequently cited is Henri de Lubac. In all probablility Beauduin was referring to de Lubac's book *Catholicism*,[20] whose subtitle, "The Social Aspects of Dogma," is the most concise summary that can be given of this masterful work. Someone acquainted with Beauduin's thought could almost have imagined this book to have been written by him. It is doubtful, however, that de Lubac really influenced Beauduin theologically, since much of what the latter quoted can be found in Beauduin's own articles, letters, and conferences prior to 1938, and most of their personal contacts were in the 1940's. Essentially, one can say that the book represented a contemporary and comprehensive summary of some of the monk's most fundamental convictions, for the chapters on the Church and on the sacraments placed special emphasis on their social nature. Ideas such as these had great influence in the French liturgical renewal.[21] One other author seldom mentioned by Beauduin, but whose ideas seemed to enter into his conferences, was his former prior at Mont César, Marmion.[22]

The CPL held an organizational meeting on May 20, 1943, at *Editions du Cerf*. The Dominicans wanted to confide the presidency to Beauduin, then more than seventy years old, but he declined. The first official session took place at Vanves in January 1944.[23] Beauduin assisted at all subsequent sessions until 1951 in the capacity of a consultant. Bishop Harscouet gave all the credit for its birth to Beauduin, although Beauduin would have insisted that such men as Aimé-George Martimort, Pie Duployé and A.-M. Roguet were more instrumental in shaping the pastoral instrument. Nonetheless Beauduin's influence is an indisputable fact. Unlike the liturgical movement of 1909, this one was not essentially a Benedictine affair. Roguet and Duployé were Dominicans, and the first meeting place, *Editions du Cerf*, was also under Dominican auspices. Only in 1953 would the CPL move its offices to Neuilly.

Vanves, the site chosen for the sessions which began in 1944, was, however, a Benedictine convent where Beauduin served as confessor. His spiritual direction and conferences made a profound impression on the nuns there, particularly his love for the Trinity, and above all his devotion to the Father. They as well as the priests who attended the sessions had a deep love and reverence for the veteran liturgist and his ideals and ideas. Peace, strength, and joy emanated from him. One felt that he was detached and completely given over to God, a soul that transcended pettiness and lived for the glory of God.

The founders of the Pastoral and Liturgical Center (CPL) realized that liturgical reform would be achieved only if the clergy received a thorough pastoral and liturgical formation. Deeply impressed by Beauduin's presentation of the liturgy as the true school of the spiritual life and the source of all apostolic action, they resolved to communicate this to others. But a concrete initiation into the liturgy such as they had experienced at Clamart, with its emphasis on topics of pastoral concern, was clearly not enough. To accomplish their goals, the initiators of the CPL pooled their resources and produced a first-rate review, *La Maison-Dieu* (1945). Beauduin, by far the most qualified of the group, was asked to describe the work of the CPL in its first issue:

> The work of the CPL is to bring the whole people of God to the authentic source of Christian life, the liturgy, which is so little adapted to the needs of the twentieth century. The present impoverishment and its former evangelical dynamism lead one to the conviction of the necessity of a renewal. The activity of the CPL will be guided by three norms:
>
> 1. The Church has the right to legislate the liturgy.
>
> 2. Centralization is good.
>
> 3. Legitimate custom can make licit what is illicit; it adapts law to the ever changing needs of society. But all liturgical laws escape the influence of custom. Liturgical initiatives that break with the

liturgical rules of the Church, therefore, cease to be specifically ecclesial and hence lose their fundamental value.[24]

Although the third point may seem rather narrow, when Beauduin's insistence on the liturgy as the official prayer of the Church is recalled, the validity of condemning an individual's claim to a more valid insight than the Church's in matters liturgical is, if not convincing, at least more easily understood.

To guard against an overly legalistic interpretation of the above points which might turn the CPL into a circle of rubricists whose paramount concern would be keeping the law rather than searching out all its liturgical implications, Beauduin added some further precisions:

1. Abstain from running to Rome with every doubt. (If obedience prejudices the good of the whole, then it goes beyond the limits of discretion and prudence.)

2. The Holy See is careful about the integrity of the liturgy and severe against unlawful initiative but encourages efforts within the framework of the law. Clerics ought to know not only the law but also its origin, evolution and history.

3. The Church is animated by a strongly hierarchic spirit; in other words, liturgical renewal will be blessed with success only if the leaders work through the bishops and prelates.[25]

Profoundly Catholic and disciplined in spirit, the CPL was dedicated from its earliest moments to making known through *La Maison-Dieu* the work of the Sacred Congregation of Rites. The members proposed to study the current state of liturgy and how it is to be understood before promoting past practices which might better express the true liturgical meaning of a feast. Concerned that the historical aspects of a liturgical feast or rite would never be dissociated from the pastoral, they agreed that all true renewal would be the product of much patient preparation. This also included a methodical popularizing of ideas which took all facets of the liturgical problem involved into consideration. Familiar changes such as the Holy Week revisions or successive modifications of the eucharistic fast are excellent examples of what such liturgical scholarship has accomplished in recent years.

Because Beauduin had successfully campaigned for the translation of the Mass into the vernacular for the faithful in 1909, many were surprised at his attitude toward its use in the liturgy itself. His position stemmed primarily from a personal opposition to the para-liturgical uses—or, more precisely, abuses—of the vernacular which sprang up in pre-war Germany and were subsequently introduced into Alsace-Lorraine during the occupation. Before long this "liturgical" innovation found its way into French usage.

Since para-liturgies existed alongside of (para) the liturgy, they were free from the restrictions imposed by the Church on her official prayers. Unlike later, more disciplined forms, these early para-liturgies lacked a solid biblical orientation and were often more accurately described as sheer religious fantasy.[26] The total freedom from liturgical restraints and the use of vernacular clearly contributed to their popularity, and because he feared that these para-liturgies would assume a greater importance in the lives of the faithful than the liturgy itself, Beauduin objected not only to their liturgical and theological excesses, but also to the use of the vernacular—a key factor in their widespread popularity.

While Beauduin did not stand alone in his condemnation of these early para-liturgies, his opposition to the vernacular Mass remains a major weakness in his liturgical career. He apparently considered it sufficient for the people to know what the priest was saying. Difficult as it is to reconcile this shortsightedness with his knowledge, understanding and love of the Oriental liturgies (traditionally in the language of the people), it proves that he directed his primary concern to restoring meaning *to* the liturgy rather than to *rewriting* it. To the very end, his love of the Roman liturgy and his conviction of its capacity to function as a valid and efficacious channel of grace in the twentieth century remained unshaken.

This difference of opinion, however, did not lessen his interest in the activities of the CPL. There were few committee meetings or study sessions at which he was not present, taking part in the discussions and giving his advice and suggestions. Some of the papers he presented later appeared in *La Maison-Dieu* or in *Lex Orandi*.[27] The latter, a significant liturgical series, published the proceedings of the study sessions, providing an accurate reflection of the center's comprehensive concern. Papers were presented by clergy and laity recognized for their academic or professional competence in the area chosen for consideration. Each problem under examination was viewed from every conceivable angle. Primary attention was given to the pastoral and theological, but the musical, architectural, historical, social, archeological and other pertinent aspects were not forgotten. The highlights of some of the debates on the pastoral implications of these papers make particularly interesting reading and can be found in *Lex Orandi*.

Writings and Talks

While Beauduin was revered by the members of the CPL, his views did not always meet with unanimous approval. At the 1946 session, he delivered a paper on the Mass as sacrifice of praise [28] only to be stoutly challenged by Bernard Capelle, the abbot of Mont César whose strongly Tridentine mentality saw the eucharist primarily as sacrifice of expiation. Beauduin refused to step down from his position and re-emphasized his insistence on the value of restoring the general notion of the Mass as a "sacrifice of praise," on the basis that Capelle's views were not genuinely faithful to tradition but rather the result of inexact opinions propounded by theologians since Trent.

In developing his thesis, Beauduin insisted that the specific function of sacrifice is not destruction but rather consecration or dedication of the victim to God. This in turn led him to challenge the view that the Mass is essentially propitiatory. On the contrary, it is more properly an act of praise and thanksgiving for the forgiveness of sin effected by Christ's death on the cross. Hence, argued Beauduin, it is ordered to disposing the sinner for God's grace. In other words, the Mass does not infallibly forgive sins. Only its proper end is attained directly and infallibly, and that end is as a sacrifice of praise.

Perhaps his most convincing point in terms of more contemporary developments was his emphasis that the thanksgiving modality of the Mass, while not exclusive, is yet the dominant idea. It witnesses to our actual and anticipated participation in the divine life. Thus, although the propitiatory and impetratory ends of the Mass cannot be denied, the most ancient tradition of the liturgy has always been *sancta sanctis* (holy things for the holy), which implies being in the state of grace.

This reappraisal of the concept of sacrifice and the balanced approach to the Mass as both banquet and sacrifice were not the only aspects of the liturgy to which he directed his energies. At the Liturgical Congress of St. Flour in 1945 he delivered a paper on the value of the sung Mass which did not pass unnoticed. Archbishop Lefebvre of Bourges praised Beauduin's admirable historical and theological lesson which justified on the level of principle the necessity of making the Mass a great, *living* assembly of all Christians. The resolutions of this congress, proposed by the CPL leaders, are not without interest:

1. That the Mass be said facing the people.
2. That the priest be heard, or at least that the lector transmit in the vernacular the words of the celebrant.
3. That the people take part in the dialogue and in the action of the Mass, i.e., offertory processions, etc.
4. That the priest give *instructive* sermons.

Among Beauduin's finer papers and articles from these last years are to be counted his articles on viaticum, *Mediator Dei* and death. In addition, he often provided very lucid and occasionally provocative commentaries on the various liturgical documents issued by the Holy See during these years, especially on the role of bishops as co-consecrators, the sacrament of confirmation and the pascal vigil. Other articles dealing with concelebration, communion outside of Mass, the necessity of giving new life to sacramental signs, and a protest against the saying of daily votive Masses for the dead suggest by their documentation that he was busy reading the Church Fathers and the councils of the Church—and not just the ecumenical councils but the local synods as well.

The article on viaticum, first presented at the 1948 CPL session at Vanves, remains one of the more noteworthy. He pointed out that the obligation to receive viaticum is more serious than that to be anointed. What paticularly struck Beauduin was that this legislation dated from the Council of Nicea (Canon 13). That the Church torn by heresy and recovering from persecutions should have seen fit to establish this canon was more than noteworthy. Most fascinating, however, is the relationship of viaticum to excommunication, which Beauduin took pains to stress. At the moment of death, Church law is suspended; however, viaticum of itself does not bring about reconciliation (in the case of excommunication). To support his position, he singled out the cases of three historical figures—Joan of Arc, Huss and Savonarola, all of whom received communion (viaticum) prior to being burned for heresy.[29]

Articles devoted to Christian life also appeared during this time. Spirituality, of course, was never far from anything he wrote, particularly if it was liturgical in nature. In considering Easter, for example, a phrase frequently found in retreat notes appears: the whole Christian mystery is a "slow resurrection" of the human mode of existence to the life of God. Fittingly enough, the topic of the last paper he presented at Vanves (1949) was "Heaven and Resurrection" (later published as "The Mystery of Death and Its Celebration" in *Lex Orandi*).

When the encyclical *Mediator Dei* appeared in 1947, Beauduin was tremendously excited and encouraged, for it recognized the contribution made by the Belgian Benedictines and gave official status to a movement in which he had been involved for almost forty years.[30] His dream in 1909 had been that it would radiate out from Belgium and engulf the whole world. Now the prognosis was indeed hopeful. In 1948 the Commission for the General Restoration of the Liturgy was established. With the restoration of the Easter Vigil (Decree of February 9, 1951) he could jubilantly proclaim it as the starting point for solid liturgical reform. The article it inspired in *La Maison-Dieu* was typically "Beauduin." Not content to rest on the laurels of success for one moment, he immediately aired a list of suggestions for further reform—stress the importance of the Amens at Mass, celebrate communion with newly consecrated hosts, eliminate the *confiteor* at communion time, and drop the Last Gospel and the prayers after Mass added by Leo XIII. He confessed that these were rather bold suggestions, although today his proposals have long since become a reality.

The year 1951 also marked the end of his exile. His last years were further brightened by the decree restoring the celebrations of Holy Week to put primary focus on the liturgy (1955), by the first International Congress of Pastoral Liturgy (1956), and by the decree authorizing and urging active participation in the Mass throughout the Roman Catholic world (1958).

Beauduin's Liturgical Legacy

Since Beauduin's death the CPL has been replaced by the National Pastoral and Liturgical Center (CNPL), an organization with a completely different structure and spirit. The original leaders of the CPL—Martimort, Duployé, and Roguet—are no longer involved. But the demise of the CPL has in no way impaired the radiation of Beauduin's influence.

Beauduin had many dreams, two of which have finally been realized. He wanted to establish liturgical schools where an in-depth study of our liturgical heritage could be pursued. His schemes never got beyond the drawing board. While Canon Camille Callewaert succeeded in snatching the one chance proffered at Louvain, his courses were dropped in 1921. The sporadic seminars on the liturgy at Mont César since 1928, augmented by Capelle's lectures at Louvain which began in 1936, were not what Beauduin intended. By 1964, however, chairs for the liturgy had been established at both Sant Anselmo and the Institut Catholique of Paris. The latter chair was endowed largely through the generosity of one of Beauduin's nieces. Bishop Jan Cauwelaert, a bishop of Belgian descent on the liturgical commission of Vatican II, also established a chair at Louvain. But the liturgical institute of Trier (1947) had been founded prior to these chairs and must be regarded as the true realization of Beauduin's dream.[31]

Beauduin's true legacy is not to be found in a chair or in periodicals such as *Liturgical and Pastoral Questions* or *La Maison-Dieu*, or even in the tributes offered him in 1953 on the occasion of his eightieth birthday,[32] or in 1959 on the fiftieth anniversary of the launching of the Belgian liturgical movement, although the papal recognition was no small achievement:

It is now half a century since Rev. Fr. Dom Lambert Beauduin— whose untiring zeal and persevering efforts the Sovereign Pontiff is pleased to recall today—attracted the attention of the members of the Congress of Malines to the importance of a liturgical life for

Christians, and thus was made, with . . . Cardinal Mercier, the promoter of a movement whose intentions aimed first at the spread of
the text of the Missal among the faithful and an ever more intense
liturgical formation of the clergy.[33]

If the contemporary liturgical movement with its pastoral orientation is in great part the work of Beauduin,[34] his true legacy is to be
found in the realization of his second dream—the endorsement and
sponsorship of the liturgical movement itself by Rome, and, even
more, by a council of the Church. Vatican II is the locus where his
true sphere of influence can be found. Already in the course of the
first session his name was raised in connection with the liturgy by
Mendez Arceo, bishop of Cuernavaca.

Of all the French bishops at Vatican II, Archbishop Henri Jenny
of Cambrai knew Beauduin the best, although Bishop Emile Guerry
attended a session of the CPL in 1945 when Beauduin gave a conference, and Cardinals François Marty and Gabriel Garonne were also
loyal supporters. Cardinal Marty's first contact with the CPL dates
from 1946. Even so, it was Archbishop Jenny who rejected the first
draft of the *Constitution on the Sacred Liturgy* on the grounds that
it contained nothing about the nature of the paschal mystery. Before
his intervention the first chapter did not even exist. That he insisted at
all is certainly due, at least in part, to Beauduin's influence on the
French hierarchy and clergy through his liturgical retreats and
his collaboration with the CPL.[35]

Canon Martimort, long associated with Beauduin through the
CPL was one of the editors of the schema on the liturgy. Various
professors from Louvain, Paris, Sant' Anselmo and other liturgical
centers—theologians who guided the bishops—were either disciples
of Beauduin's ideas or his friends—for example, Cunibert Mohlberg,
Msgr. Gerard Philips, Cypriano Vaggagini, Johannes Quasten, etc.
In fact, most of the members of the liturgical commission were friends
or admirers of the aged pioneer.[36]

Other members of the French and Belgian hierarchy, as well as
other theologians, figured prominently as promoters of Beauduin's
ideas in other conciliar documents, particularly in the ecumenical
sphere. The absence of a more direct liturgical influence on contemporary Belgian bishops can be explained simply by Beauduin's
exile and absence from the Belgian scene. Rousseau perhaps best

summed up the significance of Beauduin's influence at Vatican I
when he wrote:

> Dom Lambert Beauduin was one of the great precursors and one
> who prepared for the council. The trilogy that Cardinal Lercaro
> announced recently as the best fruit of Vatican II—"Church, lit-
> urgy, and ecumenism"—can count Dom Lambert Beauduin among
> its principal initiators for each point mentioned in this enumeration.[37]

While the following chapters will offer additional evidence in the
area of his ecumenical and theological contributions to the twentieth
century, it must not be supposed that Beauduin's liturgical influence
ends here. Giovanni Montini (Pope Paul VI), although not personally acquainted with Beauduin, first became aware of the monk's
work during a visit to Maredsous in 1928 and developed a keen interest in things liturgical. This initial exposure has been augmented
over the years by his contacts with Beauduin's disciples, Rousseau
and Bouyer, as well as with Beauduin's nephew Edouard. Thus, although in an indirect way, the liturgical pioneer's influence has extended to yet another pontiff.[38]

12

The Exile Ends

As his seemingly interminable exile dragged on, Beauduin continued to live each day as it came "in the bosom of the Father." The postwar years in Paris were marked by his involvement in a new monastic experiment, the "pastor-monk project" and various ecumenical ventures. Then in 1951, as quietly and unexpectedly as it had begun, the exile ended. Beauduin was invited to "come home." Surrounded by his sons he would watch with eagerness the ascent of his friend Roncalli, and when the latter was named Patriarch of Venice, Beauduin would have still greater expectations for him. In time he would predict both Roncalli's election to the papacy and his convocation of a council for unity. Unfortunately, Beauduin died before the council actually assembled but his disciples would enshrine many of his most cherished ecumenical and ecclesiological principles in the documents of Vatican II.

While the inception of these insights has been pointed out in earlier chapters, the increased centralization in Rome during Pius XII's long reign accentuated the need for someone to champion them. What energy yet remained in Beauduin's declining years was soon absorbed and expended in clarifying and propagating cherished ideas which are found chiefly in his unpublished notes and in the memories of his friends. In the light of his critical re-evaluation of the hierarchical structures of the Church, he stepped up his insistence on the urgent

need to resume Vatican I, a campaign begun long ago at Mont César
But now the purpose was much clearer in his mind. Only the def
inition of the episcopacy and collegiality and the recognition of th
laity's role could stave off disaster. If the Church of the twentiet
century was to function effectively as a spiritual force in th
modern world, she must rejuvenate herself.

A Monastic Experiment

From personal experience, Beauduin knew both the life of the dioc
esan priest and that of a monk. His checkered career had furthe
exposed him to every conceivable variation of clerical life. (In th
wake of his ecclesiastical ups and downs he was even offered th
position of titular abbot.) [1] He therefore appreicated the distinc
advantages of both ways of life and defended their inherent spirituautonomy. In fact, one of his rare clashes with Cardinal Mercie
had been over this very matter. Enamored with Benedictine spiritual
ity and concerned about the shortcomings of the spiritual program c
many of his diocesan priests, Mercier devised a plan whereby the
could take vows and form priestly associations. To Beauduin thi
called into question the validity of the diocesan vocation itself whic
he felt contained within it all the elements essential to a profounpriestly life. When the cardinal went to Rome in December 1924 t
obtain authorization for this association, Beauduin could not hide hi
disapproval of the whole idea. [2] How then can the pastor-mon
project be reconciled with the earlier Beauduin, since it addresse
itself to this very need?

If the pastor-monk program appears to be a compromise betwee
secular and regular life, it must be recalled that Beauduin's monasti
reforms were always directed to present needs. While he could eve
admit the possibility of hermits within the monastery (Chevetogne
living a life of prayer for union, [3] his fundamental aim was to offe
the unique potentials of monastic life to the service of the Church
In the case of the pastor-monks, he sought to strengthen diocesa
and parochial life through monastic centers created exclusively t
promote clerical spirituality.

In his last years he was very much caught up with the idea of th
local church and diocesan spirituality. During the same time that h
traced the plan for the diocesan-monks, he also sketched an outlin

for a possible book on diocesan spirituality in which one idea is frequently repeated:

> The Church of Christ by the will of her founder is constituted by a series of *particular* (or diocesan) *churches*, each having at its head a single pastor (the bishop). . . . The diocesan community is thus a divine "given" which belongs to the essential structure of the Church. . . . The *local* (diocesan) *church* is . . . a necessary organism socially constituted to introduce souls into union with God.[4]

According to Beauduin, the Christian was not an anonymous soul but an individual who had been baptized into a particular geographical community. His spiritual growth and development was intimately associated with the diocesan structure. The proposed diocesan-monks would try to reinforce this bond.

Beauduin's involvement with the group began with a visit from Jean de Féligonde, the vicar at Croissy, near Chatou, who had had requests from several confrères to form a monastic group with a specific pastoral ministry. Beauduin succeeded in dissuading de Féligonde from forming a new congregation and paved the way for the diocesan monastery which was ultimately attached to the Subiaco congregation.

At the time of Beauduin's death fifteen years later, de Féligonde described the inception of this novel experiment:

> On a certain rainy October afternoon, I knocked timidly at the door of his very modest quarters. His kind smile, enthusiastic welcome and spontaneous familiarity immediately put me at ease. I unveiled my project. . . . He pressed his lips together and nodded his head, a sign of approval that was peculiar to him, his eyes sparkling with happiness. . . . When I had finished, he said to me, his face radiant with joy: "Say, look what I've just received from a pastor in Nièvre." I scanned the paper he held out to me: a poor priest in a de-Christianized parish was asking him his advice about a project of pastor-monks![5]

One of the project's most striking features was the importance given to the bishop. For years Beauduin had considered the whole idea of exempt orders to be outmoded.[6] He considered the bishop to be the father of a particular part of the family of the Church and the source of all sacramental life for his people. On the strength of this, Beauduin argued that a much closer bond should exist between *all* priests and their bishop.

The fundamental aim of the new venture was to integrate monastic life into diocesan and parochial life while safeguarding the intensity and traditional spirit of monastic life, but at the same time penetrating apostolic life with a profoundly religious and priestly spirit. He thus envisaged a diocesan monastery which would be a center and source of the diocese's liturgical and parochial life.

In developing this idea, he insisted that the monastery be essentially diocesan from a threefold point of view:

1. The bishop (or local ordinary) would be the only head, an abbot-bishop, for he alone received the fullness of the priesthood and hence possessed the sovereignty of worship for the whole diocese.

Obviously the bishop would not reside in the monastery, although rooms would be set aside for him and he would fulfill all the functions which the Benedictine rule confers on an abbot. A prior would act as his vicar and be responsible for the details of life within the monastery and for giving a complete account of all that happened.

2. There would be only one monastery per diocese which would be the source of liturgical and parochial life for the entire diocese. Other dioceses could found their own diocesan monastery, but these monasteries would have no *juridical* link between them; each would remain a diocesan organism under the exclusive authority of the local ordinary. A moral bond and spiritual fraternity would exist between them, even support, if the local ordinaries agreed, but nothing more.

3. Its apostolate would be exercised *in the diocese*. Recruiting would also be done in the diocese. Temporarily candidates could be accepted from another diocese on this double condition:
   (a) that the diocese possessed no similar monastery
   (b) that the monk would return to his original diocese if a similar monastery were founded.[7]

The stress on staying in one's own diocese was based on a deeper reality than a simple social or cultural affinity. In baptism a definite spiritiual relationship, stronger even than that of blood, is established between the individual and the diocese, establishing certain obligations. At that moment the individual is really yet mysteriously plunged into the life of a particular diocese. As he is nourished by it in his infancy, and as he slowly matures through its life-giving sacraments, the debt of gratitude owed is ideally repaid by service to the same community which has been the source of his life.

Collaboration in the on-going spiritual and pastoral formation of the clergy provided one of the major works of the diocesan-monks. Crucial to the success of this project was the creation of an atmosphere of study, meditation, and fellowship which would offer a refreshing oasis for their brother priests as well as spiritual and intellectual stimulation. To understand the significance of this project fully, it must be placed in the context of the de-Christianized circumstances of wartime France which created the need for a new approach to the pastoral problems faced by the diocesan clergy.[8]

A new approach was necessary, but that of the diocesan-monks has not seemed to be the answer. Although the community continues to exist, the experiment has not been repeated in other dioceses. This failure may have several explanations. Perhaps it is because the primary goal, providing a spiritual oasis for the diocesan clergy, no longer poses the urgent need that it did twenty years ago. Certainly improved clerical formation and the wide publicity given to theological and liturgical trends have at least solved part of the problem. On the other hand, it may be that *Mission de France*, established by the French hierarchy on July 24, 1941, has furnished a more effective and dynamic response to the current religious crisis.

While the purpose of the diocesan-monks was to assure the maximum of priestly and spiritual life in a given area, that of *Mission de France* was more precisely evangelical: to witness in a most concrete fashion to the Gospel. This is accomplished not within the sanctuary of a monastery but by engaging fully in the life of the masses, which requires most of the teams of the mission to be self-supporting. Once ordained, they live in small communities for moral support and intellectual stimulation but function as diocesan priests for a given territory. Of particular interest is the fact that they engage in the same type of work as their parishioners and thus share a similar standard of life. They identify themselves to their co-workers as priests only when they have first gained respect and confidence on the

human level.[9] In short, *Mission de France* offers specialists who can
be moved from diocese to diocese and aims at immediate results.
The diocesan-monks offer the more traditional type of parish ministry with special emphasis on prayer.

Beauduin's attitudes toward the laity and his view of the parish
ministry are potential weaknesses in the diocesan-monk project, at
least from a lay perspective. If the guidelines made provision for the
possibility of groups of at least four monks leaving the monastery to
take up parish duties, the spirit behind them still remained emphatically monastic in inspiration and presupposed a definite monastic regularity. Vespers and lauds, solemnly chanted, as well as community
Mass, were the core around which the day was built. The schedule
was so conceived that the monks would be able to begin their parish
duties by 7 o'clock. But the parishioners were expected to regulate
their piety according to the essential demands of the priestly (or,
better yet, monastic) life of the diocesan-monks. Beauduin even admitted that the faithful might need to be educated to see their demands in the "ensemble of our priestly duties." Because this is easily
misunderstood, it presents a major weakness in the scheme.

Certainly time must be set aside for the proper spiritual nourishment of a priest. That is beyond question. The real issue is: Who
is at whose disposal? Should the spiritual treasures of the Church
be available at the convenience of the ministers or at the convenience of the people? Should schedules or convenience ever take
priority over needs? The former attitude can be accused of contributing not only to anti-clericalism but even to indifference. Beauduin, a profoundly religious man, knew that prayer was the indispensable foundation of any apostolate. Perhaps in drawing attention
to the essentials of the plan he tended to under-emphasize or neglect
some aspects of the pastoral dimension of this vocation.

In actual practice, Beauduin undoubtedly would have shown himself more flexible than the terse phrases suggest. In the light of Vatican II's presentation of both the episcopacy and the priesthood as a
ministry of service—*diakonia*—as well as Beauduin's own later reflections—one can only hope that had his involvement with this
group been more immediate and prolonged he might have modified
some points and more directly anticipated the council's emphasis.
The diocesan-monk plan was above all concerned with priestly

spirituality and pastoral formation rather than a more effective or creative use of the traditional parish structures. Others may question the almost exclusively clerical orientation of this project. The apparent contradiction of the principles which inspired Amay and set forth lay monasticism as the ideal can easily be explained by recognizing the totally different missions of the two communities. Amay was predominantly monastic and ecumenical; the diocesan community was necessarily pastoral. The priesthood was not essential to the purpose of Amay; it was indispensable for the sacramental life of the faithful on the diocesan plane.

Ecumenical Activities

Beauduin's ecumenical activities during his French exile which began in the mid-1930's are described with difficulty. His first serious Protestant contacts were with "high church" Lutherans, but almost no documentation exists because the first meetings were very unofficial and the participants wanted to protect those involved from official censure. Istina (whose seminarians had formerly spent their summer vacations at Amay),[10] the Orthodox seminary of Saint Serge, and Pastor J. M. Waltz's parish church, all in Paris, became popular meeting places for the ecumenical avant-garde of the early 1940's. Waltz formed part of the early ecumenical group into which Louis Bouyer, the first biographer of Beauduin, was introduced by Rousseau. Bouyer, at the time a Calvinist pastor, was immediately struck by Beauduin's openness at the little get-togethers. In commenting on the spirit of ecumenism among Catholics at that time, he observed:

> People don't succeed in giving much so long as they refuse to receive anything. Rare were the Catholics at this period who were disposed to admit this. Their generosity, in general, was without limit, but, to use the jargon of today, their power of receptivity was rather feeble, which made Dom Lambert's receptivity truly disconcerting.[11]

Beauduin differed radically from the typical Catholic ecumenist of his day. His seemingly limitless willingness to listen disconcerted men like Bouyer, and his sincerity really appeared too genuine

to be true. Not only would he ask for non-Catholic opinions, but he
actually gave the impression of being convinced that his Christian
brothers had something worthwhile to contribute.

The first official meeting of the Catholic-Lutheran group after
World War II was held at Istina, April 12, 1946, and monthly meetings
continued on the average of seven or eight a year until March 1949.
By common consent the participants agreed to limit their discussions
to pastoral, especially sacramental, themes. The Lutheran members
included Pastors Waltz, A. Greiner, R. Rigal, R. Blanc, Theo-
bald Suss and F. Wheatcroft (who was the equivalent of a bishop in
the Lutheran Church); the Catholics included Beauduin, Msgr.
Chevrot, and the Dominicans C. J. Dumont, Yves Congar and
Albert-Marie Avril. Beauduin's major contribution consisted of a
paper on the sacrifice of praise (June 21, 1946) and one on confession
(January 10, 1949).

Istina also provided the animating spirit behind two more ecumenical groups which attracted leading Catholic and Orthodox scholars to
similar study sessions. Apparently Beauduin had no connection with
the group owing allegiance to the Patriarch of Constantinople. G.
Florovsky and A. Schmemann played an active role in this group
before coming to America. Figuring prominently among the participants of the second group were men like Congar and Dumont or
Pierre Kowalewsky, as well as his brother Evgraph Kowalewsky
(who founded a "French Orthodoxy" and recently died a bishop),
S. Chevitok, Seraphim Rodionoff, and the lay philosopher Vladimir
Lossky (died in 1958) who was clearly the best theologian in the
Vanves circle. It was in this circle, whose Orthodox members recognized the Patriarch of Moscow, that Beauduin was found. He
particularly appreciated their discussions about the Holy Spirit and
divinization. Unfortunately, this effort at dialogue was short-lived.
The first meeting was held July 3, 1946, but the sessions came to an
abrupt halt in the summer of 1948 for several reasons, including an
official position taken by the Conference of Moscow that summer
which Catholics considered detrimental to genuine dialogue. Furthermore, the Catholics objected to the proselytizing mentality of the
Moscow Orthodox, and especially of Father Evgraph Kowalewsky.[12]
Congar, as chief spokesman for the Catholics, brought things to a
head by his insistence that unless the Orthodox members would

openly disagree with the Synod of Moscow in this matter, there was no point in holding further dialogue.[13] Since they were unwilling to take a public position, the ecumenical sessions were not continued. But this did not impede Beauduin's ecumenical contacts.

No one so convinced of his Christian responsibility to break down the barriers of ignorance as Beauduin was could possibly limit his activities to clerical dialogue. He also lectured occasionally during these years to an Orthodox lay group at St. Denis in Lille, a city in the north of France which had become home for many of the Russian refugees in the 1920's.

Another regular stop on his ecumenical circuit was the Institut Saint Serge which began sponsoring an annual liturgical congress in July 1952. These sessions attracted people from all faiths and countries. Beauduin himself attended several times. The Archimandrite Cyprien Kern, professor of patrology at Saint Serge, paid him the following tribute:

In 1929 I saw him at Jerusalem for the first time. How many times have our paths crossed. How many letters have we exchanged. My visit to Chevetogne in 1951; his somewhat bent figure on the platform at the Namur station where he came, old and tired, to meet me (what an embarassment for me). And our first liturgical week when he delivered his message which encouraged all of us and showed us the true spirit of our dialogue. One can say without exaggeration that we owe the better half of our success to Dom Lambert. It is he who is the true creator of these encounters.[14]

One cannot bring this too brief section on Beauduin's ecumenical activities to a close without suggesting what possible impact he may have had elsewhere.

From the very beginning two special periods of prayer for unity had been set aside at Amay: the nine days preceding Pentecost, instituted by Leo XIII, and the January Chair of Unity Octave (January 18–25), of Anglican origin.[15] Among some of the frequent visitors at Amay who were impressed by this ecumenical spirituality and who were destined to become ecumenists of note in their own right, mention should be made of Yves Congar and Paul Couturier (1881–1953),[16] who met for the first time at the monastery in 1932.[17]

Father Couturier, an oblate of Amay-Chevetogne,[18] was nevertheless dissatisfied with simply praying *for* other Christians; he insisted that we should pray *with* them. Upon his return to his diocese of Lyon, he began to promote his idea and eventually succeeded in giving the Unity Octave a new direction. His convictions, ably expounded in an article published in 1935, "For Christian Unity: The Psychology of the January 18–25 Octave of Prayer," in *Revue Apologétique*,[19] almost immediately caught fire in France and soon penetrated into the Protestant European countries.

Perhaps the fullest realization of the new dimension proposed by Couturier can be found in the Protestant monastic communities of Taizé and Grandchamp. Taizé is fairly well known in the United States through the theological works of one of its brothers, Max Thurian. The history of Grandchamp on the other hand remains relatively unknown. In many respects it was more closely related to Beauduin than Taizé. Originally begun in 1931 as a retreat for personal spiritual renewal, it is today the women's counterpart of Taizé. The present community came into existence in 1944, dedicated to prayer with a special stress on unity. The future foundress of Grandchamp, Généviève Michéli, was a close friend of the foundress of the Olivétans and made several ecumenical retreats at Cormeilles. In the course of one of them she was deeply impressed by a conference given by Beauduin. Years later when a telegram arrived during a reunion announcing the death of Beauduin, she and others paid tribute to his efforts for unity.

In contrast to Beauduin, Couturier had a much closer relationship to the founders of both of these pioneer Protestant groups. Sister Marguerite, a member of the community and also a close friend of the "apostle of unity," noted that he often spoke to her of "the invisible monastery" of Christians united in prayer for unity. In 1940, some months before Roger Schutz, the future founder of Taizé, had taken up residence in Taizé, Couturier wrote to Sister Marguerite:

> I have a presentiment that the first real monastery of Christian unity such as I understand it will be Protestant.

Coming from an oblate of Chevetogne, this may sound a bit strange. The motto "that they may be one" obviously has different degrees of realization. Couturier's dream of a monastery consecrated to unity was far more radical than Beauduin's. He saw Catholics, Protestants, and Orthodox living together in community and worshiping together—an interdenominational monastery whose confession of faith was Christian. Then on March 3, 1941 he wrote jubilantly to Sister Marguerite:

> Yesterday I had a profound joy. Mr. Schutz was here in my room. A part of what I have been dreaming has been accomplished. My Protestant brothers are beginning this real "monastery" that I would also like to see exist among us Catholics. . . . I will go to them on March 31 to offer Holy Mass in the church of Taizé, perhaps even at their house.[20]

Today much of Couturier's dream has been realized at Taizé. Men from all over the world, representing many different denominations, live and pray together. A man at Taizé remains a member of his original denomination while still being a monk of Taizé. Franciscan Fathers live at Taizé in close unity with the brothers. Each day they celebrate Mass, and an Orthodox priest celebrates the Divine Liturgy. Long before Taizé attained its worldwide fame, however, Beauduin gave his full support to the struggling young community and proclaimed the necessity of such an experiment and the benefits that would inevitably result.

If Amay-Chevetogne was international (and for Beauduin, "international" originally meant not completely Belgian), in confession of faith it has remained exclusively Roman Catholic. Its work, rather than a concrete realization of the unity that inspired both Beauduin and Couturier, has been, if less dramatic, at least more far-reaching. For almost fifty years it has sought to make known the causes of division, to understand these causes and to propose solutions, but most of all it has tried to foster that meeting of minds so central to Beauduin's ecumenical perspective. Taizé, on the other hand, sends small groups of brothers throughout the world and offers a much more diversified apostolate to its monks, working for unity on a more popular and perhaps individual, person-to-person level. The prior of Taizé and the community maintain contacts with the pope (Pius XII, John XXIII, Paul VI), Patriarch Athenagoras, the World Council of Churches and a large number of bishops and cardinals of different confessions.

Last Years at Chevetogne

Such, in brief outline, were some of the activities of Beauduin during his twenty-year exile. As if to signal the validity of his life and the sacrifices that it had entailed, a series of events and Roman decrees in the late 1940's and early 1950's seemed to endorse all that he had stood for. The liturgical signposts have already been pointed out. The ecumenical scene was marked by the formation of the World Council of Churches in 1948, a clear affirmation that ecumenism was here to stay. Then in 1949 Rome gave official authorization for interconfessional encounters—something Beauduin had been actively engaged in since the early 1940's.

The new decade began with the installation of Thomas Becquet as prior on July 29, 1950—the early disciple and loyal friend who himself had shared some of the founder's exile. Beauduin was invited for the occasion and given a place of honor at the head table. Becquet could not refrain from addressing some words to the venerable patriarch who listened with tears in his eyes to the expressions of gratitude and congratulations addressed to him by his son. Becquet ended his address with these words: "And now let me say, dear Fr. Lambert, that your place is here, and we will not be happy until you return to your house." After the meal was over, as Beauduin prepared to return to Chatou, his place of exile, Becquet reaffirmed his intention and, urging him to say nothing about it, promised that within a year he would see to it that Beauduin was permanently installed in Chevetogne.[21]

In honor of their twenty-fifth anniversary, the monks of Amay-Chevetogne received a congratulatory note from Pius XII (dated November 21, 1950 and signed by J. B. Montini, the future Pope Paul VI) in appreciation for all they had done to further the work of unity. This sign of recognition, plus other circumstances on behalf of Beauduin, helped to pave the way for the realization of Becquet's promise.

Once Becquet had made certain that no objections would be raised, he wasted no time. Without asking any official permission, he sent the long-awaited message to Beauduin: "Come!" Everyone assumed that this was done according to canonical procedure, but a whole year elapsed before anyone wrote to ask how it had been accomplished. When Rome heard of this, the pope asked Cardinal Tissérant to examine the matter and then to decide for the best. In February (1952) he told Becquet: "If nothing will happen, Beauduin may remain at Chevetogne." And Becquet assured him nothing would.[22]

The very year of Beauduin's return, 1951, Cardinal Jan Willebrands (then a monsignor) laid the foundation for ecumenical conferences among Roman Catholic theologians. The Roman approval that it received further enhanced Beauduin's position in the struggle to gain recognition for the ideals of unity at a moment when certain Catholics were finally beginning to take Protestant efforts seriously and to be a little ashamed of their intransigent attitudes in the past. (The year 1952 marked the official beginning of these conferences.)

For Beauduin these were years of semi-retirement. There was an almost constant stream of dignitaries, and his old Paris friends also came to visit him from time to time. In the community Beauduin gave his opinion when requested and wisely refrained from trying to impose his ideas. Community life and monastic duties left him few idle moments. In spite of growing infirmity, he made every attempt to take part in the monastic exercises which he had so missed during his exile. As his hearing began to fail, his interior life inadvertently revealed itself. His semi-audible thanksgivings after Mass were found to consist primarily of the Gloria and various ejaculations. He also loved the psalms and repeated verses when they struck him. His eagerness to maintain monastic regularity knew no bounds. When advancing paralysis made it impossible for him to move under his own power, he had himself carried to the chapel for the offices. This often imposed a slight hardship on his nurse, since, fearful of being late, Beauduin would often wake the poor monk in the middle of the night to find out if it were time to start getting ready.

The countless signs of the aged monk's love of and fidelity to his monastic vocation made a lasting impression on the younger members of the community. But his influence was not restricted to the monks. Even casual visitors to the monastery—the young, married couples, believers and non-believers—were impressed by the old monk whether they knew who he was or not. He had a gift of being present to others which old age in no way impaired. He listened attentively to whatever they had to say and entered into whatever the mood of the occasion proved to be.

Although after 1951 Beauduin published rarely, he was still found frequently with pen in hand, either taking care of personal correspondence or jotting down ideas for the future, reflections marked with an increasing preoccupation and concern for the twentieth-century Church, her weaknesses and the urgent need for reform. Repeatedly he insisted that the Church should redirect her concerns into the areas he felt most in need of exploration: the role of the bishop and, though this was less well known, the role of the laity.

A Legacy to the Laity

One of Beauduin's last trips was to Saint-Jean-de-Luz (France) where he spent the winter of 1954–1955 to escape the bitter cold of Belgium which his failing health supported so poorly. He was staying with Dr. Leon Clottens whom he had first met in 1909 at the National Congress which launched the liturgical movement. Clottens was then a Boy Scout serving as a guide for participants at the congress, and Beauduin had availed himself of the lad's services. It was the beginning of a friendship that would span a half century. Later on Clottens became his personal physician, and especially in their last years their conversations quite naturally turned to current problems within the Church.

Ever since 1934, when Beauduin reviewed a book written by a lay theologian, he had been impressed by the very real contribution to the future definition of the nature of the Church to be found in a relatively untapped potential—the laity. At the time he suggested that a course on the Church should also treat some topics from the point of view of the layman.[23] In the course of the winter of 1955, Beauduin raised the matter of the utility of publishing a lay view on the Church with his friend Clottens. He suggested a kind of *quo vadis* which would describe the present ecclesial situation and suggest future possibilities. In the notes that he entrusted to Clottens, he observed that active lay participation in the apostolate seemed to be an integral part of the constitution of the Church, an involvement which he believed to entail an inevitable corollary: intervention—

discreet and subordinate without a doubt, but active and regular—
on their part in Church affairs.[24]

This document is particularly valuable because it reveals Beauduin's
final thoughts on the nature of the Church—ideas which he realized
were perhaps too bold for his own day but which in the 1970's,
in the wake of Vatican II, have become almost standard features of
the informed Catholic's concept of the Church. Ever concerned with
the orthodoxy of his thought, however, he left the document with
Clottens, insisting that should the notes ever be published, they
should appear under the name of a layman, *in toto*, and with the
imprimatur of the Church.[25]

The document accentuated the need of the Church to renew herself
in her historically variable elements, including the modality of the
exercise of the pope's universal jurisdiction and the need to adapt
to the modern world. The document further challenged the Church
to respond to the ardent yearning, especially among the young, for
a more dynamic, relevant spirituality, and to recognize the equality
granted by baptism to all Christians and so to rid herself of a
spiritually stifling, clerical paternalism. This was not intended to be
a claim for a radical spirit of democracy in the Church but simply
a plea to respect the human dignity of each member.

In the course of his stay with the Clottens, Beauduin was joined
in February by Becquet. The two took a trip to Loyola and visited
the family castle of the founder of the Jesuits which had been
transformed into a sanctuary, heavy with gold pieces of baroque
art. Ever ready for a quip about Benedictine-Jesuit relations, Beauduin could not refrain from remarking: "If they knew I were here,
they'd be afraid!" A few weeks after their visit, a fire broke out in
the castle which made the newspapers. Beauduin and Becquet had a
few jokes about the possible culprit.

The Prophet Speaks

Finally Rome began to view the aging monk with marked veneration. In 1957 when Cardinal Tissérant came to Chevetogne for the
consecration of the Byzantine chapel, he showed great kindness to
Beauduin and personally went to the latter's room to thank him in
the name of the Church for his work for unity.[26]

Roncalli, now Patriarch of Venice, publicly declared at the Congress of Palermo that he owed his understanding of the importance of ecumenism to Beauduin:

> The principal defect of the work for union in the present hour is that it is still too little diffused among the masses which, however, are quite capable of appreciating it. My old Belgian friend, the Benedictine Dom Lambert Beauduin, said as far back as 1926 when I was at the beginning of my practical work of cooperation in the Near East: "We must create in the West, in favor of the reunion of separated Churches, a movement parallel to that of the work of the Propagation of the Faith." I had, at that very moment, just reorganized the work of the Propagation of the Faith in the world, under the inspiration of the new pope, the glorious Pius XI. I think we must return to Dom Lambert Beauduin's idea.[27]

If the Church showed signs of mellowing in her official attitude toward Beauduin, he was unable to hide his growing dissatisfaction with the way Church affairs were handled in Rome. The climax came when he confided to his monks and friends that Roncalli would be the next pope and that he would certainly convoke a council for the union of Churches. When the conclave was finally assembled, the monks gathered around the radio in a room where they had wheeled Beauduin. As the announcer named Roncalli as the new pope, the venerable ecumenist exploded with joy.[28] Unfortunately the letter that Beauduin sent to John XXIII on the occasion of his election has never been found, but undoubtedly he raised the subject of the council in it. So enthusiastic did he become when the council was finally announced on January 25, 1959 that he wanted all work in the monastery stopped so that all efforts and talents could be expended in preparing for it.

Ecumenical and Ecclesial Legacy

Unless one recalls that Beauduin began to think in conciliar terms as early as 1907 when he taught his first course on the Church, much of his excitement at the actual announcement of the council is missed. For fifty years he had maintained that a new council to complete the work of Vatican I was the only feasible solution to handle the crises of the modern era effectively. By the 1920's the conviction was clearly formulated, and he tried to have a chair on the creeds and councils established at Sant' Anselmo as a remote preparation for the council.

The accession of each new pope reopened the question for Beauduin, but unforeseen circumstances such as wars and political problems, not to mention the very make-up of individual popes, kept the long-desired council ever a thing of the future. Once the council was actually announced, however, Beauduin was full of ideas as to what it should and should not do. On one occasion he made the following remarks:

> They must not talk too much about dogma or morals at the council; they'll never get finished and they won't advance anything. Above all that, and even above the magisterium, there is the priestly power of the Church that sanctifies the faithful. She does it by *her* prayer and *her* liturgy. As long as the people will not think with the Church and will not live with her the mysteries of the paschal cycle and the Sundays, and as long as they will not pray with her, nothing will be done. The council should have for its objective the revitalization of this great prayer. That is my profound conviction.[29]

From an ecumenical perspective, Beauduin was particularly concerned that the new council do something to offset the lopsided ecclesiology of Vatican I. He suggested that the wording of papal infallibility be re-examined, and he insisted that the nature of the episcopacy be defined.

Even the bishops at Vatican I had objected to the wording of the statement on papal infallibility in its earlier stages because of what they called equivocal language which seemed to reduce bishops to simple vicars or papal delegates. Hampered by the lack of a developed theology of the episcopacy, they nevertheless sensed that their role was somehow much deeper.[30] The struggle to make their role known, with the attendant confusion in the minds of many between infallibility and jurisdiction, is one of the little known chapters in the history of the episcopacy.

Beauduin's interest in this matter was accelerated in 1928 by the chance discovery of some significant documents from the 1870's which supported his views on the inherent rights of the episcopacy. A close friend, suffering from insomnia,[31] had picked up a volume which contained correspondence and articles relating to the definition of infallibility.[32] A careful reading revealed that Protestants, especially Bismarck, had claimed that Rome would absorb the Church in the wake of Vatican I. This accusation, made in an atmosphere charged with nationalism, did not help the Church which for some time had felt her struggle for survival increasingly challenged. Moreover an official dispatch, dated May 14, 1872 and signed by Bismarck, contained seven flagrant misinterpretations of the doctrine of papal infallibility, but its publication toward the end of 1874, after circulating secretly for two years, brought swift action on the part of the German hierarchy.

Their carefully drafted pastoral released to the public toward the end of February brought prompt papal approbation (Pius' brief is dated March 2) and episcopal support. The English and Belgian hierarchies published a translation of the German letter soon afterward. In the context of these events, the German bishops' response has been called "the strongest argument which has ever been produced in Catholic tradition against the whole tendency to minimize the rights and value of the episcopacy." [33]

When his friend showed him the article in 1928, Beauduin's immediate reaction was: "We must publish it!" [34] It so happened that debate on the nature of the episcopacy was one of the problems of the day. Cardinal van Roey's republication during the following year of his paper on the episcopacy written four years earlier for the Malines Conversations was another sign of the times. Like the German bishops, he believed in the divine origin of the episcopacy and reaffirmed that no human power, not even an ecumenical council, could suppress it.[35]

Republishing old articles and letters could not settle the issue of papal primacy and the episcopacy. It is surprising, however, to note that no further polemic on this point appeared again before 1954. Even studies on these questions make no mention of any theological ferment prior to this date.[36] Nevertheless the need was never far from Beauduin's mind. In 1945 he wrote these words:

Catholics do not approve of the successor of Peter monopolizing the sovereign power. The ordinary organ of sovereign power is the episcopal body, dispersed throughout the Church and united at its head, the Bishop of Rome. The *extraordinary* organ is (a) the ecumenical council (where each episcopal member is judge and teacher under the presidency of Peter's successor; (b) the successor of Peter becoming in certain circumstances the organ for the whole Church in order to formulate the faith of the entire Church (a faith already existing in the Church but lacking a precise and defined formula)—but all this needs verbal explanations, which we will one day have.[37]

To the increased papal centralization which became a marked characteristic of the mid-twentieth century, two distinct reactions developed. One school greeted greater papal involvement in diocesan affairs with enthusiasm, considering it the harbinger of a new era, a pontifical age.[38] In other circles this same situation created a crisis of identity for bishops. New currents in the Church—the liturgical movement and the lay apostolate in particular—focused attention on the local bishop, raising the question of where one's first allegiance lay. On the one hand Rome seemed to claim priority, while at the same time the logical theological conclusions behind these new movements pointed to a diocesan-centered orientation. The fundamental principle actually in jeopardy was the fullness of the priesthood conferred in the rite of episcopal consecration. The first position mentioned above tossed the whole matter off lightly, claiming that the very notion was just an oratorical exaggeration. Not everyone was ready to agree.[39]

In 1954, two bishops spoke out. The Cardinal of Toulouse said: "A *De Episcopo* is still to be written. . . ."[40] And the Bishop of Cambrai in his book *The Bishop* took issue with a recently published work in which the following statement appeared: "Priests and bishops have equal powers."[41]

Beauduin, now over eighty, followed the public debate with undisguised interest. Recalling the clarity of the German letter, he asked Rousseau to look it up and to republish it as his (Beauduin's) contribution toward settling the question.[42] This time the idea caught on. Bishops who were worried by the conservatives found needed support in it, and even in the world of Orthodoxy, theologians took notice. An offensive was launched in favor of the sacramentality of the episcopacy, the "fullness of the priesthood" concept. It was only one step from this to collegiality, because derivation in

the fullness of the sacrament of orders, transmitted by regular apostolic succession, reattaches the episcopal body to the apostolic body
instituted by Christ.[43]

Beauduin even seemed to have anticipated the doctrine of collegiality—if at first somewhat hesitantly. As early as 1925 he noted
with interest that an Anglican commenting on Vatican I had singled
out as one of its fruits the recognition of the collegiate nature of
the episcopacy:

> The episcopacy is a college, and every college has its president
> who cannot act without his colleagues, for they have rights equal to
> his, but they cannot act without him, for he is their head.[44]

Twenty years later, discussing the apostolic constitution in which
Pope Pius XII stressed the sacramentality of the act of co-consecrators,[45] Beauduin raised one question: "If the co-consecrators are
allowed to concelebrate, why not all the bishops who are present?"[46] This query was obviously inspired by the unity of the priesthood and the shared responsibility that Beauduin saw inherent in
the very nature of the episcopacy. Subsequent reflection convinced
him that collegiality would be part of the definition of the episcopacy
of the still-unannounced council of the twentieth century.

In his opinion, the bishops united in collegial accord carry out a
twofold role. By their unanimous witness to the truths of the
Church, they exert a visible influence on believers, thereby expressing
the infallibility of the Church, and by their solidarity they help the
faithful to adhere to these same truths without reserve.[47] Their
more direct mission is to make of mankind a living and holy oblation
offered daily to the glory of the Father,[48] communicating through
their hands all the spiritual riches of Christ to his body.

Between papal infallibility and the infallibility of the Church, Beauduin made a distinction. Vatican I defined that the pope has the same
infallibility as the Church—neither more nor less. The council did
not define the infallibility of the Church because there was no need;
it had always been a truth, defined by Christ himself in his command "Go and teach; I am with you" and addressed to the whole
college, whereas the words pertaining to papal infallibility were
addressed to Peter alone.[49]

In 1957, Bishop André-Marie Charue of Namur published an article in his diocesan review.[50] How deeply the aged monk was moved is attested to by the rough draft of a letter, begun several times but apparently never finished. A reference to his birthday suggests that it was written in April 1957.

> I read and reread the theological article. One would believe it to be a conciliar document. Everything therein is exposed with sobriety and with objectivity. . . . I have the impression that without too much delay the Holy Father will convoke a council of the Catholic episcopacy to finish the exposé of the episcopal doctrine that Vatican Council [I] was unable to begin. Several theologians thrive on raising theological questions without sufficient documentation.

There followed some references to texts of Pius IX and papal infallibility, as well as questions raised in some quarters regarding the precise meaning and interpretation to be given:

> I wonder, Excellency, whether the Holy Father plans to resume the work of Vatican Council and to define the doctrine of the episcopacy which was one of the projects of the council. It is the most definable question of the whole of theology. . . . The age of the Holy Father might make one hesitate, but Pius IX was eighty years old in 1870 and Pius XII is possessed of a valor and courage that nothing can discourage. A solemn and ecumenical manifestation should not make him draw back. *Fiat! Fiat!* The Bishop of Namur should play the role of Cardinal Dechamps of Malines there.[51]

The positive tone of the excerpts given may raise a question about the honesty of this presentation. Did Beauduin's incredible loyalty to the Church never waver in the face of everything that he experienced? Not everything has been told. The consistently positive emphasis encountered in his writings is there because he was intensely aware of the negative aspects that he was trying to counteract. He died at the end of an era, but not before leaving a "last will and testament." Haltingly and partially paralyzed, he expressed in his forceful and direct way three complaints he had with the twentieth-century Church he had known.

(1) The power of the pope becomes more and more absolute,

personal, centralizing. It is uncontrolled, to the point that the episcopacy is more and more effaced and reduced to the role of pontifical civil servants. The laity are absolutely neglected and effaced. In short, the pope has become the unique and only power, and this power is more absolute than that of a dictator we have known. Such a state of affairs is absolutely contrary to the power established by Christ.

(2) The government in the Church becomes more and more arbitrary and papal (such as we've known in politics in recent times). In matters of civil power this phenomenon is evident in the evolution of the nunciature. It is especially arbitrary in doctrinal matters: without trial or warning, persons—especially writers—are denounced, censured, put aside, and discredited by the Roman power without the accused having the power to defend himself. Moreover, under administrative pretexts, persons are removed without major superiors even being informed. It is a most absolute arbitrariness that without trial discredits a writer wthout any information. These trials have evolved against the natural law. . . .

(3) Those who are to suffer from this trial must use [the necessary means] and take the required attitude to cure this evil.[52]

If his criticism thus far sounded comparable to what one might read in the press, the tone suddenly changes. Unfortunately, only phrases here and there are legible, even to those familiar with his handwriting. If faced with injustice, he urged the individual not to deny the evil or to blind himself to it, for that is not freedom. On the contrary, one must admit the evil that exists and then try to bear the consequences. Love and serve the Catholic, apostolic and Roman Church. She is the great and universal society of the children of God, and we must remain enthusiastic before this human institution. She is in great distress, but she is nonetheless essentially the society that continues, in spite of her faults, the redemptive work of Christ.

Never must we let ourselves be troubled in our souls. She has faults, she has her history, but she remains this ideal. We must remain as sons who hide the faults of a parent; not to insist on faults is not really to deny them.[53]

There are many weaknesses apparent in the exterior elements of this society which work more and more to the detriment of supernatural values, to the Church's mission. But the human side that the Church presents to the world will not destroy her spiritual riches.[54]

Into the Bosom of the Father

How thoroughly imbued Beauduin was with genuine Benedictine spirituality to the very end is strikingly expressed by his last visit to the novices. Walking in on them, he turned to their master of novices (Nicholas Egender) and said: "Tell the novices that three things are necessary: *opus Dei, lectio divina, oratio*" (liturgy, scriptural reading, and prayer).

During his last year he was totally paralyzed and suffered much from rheumatism. When the pain was more severe than usual, he would often confess that he was very happy for the extra suffering because it might help him to go straight to heaven.

Death came to the venerable monk on January 11, 1960 as the Christian world prepared for the annual celebration of the unity octave. The ardent desires of a lifetime were by then well on the road to realization. Many capable hands had already picked up his torch to carry on the work so courageously begun. Although testimonies to the greatness of the man poured into the monastery from all over the world, from Catholics, Protestants, and Orthodox, of all Beauduin's foreign friends, only Roguet, Bouyer, de Féligonde, and Father Dumont, O.P., from Istina, braved a raging blizzard to be present for the funeral. When John XXIII heard that there had been so few foreigners at the burial, he commented to his secretary Msgr. Loris Capovilla: "But we were both there in spirit." [55] Several years later on a similar inclement winter day, Metropolitan Nicodim, vicar of the patriarch of Moscow and all the Russias, came as a pilgrim to chant a panykhide over the tomb of this great man of the Church.[56]

Conclusion

Perhaps Beauduin's ecumenical contribution has nowhere been more concisely summed up than in the words of Roger Aubert: "No one has played a more decisive role in the birth of Catholic ecumenism [than Beauduin] because he knew how to conceive ecumenical activity in a clearly theological perspective." [57] His contribution was more than a striking theological intuition or the initiation of a long overdue movement within the Church—whether a liturgical renewal or an ecumenical awakening. A constant restlessness about the needs of the actual Church marked his entire life. The positive reaction that it sparked has won for him the title of prophet and given the twentieth century a worthy model for all reform and reformers.

> [Beauduin accomplished his goals] not by a criticism of the Church but by her interior renewal; not by separating but by seeking out everything which unites. Only such an attitude is capable of weakening particularism: the bad outgrowths of the counter-reform, the centrifugal forces of the Protestant reform, the unfortunate individualism and intolerance of our "Christian" Middle Ages, the innate juridicism of the West. . . . *Vir ecclesiasticus* [a man of the Church]: The venerable figure of Dom Lambert Beauduin is present to our minds as the personification of the ancient Church always renewing her youth in the full combat of the century. His work will endure, for a numerous and various progeny already continues his work which is bearing fruit in the world.[58]

In the liturgy he rediscovered the Church in her truly Catholic plenitude. His insight into her universalism found its natural expression in an ecumenism which sought to realize the only thing that mattered: the growth of the body of Christ into its full measure, a universalism which properly existed only in union with the glorified humanity of Christ. By his very life he demonstrated in a most concrete way that ecumenism is intrinsically interior and must be an indispensable condition in the life of every individual who considers himself Christian. This then is one of his major contributions: he spent himself in bringing men to a recognition that to pray Christ's prayer for unity meant that one must both desire and work "full-time" toward this unity. His constant stress on the importance of the mystical body indicates the real key to an ecumenical ecclesiology.

Beauduin sought the reasons and arguments which animated and supported his various apostolates and theological positions in papal documents and the sources of tradition. Firmly rooted in tradition, he never became involved in subtle doctrinal controversies but kept his gaze steadily directed toward the only goal that counted—the Father—and the totally undeserved invitation proffered to mankind in Christ—eternity in the bosom of the Father. His life and his work are truly a *Summa* in themselves, containing a sound doctrine and a healthy asceticism. He understood the risks involved in taking a theological position and standing steadfast behind it. "It is indeed a difficult and delicate trade which demands as much courage as prudence." [59] But his life is a fitting testimony that he was willing to take the risk—not for the sake of fame, but for the love of the Church.

Little more can be added. It is clear that Beauduin played a significant role in arresting certain potentially disastrous ecclesiological tendencies. These same concerns emerged at Vatican II and provoked a re-examination of the episcopacy and the recognition of collegiality,[60] while the *Decree on Ecumenism* stands as a milestone on the road to unity. Many of his disciples and former students figured among its illustrious shapers.

The following partial list gives some idea of the extent of his influence. Undoubtedly the most powerful echo of his ideas was through the voice of John XXIII, who already declared in 1957 that he owed his ecumenical vocation to Beauduin. Msgr. Charles Moeller, a noted theologian and disciple of Beauduin and an aide to Msgr. Gerard Phillips (who framed the rough draft of the *Constitution on the Church*), shares with Olivier Rousseau, *peritus* for the Melchite patriarch, second place in terms of devotion to the ideals of Beauduin.

Cardinals Augustin Bea, Leon-Joseph Suenens and Jan Willibrands of the Secretariat for Christian Unity were also staunch supporters of Beauduin's principles. Suenens' association with Beauduin dated from the cardinal's seminarian days at Rome when he had frequently visited Beauduin, who was then at Sant' Anselmo. Suenens was also one of the council fathers to cite Beauduin in their deliberations.

Emmanuel Lanne, a second-generation monk of Chevetogne who had known Beauduin during his stay at Paris, became a member of the Secretariat for Christian Unity before the council and cooperated in writing the *Decree on Ecumenism*. Pierre Dumont also served on the same secretariat. Many others could be mentioned, but the above suffices to indicate the extent of Beauduin's influence which certainly radiated from the many other Chevetogne monks active on various preparatory or conciliar commissions. They represented thirty o more years of remote, scholarly preparation for that "future" coun cil that their founder knew inevitably would be held to complet Vatican I.[61]

Today the same influence is still visible in his friends and in th movements he once animated with his thought-provoking observa tions about needs, lacks and abuses in the Church. Perhaps his ow words provide an even more fitting conclusion: "Celui qui dit 'Amen en mourant est éternellement vivant." [62]

13

Beauduin's Theological Legacy

In academic circles Beauduin's theological contribution will probably never be studied, for unlike such contemporaries as Rahner, Barth, or Tillich, he has not left us a systematic presentation of his thought in neatly bound and easily accessible volumes. After embarking on just such an undertaking in 1912, "Essai de manuel fondamental de liturgie," he abandoned it in 1921. Ten years later he was disciplined, and the next twenty years, which might have been his most theologically productive, were spent under ecclesiastical restrictions—including limitations on his writing. But theologically these were nevertheless very fruitful years devoted to the practical implementation of the insights he drew from living the mysteries of the faith.

Insight into the evolution of his rich and fertile thought can be traced primarily through letters to his friends, retreat notes and unedited reflections on various theological issues. It has been said that his ideas influenced the direction taken by the twentieth-century Church and the currents that prepared for and produced the documents of Vatican II.[1] While the validity of this statement has already been substantiated in previous chapters, we must admit that much of his originality is hardly recognized today. Many of the causes he championed have been so totally incorporated into contemporary Catholicism that trying to insist on their importance or boldness seems, if not irrelevant, at least banal. Perhaps the chief "defect"—

if it can be so designated—in his thought is that he lived and wrote not for a scholarly elite but for the Church. It is for this reason that Beauduin deserves recognition for his role as a practical theologian. The value of his theological contribution on the pastoral level has nowhere been more aptly summarized than in these words of Maieul Cappuyns:

> His courses in ecclesiology and liturgy, stamped with true Christianity and apostolic charity, have profoundly marked the young priests and the young monks who were in contact with him at Louvain and at Rome. A theologian in the strict sense, in love with tradition and not with convention, a bold apostle with countless achievements, he is above all a master of thought whose hold is indelible. Throughout the world professors of theology and of liturgy, parish priests, missionaries, educators, men of action, writers, and thinkers refer to his spirit.[2]

There is no doubt then but that Beauduin was a theologian—in the strict classical sense of one who meditated on Scripture and then tried to translate it into the language and lives of his contemporaries. If he failed to devise his own theological vocabulary, it is because he chose to remain faithful to the traditional language which despite its deficiencies was yet more widely and easily grasped than that peculiar to a given individual theologian. He deliberately situated his reflection not in the outer reaches of abstract speculation but in the heart of the needs and concerns of the Church of the twentieth century, for he realized that not every theological approach is suitable in ecumenical dialogue:

> We must resign ourselves to deepening revelation in terms of its . . . destination and to formulate it in relation to this economy. We must abandon the metaphysical preoccupation which wants to consider everything philosophically. This last effort only gives analogical approximations which differ enormously between Christians, while the aspect of the divine plan which directly touches the true reason of revelation draws us together in a unique fashion.[3]

Most theologians become particularly enamored with a branch of theology, or even with a given aspect of dogma within a broader discipline. The previous chapter revealed Beauduin's unfailing interest in the Church, which perhaps explains why he viewed everything from an ecclesial perspective. Inebriated as he was with the love of God and marked by an intense compassion for his fellow man, Beauduin had an insatiable thirst for unity. At first envisaged in rather narrow lines and somewhat hesitantly, unity soon became the predominant passion of his entire life.

The modest beginnings of this career indicated little to warrant his future phenomenal development. His involvement in the Belgian priest-worker experiment at the turn of the century revealed him as a social apostle. However, dissatisfaction with certain modifications in their work brought Beauduin to a serious re-evaluation of priorities. The consequent scrutiny of his goals and beliefs resulted in the radical reorientation of his life now familiar to us. Monasticism with all its positive as well as negative aspects served as a major source of inspiration throughout both his liturgical and ecumenical careers, for from the moment of his entrance into Mont César he nourished himself on Scripture and especially on St. Paul.

Commitment to liturgical renewal played a key role in the development of an indisputably ecumenical vocation, for active participation in the liturgy revealed man's true destiny. Of its very essence the liturgy taught union, uniting the faithful with one another, the congregation with the priest, the parish with the Church, and the Church with Christ. Having inaugurated action within the confines of Catholicism, Beauduin soon realized that unity conceived in such narrow terms was not really unity at all, but disunity. The prayer "that they may be one" remained an empty mockery unless prayed in the universal context in which it was uttered by Christ as head of a new humanity, a humanity without distinction of race, sex, or creed, but with one flock and one shepherd.

Thus Beauduin's ecumenical vocation came about quite naturally by way of the liturgy. He frequently reminded his friends and the public at large that every liturgist ought to be an Orientalist, at least in the broad sense, because competency in the field demanded familiarity with all liturgies. As early as 1912 he encouraged the readers of *Liturgical Questions* to read such periodicals as *Echos d'Orient* and *Rome e l'Oriente*. Both he and *Liturgical Questions* came under fire for leaning too much to the East.[4]

From the very beginning Beauduin visualized union in broad terms. Concerned that the "democratization" of the movement go beyond the circle of the specialists and interest the entire Christian people, he urged lay involvement. However, he considered a program of intellectual and moral effort alone insufficient. The theological and historical studies involved must ultimately lead to the supernatural and ascetical, placing the problem of union on the supernatural plane and in the perspective of the Christian mystique.[5]

The sound theological foundations of his ecumenism, more than anything else, qualify him as a theologian. Many others have had equally strong ecumenical motivations, but often their action sprang forth from an essentially emotional reaction to disunion or from a more dogmatically intransigent attitude. He opposed the misplaced emphasis on convert-making to the very end. What mattered was being converted to Christ so that one might have access to the Father, and this was the work of the Spirit, not of men. Through psychological reconciliation one simply paved the way for the *Spirit*—or, better yet, one surrendered the situation to the *Spirit*. This was genuine ecumenism.

Thus the chief work of Beauduin and his followers cannot easily be seen or measured. It consisted not in the statistics of conversions but in stirring up a wave of sympathy for union, an awareness of the evil of disunion, and an acknowledgment of individual responsibility. So long as a person did nothing to remove the psychological and religious barriers between spiritual brothers, personal guilt for the scandal of schism remained—a warning that remains as relevant today as in 1926.

After describing his theological sources we shall try to synthesize the essence of his thought and then consider in greater detail those aspects of his ecclesiology which anticipated more recent developments in the theology of the mystical body, the incarnation, the Trinity, the eucharist and the ministerial nature of the priesthood.

Theological Sources[6]

While all true theology necessarily originates in Scripture, conciliar documents provided Beauduin with a second and extremely valuable —although historically conditioned—reflection on and interpretation of revelation. His appreciation of these texts, particularly as preserved in the volumes of Mansi and Hefele-Leclercq, dated from his first teaching assignment in 1907. Frequently deprived of easy access to these tomes during his lengthy exile, it was with joy that upon his return to Chevetogne in 1951 he resumed his former daily habit of reading the conciliar documents. When advancing paralysis prevented him from holding the over-sized volumes of Mansi his confrères constructed a special bookstand for him, and so his studies continued to the end of his life.

From the extracts cited in the following pages, it will soon become evident how frequently and profoundly he must have meditated on the conciliar formulas and the meaning of the mysteries, particularly that of the incarnation. Few have equaled Beauduin's gift for grasping the essentials in these documents, and even fewer have succeeded in surpassing his ability to make these texts come alive for modern audiences. The early heresies often served as landmarks or models which he used, not so much to suggest the similarities with the ideas of his contemporaries but rather as a foil, sometimes almost as a caricature or with humor, to underline the deficiencies of their impoverished thought. Nestorians, Monophysites, Monothelites, Docetists and others less heterodox provided him with ideal targets for the game of pedagogical massacre.

In addition to the liturgy and reflection on Scripture and the writings of the Fathers, Beauduin was also influenced by a number of theologians—all of whom ironically enough belonged to the Society of Jesus, the order whose spirituality came in for such strong criticism from Beauduin's pen at the time of the liturgical movement. His favorites included such undisputed giants as Pétau [7] and de Régnon,[8] whose prudent reserve with regard to appropriation he greatly appreciated, particularly in the treatise on the Holy Spirit. In Christology, he made R. Prat's theology of St. Paul (1913) his bedside book; in ecclesiology he read and reread his friend Maurice de la Taille's *Mysterium Fidei* (1921) and the two volumes of Emile Mersch on the mystical body (1933). Shortly before World War II, the work of another friend, Henri de Lubac, entitled *Catholicism* (1938), delighted him; he spoke of it to everyone —a book, he used to say, that he would have liked to have written himself.

If these authors were not the real stimulus behind Beauduin's basic insights, they nevertheless encouraged his research and gave him a contemporary, scholarly assurance that he was going in the right direction. He was with them in spirit, even if his vision and the answers he formulated to specific problems were not always in harmony with theirs.

The Essence of his Thought

The late John Courtney Murray complained that "ecumenism appears as a dimension added to theology from without." It is precisely this weakness which Beauduin's ecclesial perspective avoided. The zealous Benedictine anticipated Father Murray's request "that ecumenism become a quality inherent in theology, an impulse intrinsic to Christian faith itself." [9]

The central doctrine around which Beauduin's entire thought gravitated was undoubtedly that of the body of Christ. Viewed from one aspect his accent is on the humanity of Christ; from another angle the emphasis shifts to the mystical body of Christ. An appreciation of this two-dimensional perspective is indispensable to an understanding of his ecclesiological contribution. Several important consequences immediately became apparent.

On the speculative level we realize that if Christ as head of the new humanity recapitulates in his own body the whole human race, then obviously no individual can be excluded from the Church's ecumenical concern. Likewise, since the unity of the body is the sign of man's unity with Christ, it becomes equally clear that unity and diversity, far from being in opposition, are complementary realities.

These insights were developed throughout his writings, but especially in his activity. For ecumenism to come of age, the significance of Christ's humanity had to be placed in proper focus, which explains his frequent return to the mysteries of the incarnation and of the resurrection-ascension—the alpha and omega of his Christology—to show how the cosmic reverberations of these events affect each individual. The universal repercussions of the incarnation are ratified by each individual in a unique way at the table of sacrifice, giving the Catholic a special ecumenical role.

It is not just for himself that the Catholic receives the eucharist, but for the whole world, to bring it more immediately into contact with Christ. The body of Christ achieves its true dimension only when sealed in an existential context of communion with all men—hence the eucharist's ecumenical dimension. The sacred species enflesh Christ in the Christian, initiating his slow resurrection into Christ's glorified humanity. Since Christ comes for all, the true Christian receives for all men and willingly gives himself up for them. The vital role played by the eucharist demands some unique mediation, for it transforms human beings into supernaturalized beings, and such power is not within the realm of human possibility. Christ therefore prolongs his mediatorship through the ministry of especially deputed and ordained priests, chosen by God and not by man.

Human mediation tends to become formalized into visible rites and systems, but a smoothly run operation is not Christ's ultimate goal in establishing his body here on earth. All men have a single goal—life *in the bosom of the Father*. Structures are given as aids; as such, they are neither absolutely essential nor absolutely immutable, a point dramatically demonstrated in liturgical reform since Vatican II. While perhaps not all would have been to his liking, the pastoral inspiration of the changes certainly would have met with his approval.

So long as the essence of the redemptive act is maintained in its purity and made accessible to mankind, the objective of Christ's sacrifice can be achieved. Beauduin therefore placed a great emphasis on living these key doctrines and none at all on convert-making, believing example to be a far more powerful influence than any theological arguments. Since visible membership is not a sure sign of salvation, the far greater urgency obviously is not more members but a deeper penetration into the mystery of redemption. A poorly understood Catholicism which borders on the magical or a conversion of convenience can effectively inhibit if not prevent an authentic relationship with the Father, whereas the Christian living *in the bosom of the Father* radiates the fruits of the resurrection and brings humanity that much closer to its universal fulfillment.

No matter how one approaches Beauduin's ecclesiology, Christ is always at the center—either in his glorified humanity, or in the eucharist which makes his humanity accessible to man, or in the priesthood which makes him present in our midst as priest and victim. These doctrines reaffirm his prayer "that they may be one." Their sole purpose is to draw all men into Christ, who points beyond to his Father. As our priest, Christ's desire is that he may lead us *into the bosom of the Father.* This then is the theological essence of Beauduin's ecclesiology. Ecumenism, far from being a postscript in his theology, became an inherent quality of it, an impulse intrinsic to his Christian life and faith. Recent literature echoes his concern, for men like G. E. Wright and W. Pannenberg have emphasized the danger of Christomonism and the necessity of going beyond Christ to the Father.

Not content with the doctrine and theological debates of his day as presented in the standard texts, Beauduin demanded more stimulating material which he ferreted out not only by going back to the traditional sources of the Roman Church but also by familiarizing himself with the theological contributions of other ecclesial communities, Protestant as well as Orthodox. Inspired by their theological traditions and by a respect for the insights of every age and culture, Beauduin found valid intuitions outside the confines of Catholicism and admitted it—a thing almost unheard of at the time. From such a broad spectrum of influences he formulated the principles of his theological thought. Orthodoxy provided one of the richest mines for both liturgical and ecclesiological reflections,[10] Protestantism added additional insights,[11] and he appears to have received his first solid insight into collegiality from an Anglican.[12]

Beauduin's ecclesiology rested on two fundamental principles of the Christian tradition: the recapitulation of all humanity in Christ's humanity and the canonization of a plurality of members (parts) as seen in the symbol of the body. Although he was ready to admit that Orthodoxy, Anglicanism and Protestantism represented three distinct problems, he refused to see them in isolation one from another, which was what his adversaries demanded. To extend the hand of fellowship in just one direction was not ecumenism at all. All mankind was called to an equal participation in Christ. No one had the right arbitrarily to decide a priority in this matter for a particular group. Nor could the distinctive problems of one ecclesial group be grasped if taken out of the universal context of disunion. Malines had taught him two things: what is different in other Churches from Roman Catholic tradition or custom is not *de facto* anathema, and the challenge of union, as well as the responsibility for it, is directed to every single individual—on both sides. All of his subsequent activity was colored by this conviction.

Thus, in passing from the speculative to the practical, the ecumenical quality of Beauduin's ecclesiology is further strengthened. His ideas on the actual structure of the Church reveal a concern for a more vital ecclesial life which will have no part in religious chauvinism or vested interests. While the spiritual renewal of both clergy and laity would heighten the hierarchic nature of the Church, this achievement should not be limited to a merely visible face-lifting. A deeper probing into the meaning of Christianity could only result in a fuller ecclesial life for all—bishops, priests and laity. And even here he placed the benefit to be derived in the broader context of ecumenism. Before profitable dialoguing with another was possible, one's own ecclesial role needed to be clarified and true community established within the family.

Faced with the justified criticism of other Christians who, perhaps because of their distance, were capable of greater objectivity and more aware of contradictions within the institutional Church, Beauduin did not hesitate to call a spade a spade. As a Roman Catholic he was careful to distinguish between the mutable and the immutable, something which the Orientals of his day often failed to do in their rejection of Rome. On the other hand, he was the first to condemn abuses (the external elements of religion, particularly in matters of canon law pertaining to liturgy and to interpersonal relations—e.g., the problem of authority, etc.) which were in opposition to the principles of Christianity on which they were supposedly based. Not content with a humble admission of fault within the Church of Rome, he went to the heart of the matter and tried to remedy the situation, urging that those variable elements of the Church which alienate others be eliminated "for the spiritual life . . . of all men."

The Mystical Body

Perhaps the most pertinent problem in ecumenism today is the notion of hierarchic authority, a matter best understood in the context of the mystical body which recapitulates the hierarchic nature of the Church. Unfortunately, in the first decades of this century, the Church as the mystical body of Christ was not even mentioned in many theological treatises on the Church, undoubtedly due to the voices raised against it at Vatican I as too vague and mysterious a concept. Some few, however, did give it a brief postscript in a *scolion dogmaticum.*[13] In Beauduin's system, its importance was capital:

> The idea of unity is more than a material unity. . . . There is only one doctrine which concerns union: that of the Church, of the mystical body. . . . It is the growth of the body, the full measure of Christ, that alone interests us. . . . This unity is the supreme desire of Christ; thus there is no more "catholic" work than that of union. [14]

It is therefore important to note the emphasis that Beauduin gave to this doctrine from the beginning of his teaching career. He had even given serious thought himself to a major work on the nature of the Church to remedy this lack, but his wanderings and his many activities thwarted any such project.

In 1926, however, one of his former students, Bruno Reynders, asked for an outline on the mystical body of Christ and received the following letter and outline: [15]

> I've thought much about your thesis topic, but in the midst of a thousand disparate occupations, I have had difficulty collecting my thoughts. I ought to say that it's my deep affection for you which has helped me to come up at last with this sketch. I give you my most intimate thought on the Church, the idea that I would have liked to have developed in a treatise. You will do that better than I. . . .

The Church: The Body of Christ

I. *Doctrinal part*
   1. Revelation on this question: St. John and St. Paul.
   2. Tradition on this question: St. Ignatius of Antioch, St. Irenaeus, St. Athanasius, St. Gregory of Nyssa, St. Augustine and St. Ambrose, Peter Lombard, and St. Thomas.
   3. The teaching of the Church on this question, especially the Council of Florence,[16] the Council of Trent and the Vatican Council.

II. *Theological speculation on the corpus Christi mysticum*
   1. Figurative explanation: insufficient.
   2. Humanity of Christ, instrumental cause of our entire spiritual life; channel of every grace; in this sense all the faithful would be as his members (still insufficient).

3. Humanity of Christ, exemplary cause: which contains under this heading, all the initiations which reflect it; also under this heading, the humanity of Christ contains in it every individual humanity (true sense of this aspect of the *corpus Christi mysticum*).

4. Explanation founded on the hypostatic union of the humanity with the Word. Under this heading the humanity of Christ acquires a universality communicated by the Logos to the flesh which he has assumed. Thence a certain incorporation of every individual humanity in Christ, (reminiscent of universals and Platonic ideas). These are theological speculations which are very useful and fruitful, but free.

III. The doctrine of the *corpus Christi mysticum* in Catholic, Orthodox and Protestant ecclesiology. Conclusion for the idea of the union of Churches.

Since the humanity of Christ recapitulates in itself all humanity and the Church is none other than the whole Christ, the incarnate God mystically united to the members of his Body, Beauduin's ecclesiology was intimately linked to his Christology.

The Humanity of Christ

While many factors explain the weakness of ecclesiology at the turn of the nineteenth century, Beauduin seemed to single out a deficient Christology as the principal cause for this situation. All Monophysite tendencies and Mariological exaggerations called forth strong words of condemnation on his part. He considered some highly esteemed authors in his day to be tottering on the brink of heresy. The misplaced stress on Christ's divinity in recent centuries had spawned a form of practical Monophysitism from which Christ's manhood had lost its true place.[17] Beauduin was one of the first to react against this theological error. With the devaluation of Christ's human nature, Mariology assumed an ever increasing and, to Beauduin's mind, totally disproportionate importance.

One day, conversing with Guardini, the two fully agreed that unless something was done the future heresy would be Mariolatry.[18] In spite of the arguments offered in its favor, one title particularly abhorrent to Beauduin was that of "mediatrix." The idea of a

Marian mediation toward the Father, an idea actively promoted by
Mercier, shocked Beauduin and brought him once again into conflict
with a man whom he deeply respected.[19] He preferred to honor
Mary at her Son's side where through her *fiat* she introduces us into
the mystery of the Church. Some Mariologists, according to Beauduin, were guilty of emptying the incarnation of its profound
theological content:

> The Holy Virgin is closer to us than our Lord—what a blasphemy
> against the whole economy of the incarnation . . . and the effect of
> this Mariology on our separated brothers. . . . You probably think I
> am willing to sacrifice truth for the sake of reconciliation. But this
> is very serious: there is only one priest . . . one victim, and it is
> this singular sacrifice of the only priest which has reconciled us.
> *No* creature can intervene in order to add some additional efficacy
> to this redemption by the only eternal priest. . . . Christ, *man-
> mediator* between us and his Father—that is the great truth. What
> is serious is that for this unique, visible, human, divine, eternal,
> priesthood, they substitute a sanctifying action, invisible and trans-
> cendent, in which Mary and the Holy Spirit collaborate mysteri-
> ously outside the visible and priestly economy of Christ and his
> Church. . . . It's a kind of Catholic Protestantism.[20]

Happily the warnings of John XXIII and the precautions of the
council averted this danger. The title of mediatrix was recognized,
it is true, but only in a series of other titles, and the conciliar fathers
took pains to underline that nothing could be taken away from
Christ as sole and universal mediator (*Constitution on the Church*,
n. 60).

A prelate, provoked by such declarations in this vein, one day
asked a friend of Beauduin's what the latter would say if suddenly the
Virgin appeared to him. When this remark was reported to him,
Beauduin was quick to reply: "What would I say? 'Most Holy
Virgin, I love you very much, but I still love your Son much more.'"
This response is not unrelated to a remark he made several times to
his disciples: "I love Christ to the point of madness!" (*J'aime le Christ
à la folie!*) And by that he meant Christ, God and man. "We are not
Nestorian enough," he declared one day during a retreat for priests
in an attempt to make them understand the tragic loss of a sense of
the humanity of Christ in modern piety.

Another devotion which he seemed to appreciate very much before his liturgical conversion—devotion to the Sacred Heart—became a thorn in his side when he realized that the sentimental surcharge, brought about by the way in which this devotion was little by little spreading, put the true character of the humanity of Christ in the dark. Thus, what should have been the true cult of the Christ-man rarely saw the light of day. His efforts to correct this loss of proper perspective were left unfinished, but his initial contribution traced the influence of St. John Eudes before the exaggerations of the devotees of Paray-le-Monial appeared on the scene.[21] These anecdotes show how constant was his preoccupation that the mystery of Christ's humanity not only be appreciated but also—and even more important—that it form the heart of the Christian's daily meditation, for the significance of the Christian life would never be grasped in isolation from this mystery.

The Christmas liturgy also provided Beauduin with a fundamental argument for and ideal résumé of his doctrine of the humanity of Christ. Its emphasis on the social and collective nature of the redemptive mystery inaugurated through the incarnation clearly established Christ as the source of a new relation between God and humanity.[22] For Beauduin, this mystery is a revelation of God's intense will for union with man. Faced with man's refusal through sin and rather than impose his will, God accomplished this union with the cooperation of man through the incarnation. Christ became *true man* and conferred through this mystery a veritable consecration on the whole of humanity.[23] The essence of this mystery is:

[Christ] makes this image of the Father, which he is, accessible to us. This human birth transposes the eternal begetting of the Son by the Father into the order of realities where we move about daily.[24]

The trip to the Holy Land in 1929 impressed Beauduin, as nothing else had, of the theological urgency to come to grips with the reality of Christ's humanity:

What a Christian revelation it is to spend some time here! Now I know our Lord much better. He is truer, more human, more materialized. Here the mystery of the incarnation stands out in relief.

Verbum caro hic factum est. [Here the Word was made flesh.]
And so too with the whole economy of the Old Testament: the
entire preparation for Christianity by the old law becomes an
integral part of the redemption. We are not Jewish enough and
too Monophysite: those are two impressions from my stay here.
. . . A Christ not *man* enough and not *Messiah* enough—that, it
seems to me, is the defect of our Christianity.[25]

Because of the centrality of the humanity of Christ in his theology,
Beauduin demanded great precision in its presentation and did not
hesitate to criticize weak or ambiguous statements. A series of letters
to Charles Moeller, one of his special disciples, who subsequently
became secretary of the Congregation of the Faith, best illustrates this
concern. He singled out the following line from one of Moeller's
articles: "No doubt, the soul of Jesus never acted separately from
the divine will," [26] and then in a friendly manner expressed his
reservations.

No doubt what follows corrects this expression; but "never acts
separately" seems to diminish the capital truth of the human and
free will, distinct from the divine will. I should have preferred
"contrary" to "separately."

Having made this point, Beauduin then developed the Monophysite
danger he sensed in the article:

I am stupefied to notice how this concern for apologetics and controversy in order to demonstrate the divinity of Christ warps many
minds and almost prevents them from insisting on the specifically
human acts of redemption. I do not like your sentence: "We then
have a tendency to see in him only the man, the perfect model of
humanity." But it's by that that we must begin! The apostles at
first saw only a man; by following him they saw his wisdom, his
goodness and his miracles, and finally, after a good many hesitations,
they concluded to his divinity. . . . Man first, who leads us to God:
in short, the incarnation.[27]

In a later letter, Beauduin returned to the same topic:

I feel that your key idea is *to restore the sense* of the humanity of
Christ which has totally disappeared; in my opinion, this is the

great dearth, the singular want of modern Christian life; there is no longer any human mediator to go to the Father; therefore there is no longer any Christianity; we have arrived at a religion of the good God as subject, object, end, and means of our whole religion.

The Lateran Synod of 653 and Constantinople III (680–681) received high praise from Beauduin for the strong anti-Monothelite positions taken. But the errors condemned in the seventh century still threatened the true manhood of Christ in the twentieth century. In comparison, Chalcedon seemed to have stuttered and hesitated before this great mystery of the incarnation, handicapped as it was by an inadequate philosophical framework, a theological vocabulary just in the first stage of development and as yet incapable of capturing and expressing East-West differences, and the undue influence of Cyrillian theology. It is interesting to note that he made a similar criticism of St. Thomas. Of all the tracts of the Angelic Doctor, his treatment of the incarnation in the *Summa* is the poorest because it favored Monophysitism:

It is the apostolic glitter of this illustrious falsifier Denys which troubled the vision of St. Thomas. The humanity of Christ, instrument of the divinity! That's pitiful. . . . I am psychologically convinced that Severus of Antioch is the author of Pseudo-Denys: it's exactly his method and way of acting. I have also well understood . . . the somewhat Monophysite character of the Byzantine liturgy; while in the Latin liturgy everything is: per Dominum *nostrum* (through *our* Lord). . . . You have put into form the vague intuitions of my whole life.[28]

Monophysitism was not the only contemporary danger that Beauduin attacked. Docetism, which led to a minimizing of the importance of Christ's physical body in the spiritual life, was another modern resurgence of the ancient malady against which he vigorously warned.[29] In trying to make the reality of this physical body more apparent to his audiences he carefully avoided any theological ambiguities. The Christ he spoke of was the Christ he knew, the living Christ and hence the glorified Christ. This precision is fundamental in his theology.

Although he did not contract original or actual sin, the Word is true man . . . with all the faculties of the human soul. . . . He is a man, not a human nature. He did not come to be adored but to teach us to adore the Father. Our whole spiritual life of union with God, with the Father, is *in* Christ Jesus. Where is this Christ? In glory. We contemplate the historical Christ only after first entering into intimacy with the glorified Jesus.[30]

The theme of the consecration of humanity associated by Beauduin with the mystery of the incarnation is closely connected in his writings with the principle of solidarity which makes Christ's life and death ours:

[It] groups all humanity into a vast moral organism of which Christ is the head. . . . His whole terrestrial work is above all collective and belongs to the whole of humanity.[31]

If the language he used in 1919 appears dated today, the same thoughts can be found expressed in a more contemporary manner in 1942:

I would like to understand more and more thoroughly the two thoughts of which we have spoken so much: the *cosmic* character of the work of the new Adam, divine life having touched human nature in one of its points which is the singular human nature of Christ; the whole race and even the whole universe, each according to its own nature . . . participates in this divine contagion. And besides, the event of the incarnation already confers a consecration to our race.[32]

The gravity of the Christological crisis such as it was sensed by Beauduin is best expressed in the following excerpt from a letter summing up the theological disappointments of a lifetime:

There are many things which sadden me in theology, not to mention the doctrine of the incarnation. You know the essentials. But how completely different and secondary they appear to contemporary theologians with Monophysite leanings.
(a) The word *substantial* applied to the union of the human nature to the person of the Word. If there were a fusion of the two natures, one would not express it differently. Isn't there a Monophysite hint in this invocation in the Litany of the Sacred

Heart: Heart of Jesus substantially united in the Word of God (*Cor Jesus verbo dei substantialiter unitum*)? It is at least equivocal, because for many "substantial" is a synonym for nature. Would not the word "ontological" be less dangerous?

(b) And this *substantial* sanctity which the man Jesus ought to possess by the unique fact of the hypostatic union, how much I distrust it; yes, an infinite exigence for his human nature to be sanctified by the gift of grace, the gift which divinizes man. But this substantial sanctity is then ontological by the very fact of the hypostatic union. It is indeed dangerous, all the more so since sanctifying grace in him is treated as an *accident* (a dangerous word that many theologians willingly juggle about in discussing this created grace).

(c) And the whole question of the knowledge of Christ, what a swarm of little (human) Monophysites and what a dangerous hornets' nest. All these apologists have only one concern: to save the divinity; the humanity is secondary. The incarnation bothers them.[33]

Although occasionally criticized for an improper use of theological terms, Beauduin nevertheless consistently gave evidence of an awareness of and a genuine sensitivity to the true meaning of these technical words as well as a serious concern about the subtle abuses to which they are so easily lent in the hands of a careless practitioner.

Beauduin found it impossible to consider the incarnation apart from the paschal mystery, since through the paschal events the reality of the incarnation, the principle of solidarity in Christ, became theologically evident. While Easter marked the birth of a new humanity,[34] the ascension stressed the mystery of Christ's return to the Father and the entry of his transfigured humanity into a glorious and everlasting reign. This principle of solidarity in Christ can only be grasped in its fullness in terms of this eternal triumph, for the Son's return and the Father's acceptance of his Son's humanity become an everlasting pledge to man not only of the divine acceptance of the human condition but of the radical elevation of this limited reality so that it may participate forever in infinity.

Because this new humanity is the core around which Beauduin's ecclesiology moved, one cannot understand the Church without first penetrating into the inner sanctuary, into the glorified humanity of Christ.

And the center of the mystery of the Church, the unique point of convergence, is the glorified humanity of Christ . . . of which the Church is the fullness and continual realization until he will have attained his full stature. The Church is the resurrection of the dead, and, following the example of the first-born, it is the great mystical cosmos, this great reality in which everything is renewed each day a little more here below, which we are to see, contemplate, and love, for which and in which we are to live. The spirit of the faith gives us eyes only to see that; everything else, all the physical, psychological, ethnic phenomena which make up the apparent world—the only reality for animal-man—all else is nothing for us. There is only one single reality, the risen one who re-creates the world of the first Adam, who restores all things in himself, who by his spouse has brought forth his new humanity. The one who sees and lives this alone has faith; the one who does not penetrate through the shadows which surround this great supernatural cosmos believes perhaps in some dogmatic formulae but he does not have living faith; he does not see. . . . They contemplate the cathedral from the outside; but one must enter into the sanctuary to see the mystery of the Church: and the true Church is in heaven because the substantial sacrament and the source of all is there.[35]

The whole of the great supernatural organism, of the tremendous reality of the invisible world (but much more real than the visible world), of the mystical body which envelops us, is the glorified body of the risen Christ. He is the man seated at the right hand of the Father, our contemporary, *our all*. The historical, suffering, eucharistic Christ . . . the glorious Christ, in heaven, the only definitive reality, absolute, central, and source of the entire supernatural order.[36]

The same cosmic dimensions recognized by Beauduin in the incarnation are also found in the resurrection. Contrary to what might be supposed, the frequent use of this term "cosmic" is not the reflection of some Chardinian influence but the expression of a Thomistic perspective.[37] The whole Christian mystery is therefore seen as a gradual resurrection of the human species into the life of God. The consecration of mankind, inaugurated by the incarnation and accomplished in Christ through his glorification, is continued by the Holy Spirit in the Church.

His masterpiece is the God-man, from the moment of his formation in the womb of Mary even to the glorification. He [the Holy Spirit] reproduces this masterpiece in every member of the Church. The Church is the great sacramental in which he acts, the body in which and by which he accomplishes his mission as herald of Christ.[38]

Beauduin's theology of the resurrection, with its redemptive and ecclesial connotations, was clearly developed by 1920. Firmly convinced of the doctrinal advantages offered by a realized eschatology (to be understood in terms of a dynamic "taking place now"—in other words, initiated but not completed), he recognized that only a *living* faith makes the reality of this truth evident. The Church clearly had a vital role to play in this matter:

Easter marks for the whole of humanity the end of an era and inaugurates a new economy, a collective triumph. . . . The mission of the Church is to realize these salvific events in us, to associate us intimately with them, to make us enter into their reality, and to make them present, tangible and contemporary.[39]

Hence, an understanding of the role of Christ's humanity as the link tying man to the Godhead in a new relationship was basic to Beauduin's theology and the source of the deepseated unity which harmonized the profound tendencies in his life. This unity was revealed to him by his thorough knowledge of the traditional doctrine of the Church as the mystical and social body of Christ, but it was never divorced from his profoundly trinitarian spirituality.

The Trinity

Beauduin delighted in disconcerting people and particularly in teasing novices with the disarming query: "Do you believe in God?" To the only logical answer his victims ever offered, he would reply with gentle humor and a very knowing look: "But there is no God—just Father Son and Holy Spirit."

At the end of the nineteenth century, de Régnon reopened the issue of the nature of this relationship. In its broadest terms the question was: Does the Christian stand in a proper person-to-person relationship with the three persons of the Trinity or is he related to the Godhead as a whole? Another way of inquiring into this relationship was to ask whether the Christian could be properly called a "son of God" or a "son of the Father"? Here it is not the controversy in itself but Beauduin's position on the matter which interests us. One sensed that for him there was no question at all about the nature of the relationship. His spiritual life drew its nourishment from three very real and very personal friendships.

It is not surprising then that the theme of the Trinity was never far from the tip of his tongue, for it concerned not a dry, academic debate but the very reality about which his entire life was centered. His only purpose through his talks and retreats was to plunge individuals more profoundly into the mystery of life which for him was summed up beautifully in the mystery of the Trinity, wherein we first encountered the Holy Spirit who incorporated us into the Son, and then through the Son were led into the bosom of the Father—*in sinum Patris,* our true goal.

> This same and unique life, according to an eternal decree, is communicated by *grace* to creatures . . . [angels and men], whence the *Church,* the extension of divine life to a group of creatures. The glorious life of the Father becomes, by grace, a good common to God and to all those he calls to share in it: *that is the Church.* The very life of God, God's way of living, the very objects of the life God shared, the divine society itself, the family life of God extended to humanity—all this proceeds from the *bosom of the Father* (Jn. 1:18). The Church then is the community of those who are called to enter into part of the heritage of the Father and of the goods of the alliance.[40]

Through his studies of Scripture and the Fathers, Beauduin early discovered a certain theological inconsistency in trinitarian doctrine.[41] The theological development of processions and relations found in the theological textbooks of his day somewhat failed to express the profound implications of the teaching in St. Paul and the early Roman liturgy. Because in the incarnation an individual human nature entered into a unique relationship with the divine nature, every human nature is in a potential relationship with Father, Son, and Holy Spirit. The full significance of this fundamental insight slowly dawned on Beauduin. In 1932 he realized that a certain understanding of the mystery of divine filiation is an indispensable prerequisite preceding any penetration of the mystery of the Trinity.

Referring to the prayer before communion which speaks of the action of the Trinity *ad extra*, Beauduin voiced a position not generally held by Western theologians in the 1920's and 1930's on the matter of appropriation versus propriation. The standard view saw man in one relation only to God who is Father, Son and Holy Spirit. Like de Régnon, Beauduin envisaged three distinct and proper relations which can be explained as a single relationship to three divine persons:

> Our sanctification is not only the projection in time and in our race of the activity *ad intra* in the bosom of the Father. The action of Christ in the present phase of the realization of the great plan of the Father is to send us the Holy Spirit—that is, to transmit to us his whole life and all his riches by the action of the Holy Spirit in the Church, in the sacraments, and in the souls of the faithful. This mission is not an attitude taken at one moment and transmitted like an order but a continual operation and an intimate and profound cooperation, a continual fruitfulness [in our regard].

This relationship to the Holy Spirit is not to the detriment of our relationship to Christ. To live in intimacy with the Holy Spirit is to live in intimacy with Christ.

> Intimacy with Christ is acquired only in the Spirit. Thus there is a double mission, just as there is a double procession in the life *ad intra* . . . without impairing . . . our relationships with the three persons. The sacraments are the instruments adopted by Christ by which the Holy Spirit accomplishes his mission. This is especially true in the holy eucharist: the body of Christ acts in us by the action of the Holy Spirit.[42]

Beauduin's initial insight into this complex area of theology appears in a developed treatise on the Trinity as the object of the liturgy in a chapter of *Essai* written in 1914. Starting from the premise that Christian life begins and ends in the name of the Trinity and that no end other than the Trinity is proposed by the Church for worship, Beauduin concluded that the liturgical formulae properly known as presidential prayers [43] are affirmations of trinitarian unity as well as of a real indispensable distinction of persons. Moreover, if Christians fail to live the dogma of the Trinity, then their religious life will insensibly degenerate into an impersonal monotheism, a vague Christianity.[44] Continuing in the same article, he discussed the matter of appropriation and carefully pointed out that the liturgy does not always use the term in a strictly theological sense:

But notice, and we insist on this remark, we do not use the word "appropriations" here in the exclusive sense which theology gives it, in opposing it to the operations strictly proper to each person. The liturgy constantly appropriates, leaving to the scientific study of dogma the concern of determining in which cases the appropriated work is truly proper to a certain person; in which cases . . . we are in the presence of a logical process, justified without doubt by the objectivity of the mystery and our powerlessness to express it perfectly, but without reality in God.

Thus for the liturgy the Father is creator, the Son is redeemer, and the Holy Spirit is sanctifier. In the first case, it is an appropriation in the theological sense of the word; in the second, a work strictly proper to the Son; in the third, the Church has not pronounced. . . . Happily the ancient opinion of a proper work seems to prevail. . . . We will call the method of appropriation in the liturgy the process which consists of assigning to each person of the Holy Trinity a role formally distinct in our supernatural life, whether that role is strictly proper to that person or not.[45]

To support this position Beauduin argued more from expediency than anything else:

If the properties which distinguish the persons in God are not concretized, made living and perceptible in the operations and works that we see and touch, the dogma of the Trinity will enter neither into the understanding nor into the hearts of the faithful. Since the liturgy and the Gospel are not metaphysical speculations reserved for an intellectual elite, but truths put into act and translated into acts of faith and love by the Christian people, the divine persons have to be humanized and clothed, each with a person and independent activity.[46]

Appropriation therefore helps to preserve a distinction of persons in the unity of the Trinity. Beauduin was actually grappling with a much deeper problem than he realized: the effect of a centuries-old tradition of predominantly non-trinitarian piety. Piety, in his vocabulary, was not a spiritual anesthetic or vague euphoric feeling but the most vital aspect of man's life here on earth which drew the dynamism from doctrinal, not emotional sources. While it is difficult to assess the impact of de Régnon on Beauduin's thought, since only one reference in this essay is given to the trinitarian scholar, Beauduin's whole life was certainly one enthusiastic *Amen* to the Jesuit scholar's rhetorical question:

> Wouldn't it be opportune to refresh our teaching at the primitive sources, to reawaken in the Christian people their former familial life with the Father—by the Son—in the Spirit of the Father and the Son? [47]

It should be evident from the quotations given that Beauduin had his own distinctive position on appropriations derived primarily from the liturgy, an understanding which is perhaps more closely related to the contemporary discussion of appropriations and which corrects it. In 1914 he had said: "The method of appropriation in the liturgy is the process which consists of assigning to each person of the Holy Trinity a role formally distinct in our supernatural life." By 1946 his position was clearly defined.

> In the supernatural order, they make an appropriation of language in saying that the Father is God, the Son is Wisdom, and the Holy Spirit is Love. . . . That's appalling. . . . *there is no appropriation in the supernatural order.* . . . The Father has sent us his Son and the Holy Spirit. *It is the Father who sends his Son, not the good God, and that's the heart of the whole matter.* Therefore, in the domain of truths which God had come to reveal to us, we are in the divine order, we are in the divine life, and we must no longer speak of appropriation. . . . Our Lord appropriates nothing; he applies all to the Father and to the Holy Spirit. It is the incarnation which makes the order supernatural and is proper to the person of the Son. . . . There is no longer anything but the supernatural order which Christ came to establish. . . . Appropriation is the negation of all great dogmas.[48]

It is the Holy Spirit who accomplishes the definitive taking possession of the world inaugurated by the incarnation. He is not a
footnote to the divine plan but a vital and indispensable part of it;
yet this fundamental truth continues to struggle for recognition in
the West. Beauduin thus stands out for his attempts to draw attention to the role of the Holy Spirit in the divine economy and to
replace the general vagueness that has obscured the person of the
Holy Spirit in the minds of the faithful for centuries with some
small idea of the dynamic force that the Spirit has played in the
world since his activity first burst forth in the Person of Christ. Such
efforts gained wider publicity in the debates at Vatican II and in the
action taken by the council fathers and the post-conciliar commissions
they established.

Subsequent liturgical reforms have included the ancient *epiclesis*
or calling down of the Spirit in several of the new eucharistic prayers,
but widespread skepticism frequently greets any mention of the
prophetic element in the Church or any encouragement or endorsement of pentecostal groups. The consistently cool reception offered
to the Holy Spirit in the life of the Church, in her liturgy, theology
and spirituality, has led some to conclude that we need yet another
council to define the role of the Holy Spirit.

In his campaign on behalf of the Holy Spirit, Beauduin was thinking primarily in terms of how he takes possession of man through
the sacraments and pre-eminently through the eucharist. Thus, for
true life, man must be animated by the Holy Spirit. For Beauduin,
the eucharist was synonymous with the Church penetrated with the
same Spirit that filled Christ because it was the body of Christ. Its
true meaning, therefore, and value, weakened by centuries of neglect,
needed to be reaffirmed, and it was imperative that a eucharistic piety
which had become marginal be put into proper perspective.

The Eucharist and its Liturgical Dimension

Beauduin never tired exploring the theological riches of the eucharistic sacrifice, for the principal message of liturgy was the theme of his
whole spirituality: through Christ's glorified humanity we are related to the Trinity. But its significance was even deeper, for in
the liturgy the Church's collective character received its maximum

intensity. Thus the eucharist did more than symbolize the Church; it *made* the Church, which once again highlights the social aspect of Beauduin's thought.

> This eucharistic theme traced with grand strokes by the Fathers— how full of meaning was this mystery! The eucharist—commemorative, sacrificial, *communal*. This last aspect is especially rich; the ecclesial body of Christ realizes itself by this divine principle, acting in a permanent manner in the very heart of the society of the faithful: truly, the eucharist makes the Church.[49]

In an age which emphasized the destruction of the victim and the propitiatory value of the Mass, [50] Beauduin was remarkable for the positive stress he placed on the notion of sacrifice and the ends for which it is offered. Preferring to develop the Mass from its aspect of banquet as a sacrifice of thanksgiving and of praise, his most detailed treatment is found in *Essai*. It insisted primarily on the theological foundations and predated by some twenty-five years his debate with Capelle on the subject.[51]

Sacrifice is a religious act, formally social, and accomplished by a priestly minister who represents a community unanimously united in an act of worship which is thereby both public and hierarchic. It seals the reciprocal exchange of love and fidelity. If there is no perceptible sign of the convergence and unification of the worshiping dispositions of the whole community, the sacrifice is deprived of its social character. Beauduin's understanding and appreciation of the eucharistic transformation clearly foreshadowed the modern emphasis which insists upon the paramount importance of the social dimension of sacrifice.

> By this transformation, the matter becomes the expression of the worship of the whole community; it is clothed with a cultic significance; it receives a sacred destination; it synthesizes and incarnates the religion of the collectivity. And this identification is so intimate that the true victim of the sacrifice is in all reality the community itself, much more so than the material oblation which is reduced after transformation to the role of symbol.[52]

The choice of the verb "reduced" is unfortunate, open as it is to a minimizing interpretation of the gifts involved. However, if we give "symbol" its maximal meaning—as a real participation in that which it signifies—any serious equivocation in Beauduin's statement can be avoided. His emphasis is essentially pastoral to awaken in the worshiping community an intense awareness of their total involvement in the action at the altar. In contrast to the rather passive role of the bread and wine, they, the people of God, are called to give themselves actively to the Father, to one another and for one another, just as Christ freely and unreservedly gave of himself.

One of the greatest evils of modern piety, the misunderstanding of the true meaning of sacrifice in the eucharist, had been unwittingly fostered by Trent. Once essentials had been defined, interest shifted to non-essentials and theologians eventually lost sight of the relative value of their peripheral discussions, mistaking them for essentials to orthodoxy.[53] Theology, instead of contributing to the spiritual vitality of the Church, became in part responsible for its stagnation. Deprived of a sound understanding of sacrifice, the people became confused over the actual purpose for which Christ instituted the eucharist. Few were aware that his primary intention was to insure the incorporation of members into himself so as to consummate the sanctification of the new humanity, and consequently they remained ignorant of their social responsibility in, to and for the world.

Beauduin accentuated the positive. The Mass was a transformation rather than a destruction, and a transformation of cosmic proportions in that the entire community and even the universe itself were to some extent transformed by the action at the altar. He summed up the underlying principle concisely in these words: "The Cross merited everything and applied nothing; the Mass merits nothing and applies everything." [54]

The eucharist as the *lieu par excellence* for our encounter with Christ's humanity was important in Beauduin's thought not only for its theological and pastoral value but also as a center from which his ecumenical inspiration radiated. Because of the universal dimension of redemption, no one could be excluded from the beneficial influence of the eucharist. Especially its communal aspect as principle and root of Catholic unity became the premise on which rested the whole structure of his ecumenical position. If the transformation into a unity of cosmic proportions symbolized by the sacrament is not at the heart of one's reception, then eucharistic life remains embryonic.

He therefore concluded that the eucharist exists *in votum* (in desire) in the Protestant Churches as the only logical explanation of their serious ecumenical efforts.[55]

To achieve unity, therefore, psychological reconciliation alone is insufficient. Only when it is joined with a generous and intelligent reception of the eucharist will Christ's wish that they may be one be achieved:

Thus each Christian soul will become in the mystical body of Christ a source of unity; and here the most humble will be the most powerful. To bring this unity about, however, there are three necessary dispositions:

(1) *a profound regret for broken unity*. If we do not suffer from this separation . . . our prayers will be without *élan*, without ardor.

(2) *a need for penance and expiation*. The solidarity of the communion of saints goes both ways and is not diminished by distance in time or space. An *élan* of generosity and of fervor [through penance] will merit for us the tremendous grace of a return to unity. We must develop the supernatural concept of the Church in souls eager to associate themselves to this movement. There is in fact only one doctrine . . . in terms of which we can think the concept of religious unity . . . in all its depths and richness—that of the mystical body. And this quite interior point of view gives to . . . unity . . . an atmosphere which touches indisputably what is purest and most religious in the depths of souls.

(3) *an overflowing charity*. It is not a question of a superficial prayer . . . but a profound and supernatural state of soul of which prayer is only the faithful expression. True charity is the charity of Christ who did not hesitate to cement this union with his blood.[56]

Every Christian cements his participation in the communion of saints and reaffirms his membership in the mystical body when he receives the eucharist, for he places the problem of unity in the very context where Christ confronted it: the Last Supper. Thus in and through the eucharist, Christ puts at the disposal of each Christian the only means that he himself had: the total gift of self in love and an earnest appeal to the Father.

When the faithful are no longer content just to pray in church but seek a conscious union in Christ with their brothers and the priest, then, and only then, will they create a true community—the primary goal of the liturgy. But worship must be true to the nature of God *and* of man.[57] According to Beauduin, the success of the liturgy depended not on its becoming better understood but rather more human.[58] Of course, unless it remains in touch with the entire Church, its vitality will be seriously threatened. Only if these conditions were fulfilled would the liturgy be able to exercise its fundamental role:

The liturgy, especially if it is well understood and one day rediscovers its traditional plentitude, can contribute . . . in harmony with all the works of the apostolate, to remake not only individual Christians, but a true Christianity.[59]

Interested as he was in externals, Beauduin was much more concerned that there be first something within (a profound interior life) capable of being exteriorized. He realized it was the liturgy's task to cultivate this when many, even in clerical circles, failed to associate it in any way whatsoever with the spiritual life. The Church's official worship was therefore much more than a simple external act of ritual. The Christian who faithfully lived the liturgy developed in himself the very life of the Church. This conclusion, far from being the product of a clerically centered mentality, resulted from a profound conviction that the liturgy is the *religion of the spouse of Christ,* and hence *the* means of union with him, of living *in the bosom of the Father.*

Spurred on by his convictions, Beauduin campaigned for two liturgical innovations which he felt would develop true eucharistic piety. Without any difficulty he was able to demonstrate that these so-called innovations—concelebration [60] and the distribution of communion during Mass [61]—were not only based on sound theological doctrine but had once been standard practice in the Church.

The capital reason for the eucharist *at* Mass is the notion of sacrifice and the natural union of parts with the whole. Communion is part of the sacrifice; it is its consummation and participation. . . .

Eating is the physical act by which we identify with the victim, transform it into our life, signify our solidarity with it, and affirm that the acts of religion expressed by the victim are ours. On the cross Christ was humanity; that is why he should not be alone at Mass. The Mass is our chance to participate.[62]

Undoubtedly it would have been theologically more precise to say that we are transformed into the victim whom we receive and that our acts of religion become his. Once again Beauduin's concern is primarily pastoral, to insist upon identification with the action of the Mass. But if the liturgy provided a point of contact between God and man, it also provided a meeting place for men.

The eucharist remained the center from which radiated all his efforts for Church unity. It was only natural then that he should make the liturgy the focal point of his foundation at Amay-Chevetogne where the co-existence of the two rites was to teach his monks to pray with other cultures and to enter into different traditions of thought and spirituality, stimulating in turn a mutual growth and hastening a common participation in the eucharist.

Rarely did Beauduin lift the veil on his own interior life; however, thanks to the foresight of several of his friends who preserved his letters, yet another dimension of his eucharistic piety has been preserved. To them he revealed his own priestly consciousness.

The Ministry of the Priesthood

In the light of Beauduin's long-standing interest in clerical education and spiritual formation, it is not surprising that true priestly piety for him centered on the Mass (which included a humble surrender to the mind of the Church) and found its extension throughout the day in the Divine Office. Certainly he would view with alarm the growing disenchantment with the breviary in clerical circles today, as well as the disregard of liturgical norms. Prayer was the very heart of any Christian vocation, and if the ministers themselves failed to inculcate a sense of humble dependence through their own prayer life, what hope was there for a healthy lay spirituality?

Anticipating Vatican II's reminder to priests of their ministerial role in this regard by over thirty years, and with the memory of his own experience with the Labor Chaplains still fresh in his mind, Beauduin could not insist enough on the true nature of the priest's social ministry.

> Each order confers on us a ministry, a function in the sacrifice which is the essential of the life of the Church. And as the Church is visible, she introduces us into our social functions by a public act, visible to all; by an investiture we are invested with our functions. And this investiture by a society that is at once visible and invisible produces this double effect, *ex opere operantis ecclesiae* [by the work of the Church operating]. She places you at the visible and invisible height of your functions. You must see your new order in the grandeur and love of Holy Mother Church: it is for her and not for yourself that you enter into orders.[63]

The priesthood is therefore not primarily a reward or a privilege for the one who is called to ordination but a challenge and a task. The candidate has a lifetime mission to sanctify and consecrate:

> And then our whole day by this oblation (*our* Mass, our offering poured out each day with Christ's offering) is consecrated to our Lord, is *sacri*-ficed, is *sancti*-fied: all of that is the same thing. And that is not only for us but for all our brothers, for the whole mystical body and especially for those whose sanctification will be confided to us later.[64]

This sanctification can be accomplished only if proper preparations are made, and Beauduin was adamant in his insistence on the necessity of continuing one's theological formation as well as deepening one's spirituality. Only one concern motivated him: the responsibility that a priest accepted to nourish the life he was called on to communicate.

> You must ask the Holy Spirit to preserve this gift of a taste for theology and always to find therein nourishment for your spiritual life; this will be precious for your whole priestly life. Don't worry too much about obscure points and theological arguments. What is important for us is to assimilate the substance of the revealed truths and to permeate our being with it. Proofs can come in second place. We are not made, I believe, to defend dogma apologetically

against adversaries; there are enough apologists for whom theology appears only under this perspective; as for us, we want to live from it substantially and to have others live from it too.[65]

Two mysteries central to the Christian dispensation, the resurrection of the body and the eucharist, had particular relevance. For this reason he urged that they be made the heart of any priestly spirituality—but once again it was in view of the immediate benefit that it could mean for *others*.

And moreover, nothing is accomplished if our Father does not hand over to his Son, and to us in Him, all the riches of life, body and soul. . . . Above all I believe that for the young today, the dogma of the *carnis resurrectio* [resurrection of the body] well understood can give them such a respect for themselves, such an enthusiasm, and such a spirituality that virtue would become less burdensome for them—all the more since the eucharist has the same sense: *pignus vitae aeternae* [a pledge of eternal life].[66]

When his friends approached the moment of ordination, he tried to share with them the awe, the mystery and the challenge of the priestly vocation. On the eve of one young man's ordination, Beauduin reminded him of his share, along with all his brother priests, in the priestly role of Christ.

You will enter into the unique High Priest and you will produce with him, as him, the fruits of life. You give by this step without return the whole sense and fullness of the Christian life; you give yourself up without reserve to Christ in order to prolong in his mystical body the only work that counts here below: the slow resurrection of the human world into the life of the Father. It is a full life, a real life, a life without limit and without end that will interest you from now on—for you and for others: the interests of the Father with Christ, *pro Christo legatione fungimur* [for Christ we enjoy our mission]. . . . I feel that our hearts beat in unison, that we will spend this whole week and the days which follow the tenth of June, together exploiting without reserve the communion · of saints which is the true rendezvous of friends. And don't forget that you will receive the priesthood of unity; that the prayer of the High Priest at the Mass of the Last Supper was "that they may be one"; may this sacrament of unity take in your hands its full meaning.[67]

A priest whose day did not gravitate around and draw its inspiration from the liturgy had not yet discovered the rich treasure that was his or accepted the serious obligation conferred upon him in Holy Orders.

The careful reader will have noted the fundamental unity to Beauduin's theology. All the topics treated—mystical body, humanity of Christ, Trinity, eucharist, priesthood—are intimately related and interrelated. Compartmentalization was foreign to his thought as well as to his ecumenism. In the final chapter we shall see how these facets inspired what might be more properly called his ecclesiology and led him to criticize, sometimes rather sharply, those aspects most guilty of destroying or endangering that unity willed by Christ.

14

Toward a Reformed Church

Beauduin's ecclesiology merits attention today, not only because it summarizes one hundred years of ecclesiological developments, from 1870–1970, but also because it anticipates developments yet to come. Some will perhaps be disappointed in the contents of the pages to follow. In the light of post-Vatican II discussions, there is the danger that the casual reader will underestimate the boldness of Beauduin's thought. His ideas are pre-conciliar, and yet at a time when prudence dictated caution, Beauduin spoke out, forming minds for the future. (One of the first books on the lay role in the Church, by the German writer J. Thome, was put on the Index. In the light of more recent developments, it seems quite harmless today.)

Beauduin's stature as a prophetic figure of the twentieth century is already assured by the realization of so many advances, changes and modifications in things liturgical, ecumenical and ecclesial foreseen by him long before his death in 1960. At a time when truly ecumenical outlooks were still viewed with suspicion, his theology was universal in *conception*, drawing its inspiration from the whole body of tradition, in *comprehension*, relating its conclusions to the total Church, and in *extension*, going beyond the traditional limits of ecclesiastical concerns to the spiritual needs of mankind itself. Prior to him, no ecclesiology for centuries had incorporated as fully the social outlook of Christ or interest in the theological insights of other Christian ecclesiologies, nor had the doctrine of the mystical body assumed such ecumenical importance and extension.

It was with reason, then, that he reiterated time and again the necessity of strengthening a truly ecclesial mentality through a solid theological diet:

> I believe that the great work to accomplish for the reform of our customs is to revive an ecclesial mentality. The mind is sick, and since our spiritual life is rooted in the intellect, everything else is affected by it. To live in the Church, from the Church and for the Church—do you not think this is the true modality of the law of love of God and of neighbor? [1]

> The principal object of your intellectual preoccupations is to acquire the true ecclesial mentality whose base is constituted by a profound, complete and supernatural comprehension of theology.[2]

Beauduin saw a new world rising from the upheavals of his day and asked whether the Church should not also experience a profound evolution. Since men are free to modify their civil regimes according to the needs of the age and to suit the dispositions of the people, does not the Church of Christ have the same possibility? Emphatically not, for the Church has received from Christ a definitive and irrevocable constitution which no current of opinion or human demand had the power, let alone the right to modify. Heaven and earth will pass away, insisted Beauduin, but not the reality of the Church. While nations rise and fall the Church remains immutable. Without further clarification, such views might suggest an extreme narrowness and inflexibility. But in "Prophetic View of the Future Church," his finely nuanced presentation actually opens up untold possibilities:

> Without speaking of revolution in the political and human sense of the word, one can, one ought to envisage the legitimate and necessary evolution which the Church ought to, and can, realize under pain of remaining foreign to and dissociated from the profound modifications underway and thus failing in her ecumenical mission.[3]

The Hierarchic Nature of the Church

While many invariably relapse into impersonal terms in discussing the

Church, as if she were simply an institution, Beauduin carefully distinguished between the Church as an institution and the Church as the body of Christ. For him there was not the slightest question but that the Church as an institution was not absolutely necessary. He carefully distinguished three spheres of activity—or, as he called them, zones:

> First the central zone which is the ensemble of the countless people invited by Christ. Next the sacramental zone in the broad sense, which includes not only the sacraments but the Church, the sacramentals, the magisterium and ecclesiastical government. Finally, the third zone, historical and essentially variable. The last two zones are not absolutely necessary to the work of Christ when the tremendous good of human freedom is at stake. In certain cases, Christ applies his merits in spite of the absence of the last two zones.[4]

In discounting the absolute necessity of the visible institution, Beauduin did not exclude mediation by members of Christ's humanity, for an individual could quite conceivably be attracted to Christ through some external, visible mediation of Christ's humanity without being infallibly drawn to the institutional Church.

Beauduin much preferred, however, to describe the Church in terms of the glorious humanity of Christ, although the term "mystical body" was not foreign to his writings. Mystical, for him, meant something real but invisible which requires a sign of presence mysterious in nature, as in the case of the sacraments where an outward sign produces an effect disproportionate with the instruments.[5] Concerned that the essential visibility of the Church be recognized as fundamental to the nature of the Church, Beauduin strove tirelessly to bring the visible and invisible dimensions of the Church into a harmonious balance. Since the Christian is by definition a member of a body, his point of contact with the latter should be sensible.[6]

The imbalance brought about by the premature cessation of Vatican I was a prime factor behind this concern, and consequently his chief ecclesiological contributions lay in the pastoral application of theological conclusions long recognized as valid, although frequently ignored. His battle against a clerically dominated and oriented Church

is not yet over, but his strategy remains valid: to reintegrate the
mystery of the Church into the lives of Christians. This can be accomplished only if the mystery itself is placed at the very center of
each individual's life.

> [A] life which is in principle *in the bosom of the Father*, and which
> has brought forth fruit in the mystery of God, communicates it-
> self to us and makes us live with Christ in God a life which is the
> family life of the Father himself. The whole theme of St. Paul is
> the plan of the Father for the world through the Church. Faith
> and charity are the infinite gifts which enable us to live this family
> life of God himself. It is the life of God, transplanted, grafted on
> to us, inviscerated (*sic*) into our own human flesh, into our own
> human nature which gives us the capacity of activity properly
> divine, to adopt the views of God, the knowledge of God.[7]

His point is painfully clear. When a truly familial spirit prevails, arbitrary and occasionally abusive uses of power will no longer mark or
mar relations within the Church. Instead love, trust, consideration and
respect will prevail. Mature men will at last become free men, the
legacy bequeathed to them by their brother on Calvary.

Beauduin's conclusions regarding the structural side of the Church
provide perhaps the most provocative and timely part of his entire
ecclesiological contribution. They show him as profoundly engaged
in the reform of ecclesial structures as he had once been in the reform
of social institutions and liturgical practices.

Vatican I's proposed schema on the Church, *Pastor Aeternus*, which
had been drawn up by Schrader, a disciple of Franzelin, [8] first made
Beauduin acutely aware in 1907 of the serious structural imbalances
in the then current concept of the Church. In the light of the schema
he suddenly realized the pitiful inadequacy of standard texts on the
Church. Even though the schema reflected post-Tridentine Scholas-
ticism, the fact that the author remained open to the patristic tradition in his effort to expose the Church's properties and powers made
the document a particularly useful tool.[9]

While one might quite logically be tempted to point to Beauduin's
trial, sentence and exile as the source of his disenchantment with
Roman bureaucracy—and it most certainly reinforced his conclusions

—the decisive change in his thought dates not from the 1930's but from his professorship at Rome during the years 1921–1924.[10] It was within the very shadow of the Vatican and of the Curia that he began his campaign for a decentralization of authority within the Church, before the conception of Amay or any serious clash with Roman officialdom had occurred.

Even as he left Belgium in 1921 for his new assignment in Rome as professor of ecclesiology, he considered himself Roman in every sense of the word. The Roman Catholic Church was the true, infallible Church, possessor of the truth and defender of true Christian orthodoxy. Fortified with the same notes he had used before the war at Mont César, he had every intention of basing the course of the schema of Vatican I, but Eastern contacts and a veritable Eastern awakening on his part soon alienated his loyalties from the conciliar draft of 1870. The schema remained central but he no longer presented it in his former uncritical fashion.

Although presented from a sociological angle, the document clearly viewed the Church in terms of a human rather than a divine society. The lack of proportion between passages on the pope and those on the episcopacy was particularly disconcerting. That the ecclesiastical interest of 1870 centered around the power rather than the life of the Church was characteristic of the times. With the office of the bishop regarded almost exclusively from a juridical aspect, the hierarchy had become isolated from the community. The whole emphasis was at odds with Beauduin's new insight into the essence of the Church as a community of believers.

Granted all these historical and ideological limitations, one may well wonder why he continued to use *Pastor Aeternus* as an outline for his course. That he did is an indication not only of the non-existence of any serious text on ecclesiology in his day but also of his respect for the teaching authority of Church councils. Even if the document had never been officially promulgated *in toto*, he firmly believed that it must be accepted as a theological source in order to preserve doctrinal continuity. All future ecclesiological developments would have to spring from this unfinished conciliar draft plus the whole body of past teachings on the nature of the Church of which no synthesis existed in his day.

Beauduin presented this schema as *Constitutio Prima de Ecclesia* (the *First* Constitution on the Church)—the first of a series to come, and not as the Church's definitive teaching on the subject—and he made it the primary purpose of his course to counteract the obvious inadequacies in the proposed schema. From the Middle Ages, Western emphasis on the legislative and administrative aspects of the Church tended to obliterate the true concept of the mystical body of Christ. In his analysis he ultimately traced the outline of a Church yet to come. His interest in the episcopacy has been amply documented. It is time now to show more precisely how his ecclesiology received its radical redirection during these important years.

A New Direction

Through his contacts with the Oriental circle, the conferences he attended and his own research, Beauduin made two overwhelming discoveries which led to the revision of his own concept of the Church, a concept which he soon proclaimed from the podium of his classroom and continued to stress in articles, conferences, and conversations throughout the rest of his life.

The first challenge to his Roman concept of the Church was offered by a closer examination of Eastern ecclesiology which proved to be founded on a principle of decentralization—the exact antithesis of Roman ecclesiology. And yet Rome not only recognized the apostolicity of the Eastern Churches but admitted a greater antiquity to their ecclesial structures.

Moreover, in preparing the paper on the pallium for Cardinal Mercier and the Malines Conversations, Beauduin made yet another discovery—the authentic nature of the patriarchate. He saw that the Eastern Churches (or patriarchates) remained truly independent, yet nevertheless enjoyed intercommunion. Further investigation also made it clear that these patriarchates arose not because of distinct apostolic origins but because of the political autonomy of the great cities with which they were originally associated: Alexandria, Antioch, Rome, Constantinople, and Jerusalem.

Far from representing a disintegration of Christian unity, this lack of uniformity had been recognized from the very beginnings of Christianity. The first councils had even established the hierarchical order of these sees. A highly centralized Church, therefore, such as Rome was increasingly becoming in the 1920's, certainly could find no support for the divine origin of this state of affairs, at least from the witness of the patristic period. The evidence clearly supported quite the opposite conclusion: that independent Churches bound together in a common faith and communion under the primacy of honor acknowledged in the successor of Peter was an ancient and accepted norm. This idea of structural pluralism clearly delighted Beauduin and he would make it one of the foundation stones of his own ecclesiology.

Moreover, earlier studies on the nature of the pallium had proposed additional nuances which he had unfortunately overlooked. In the East the pallium was never *given* to the patriarch; it belonged to him by virtue of his office.[11] In the West, however, a distortion or at any rate a radical modification of the custom had crept in, for the pope both gave and controlled the recipient. (In recent centuries, for example, the pope has given the pallium to Uniate patriarchs.)

Had Beauduin been better informed of this fundamental distinction, he could have used it to his advantage to strengthen his argument and would then have anticipated even more decisively paragraph 23 of the *Constitution on the Church* where episcopal conferences were intentionally compared with the ancient patriarchal sees.[12]

These insights of mid-career lay behind his distrust of any centralizing ecclesiology which might jeopardize the ancient structures which had maintained unity between Churches for so many centuries. They provided the fuel for his long campaign on behalf of the definition of the episcopacy and for his interest in the re-evaluation of the local (or particular) church i.e., the diocese. This concern extended even to the parochial level, an interest which admittedly had originally sprung from the liturgical movement but which took on even greater force in the light of his new understanding and appreciation of the episcopacy.

Much of what he wished for the episcopacy in terms of greater local jurisdiction has begun to be realized. The acceptance of the concept of collegiality is also making headway. The more profoundly pastoral dimensions, however, remain quite dependent on the individual bishop and whether or not he is willing to assume his full responsibility as father, liturgical leader and teacher. In none of these areas can Beauduin be considered an innovator, for he simply reminded the Church—Rome in particular, and bishops in general—of the broad lines of the episcopal vocation as traced so majestically by the early Church Fathers, many of whom successfully combined the office of bishop with that of liturgist and theologian.

The creative and intuitive nature of his decentralist thinking becomes most evident as soon as we shift our attention to his writings and ideas on the papacy and laity. Although it can be justly argued that there is historical precedence for most of his suggestions in these areas, there is one basic difference. While exceptionally outstanding bishops have existed in every century who certainly understood their vocation as expounded by Beauduin, it is hard to build an equally convincing case for the universality of his key proposals concerning the papacy and laity.

Beauduin recognized the necessity of continuity and the unchanging inner essence of the Church, but he never implied that the Church's mode of life in the first century was necessarily the ideal which the twentieth century ought to imitate. Adaptation to changing circumstances was imperative, and in the re-examination of the papal and lay roles we have his most strikingly prophetic contribution.

No more than humanity can the Church change her nature, but, living and conquering, she ought to adapt herself to this new world, to shake herself up, rejuvenate and renew herself under pain of denying her history and knowing a long eclipse. . . . To maintain without change a centuries-old routine, crystallized into an archaic administration and old-fashioned formulas, impoverishes the source of spiritual life, especially at an hour when all men and things want to be reborn. . . . The empire and the Church are not subordinated one to another, but both are God's creation. One is civil man's guide; the other is spiritual man's. Both are eternal since they come from God. In spite of all its anguish and misfortune, the present hour invites noble hearts to a grandiose work.

Every change in the life of the Church establishment must be rejected *a priori*. Besides, Church authority alone is the judge of eventual wished-for reforms. Without a doubt, in the Church there is an immutable element which concerns the foundations of her doctrine, her government, and her sacramental institutions—her essential constitution. But next to this invariable nucleus is a variable historical element—her human physiogonomy. In each country, in every era of her history, wherever she wants to exercise her power of expansion, she adapts herself. Her discipline, her law, her cult, even her theology—this whole ensemble of the ecclesiastical institution is variable.[13]

The Papacy

Until Pope John XXIII shocked and delighted Christians throughout the world by his radical departure from Vatican traditions (some of which only dated from the late nineteenth century), many Christians, particularly from the East, saw the Bishop of Rome more as an obstacle to unity than as a symbol of unity. For these the pope provided the most glaring ecclesiological contradiction imaginable: not only did he seem to claim a privilege incompatible with his human origin (infallibility was initially misunderstood as impeccability in the East), but of his own free choice he had deprived himself of all concrete pastoral contact with the people of his local church.[14]

Along with the problem of papal infallibility were included a number of related issues: the jurisdiction of Peter and his successor, the power of ecumenical councils, and the divine origin and non-delegated but ordinary jurisdiction of the apostolic (episcopal) college, plus other traditions and historical elements of the constitution of the Church.[15]

While many Orientals were willing to acknowledge the historical hegemony of Rome, and some few even to recognize papal primacy, none accepted the dogmatic basis for primacy decreed by Vatican I, at least as they understood it. Beauduin felt that papal infallibility could be justified only when understood in the full context of *Pastor Aeternus*. The very title was subject to misinterpretation: *The First Dogmatic Constitution of the Church of Christ*. Too many ignored the key word—*first*—and concluded that papal infallibility was the total and final dogma of the Church—that the pope, in fact, was the Church. They failed to realize that the complete Constitution had fifteen chapters and that only one small section, papal infallibility, had been acted upon.

The definition itself was really more moderate than the maximalist interpretations of some, including Pius IX, led the general public to believe. Papal infallibility had clearly been defined in terms of the infallibility of the Church, but due to historical circumstances (the outbreak of the Franco-Prussian war) the infallibility of the Church (the subject of chapter nine of the proposed schema) had never been defined. However, the basis of that infallibility rested on the words addressed to all the apostles collegially united.[16]

Papal supremacy, to be acceptable to the Eastern Churches, must be seen as part of a more developed ecclesiology. Beauduin believed that this was possible if the definition of 1870 were reopened for discussion and possible rewording.[17]

> By the will of her founder, the universal Church is composed of a series of particular churches (dioceses), episcopal-communities, each one governed by its own pastor, its unique bishop who feeds his own flock under his own responsibility and in virtue of ordinary powers attached by Christ to his apostolic function.[18]

Of great importance is the fact that these powers came *directly* from Christ to the bishop; they were not conferred on the bishop by the pope. Thus papal power ought not to prejudice the immediate divine and ordinary power or authority of the bishop. Under these conditions, infallibility posed no intrinsic problem for Beauduin. Its true role was to watch and conserve, not to invent and create, providing an organ in the teaching Church and a life and an end in the Church taught.[19] Much of the confusion surrounding infallibility could be removed by clarifying the broader question of Roman centralization:

> The truly Catholic point of view sees Roman centralization as of divine origin, but the laws and institutions to implement it can vary according to the times, places and needs. The human and historical elements envelop and guarantee the essential and divine elements. . . . There is an important difference between the end and the means of centralization. The spiritual authority that is exercised seeks to protect the venerable tradition in three domains:
> (1) in doctrine, permitting divergent theological opinions;
> (2) in ministry, permitting free discussion in the field of sacramental theology and a variety of rites and liturgies;
> (3) and especially in government; the spirit of centralization is

not in Roman tradition. (e.g., the 1918 Code of Canon Law applies only in the West).[20]

If the East viewed this dogma and the apparent drives toward an ever greater centralization as a threat to episcopal power, their uneasiness was understandable, since the divine constitution of the Church opposed such centralization. For the same reason Beauduin repeatedly criticized the common practice of frequent recourse to Rome in search of answers to problems that could be handled at local or regional levels. Such a procedure restricted the authority of others and stifled individual initiative. The decisions of Rome were meant as general solutions, and the whole system was thrown off balance when they were given for a particular local case.[21]

Because Roman centralization created an almost insurmountable obstacle for the Orthodox, the theological issue posed by papal primacy had profoundly affected ecclesiology. It gave definite juridical overtones to the concept of the Church in the West which paled before the Eastern notion of a mystical, spiritual society founded on the mystery of the communion of saints.[22] For this doctrine to achieve its full flowering in the West, the concept of collegiality offered interesting possibilities not only because of its obviously apostolic origin but also because of its similarity to the Orthodox concept of sobornost.

The sobornost theory had been proposed in the mid-nineteenth century by the lay theologian Alexis Khomiakov and elaborated by Sergius Bulgakov to supply the need for an infallible organ. According to this theory, the ultimate repository of infallibility is the community of the faithful; bishops, even when gathered together in council, only witness to the faith of their respective flocks. Decrees are hence to be considered infallible only if accepted by the laity at large.[23] (There was historical precedence for this view, e.g., the popular rejection of the union decrees signed at the Councils of Lyon and Florence.)

In the light of Vatican II's acceptance of the idea of collegiality, it should be pointed out that Beauduin conceived collegiality in a somewhat broader fashion than it has yet been utilized. For him, it could imply not just the union of bishops, but the coalescence of churches (in the sense of dioceses) in a kind of conciliarity. This union, comparable to the sobornost, is thus the root of the immediate and universal jurisdiction of Rome.[24] In short, Beauduin implied that the pope in a very real sense is dependent on the consensus of the faithful and hence in no way an absolute monarch. The nature of the Church demands an active collaboration between the teaching Church and the Church taught. While this principle is slowly gaining wider publicity, the exchange still remains woefully limited. It represents, however, one of his major prophetic insights, drawn from a recognition of the rather stifling clerical domination encountered by the laity at all levels in the Church and the realization that if the Church was to endure, the structures as he knew them would have to go.

But even more important than all this theologizing is the fact that *all*, from the pope on down, must live the mystery of the Church, drawing their nourishment from a truly ecclesial piety. The key to this mystery obviously lay in the doctrine of the mystical body from which one could easily infer the need of a hierarchic structure. But all attention within this structure must be focused on Christ as head, on Christ who had personally equated the role of leadership with that of servant—a total commitment to a life of ministry to the needs of others.

The accumulation of power and princely rank was utterly foreign to the office of Peter as originally conceived and described in the New Testament. Peter remained simply Christ's representative. In fact, the pope was originally called the vicar of the apostles rather than the Vicar of Christ.[25]

The whole problem posed by the papacy might be solved more easily if the pope would relinquish his "recently" acquired prerogatives of primacy and infallibility. At least such is the consensus of many eminent Protestant and Orthodox theologians cited individually by Beauduin.[26] His own suggestion is truly prophetic:

> To take an example as meaningful as it is delicate: the universal jurisdiction of the Bishop of Rome is an essential element in the Roman ecclesiastical structure. But the modality of this jurisdiction is extremely variable. Today very centralized, formerly more centrifugal; in the East hardly felt at all, in the West more unified; in this peripheral zone nothing is absolute or intangible. Christian truths can grow old if they are not continually rejuvenated by an ever new vision and presented in a living form.[27]

Since Vatican II the feudalistic notions which surrounded the office of bishop, epitomized in the title "prince of the Church," have been eclipsed by an increased emphasis on the more scriptural concept of service and the title of shepherd, as well as a de-emphasis on the "pomp and circumstance." Moreover, the idea of retirement goes hand in hand with that of service. When a servant can no longer fulfill his function, he is replaced. The adoption of a policy of papal resignation (there is a precedent in Celestine V and Gregory XII) would be an eloquent testimony that the office of pope, as of any bishop, is primarily to serve the Christian community. And an actual resignation might help to weaken one of the last remaining barriers to union.

A reconsideration of the *function* of the papacy, especially in collegial terms, has generally received an enthusiastic hearing in non-Roman circles. To quote just one witness, we cite Archbishop Ramsey in a recent interview in *Church Times*:

> If the papacy were to evolve in the direction of collegiality, it is possible that the Roman Catholic Church will present fewer difficulties to the Orthodox. . . . I doubt that union would have been possible in terms of the definition of the papacy of 1870; but if the context of the collegiality of the pope's authority continues to grow within the Roman Catholic Church, the situation could become different.[28]

The Laity

It must be confessed that Beauduin's earliest interest in the laity tended to be of a paternal-pastoral nature. Dismayed by the apparent lack of concern in creating and nourishing a solid spirituality among the faithful, he launched the liturgical movement and did his utmost to foster a profoundly religious spirit among all those with whom he came in contact. Those pastors content with providing a liturgy that catered to the lukewarm particularly enraged him, and if they read his articles or heard him speak, they could not but wince at the words directed to them. He considered such priests to be a discredit to the ministry, for they appeared willing to substitute the equivalent of an automat for the family meal.[29] Parochial and spiritual renewal thus provided the first phase of his activity. To prefer an "individual piety" was to choose to live on the margin of the Church, and

Beauduin was convinced that unless someone created an awareness of the infinite riches at the disposal of every Christian for growth into Christ, the twentieth-century Church would be doomed to an atrophied existence.

By the end of World War I his attitudes toward the laity became less clerically biased. His many contacts had further convinced him of the very real role and contribution that the mature layman had to make on practically every level of ecclesial life. This new appreciation is reflected in the liturgical periodical *Liturgical Questions*, for the subtitle "Reserved for the Clergy" was suppressed when publication resumed after the war. In the years that followed, Beauduin became increasingly involved in promoting a certain relationship of equality or collaboration between the various hierarchic ranks within the Church.

Initially, however, his emphasis was on the parish liturgy, for it played a key role in fostering the spiritual health of the Church and served as an effective gauge of both parish and family vitality.

> The parish is the normal organism created by Holy Church to develop in the mystical body of Christ this collective life and perfect unity which gives it its strength. Regular and active participation at the same altar by the full and solemn assembly of the whole parish family, especially on the Lord's Day, constitutes the first and indispensable source of this parish life.[30]

Moreover, to counteract the increasing disappearance of family spirit, two remedies were proposed: attachment to parish life and the introduction of a liturgical life into the home. The most powerful expression of the spirit of union, so lacking in many families, was to be found, according to Beauduin, in the parish High Mass where, united in a common worship, the members rendered official homage to God. Furthermore, the restoration of old family traditions like the paternal blessing might well succeed in extending the Sunday experience throughout the ensuing week.[31] Many of these ideas have since been actively promoted by such groups as the Christian Family Movement and the Cursillo Movement whose programs actively endorse Beauduin's insistence that "the best remedy to individualism is to live the dogma of the communion of saints through the liturgy understood and practiced with fervor." [32]

In exploring the layman's role, Beauduin inevitably was led to a consideration of the Christian's priestly role, anticipating by more than twenty years the endorsement of the idea by the encyclical *Mediator Dei*. For Beauduin the piety of the Church depended on two fundamental principles: the priestly power of Christ and the principle of solidarity. Through the liturgy, then, each one places himself under the sanctifying influence of Christ's priestly power who, as our common representative, binds us together, teaching us how to praise the Father. The key to the Catholic doctrine on the priesthood lay in the modality of Christ's priestly power as it is *now* exercised through the ministry of a visible priestly hierarchy.

> The hierarchy . . . is the unique channel through which divine life is poured out on humanity. That is the whole priesthood of Christ. . . . Consequently, for every Christian the *authentic mode of union with the priesthood of Jesus Christ* is in a close union with this hierarchy in the *exercise of its priestly power*. That is the first and indispensable source of supernatural life. . . .

> To develop in oneself this liturgical piety, as we have said, is to surrender one's soul to the priestly influence of the hierarchy, and, as a consequence, to the action of the eternal priest on our soul. . . .

> The more intimate, active and frequent our participation in these [liturgical] acts, the more will the priesthood of Christ act in our souls. On the contrary, to reduce to a strict minimum our participation in liturgical acts is to withdraw to a degree from the action of the Church and to isolate oneself from the adoration and prayer of the spouse.[33]

Closely related to this mutual responsibility of the clergy and the faithful to give their all in the liturgy was the concept of spiritual fatherhood. However, unless the hierarchy is viewed as much more than an administrative machine or a watchful guardian of dogma and morals, and unless lay people try to see beyond the sometimes too obvious personal defects of their ministers, there can be no grounds for the sentiments of respect, filial confidence, and supernatural obedience which should be inherent in the clergy-lay relationship.

> Liturgical piety, properly understood, is the weapon for combating this evil. . . . It places us under the active influence of the

priestly power of the Church. In it the hierarchy exercises its
spiritual fatherhood; and the faithful, nourished at the family table,
draw thence the filial respect, the loving obedience, and the *esprit
de corps* which constitute their strength.

Do we reflect on this truth sufficiently? All the liturgical books that
day by day regulate our sacrifices, our adorations . . . draw all their
powers of praise [and] of sanctity from the fact that they are
given us by the supreme head of the hierarchy. . . . Their tran-
scendent and incomparable title in the eyes of the Father who is
in heaven, and in the eyes of the faithful, is that they form the
great prayer presided over by the vicar of Jesus Christ, the reigning pontiff.[34]

Obviously, for Beauduin, true liturgical piety is practically synono-
mous with filial piety. What is true of the individual's relationship
with the Holy Father applies equally to his relationship with his own
bishop. If these already existing bonds are recognized and the Christian faithfully lives the liturgy, developing in himself the life of the
Church, then, should he be faced with a crisis of obedience, there will
be no insurmountable problems.

It is a matter of certainty that the Christian soul, united by means
of the liturgy, by reason of spiritual habits long grown dear, to
the life and the thought of the Church, will find easy and sure
guidance in a sense of filial obedience that is both complete and
sincere.[35]

Beauduin wrote these words in 1914. After a lifetime of crises, his
attitude had not changed. The priesthood was still the source of
sanctity for the Christian.

As St. Thomas says, every rite of the Christian religion is derived
from the priesthood of Christ. The priesthood of Christ, source of
all sanctity, is visibly and sacramentally in the Church, and every
action of the Holy Spirit operates only in this visible priesthood.[36]

When the encyclical *Mediator Dei* appeared, a doctrinal work
which established the transcendence of priestly activity in the
Church, [37] Beauduin repeated his main ideas on the topic. Upholding

the traditional teaching on the ordained priesthood, he now found papal support for his frequent insistence in the past that all Christians participate in the priestly mission of Christ. He suggested that the words *sacerdos alter Christus* (the priest is another Christ) be avoided because *Christianus alter Christus* (the Christian is another Christ) was more authentic. The conferral of holy orders, the visible and external priesthood of Christ, did not make a man a more complete Christian, for full Christian dignity had already been bestowed in baptism, confirmation, and the eucharist.[38] Democratic as this may sound, Beauduin still saw a sharp distinction between the priesthood of the faithful and that of ordained ministers. Ordination did not emanate from the people, nor were the powers it conferred delegated by the laity. Prior to representing the people before God, the priest was the envoy of Christ, the head of the body; thus he represented God to man. He was, therefore, a sacramentalized instrument of Christ's priesthood, while the layman remained a priest in quality of member, not of instrument, with an active and organic participation in the offering of Christ.[39]

If a false emphasis on the priesthood of the laity threatened to impoverish the significance of the priesthood within the Church, the principle of solidarity made Christ's priesthood a collective reality. It was this reality, this collaboration of men in the sanctification of humanity, that Beauduin wanted to safeguard. Interesting as these theological issues may be to some, Beauduin's most valuable insights are to be found in his understanding of lay spirituality.

Christian Spirituality

Down through the centuries, the true nature of asceticism and its relationship to monasticism had often been lost sight of, permitting a gradual divorce to creep in between the lay state and the clerical-religious state, between the Christian and his ascetic vocation. In actual fact, monasticism was conceived by laymen and intended for laymen desirous of living the Gospel more fully. For centuries the so-called three states of life within the Church—clerical, religious, and lay—were regarded just as that: as ways of life, of reaching God. According to Congar, by the thirteenth century the clerical way of life was regarded more as a function; hence the bond between the lay and religious was closer than that with the clerical, since neither layman nor monk, by virtue of his way of life, had the power of the jurisdiction of orders.[40]

It is possible that Gratian started the trend of looking down on the laity; he refers to lay life as a concession to human weakness.[41] Such spiritual snobbery was foreign to Beauduin. In trying to re-integrate the liturgy back into its rightful place in every Christian's life, he indirectly paved the way for a full recognition of the lay state and its role in and contribution to the life of the Church. He therefore invited everyone to meet the challenge offered by self-discipline for a spiritual motive, traditionally referred to as asceti-cism. For this reason his writings on the subject deal primarily with fundamentals. They are not only intelligible but applicable to clergy, lay and religious. Given his balance, it is unfortunate that he has not left us more.[42]

Asceticism is not principally scourgings, fastings, sleepless vigils, and endless mortifications of one kind or another; it is living the Gospel message of *love in community*. Every Christian is called to this vocation of true Christian asceticism, the only path to truly human fulfillment. Living beyond the commandments and accepting the challenge to risk propriety and to be a fool for Christ requires special strength, and in Beauduin's eyes the best support for such a life was the liturgy. The very purpose of his democratization of the liturgy had been to foster active participation among the laity so that they might rediscover the fundamental principle of true Christian asceticism: that the liturgy is the means whereby our life is plunged into the mystery of Christ who alone will lead us to the Father.

The spiritual life is consequently not uniquely oriented to monks, nor need it follow a closely regimented program. In one of his notebooks Beauduin bemoaned the illusion that sanctity is acquired by moral efforts which master our faults and lead us to virtue.

Intimate union with our celestial Father is a *gift* which the Father gives us; it doesn't come from us. Not that we should not be concerned about virtue, but it is because we are sons of the Father that we must be perfect—we do not practice virtue to become holy but *to stay holy*. It is divine reality—the love of the Father—that showers us with his gifts. This reality sanctifies us; the imitation of Christ is imperative because we are sons of the same Father.[43]

In pre-conciliar books of piety the gift aspect of spiritual growth was rarely stressed, which accounts for Beauduin's basic criticism of these works. They spent too much time telling what to do rather than explaining the true nature of sanctity.

> The spiritual life is confused with the practice of virtues, with the imitation of Christ. These only condition and preserve sanctity; they don't create or constitute it. Sanctity draws all its being in contact with the glorified man—the only true Christian—and all this comes from the Church. The practice of virtues, the imitation of Christ, etc., are imposed not by obligation but *because we are saints*.[44]

Beauduin's consistently positive view of human nature and of the holiness to be found there because of the mystery of redemption helps to explain the strong anti-Jansenist, anti-Manichaean bias in his approach to the spiritual life, indeed, in his total theological perspective. What is significant in the above excerpt is the choice of words, e.g., "contact with the glorified man." Beauduin could have simply said Christ, but he sought to draw attention to the tension between the divine and the human which lies at the very heart of a disciplined life. Alarmed by the Monophysite tendencies of the day, Beauduin laid particular emphasis on the humanity of Christ in his retreats and articles because he was persuaded not only that it most needed recognition, but also that it provided the most powerful remedy to the spiritual ills of modern man.

Beauduin opened a retreat given in 1920 at Mont César with a plea that human nature be reintroduced into monastic life in the disciplines of prayer and work—traditionally the chief means of sanctification. At least three conferences returned to this focus on the human dimension. Monastic asceticism, he declared, must always be seen in the light of the social character and the principle of moderation that St. Benedict sought to instill in his sons.[45] (Because Beauduin approached the Benedictine rule as a sociologist, showing its social dimension, this particular retreat aroused quite a strong reaction.) His main point, however, whether preaching to monks or writing to the general public, remained the same: the Christian way of life should produce mature men.

Although some of his remarks may leave the impression that a real distinction exists between Christian life and ascetic life, he was trying to counteract current prejudices. He therefore started from the negative statement of the question which supposed a real dichotomy. The debate has yet to be resolved. Many ascetical theologians still defend the thesis popularized by John of the Cross that the way of renunciation is the higher way and alone leads to perfection. Since the burden of Beauduin's argument was intended to encourage the layman to lead a more demanding Christian life rather than to discourage him from even trying, Beauduin carefully avoided such insinuations.

To offset the common view, he declared that the ordinary person was an ascetic without even being aware of it. Whoever wanted to lead an ordinary Christian life necessarily observed the precepts of God and Church and practiced the virtues demanded by these precepts. This automatically placed the individual in the first degree of asceticism (according to his schema in the 1920 retreat). Growth meant taking another step in the same direction rather than a radical reorientation of one's life. Beauduin saw sufficient possibility for renunciation in ordinary lay life. To impose something in addition went contrary to the nature of genuine Christian life as described in the Gospels. It somehow made the spiritual life appear artificial and withdrawn from reality.

And who can deny that this ordinary discipline, faithfully practiced, represents, especially in today's world, a considerable amount of effort and renunciation? Equity and justice, temperance and continence, charity and forgiveness and so many other virtues make at certain times heroic demands and require continued efforts at every age and in every state of life. A sincere reading of the Sermon on the Mount . . . suffices to give an awareness of the demands of the spirit of Christ and to show that every true Christian is an ascetic.[46]

The *Pastoral Constitution on the Church in the Modern World* in many respects seems to be an extended commentary on Beauduin's view of Christian asceticism, developing these same themes of equity and justice, temperance and continence, charity and forgiveness.

Asceticism brings to fruition the mystery of life and death within the Christian, the mystery into which baptism initiated him, when he received the germ of spiritualization, the possibility of resurrection and glorification, of the "transformation of our decrepitude into a renewal of eternal youth." But what, in fact, is the actual experience of the Christian? He is the victim of a decadent moral theology. A moral theology that has separated itself not only from asceticism and thus from contemplation of the summits toward which man should tend, but also from the study of doctrine itself.

> It has become, practically speaking, the science of the *minimum*, teaching the art of the "just enough," not to mention the "least possible," the art of how "to satisfy." [47]

As a result many lose sight of the beauty and moral ideal of Christianity: the divine transfiguration that the adoptive sonship demands and realizes in us. Moreover, as soon as things are set up in the form of laws, the typical human reaction sets in—to see how much one can get away with, or how cheaply one can get by.

How thoroughly he understood and loved human nature is revealed by Beauduin's reaction to this situation. No accusing finger is pointed, no anathemas are hurled; only an anguished cry of regret is uttered over the spiritual riches being missed. One immediately senses from the very conciseness of his words that here was a man who had truly and profoundly experienced these riches and knew how frequently the accessible was made inaccessible through sheer human insensitivity.

> This defensive attitude is human and justifiable; but when it is systematic, when it becomes an obsession for the minimum, it narrows our horizons, breaks our élan, and dries up the soul; we become slaves under the whip. And it is, however, under this austere aspect of painful duty that our most noble privileges are presented to us: the duty to believe, to pray; the duty to love, to sacrifice, to repent and so many others. [48]

Beauduin found such gross distortions of truth unbearable. Aroused to action, he undertook the task of convincing Christians that this duty is also a privilege. The special rights conferred originate in, are nourished by, and grow in the liturgy:

[Baptism confers] the right to know the secrets of the Father and
to adhere by a divine act that is called believing; the right to
regenerate ourselves in the merits of our head; the right to make
ours his sacrifice; the right to be an ascetic in whatever state we
are; the power to take off the old man and put on the exuberant
youth of the new man in light and in love.

It is not a question of a specialty. The only religious profession
that confers on us this right and imposes on us this duty is our
baptism. One is Christian only at this price.[49]

Baptism does not introduce the Christian into a static state. The
rights and powers conferred are dynamic. Elsewhere in his writings,
Beauduin stressed the source of this growth which is so vital for
true Christian asceticism:

And since for the Christian ascetic the eucharistic altar must be
the tryst whither he comes daily to receive the basic lesson of the
oblation of self by virtue of the example of the gift of his master,
is it not true to say that the liturgy, in giving to the eucharist as
sacrifice and sacrament all its powerful efficacy over our souls, is
the *universal and official school* of true asceticism? [50]

Lest one be misled into assuming that contemplation of the eucharistic
Lord suffices, Beauduin continued:

The ideas of the faithful are not sufficiently enlightened upon this
point, and more than one pious soul would perhaps be scandalized
to hear that the *chief* aim of our Lord in instituting the eucharist
was not that of being a permanent host in our tabernacles, but
that of *realizing every day and in every member of Christ the
mystery of the death and the life of the head by means of the
eucharistic sacrifice and sacrament.*[51]

There is no other way to achieve this than by the individual's full
participation in the liturgical act. Full participation went far beyond
physical involvement. It presupposed an ever greater spiritual awareness and appreciation of the mysteries enacted, a veritable participation in the intention of Christ himself.

After a detailed description of what Christian asceticism is not—
the negative forms of Jansenism and legitimate penitential asceticism,

a spiritual "elective"—Beauduin enlarged upon the nature of true Christian asceticism. His emphasis on the paramount importance of the Holy Spirit and the honorable role of the human body remains particularly noteworthy.

[The human body is not] a shameful and bothersome envelope which can only hinder our divine transformation and which must be annihilated and made inoffensive. In virtue of our substantial unity . . . it must collaborate with docility in the common task, as it will participate later on in the final transfiguration.[52]

Two notions in opposition in his day, humanism and asceticism, are thus successfully reconciled. In the daily routine, the aspirations of the true humanist find their full satisfaction in authentic Christian asceticism.

Although this article was written long after his first days at Mont César, it reflected and crystallized the attitudes expressed informally in earlier years. The human element continued to be extremely important, for the individual was never in isolation. Each person was part of a social organism, a community. Asceticism could therefore not be discussed in any depth apart from its communal dimension and consequences.

Theological, liturgical and practical considerations all led Beauduin to realize more and more not only the importance of an active laity but also its absolute necessity. Unless the laity shared in the concerns and problems facing the Church, and unless their talents were at the service of the Church, the perfection toward which she had been striving would never be fulfilled. Vatican II repeatedly reaffirmed this conviction in its many documents relating directly to the laity. Moreover, it is a theme heard with increasing frequency today from the lips of every significant Church leader.

As early as 1934 Beauduin had proposed that in a course on the Church some topics be treated from the point of view of the laity, for the laity too is called to theology.[53] Some of these same ideas appeared in notes already mentioned (Chapter 12) which came about as the sequel to his discussion about the utility of publishing a lay view on the Church. It is in additional notes taken by Dr. Clottens that some of Beauduin's more practical—and still prophetic —views on the role of the layman in the Church come to light.

Admitting the very legitimate and human hopes for prosperity, justice and peace by his contemporaries, Beauduin was nevertheless concerned that they recognize not only their duty to collaborate in the mission of the Church but also that they preserve a proper perspective for what is really essential. Action and involvement in the temporal work of the Church, necessary as it is, must never eclipse the higher mystique to which they are called.

In tracing the line of action potentially open to the layman in terms of the nature of the Church as he understood it, Beauduin discussed in detail the various types of power in the Church—doctrinal, administrative and priestly—and carefully pointed out where the spiritual priorities lay. In each instance, he spoke in terms of a place which rightfully belonged to the layman but which had been lost—often through an exaggerated reaction (as in the sixteenth century) which led to their exclusion from offices or functions formerly open to them.[54]

In doctrinal matters, the lay theologian has finally emerged, although he is not always well received in clerical *or* lay circles. While Beauduin lived, the layman was still excluded from obtaining theological degrees in pontifical institutes. By the 1950's the climate had begun to change; now even women may apply.

Concerning administrative affairs, Beauduin had much to say. His main point was to insist that administration and control of the goods of the Church belongs to the laity because the entire burden of support rests on them. Another administrative aspect which called forth sharp criticism was the Vatican diplomatic corps which in principle seemed to represent a serious break with an earlier and happier state of affairs. Until the eleventh century, a simple relationship of communion existed between Churches. Now the general administration of the entire Roman Catholic Church is assured and in some ways controlled by the Roman personnel who have usurped —unconsciously though it may be—the prerogatives of the local bishops. In this latter case Beauduin could only urge the bishops to know their local rights better and to assert their rightful independence.

We have seen the importance that Beauduin gave to the priestly function of the laity. In 1955 he only reiterated what he had said earlier, warning lay men and women that unless they collaborate totally in the liturgy they risk performing acts empty of meaning. Once again he stressed the priesthood of the father of the family, and, perhaps aware of the nascent movement for women's liberation, explained that his special emphasis of the father's role was not to be interpreted as an anti-feminist measure but simply as a recognition of the hierarchical order within the family.

The formation of priests also came in for some consideration, since in many instances the fervor of the faithful rises and falls with that of their clergy. Of all the virtues he could have listed, Beauduin singled out the need to know the life of the faithful and to become familiar with the pressures and tensions that modern man faces and lives with as of special importance.

The emphasis in Beauduin's writings on the lay state is strongly positive. Although the hierarchical motif frequently recurs, any hint of a clerical monopoly or divisiveness is clearly seen as an abuse. The members of the Church, bound together with a common life, ideally fulfilled their respective roles in an atmosphere of love and harmony. But Beauduin was realistic. Although human pettiness remained an ever present threat, he firmly believed in the divine nature of the Church as body of Christ, and his invincible confidence reassured the wavering faith of others.

If much outside the institutional Church seemed preferable to what was within, he nevertheless insisted that the best fashion of serving the great causes in the Church was not revolt but submission. This conviction explains both his own acceptance of exile at En Calcat and his energetic efforts toward a structural renewal within the Church. The anguish of sincere Christians who suffered as he did from the visible disunity of Christendom caused him to search tradition for ways and means to revitalize ecclesiastical institutions. Beauduin was looking for structures that would give visible witness to the hierarchical nature of the Church while changing her image from a highly organized, juridical society. Not every reformer, however, possessed as much patience as Beauduin. The sad experience of departures from Amay which had been touched off by exasperation with Rome led him frequently to caution as well as to encourage younger liberals to work from within, even submitting when necessary. "Cheer up, it doesn't kill you; I'm eighty years old," he once noted with a knowing nod and a wry smile.[55]

Conclusion

In trying to do justice to Beauduin's ecclesiology, we have run the risk of distorting his essentially unified outlook. Compartmentalization was foreign to him. If the attempt to highlight key doctrines or themes created the impression that Beauduin treated any one doctrine in isolation from all other doctrines, the fault is ours. The Church was (and still is) a living reality which he never subjected to dissection. Hopefully, the interrelationships existing between these doctrines—the glorified humanity, the Trinity, the eucharist—were equally apparent in the considerations of this chapter on the Church. Other doctrines such as the priesthood or the mediatorship of Christ also could have been developed. His position has at least been suggested in this presentation of the clerical, lay and episcopal roles within the Church as viewed from the perspective of their respective priestly functions. For a first attempt at a synthesis, it seemed legitimate to limit this discussion to these several concepts so fundamental to an understanding of the ecumenical dimension of his ecclesiology.

In the practical application of his ecumenical insights many tended to write Beauduin off as a hopeless idealist. Yet in view of Vatican II's definition of the Church, how can anyone be excluded from the Church's concern? And if this Church is indeed a pilgrim Church, how can anyone remain closed to the possibility of future structural modifications? Many of the documents of Vatican II give ample testimony to the validity not only of his reflections but also of the activity that they stimulated.

Were he still alive, it is not hard to imagine where Beauduin would direct his energies. Ecumenism and liturgy have been "democratized." Lay people not only participate when invited, but increasingly they initiate action, which has created new problems and needs within the Christian community. The old clergy/lay divorce has been replaced by a new cleavage among laymen themselves. Increased lay initiative occasionally results in actions that appear irresponsible, arousing suspicions about lay competency. Hence the greatest need today in the Christian community is adult education—both clerical and lay.

Scholarly journals, so much a part of every one of Beauduin's undertakings—even popularized versions—are not the solution. They have always been inadequate in terms of mass education. Today with the mass media, more effective means are just waiting to be utilized, but they depend on even more basic resources: the handing down of authentic tradition. Beauduin has passed the torch on to a new generation and Chevetogne remains a rich source for any such activity with its extensive library so rich in biblical, patristic, ecclesial and ecumenical sources, but the dedication of a few is no longer sufficient to stem the tide of religious confusion and indifference. This is the age of the laity, and Beauduin has left them a plan of action. Will they heed his challenge?

Beauduin never confused his personal identity with his activities. He lived in, with and from the Church, and in this way he anticipated most major developments in the twentieth-century Church—including the definitions of the Church and collegiality. Because he lived for the Church and not for himself, he was unafraid of relinquishing authority in an activity when the Spirit called him elsewhere. Hopefully this same Spirit will raise up one like Beauduin to be a catalyst for the decades ahead, someone who like Beauduin will make of his life one prolonged AMEN.

"Celui quit dit 'Amen' en mourant est éternellement vivant." [56]

Abbreviations

AAS	*Acta Apostolica Sedis*
BNDSE	*Bulletin de Notre Dame de la Sainte Espérance*
BMOS	*Bulletin mensuel des oblates séculières et de l'union spirituelle des veuves de France*
CCSL	*Cours et Conférences des Semaines Liturgiques*
CM	Charles Moeller
Col M	*Collectanea Mechliniensia*
CPL	*Centre de Pastorale Liturgique*
CSFR	*Cahiers de Sainte Françoise Romaine*
ECQ	*Eastern Churches Quarterly*
ETL	*Ephemerides Theologicae Lovanienses*
Irén.	*Irénikon*
JES	*Journal of Ecumenical Studies*
JJ	Jean Jadot
LB	Lambert Beauduin
Lit. Tijd.	*Liturgisch Tijdschrift*
MC	Maieul Cappuyns
MD	*Maison-Dieu*
NRT	*Nouvelle Revue Theologique*
OR	Olivier Rousseau
PL	Paul Leyniers
QL	*Questions Liturgiques*
QLP	*Questions Liturgiques et Paroissiales*
RB	*Revue Bénédictine*
RCIF	*La Revue Catholique des Idées et des Faits*
RGB	*La Revue Générale Belge*
RHE	*La Revue d'Histoire Ecclésiastique*
RLB	*Revue Liturgique et Bénédictine*
SE	*Sanctae Ecclesiae*
TB	Thomas Becquet
TD	*Theology Digest*
TS	*Theological Studies*
VLsm	*La Vie Liturgique, supplément mensuel*
VS	*Vie Spirituelle*

Notes

1. Cardinal Suenens, "Toward Unity and Freedom in the Church," *National Catholic Reporter*, May 28, 1969, p. 7.

2. Louis Bouyer, *Dom Lambert Beauduin, un homme d'Église* (Tournai: Casterman, 1964), pp. 13f. The author wishes to acknowledge a great indebtedness to Fr. Bouyer for many details borrowed from this book, as well as for the investigatory leads it contained. With the present generation, the Beauduin properties (the paternal estate) have passed to other hands.

3. Letter of E. Beauduin to the author, May 21, 1971.

4. Notes to the author from O. Rousseau (henceforth OR), May 1971.

5. According to Bouyer, *op. cit., p. 15*. Roger Aubert identifies this monastery as that of Forges; cf. "Un homme d'Église, Dom L. Beauduin," *Revue Nouvelle*, Vol. 31, No. 3 (1960), p. 225.

6. Cf. *Ephemerides theologicae lovainienses*, Vol. 4, No. 3 (1969), pp. 456–66 for two interesting letters written by Beauduin in 1893 to Paul Halflants revealing his piety and his social concern.

7. André Haquin, *Histoire du renouveau liturgique belge (1882–1914)* (Louvain: Université catholique de Louvain, 1966), p. 126. Also see his *Dom. L. Beauduin et le renouveau liturgique au touranant du xxe siècle* (Paris: Editions J. Duculot, 1969).

8. LB to OR, Amay (?) 1/7/27.

9. Letter of E. Beauduin to the author, May 21, 1971.

10. Haquin, *op. cit.*, p. 128. By 1891 Louvain also had a school of social and political science.

11. Bouyer, *op. cit.*, p. 16. Cf. C. Cardolle, *Un précurseur, un docteur, un pionnier social Monseigneur Pottier (1849–1923)* (Brussels, 1951); A. Pire, *Histoire de la congrégation des Aumôniers du Travail* (Charleroi: 1942), pp. 14–16.

12. Bouyer, *op. cit.*, p. 7.

13. The actual initiator was Father Reyn, a priest of the congregation of the Sacred Heart of Issoudun, who received every encouragement from his provincial, Father Allard. Bouyer, *op. cit.*, p. 17. This perhaps explains Beauduin's devotion to the Sacred Heart and later reaction to its absence at Mont César.

14. Haquin, *op. cit.*, p. 128.

15. Bouyer, *op. cit.*, p. 17.

16. Pire, *op. cit.*, pp. 128f.

17. *Ibid.*, pp. 87f.

18. A. Pire, *op. cit.*, p. 13. For Beauduin's "Rapport sur les Oeuvres de Seraing," delivered at a Congress for priests affiliated with the Labor Chaplains, cf. Haquin, *op. cit.*, p. 28.

19. M. Cappuyns, "Dom Lambert Beauduin (1873–1960): Quelques documents et souvenirs," *Revue d'Histoire Ecclésiastique*, 61, No. 2 (1966), p. 429.

20. Bouyer, *op. cit.*, p. 20.

21. R. Aubert, *op. cit.*, p. 286.

22. Cappuyns, *op. cit.*, p. 428.

23. Pire, *op. cit.*, p. 124.

24. Bouyer, *op. cit.*, pp. 18–19.

25. Future auxiliary bishop of Liège and former superior at Saint-Trond.

26. *Christ: The Life of the Soul* (1917), *Christ in His Mysteries* (1919) and *Christ: The Ideal of the Monk* (1922). Benedict XV, speaking of them to Bishop Szepticky, said: "Read this; it's the pure doctrine of the Church." And Cardinal Mercier would say: "Dom Columba (Marmion) puts you in touch with God." Marmion, *Le Christ vie de l'ame* (Maredsous: Editions de Maredsous, 1949), pp. vii–viii.

27. T. Delforge, "L'Influence de Dom Marmion," *Lumière du Christ*, No. 159 (1960), pp. 66–67, cites and translates testimony of Cunibert Mohlberg in *Schwezerische Kirchenzeitung*, March 24, 1960.

28. Lambert Beauduin, "Dom Marmion et la Liturgie," *VS* 78 (1948), p. 45. The new Roman breviary is a fitting comment if not tribute to Marmion, for selections from his works are included in the lessons for Morning Prayer, thus placing him in the select company of the great theologians and liturgists of the early Church.

29. F. Vandenbroucke, "Dom Lambert Beauduin," *Lumière du Christ*, No. 158 (1960), pp. 32–33.

30. L. Beauduin, "Mise au point nécessaire, Réponse au R. P. Navatel," *QL* 4 (1913), pp. 98–100.

31. *Idem.*

32. Words from Pius X's famous motu proprio of November 22, 1903—*Tra le sollecitadini*, *AAS* 36 (1903), pp. 328–339—that Beauduin never tired of quoting.

33. See the restrictive responses of the Pontifical Biblical Commission from 1905–1933. It was only in 1948 that some of the negative decisions were admitted as being the product of historical conditions and no longer binding. Cf. response to Cardinal Suhard, *AAS* 39 (1948), pp. 45–48; *Rome and the Study of Scripture* (7th edition; St. Meinrad: Grail Publications, 1962), pp. 150–153.

34. See Chapter 14.

35. H. Duesberg, of Maredsous, one of Beauduin's pupils, took the course in 1911–1912 and still has very complete notes. The course treated the following topics: nature of the Church, primacy of the pope, bishops, magisterium, members, and marks of the Church. The last section, treated in apologetic fashion, was very severe on the non-Catholic Churches, or sects as he preferred to call them. Aubert, *op. cit.*, claims that the substance of this first course is to be found in *Liturgy: The Life of the Church.*

36. For Guéranger's role, see S. Hilpisch, *Benedictinism in the Changing Centuries* (Collegeville: Liturgical Press, 1958). The history of Solesmes will be found in P. Guéranger, *Essai historique sur l'Abbaye de Solesmes* (Le Mans, 1846), and *Le Monastere Saint-Pierre de Solesmes* (Solesmes, 1955). Cf. O. Rousseau, *Progress of the Liturgy*, pp. 76f. and n. 18, pp. 184f.

37. Bouyer, *op. cit.*, p. 37.

38. Beuron: U. Englemann, *Beuron* (Munich-Zurich, 1957); H. S. Mayer, *Benediktinisches Ordensrecht in der Beuroner Kongregation* (4 vols.: Beuron, 1929–1936). Maredsous: H. de Moreau, *Dom Hildebrand de Hemptinne* (Maredsous, 1930). Dom Hildebrand was abbot during the years 1809–1909 and later primate. Mont César: *Le Mont César*, 1899–1949 (Louvain: Editions de l'Abbaye du Mont César, 1949.) David Knowles, *Christian Monasticism* (New York: McGraw-Hill Book Co., 1969).

39. Cappuyns, *op. cit.*, pp. 441–442.

40. O. Rousseau, "Un homme d'Église Dom Lambert Beauduin, Initiateur Monastique," *VS* 104 (1961), pp. 46–47.

41. *Ibid.*, p. 49. Cf. Bouyer, *op. cit.*, p. 104.

42. Bouyer, *op. cit.*, p. 31—cited by Bouyer, source not given.

43. *Ibid.*, p. 33.

CHAPTER 2

THE BELGIAN LITURGICAL MOVEMENT

1. See Bouyer, *Liturgical Piety* (Notre Dame: University of Notre Dame Press, 1954), or Ernest Koenker, *Liturgical Renaissance in the Roman Catholic Church* (St. Louis: Concordia Publishing House, 1954) for good, substantial studies on the liturgical movement. Also, O. Rousseau, *The Progress of the Liturgy* (Paramus: Newman, 1951).

2. *Congrès eucharistique international, Bruxelles, 13–17 juillet 1898* (Brussels, 1899), p. 106, quoted by Haquin in *Dom L. B. et le Renouveau Liturgique*, p. 38. Godefroid Kurth (1847–1910) at the time of the National Congress in

1909 was professor emeritus at the University of Liège, director of the Belgian Historical Institute in Rome, a position he had held since 1907. His area of specialization was the social and literary history of the Middle Ages. Since 1899 he had edited *Archives Belge*. His principal work, *Les origines de la civilisation moderne*, was published in 1866. Another work by Kurth which saw several editions was *L'Église aux tournants de l'Histoire*. O. Rousseau treats the history of the Louvain liturgical movement in some detail in "La revalorisation du dimanche dans l'Église catholique depuis 50 ans," in *Miscellanea Lercaro*, Vol. I, Rome, 1966, pp. 525f. Of interest to Americans is the fact that in 1888 an anonymous article in *Catholic World* suggested that a close relationship existed between lay passivity and leakage; as a remedy it called for more active participation in the liturgy. An 1889 article urged the Church to use the talents of the laity and to give them a vital role. Many articles in favor of congregational singing appeared at this time; cf. D. Callahan, *The Mind of the Catholic Layman* (New York: Chas. Scribner's Sons, 1963), pp. 64f.

3. Bouyer, *Liturgical Piety*, pp. 62f.

4. Haquin, *Dom L. B. . . .* , pp. 75–76, relates Mercenier's memoirs on the creation of *Liturgical Life*.

5. Haquin, *Histoire . . .* , p. 136; this question was posed by M. Cappuyns, O.S.B., January 18, 1959.

6. The letter is dated July 6, 1909 and was first published by Haquin in 1966.

7. "Message de dom Lambert Beauduin," *QLP* 40 (1959), p. 200.

8. O. Rousseau, "Autour du jubilé du mouvement Liturgique," *QLP* 40 (1959), p. 204.

9. *Le Patriote*, September 27, 1909.

10. The account from *Le Patriote* as well as that in Rousseau's article cited above can be compared with the original of Beauduin's paper, "La vraie prière de l'Église, Rapport au Congrès de Malines de 1909," in the proceedings for the *Congrès de Malines* (Brussels: S.A.), Vol. 5, pp. 1–6, or in the resume printed in *QLP* 40 (1959), pp. 218–221. This congress was unique not only for its liturgical breakthrough—it was also the first Catholic Congress to deal with the missionary problem. Moreover, it even had a section for women and their works!

11. Bouyer, *op. cit.*, p. 41.

12. Haquin, *op. cit.*, pp. 154f.

13. These pamphlets were subsequently collected and published by Mont César as a Sunday missal. St. Andrew's Abbey at Bruges, more familiar to Americans, began after World War I to publish a daily missal—the *Saint Andrew Bible Missal*. This same work is carried on in the U.S.A. One might say that it was imported by such men as Fr. William Busch, ordained at Louvain in 1907 and associate editor of *Orate Frates* (now *Worship*) and author of *The Mass Drama* (2nd edition, 1933), and Virgil Michel, O.S.B.,

who studied under Beauduin at Sant' Anselmo and frequently mentioned him in his letters; P. Marx, *The Life and Work of Virgil Michel* (Washington, D.C.: Catholic University of America, 1953): "All of Dom Lambert's interests became Father Virgil's, not least among which was his work with Anglicans and Orthodox in furtherance of Christian unity" (p. 33). Ermin Vitry of Maredsous (one of Beauduin's students at Louvain), a specialist in plain chant, was later invited to Collegeville, Minn., and exercised a notable influence on the revival of Gregorian chant in America. He died in 1960.

14. Haquin, *op. cit.*, pp. 148f.; also see pp. 80f. in his *Dom L. B.* . . .

15. Notes from T. Becquet to the author, May, 1971.

16. Haquin, *Histoire* . . . , pp. 232f. Haquin suggests some of the historical reasons for the failure to realize this project. Personal rivalries also entered in; see his *Dom L.B.* . . . , pp. 146f.

17. Haquin, *Dom L. B.* . . . , pp. 138f.

18. Haquin, *Histoire* . . . , p. 252.

19. Bouyer, *op. cit.*, p. 48.

20. Three unsigned articles appeared in *Le Patriote*, a Belgian daily, in September 1912, symptomatic of the growing resentment. Ironically they came from a fellow Benedictine, Jerome Picard of Maredsous; cf. Haquin, *Dom L. B.* . . . , p. 174.

21. L. Beauduin, "Grief contre le movement Liturgique," *QL* 2 (1912), pp. 529–536.

22. Archives of Chevetogne, To the Director from J. M., Carthage, 6/29/1914.

23. L. Beauduin, " 'Liturgie catholique' par Dom M. F. Festugière (recension)," *QL* 3 (1913), pp. 391–394.

24. J. J. Navatel, "L'Apostolat liturgique et la Piété personnelle," *Etudes* (November 20, 1913), pp. 449–478.

25. L. Beauduin, "Mise au point nécessaire," *QL* 4 (1913), pp. 83–104, parts of which are cited at the beginning of this section.

26. LB, "Liturgie catholique . . .", Dom Festugière's definition, p. 393.

27. *Ibid.*, p. 394, quoted by LB from Mercier's *Oeuvres Pastorales* I, p. 322.

28. The original edition was re-edited in 1922, and the title was changed (without Beauduin's knowledge) to *La Piété Liturgique* because of the uproar over the original title, but later editions returned to the original title.

29. L. Beauduin, *Liturgy the Life of the Church*, trans. V. Michel (Collegeville: Liturgical Press, 1926), p. vii.

30. See chapter 11 and the *Centre de Pastorale Liturgique*.

31. "La Lettre de S. em. le Cardinal Tardini a S. Em. le cardinal van Roey," *QLP* 40 (1959), pp. 197–198.

32. L. Beauduin, "L'Esprit paroissial—autrefois et aujourd'hui," *QL* 2 (1911), p. 261.

33. L. Beauduin, "Dom Marmion et la Liturgie," *VS* 78 (1948), pp. 35–37.

34. Bouyer, *op. cit.*, p. 75.

35. Haquin, *Dom L. B. . . .*, pp. 55f.

36. *Ibid.*, pp. 16of. According to Canon Martimort the two had known each other since 1898 at Rome where they first met. The author has been unable to verify this or find out about the nature of Beauduin's trip to Rome. Cf. *QLP* 40 (1959), p. 244.

CHAPTER 3

WORLD WAR I AND THE POSTWAR PERIOD

1. Cf. Bouyer, *op. cit.*, pp. 83–102, for a more detailed description of Beauduin's wartime adventures, to which this chapter is heavily indebted.

2. F. Vandenbrouck, "Un portrait de dom Lambert Beauduin," *QLP* 55 (1964), p. 202. Vandenbrouck disagrees with Bouyer who gives Rheinbrecht the rank of colonel. Becquet suggests "commandant" and adds that every September 8, the monks are reminded of the incident by the account read in the chronicles of Mont César.

3. Bouyer, *op. cit.*, p. 86.

4. *Ibid.*, p. 87.

5. *Idem.*

6. Cappuyns, *op. cit.*, p. 435. The bishop of Namur was the only one not to invite him to dinner.

7. L. Beauduin, "Autour de la lettre *Patriotisme et Endurance*," *Revue Cardinal Mercier* (April 1951), pp. 33–44, later reprinted as "Le Cardinal Mercier et ses suffragants en 1914," in *Revue Générale Belge* (July 15, 1953), pp. 410–419. This is the only account Beauduin ever published of any of his war-time experiences.

8. Cappuyns, *op. cit.*, p. 325.

9. One of these seminarians, Thomas Becquet, later joined Beauduin's community at Amay.

10. L. Beauduin, *op. cit.*, p. 418.

11. Ibid., p. 419.

12. Quoted in a letter from Rousseau to the author, April 15, 1971.

13. Thomas Becquet, "La figure et l'œuvre de Dom Lambert Beauduin," *La Revue Générale Belge*, (April 1960), p. 8, with some details added by Becquet in a letter to the author.

14. This name perhaps comes from his days at Saint-Trond. The sudden replacement and disappearance of M. Fraipont, director of the seminary, is recounted in a letter of May 7, 1893; cf. *Ephemerides Theologicae lovainiences*, No. 3 (1969), pp. 458f.

15. The military tribunal, according to Becquet, was located at Malines. Bouyer locates this incident in the vicinity of Maeseyck, p. 93; Vandenbroucke at Maredret, *QLP* 55 (1964), p. 202; Moeller at Maredsous, *La Libre Belgique* (July 15, 1964), p. 8. Reynders disagrees with Vandenbroucke and Moeller; agreeing to an extent with Bouyer, he locates the latrines at Maeseyck and the

tribunal at Diest or in the environs—in some undated notes sent to the author in the summer of 1967.

16. Cappuyns, *op. cit.*, p. 437.

17. Summary of de Régnon's four volumes: Vol. I presented an exposition of trinitarian doctrine as held by the fourth-century Latin and Greek fathers, positions determined in great part by the heresies of the day. Vol. II, treating the Scholastic theories of the divine processions, underlined the variety of theories generally ignored in standard texts. Moreover, de Régnon maintained that the genius of a man can only be fully appreciated when seen in the context of his milieu and age. Richard of St. Victor is treated in depth, since his theory differed considerably from the classical one systematized by Thomas and imposed on moderns as *the* theory. The author's point: much of Thomas can only be understood by a comparative study of his contemporaries. Vol. III developed the Greek theories of the Father and Son; Vol. IV, of the Holy Spirit.

18. R. Aubert, *op. cit. (La Revue Nouvelle)*, p. 234.

19. O. Rousseau, "In Memoriam: Dom Lambert Beauduin (1873–1960)," *Irénikon* 1 (1960), reprinted in *Dom Lambert Beauduin in Memoriam*, p. 50.

20. Navatel had gone to England to teach Church history to the French Jesuit scholastics at Hastings. Bouyer incorrectly locates this episode in Holland, *op. cit.*, pp. 100f. I am indebted to Rousseau who verified that Navatel was never in Holland, notes to the author, May, 1971.

21. Cappuyns, *op. cit.*, pp. 432–433.

22. OR to author, April 15, 1971.

23. *Idem.*

24. Bouyer, *op. cit.*, p. 103.

25. According to Becquet in a conversation with the author in the summer of 1970. Cf. Cappuyns, *op. cit.*, pp. 441–442.

26. Szepticky and the significance of this visit as well as his overall contribution will be discussed in detail in Chapter 5.

27. Cappuyns, *op. cit.*, p. 440.

28. At Mont César he taught *De Ecclesia, De Fide et De Vera Religione* as well as a course on the liturgy.

29. Aubert, *op. cit.*, p. 235. When Abbot Schuster (later Cardinal of Milan) was unable to find professors, Benedict XV finally confided this Institute to the Jesuits. Its purpose was to counteract the incompetence and prejudice concerning the Orthodox current in seminaries and in the Latin Church at large.

30. In 1897, Leo XIII entrusted its direction to the Benedictines.

31. Notes to the author from Becquet, May 1971.

CHAPTER 4

THE MALINES CONVERSATIONS

1. J. G. Lockhart, *Charles Lindley Viscount Halifax* (2 vols., London, 1935–1936); Earl of Birkenhead, *The Life of Lord Halifax* (London, 1964).

2. Hyppolyte Hemmer *et al., Monsieur Portal, Prêtre de la Mission (1855–1926)* (Paris, 1947); Arthur T. Macmillan, *Fernand Portal (1855–1926), Apostle of Unity* (London, 1961).

3. Roger Aubert was among the first to publish these documents. We are much indebted to several of his articles: "Quelques mots sur l'Église Anglicane," *Collectanea mechliniensia* 52, No. 1 (1967), pp. 3–6 (henceforth referred to as *Collectanea . . .*); "L'Histoire des conversations de Malines," *ibid.,* pp. 43–54; "Les Conversations de Malines Le Cardinal Mercier et le Saint-Siège," *Bullétin de la Classe des Lettres et de Sciences Morales et Politiques* 53 (1967), pp. 87–159 (henceforth referred to as *Bullétin . . .*).

4. L. J. Swidler, *The Ecumenical Vanguard* (Pittsburgh: Duquesne University Press, 1966), p. 43.

5. J. de Bivort de la Saudée, *Anglicans et catholiques, Le problème de l'union Anglo-romaine; 1833–1933* (Paris-Bruxelles: 1949).

6. J. J. Hughes, *Absolutely Null and Utterly Void* (Washington: Corpus Books, 1968), p. 35, where Hughes quotes a letter from Portal to Paul Thureau-Daugin, dated December 3, 1910.

7. Dalbus was none other than Portal; cf. *RCIF* 31 (October 23, 1925), pp. 15f., where a letter from Cardinal Rampolla gives Leo XIII's reactions.

8. Swidler, *op. cit.,* p. 43.

9. *AAS* 29 (1896), pp. 193–203. The decision of the commission which examined the issue was not unanimous. Men like Gasparri and Duchesne gave a favorable judgment on the validity. Cf. Swidler, *op. cit.,* p. 44. The issue itself has recently been reopened to examination at Rome; cf. Aubert, "Quelques mots sur l'Église Anglicane," *Collectanea . . . ,* p. 5.

10. Cf. Hughes, *op. cit.,* for a very thorough treatment of the question.

11. *ASS* 29 (1896–97), pp. 198–201, and Hughes, *op. cit.,* pp. 58f.

12. The author is indebted to Rev. A. M. Allchin of Pusey House, Oxford, for some of the historical details and clarifications in the above, as well as the following paragraphs.

13. Lord Halifax confided to a monk of Amay (D. A. de L.) in 1926 that he first went to Cardinal Bourne by whom he was poorly received. It was then that he urged Portal to approach Mercier.

14. Aubert, *op. cit., Collectanea . . . ,* pp. 45–46.

15. Quoted by Aubert, *ibid.,* p. 47.

16. Bell (1883–1958) subsequently became Bishop of Chichester in 1929 and was one of the most influential Anglican figures in the foundation of the World Council of Churches.

17. Under Pius XI, d'Herbigny became an extremely powerful man. His real interest, however, was to be the Russian question. See Chapter 5.

18. Aubert, *op. cit.,* p. 48. It seems clear from a letter to d'Herbigny that the cardinal was at first unaware that the Jesuit wanted to participate himself—cf. Aubert, *op. cit., Bullétin . . . ,* pp. 98 and 135, and especially Mercier's letter to d'Herbigny.

19. In the archives of Lambeth Palace in Box 189 are preserved d'Herbigny's correspondence and action concerning the proposed parallel to the Malines

Conversations. The correspondence, including letters from another Jesuit, Fr. Leslie Walker (1877–1958), dates from April 1922 to February 1923.

20. E. Beauduin, *La Vie du Cardinal Mercier* (Tournai: Casterman, 1966), pp. 128–129.

21. Aubert, *op. cit., Collectanea ...*, p. 49.

22. Mercier in a letter to Beauduin, February 15, 1925, stated that from the second conversation the importance of the pallium was insisted on as of great significance in an eventual reunion. Cf. *Irénikon* 3 (1927), pp. 150–151.

23. Aubert, *op. cit.*, pp. 49–50.

24. The points of agreement reached in the third conversation were, from the Anglican point of view, extremely important. They greatly influenced a young theologian, A. M. Ramsey, now Archbishop of Canterbury. See Appendix I of his *The Gospel of the Catholic Church* (London: Longmans, Green, 1956).

25. D. J. Mercier, "Les Conversations de Malines," a sixteen-page letter reprinted in *Oeuvres Pastorales* 7 (1929), pp. 289–305.

26. Cf. Aubert, *Bullétin ...*, pp. 112–113, for details behind this suppression and letters from Gasparri denying responsibility (pp. 145–149).

27. *Ibid.*, pp. 149–151. Sordet, a Redemptorist in residence at Rome, had been the cardinal's secretary at the conclave in 1922.

28. Born in 1877, he died in 1970. Since 1912 a member of the section of the Secretariat of State which dealt with extraordinary ecclesiastical affairs, he became its under-secretary in 1919. Named a cardinal in 1937, he later, as head of the Holy Office (1951), took severe measures against the priest-workers.

29. *AAS* 15 (November 12, 1923), pp. 573–782.

30. E. Beauduin, *op. cit.*, p. 130.

31. *AAS* 16 (1924), pp. 123–124; Aubert, *op. cit.*, pp. 116–117; *RCIF* (Oct.-Nov.), 1925. In the first, a letter by Mercier appears; in the second, the letter is republished with a footnote (Gasparri's note) giving the pope's tacit approval.

32. Letter of Gasparri to Mercier, 3/30/23, cited in Aubert, *op. cit.*, p. 105. Cf. p. 144 for his reply to Mercier's plan (given on pp. 142–143).

33. Archives of Lambeth Palace, Box 187, "Material from 1923–25." Memorandum for Malines by C. G. (Gore), Christmas 1924; see the postscript. (Gore had been chosen as a counter-balance to Halifax. He had little sympathy with the latter's pro-Roman views.)

34. P. Battifol's response, pp. 19, 21 and 22. Archives of Lambeth Palace, Box 187.

35. Pius XI in speaking of the Lateran on its anniversary (1924) evoked the memory that Augustine of Canterbury had been consecrated in the Lateran and given the pallium and therefore, the jurisdiction of all English churches; cf. L. Beauduin, "Omnium ecclesiarum mater et caput," *QLP* 9 (1924), p. 173.

36. "Includamus hunc in orbe nostro quasi alterius orbis papam," *Mansi, ACC*, Vol. 20, p. 948.

37. Cf. Halifax, *The Conversations of Malines* (London: Phillip Allan & Co., 1930), pp. 241–261.

38. Aubert, *Bullétin ...*, p. 156, letter dated January 31, 1925, Rome.

39. *Ibid.*, pp. 157–158, letter dated February 15, 1925, Malines. Seredi was one of the principal collaborators of Gasparri in the elaboration of the 1917 Code of Canon Law. He was named Archbishop of Estergom and raised to the rank of cardinal. He died as a result of harsh treatment during World War II.

40. *Ibid.*, pp. 158–159, February 20, 1925, Rome.

41. XXX, "La Vie Catholique, Les Conversations de Malines," *La Revue du Siècle* (Paris, May 13, 1934), p. 87.

42. Halifax, *op. cit.*, p. 256.

43. Cf. note 32.

44. Bouyer, *op. cit.*, pp. 126–27, although several in the nineteenth-century Oxford movement saw parallels.

45. Gratieux, *L'Amitié au Service de l'Union* (Paris: Bonne Presse, 1950), p. 259. One of the bitterest of Beauduin's critics was Fr. Woodlock; cf. "The Malines Conversations Report," *The Month* 155 (1930), pp. 238–246, and "Topics of the Month: Malines Once More: Dom Beauduin's *ballon d'essai*," *The Month* 155 (1930), pp. 267–279. Beauduin replied to the second article in *Irénikon* 7 (1930), pp. 471–473.

46. R. Aubert, "Un homme d'Église, Dom Lambert Beauduin," *La Revue Nouvelle* 31 (1960), p. 241.

47. Halifax *et al.*, *Conversations at Malines* (London: Oxford University Press, 1927), p. 32.

48. *Ibid.*, p. 91.

49. XXX, "La Vie Catholique, Les Conversations de Malines," *La Revue du Siècle* (Paris: May, 1934), p. 86.

50. *The Tablet*, Vol. 224, No. 6766 (January 31, 1970), p. 98. Cf. Frere's *Recollections of Malines* wherein he recalls this point.

51. Note by G. K. A. Bell preserved in Lambeth Archives, Box 187.

52. Malines Archives.

53. Lambeth Archives, Box 187. Halifax's speech also appeared as an appendix in *Reunion and the Roman Primacy. An Appeal to the Members of the English Church Union* (London, 1925), pp. 33–36. Woodlock's public criticism appeared in *Les Etudes*, Vol. 184 (August 10, 1925), pp. 304–310.

54. Gratieux, *op. cit.*, pp. 273–282.

55. XXX, "La Vie Catholique, Les Conversations de Malines," *op. cit.*, pp. 84–86.

56. Archives of Chevetogne.

57. Basile Mercier in a conversation with the author in the summer of 1966.

58. The highlights of this trip to the Near East were Egypt, Palestine, Constantinople, and Greece, including a stay at Mount Athos; for details see Chapter 9.

59. E. Beauduin, *op cit.*, pp. 131–132.

60. The trial which dealt with his refusal to accept a restricted concept of ecumenism as the work of his monastery resulted in a sentence of two years of penance at En Calcat (1932–1934) and an exile from Belgium which lasted until 1951. The legality of this trial is highly questionable. The very man who

signed the sentence (Cardinal Pacelli) apparently had no idea what it was all about. See Chapter 10.

61. E. Oldmeadow, *Francis Cardinal Bourne* (2 vols.: London, 1940–1944), Vol. 2, p. 377. The section pp. 353–414 is a detailed criticism of Beauduin's Proposal.

62. Cf. LB's articles in *Cahiers de Sainte Françoise Romaine.*

63. Notes from a conversation with LB, July 20–24, 1958, Chalivoy.

64. LB, "Les Patriarches," *Irénikon* 1 (1926), pp. 239–244, 267–274.

65. Cf. *Irénikon* 3 (1927), p. 150. Also *L'Unité Chrétienne* (collections 3 and 4), *Irénikon* 2 (1927), contains letters between Mercier and the Archbishop of Canterbury relating to the conversations, as well as Mercier's *Pastoral* of January 18, 1924.

66. *Lambeth Conference 1930* (London: 1930), p. 131.

67. J. W. Doyle 1786–1834, Roman Catholic Bishop of Kildare, in 1824 voiced his willingness to renounce his see without pay, pension, fee or ambition—if it would help unity. Cf. G. Tavard, *Two Centuries of Ecumenism: Search for Unity* (New York: New American Library, 1962), p. 46.

68. Cf. *Concilium*, Vol. 4, No. 6 (April 1970), *Post Ecumenical Christianity*, especially Congar's "Do the New Problems of Our Secular World Make Ecumenism Irrelevant?" pp. 11–21.

69. *The Tablet*, Vol. 224, No. 6766 (January 31, 1970), p. 98. Mention might also be made of Bishop Butler's "United Not Absorbed," *The Tablet* (March 7, 1970), pp. 220–221 and "Bishop Christopher Butler Proposes a Model for the Reunion of the Roman Catholic and Anglican Churches," *The Listener* (April 2, 1970), pp. 441–442. The implications of these articles are discussed in *JES*, Vol. 8, No. 2 (1971), pp. 278–285.

70. Cf. J. Willebrands "Ecumenical Significance of the Visit of Archbishop of Canterbury to the Holy Father," *Unitas* 19 (1967), pp. 8–17; *One in Christ* 3 (1969), p. 315.

71. Cf. note 38.

CHAPTER 5

LOOKING EASTWARD

1. A. Schmemann, "Orthodox Tradition: The Church," *Convergence of Traditions—Orthodox, Catholic and Protestant* (New York: Herder & Herder, 1967), p. 12, edited by Elmer O'Brien.

2. Jean Meyendorff, *Orthodoxy and Catholicity* (New York: Sheed & Ward, 1966), p. 116.

3. A. Szepticky, "Eastern and Western Mentality" originally printed in *Pax* (January and April, 1933); reprinted in *ECQ* 9 (1952), pp. 395–396.

4. The terms "Uniate" or "Uniatism" originated as pejorative terms used by the Orthodox to describe those Orthodox who had returned to Rome (who actually prefer to be called Eastern Catholics). No pejorative overtones are intended by our use of the word. The Uniates often originated as a progressive movement within Orthodoxy at a time of crisis when reform was

deemed necessary. We might compare them to the Oxford Movement of the preceding chapter. For the question of Latinization, see the numerous articles by C. Korolevsky in *Stoudion* (1922–1929). His controversial brochure *L'Uniatisme* (*Irénikon collection*, Nos. 5–6; Gembloux, 1927), is another excellent source.

5. Nicolas Zernov, *The Russians and Their Church* (London: SPCK, 1964), pp. 168f.

6. Peter Mogila, the Metropolitan of Kiev and a Russian Orthodox Thomist, founded the Ukrainian school of theology. His profession of faith against the Calvinists remains a classic. For sharply contrasting views on the nature of the union of Brest, see O. Halecki, *Poland and Christendom* (Houston: University of Saint Thomas, 1964), p. 9, for the Polish Catholic view; and A. Schmemann, *The Historical Road of Eastern Orthodoxy*, translated by Lydia Kesich (New York: Holt, Rinehart and Winston, 1963), p. 325, for a Russian Orthodox evaluation. Moscow abolished the see of Kiev in 1686.

7. When the Marxist government ordered the confiscation of all Church property, Pius XI with the support of American millionnaires offered to pay the full value so that it might remain in the possession of the Russian Orthodox Church. Although this offer was rejected, some relief to the famine-stricken was permitted until it became apparent that the pope was only interested in relief and not politics. The subsequent Roman Catholic indictment of communism led the Soviet press to accuse Rome of wanting a universal Church. It also touched off persecution of Roman Catholics. The Orthodox Patriarch Tykhon told his priests to hand over everything but consecrated objects. There were 691 who died rather than disobey. Others refused to comply, broke away, and formed the Living Church. M. Miller, "The Confiscation and Destruction of Church Property in the Ukraine," in *Religion in the USSR* (ed. by B. Iwanow; Munich: Carl Gerber Grafische Betriebe KG, 1960), p. 50 and J. Meyendorff *The Orthodox Church*, translated by John Chapin (London: Darton, Longman & Todd, 1962), pp. 121–141.

8. As émigrés continued to flow out from Russia, many found their way to England where they were welcomed by some of the ecumenists of the day. Two of the principals from the Malines Conversations, Bishops Gore and Frere, founded with the Orthodox the Fellowship of St. Alban and St. Sergius in 1927, which became an unofficial yet important channel for relations between Orthodox and Western Christians. Cf. N. Zernov, *op. cit.*, pp. 174–175. A center established expressly for ecumenical work, it was conceived of by a former Benedictine monk of Farnborough and secretary of Szepticky.

9. Rousseau, "In Memoriam: Dom Clement Lialine (1901–1958)," *Irénikon* 31 (1958), pp. 166–167.

10. C. Korolevsky, *Le Métropolite André Szepticky* (Grotta Ferrata, 1920).

11. V. Vancik, "Death of Metropolitan Sheptitsky," *Catholic Mind* 43 (1945), p. 144 (reprinted from the *Narod*, Chicago, December 10, 1944).

12. On October 14, 1929, in a conversation with Fr. Antoine Delpuch, superior of the White Fathers' seminary in Jerusalem, Beauduin and Becquet learned that the superior had seen the authorization signed by Pius X in the hands of Szepticky himself. It actually gave him the authority to receive Rus-

sian Orthodox priests into the Roman Catholic Church who, while maintaining their ministry to the Orthodox, would be Catholic *de facto* without any manifestation of their Catholicism, e.g. they could concelebrate with their own Orthodox bishops, etc. We had not yet reached the age of ecumenism! From "Notes on Dom Lambert Beauduin's trip to the Near-East," p. 11, taken from Becquet's diary of the trip.

13. F. Mercenier," "Le Métropolite André Szeptycky," *Irénikon* 19 (1946), p. 59.

14. *Ibid.*, p. 61. This conference of February 18, 1921, was published in *Stoudion*, pp. 10–12, 33–40 in 1923; the thesis of the talk would be taken up by Beauduin in *Equidem Verba*; see Chapters 6 and 7.

15. D. Attwater, "Andrew Szepticky," *Blackfriars* 29 (1948), p. 56.

16. His brother, Clement Szepticky, superior general of the Studites, had made his novitiate at Beuron.

17. In 1939 only twenty of the two hundred monks were priests. Since then the order has experienced a rapid decline. Toward 1949, the remaining group of about fifteen spent several years at Chevetogne. After a sojourn in Canada, they returned in reduced numbers to their present site in the suburbs of Rome.

18. Attwater, *op. cit.*, p. 55.

19. The Basilians had been radically changed from a contemplative to an active congregation in 1882 by the Jesuit reform; cf. F. Beyda, "The Szepticky Museum," *ECQ* 9 (1952), p. 408.

20. Bouyer's criticism of Korolevsky is not justified. He cites a contemporary who claims that Korolevsky's book on the liturgy is "nothing but a collection of flagrant errors and impudent lies": *op. cit.*, p. 113. American reviewers at least seem more appreciative of his scholarship: D. J. M. Callahan, S.J., writing in *TS* 16 (1955), p. 626, says: ". . . a clear, succinct, timely assemblage of historical documents . . . treated with gratifying thoroughness and ample documentation." J. Murray, S.J., in *TS* 19 (1958), p. 123, claims that Korolevsky "writes for the 'intelligent' reader . . . a more involved historical inquiry" than average. His two-volume work (a third was never published), *Histoire des patriarcats melkites depuis le schisme monophysite de 6 ème siècle jusqu' à nos jours* (Paris: Picard, 1911), was praised by Fortesque for its care in the verification of facts, patience in research, and accuracy in theological and liturgical lore—"a work which any other in Christendom may envy." In short, he has produced much more than Bouyer gives him credit for, and apparently he did a scholarly job of it. The writer of the obituary notice felt justified in claiming that Korolevsky had done more than any other "private" person to open Western eyes to the Eastern Churches, their history and tradition. Also see Cappuyns, *op. cit.*, p. 449, for further comments on Korolevsky's contribution.

21. Obituary notice: "Cyril Korolevsky," *ECQ* 13 (1959), pp. 88–89.

22. In reality Korolevsky's earlier and more direct influence on Olivier Rousseau lasted but a short while. There were two stages to his impact on Beauduin: (1) at the end of 1921 when he passed on the documents on Sant' Anselmo; (2) in 1923–1924 when he prepared a typikon for Amay which in

the end Beauduin did not want. (This typikon is today in the Archives of Chevetogne.) From this moment on he had no further influence on Beauduin.

23. M. d'Herbigny, "Seize jours à Moscou, Oct. 4–20, 1925," *Etudes* 185 (1925), pp. 513–540, 658–676.

24. M. d'Herbigny, "Pâques 1926 en Russie," *Etudes* 188 (1926), pp. 257–282 (from April 1 to May 15) and 421–447.

25. M. Cappuyns, *op. cit.*, pp. 441 and 761. Prior to his Oriental career, d'Herbigny produced a theology of the Church, *Theologica de ecclesia* (Paris: Beauchesne, 1920) and *Un Newman russe, Vladimire Soloviev* (Paris, 1911). At the peak of his career he produced several books and a number of articles: *L'âme religieuse des Russes d'après leurs plus récentes publications* (123 pages, reviewed in *Etudes* 182 (1925), p. 111; *La Tyrannie soviétique et le malheur russe* (254 pages), *Etudes* review, 182 (1925), p. 249; also reviewed in 176 (1923) p. 373. Some additional articles—"L'Église vivante de Russie ou le clergé rouge," 174 (1923), pp. 257–275; "Les préludes de la révolution russe, d'après les memoires du Comte Witte," 180 (1924), pp. 5–29. At the end of his career he wrote *"Les Sans-Dieu" militants et la propogande mondiale du communisme* (Paris: Fédération nationale catholique, 1938).

26. N. Teodorvich, "The Roman Catholics," p. 86, in *Religion in the USSR*.

27. J. Ledit, S.J., *Acta Romana Societatis Jesu* 8 (1935–37), p. 540.

28. Data taken from *Catalogues of the Members of the Champagne Province of the Society of Jesus* (1898–1958) and *Acta Romana Societatis Jesu* 7 (1932–1934), p. 90 The author is indebted to Fr. James J. Hennesey, S.J., formerly rector of Fordham, now a professor at Berkeley, who provided this data.

29. Cappuyns, *op. cit.*, pp. 441 and 791f.

30. *AAS* 27 (1935), pp. 65–67, motu proprio of Pius XI *Quam Sollicita*.

31. 1934–1937: he is listed as a bishop living in Brussels and giving retreats. 1937–1940: beginning with 1937–1938 he is listed simply as "Fr. Michel d'Herbigny," a writer at Florennes, Belgium. *Woodstock Letters* 77 (1948), p. 228, indicates that he resigned as bishop in 1937; in 1939 his see of Ilium was given to James Maguire, auxiliary bishop of Dunkeld, Scotland. 1940–1955: listed as "Fr. d'Herbigny," resident at Mons (France), a Jesuit novitiate. 1956–1957: novitiate moves to La Baume Ste-Marie; he died December 24. From catalogues *loc. cit.*

32. Bouyer, *op. cit.*, p. 116.

33. S. Quitslund, " 'United not Absorbed,' Does It Still Make Sense?" *JES*, Vol. 8, No. 2 (1971), pp. 278–285.

34. Abbott, *The Documents of Vatican II*, p. 374, paragraph 3.

CHAPTER 6
THE PRE-HISTORY OF AMAY

1. Bouyer, *op. cit.*, p. 110.

2. Letter of Leo XIII to Cardinal Dusmet, dated January 4, 1887, cited in *Stoudion* 1 (1924), p. 103. (This periodical was founded by Korolevsky.)

3. Haquin, *op. cit.*, p. 27, letters of van Caloen, March 13, 1887. In 1878 van Caloen undertook the translation of the missal for the laity. He also restored the Benedictine Order in Brazil, working on the spot from 1895–1919. On November 4, 1909, Abbot de Kerchove wrote him saying: "we are quite disposed to form priests for the Rio Branco. I believe dom Lambert would make a good rector." Cf. Haquin, *op. cit.*, pp. 6–29, 109.

4. Van Caloen, *Revue Bénédictine* 8 (1891), pp: 117–129.

5. Charles de T'Serclaes, *Le Pape Léon XIII*. (2 vols.; Paris: Desclée, 1894), pp. 594–596.

6. *Orientalium dignitas*, *AAS* 27 (November 30, 1894), p. 260.

7. LB, "Rapproachement anglo-oriental," *Irénikon* 1 (1926), pp. 166–168. Rome, as late as Vatican II, had seen no problem in granting intercommunion with the Orthodox, but the Orthodox see insurmountable obstacles and generally oppose intercommunion unless there is total unanimity of faith. As Meyendorff summed it up: "All theories of intercommunion presuppose either relativism or theological disjunction between the sacramental presence of Christ and his revelation as unique truth"; *Orthodoxy and Catholicity*, Chapter 7. Haquin suggests that Beauduin's interest in Oriental rites may have dated from 1913 and the decree *Tradita ab Antiquis* which authorized communion in both rites, Latin and Oriental: *op. cit.*, p. 180.

8. LB, *Retraite Liturgique "Ut unum sint"* (Louvain: Mont César, 1913), 120 pages. A liturgical retreat centered around the liturgy of the day, bringing the retreatants (priests) together for the chanting of the Divine Office, celebration of the Mass, and workshops on how to bring the liturgy into their lives and the lives of those entrusted to them.

9. A second liturgical career would begin in the 1940's, in France.

10. To cite only a few of the earliest examples in *Liturgical Life*: 1909: "L'année ecclésiastique" compares the Roman celebration of advent with that of the Greeks (p. 15); 1910: "Explication de la messe"—Greek customs concerning catechumens, liturgy, and concelebration, continued down to the present (pp. 29–34); "Messe des catéchumènes"—use of litanies, importance of role of deacon (pp. 130f.), etc.

11. LB, private memoirs written at En Calcat in 1932, entitled: "L'Union des Eglises—Fondation d'Amay. Apostolat unioniste," p. 1.

12. Some differences of opinion seem to exist; cf. Bouyer, *op. cit.*, pp. 104–105. R. Aubert "Un homme d'Eglise, dom Lambert Beauduin," p. 236, recounts both the Mont César visit of 1920 and the renewed acquaintance-ship of 1922—1923. A. Ostoya, "Poland, the Ukraine," *Catholic World* 174 (1951), p. 106, dates Szepticky's tour of Belgium as 1921.

13. LB, *"Memoirs,"* pp. 3–4.

14. He became rector of the Greek College in 1919.

15. In 1916 Antoine Delpuch had suggested the creation of an Oriental congregation to some prelates; Benedict XV presented the idea to the

cardinals who immediately accepted it. Delpuch served for a time as president of the Pontifical Oriental Institute which was eventually turned over to the Jesuits. Originally it drew its professors from as many orders as had qualified men and were willing to assign them to the work.

16. *Memoirs,* En Calcat, 1932, p. 1. Msgr. Papadoupoulos was the Catholic bishop of the Byzantine rite in Constantinople; Ostoyan, *op. cit.,* p. 410.

17. Attwater, *op. cit.,* pp. 54–56; Vancik, *op. cit., p.* 145; Ostoya, *op. cit.,* pp. 105–106; Bouyer, *op. cit.,* p. 120.

18. LB to OR, Mont César, 9/29/23.

19. *AAS* 15 (November 12, 1923), pp. 573–582.

20. R. Aubert, "Un homme de'Eglise, Dom Lambert Beauduin," *La Revue Nouvelle* 31 (March 1960), p. 236.

21. According to Bouyer, Beauduin not only was the author of the projected plan submitted by the cardinal to Pius XI, but also of the cardinal's cover letter; cf. *op. cit.,* p. 121.

22. The text of this papal brief never appeared in *AAS.* It incorporated the major ideas of Szepticky's 1921 address on union and monasticism.

23. LB to OR, Chatou, 2/9/43.

24. Mercier to LB, 12/11/23. The document was entrusted to d'Herbigny to be passed on at the "psychological" moment.

25. LB to OR, Rome, 12/7/23.

26. LB to OR, Rome, 2/13/24.

27. LB to OR, Rome, 3/16/24.

28. LB to OR, Rome, 4/25/24.

29. LB to OR, Rome, 5/29/24.

30. L. Beauduin, "Projet d'érection d'un institut monastique en vue de l'apostolat de l'union des Eglises," 1924, Archives of Chevetogne. Paper sent to Cardinal Mercier who subsequently sent it on to Pius XI.

31. André Stoelen was the monk released by the abbot.

32. This letter belongs to the dossier of Bruno Reynders, who was one of the monks assigned to destroy certain confidential papers at the moment of Abbot de Kerchove's death. Realizing its historical significance, Reynders first copied it and then burned the original.

33. Perhaps he refers here to the Oriental foundation by Latin monks proposed in the project.

34. Bouyer, *op. cit.,* pp. 122–124.

35. LB to OR, Rome, 6/13/25.

36. LB to OR, Belgium, 8/20/25.

CHAPTER 7
THE FOUNDATION OF AMAY

1. Pius XI seriously considered a council to complete the work of Vatican I. However, the Roman question first had to be settled. When that was ac-

complished in 1929, efforts for a council were further delayed by all the administrative reorganization involved. Pius XI's death, his successor's different views on the matter, World War II and other events all served to further postpone the realization of this matter; cf. *Irénikon* 33 (1966), p. 409. Also, G. Caprile, *Il Consilio Vaticano II*, Vol. 5, pp. 681f. (Rome: La Civilta Cattolica, 1969).

2. LB, "Une visite à la laure orthodoxe de Potchaiev," *Pages de Gloire* (6e séries, Bruges: Desclée de Brouwer, 1927–1928), pp. 48–56.

3. Second Edition, Prieuré de L'Union, Amay-sur-Meuse, 1926, 32 pages (first edition: Mount César, 1925, published the day he received final approval from Mont César—May 25).

4. T. Becquet, *L'Union des Eglises Le Mouvement Actuel* (Collection des Etudes Religieuses #157) (Liège: Pensée Catholique, Imp. St-Jean, n.d.), 36 pages.

5. LB, *Une Oeuvre Monastique. . . ,* p. 9.

6. Consistoral allocution of December 18, 1924, *AAS* 16 (1924), p. 495.

7. LB, *op. cit.,* pp. 9–10.

8. Solesmes (France), Beuron, Maria-Laach (Germany), Mont César, Affligem (Belgium), Saint John's (U.S.A.), Downside (England), to name only a few.

9. Polycarp of Smyrna and Pope Anicetus at Rome circa 150. Congar, *After Nine Hundred Years* (N.Y.: Fordham University Press, 1959), p. 391, and O. Rousseau, "La question des rites entre Grecs et Latins des premier siècles au concile de Florence," *Irénikon* 22 (1949), pp. 233–269.

10. "Note on Amay," September 1942, p. 5, and "Note on Historical Circumstances of Amay," 1950, p. 2.

11. Note of 1950, p. 2.

12. LB, *op. cit.,* p. 15.

13. *Motu proprio* of Benedict XV: *Dei Providentes* of May 1, 1917: *AAS* 9 (1917), p. 530. This same idea is to be found in the Vatican II *Decree on Eastern Catholic Churches,* n. 3.

14. The work begun by Amay in this domain continues today at Chevetogne in studies on Eastern theology and related topics.

15. LB, "Note sur Amay," September 1942, p. 3.

16. *Ibid.,* pp. 1–2 (emphasis added).

17. Chevetogne remains predominantly clerical today, but concelebration has helped to solve at least one problem, that of making the community Mass a truly communal celebration. Nevertheless, in the young generation, the idea and the practice of lay monks is growing.

18. Just five days prior to its publication, Mercier had read Beauduin's *Proposal* at the Malines Conversation.

19. LB to Gommaire Laporta, Amay, 10/4/25, dossier of Bruno Reynders.

20. Memoirs of Thomas Becquet to the author, 1967, p. 1. The pontiff singled out Mexico because of the particularly bloody religious persecution going on at the time.

CHAPTER 8

THAT THEY MAY BE ONE

1. LB, "L'Union des Eglises et le Concile du Vatican," *RCIF*, Vol. 5, #31 (October 23, 1925), pp. 10–13.

2. "Le Problème de l'Union au Point au Vue Orthodoxe"—the conference was never published. Both Olivier Rousseau who heard the talk and Theodore Strotmann (also of Chevetogne) attest to the impact that it made on Beauduin. Cf. O. Rousseau, "La Semaine Unioniste," *Irénikon* 12 (1935), pp. 599–611 for a résumé of the week and evaluation. The more important talks were published in *RCIF*, October 23 and November 6, 1925.

3. M. Cappuyns, *op. cit.*, p. 441. The families of Viscount Henri Davignon and Baron del Marmol originally offered the land to Maredsous in 1914. An interesting point to note is the fact that later on, when groundwork was begun for construction, it was stopped by the military. The property was right on the Belgian "Maginot" line, and the fort that was built near the place where the future monastery might have stood was the last to fall, surrendering only after the Belgian capitulation when the Germans were already at Abbéville. Before thinking of Tancrémont, Beauduin went to see the monastery of Chevetogne abandoned by the monks of Ligugé in 1923, but it had just been rented. In 1939 it would again become available, at which time it would be acquired by the Monks of Unity.

4. Father De Groot, S.J. sent a wire to Beauduin in the autumn of 1925, inviting him to meet him at Louvain. Beauduin sent Becquet. At first Beauduin paid no attention to Becquet's report. When he finally did visit Amay, he immediately became enthusiastic.

5. Cappuyns, *op. cit.*; cf. p. 448 for the letter to de Kerchove, dated 12/16/24; pp. 453–454 and 762 give more details about these financial arrangements.

6. LB to OR, Amay, October 1926.

7. Cappuyns, *op. cit.*, pp. 450–451, for the letter to de Kerchove, dated 5/21/25.

8. Beauduin especially liked to stress this international flavor. In 1954, in an article that overlooked precise chronology, he wrote: "Among the first novices of the monastery may be noted a Frenchman, Basile Mercier, who has since won fame as an Orientalist, and is professor of Armenian and Georgian Christian literature at the Institut Catholique in Paris. Other pioneers who grouped themselves around the founder were (Canon) Theodore Belpaire of Antwerp who sacrificed a brilliant career to give himself up entirely to the apostolate of the East; Gregory Bainbridge from Australia; Thomas Becquet, present prior of the monastery; Olivier Rousseau who has specialized in a study of the liturgy and of the Eastern Fathers; Mercenier, now director of the new *Didascalia* of Alexandria; Clement Lialine who comes from an ancient Russian family and who has specialized in the theology and history of Orthodoxy; Theodore Strotmann, one of the many in Holland devoted to reunion." Cf. LB, "Thirty Years After," *Pax* 44 (Spring, 1954), p. 24.

For the sake of historical accuracy, here is the official list of the original community: the first group came between December and July—Ildephonse Dirks, Thomas Becquet, Michel Schwartz; those who came near July—André Stoelen (died 1971), David Balfour, Anselm Bolton, Andrew de Lilienfeld, Jose Porron, Irénée Doens the first novice; and those who arrived in September 1926—Pierre Dumont (died 1970), Theodore Belpaire, Cyrille de Ruyck (died at Chevetogne, December 16, 1971), and Franco de Wyels. Others also came from every persuasion, but not all stayed.

Of those mentioned in the above article, Belpaire celebrated the sixtieth anniversary of his priesthood in September 1966 and died in October 1968. Becquet is pastor at Loddes in southern France; before the council he served on the preparatory commission of the Oriental Church. Lialine died April 26, 1958, and Mercenier died in 1965. Bainbridge is now in England and Mercier is a chaplain in a convent. Only Strotmann, Jose Porron (a lay brother who during World War I was a monk of Ligugé at Chevetogne) and Rousseau (peritus for the Melchite patriarchate during Vatican II) now reside at Chevetogne.

9. This entire section on "Life at Amay" is very much indebted to some notes from Becquet, one of the original members of Amay and secretary to Beauduin. From "Notes to the Author" May 1971, pp. 4–9. Cf. O. Rousseau, "Dom Lambert Beauduin et la vie monastique," *Revue Mabillon*, Vol. 50 (1961), pp. 265–278.

10. O. Rousseau, "Après dix ans: la semaine unioniste de Bruxelles en 1925," *Irénikon* 12 (1935), p. 605. The very title of the publication was inspired by the title of a collection of Pusey's tracts, one of the originators of the Oxford Movement.

11. Archives of Chevetogne. Portal to Beauduin, 4/28/26.

12. Cf. cover of the first edition of *Irénikon*, April 1926.

13. LB, "De quoi s'agit-il?" *Irénikon* 1 (1926), p. 6.

14. LB, "Le vrai travail pour l'union," *Irénikon* 3 (1927), pp. 5–6.

15. Becquet, notes from his diary, to the author, July 18, 1970.

16. In 1929 Etcheverry wanted to suppress *Irénikon*. He asked Chibas-Lassalle, prior of the Benedictine monastery on the Mount of Olives in Jerusalem, who in turn asked Delpuch whether there was cause for action. Delpuch replied: "If you touch the monks of Amay there will be a revolution in the Orthodox world" (from Becquet's journal). When Beauduin met Delpuch on his trip (see next chapter), Delpuch recounted the details to him.

17. J. D. Mansi, *Sacrorum conciliorum nova et emplissima collectio* (31 vols.: Florence and Venice, 1757–1798), new printing and continuation published by L. Petit & J. B. Martin in 60 vols., Paris, 1899–1927.

18. Cf. *Irénikon* 3 (1927), p. 313, as pointed out in an unpublished article by O. Rousseau, "Dom Lambert Beauduin et les conciles." The notice stated that they had received fifty-five volumes.

19. De Wyels' articles appeared in *Irénikon* 5 (1929), pp. 366–396, 488–516, and 655–686.

20. OR to the author, August 1971.

21. OR to the author, 4/15/71.

22. The reply, although dated July 4, 1927, only appeared in *AAS* 20 (1928), pp. 26–27; cf. Cappuyns, *op. cit.*, p. 762.

23. LB to OR, Amay, 8/19/27.

24. Cf. note 22.

25. The term "return" frequently used in pontifical documents in the first part of this century concerning the Russian Orthodox tends to be misleading. Pius XII stated in *Sacro Vergente Anno* of 1952: "Up until 1948, no official document declared your Church [Russia] to be separated from the Apostolic See": Tavard, *op. cit.*, p. 181.

26. LB to OR, Amay, 8/21/28.

27. In 1957 the Holy See invited the monks of Chevetogne to take over the direction of the Greek College.

28. *AAS* 20 (1928), pp. 5–16.

29. Bouyer, *op. cit.*, p. 150.

30. LB, "L'Encyclique '*Mortalium Animos*' du janvier, 1928," *Irénikon* 5 (1928), pp. 81–91.

31. *Ibid.*, p. 91, quoted from Mercier's discourse at the Unity Week of Brussels, September 25, 1925.

32. W. A. Visser't Hooft, "Nathan Soederblom, figure de prophète du Mouvement Oecumenique," in *Oecumenica* 2 (1967), p. 145.

33. Bouyer, *op. cit.*, p. 151. For further details, cf. Cappuyns, *op. cit.*, p. 767.

34. A member of the Subiaco Congregation, noted for his fairness, he was proud of having dismissed *twelve* Benedictine abbots! He died in 1937.

35. Becquet, notes to the author, May 1971, pp. 9–10. Cf. Cappuyns, *op. cit.*, p. 763; Bouyer, *op. cit.*, p. 152.

36. LB to OR, 2/12/28, quoted in notes to the author from Rousseau, May 1971.

37. Cappuyns, *op. cit.*, p. 765, letter of LB to Pierre Dumont 12/15/28.

38. Cahiers III and IV, of Rousseau.

39. LB to OR, Amay, 8/19/27.

40. "Note sur Amay," 1942, p. 2, a condensation. The Latin phrases: "Especially and now lovingly our mind turns to the inhabitants of Russia." "They should undertake the unity with the Catholic Church among the dissidents, especially the Russians."

CHAPTER 9
THE NEAR EAST

1. T. Becquet, "Dom Lambert dans le Proche-Orient," p. 2, notes sent to the author, 1969.

2. LB to OR, Rome, 2/1/29.

3. Much of the following pages were taken from the detailed diary Becquet kept of his trip with Beauduin in the Near East. The two were together from

September 22 to November 1, 1929, at which point Becquet returned to Belgium and Beauduin went back to Jerusalem. Some supplementary material was sent the author on August 4, 1971. No attempt has been made to double-check facts and figures in the diary, since the interest and emphasis of this chapter are on the human rather than the historical dimension of Beauduin.

4. This Coptic priest was the Coptic patriarch's delegate to the Life and Work Conference at Oxford, 1937.

5. When Etcheverry asked Chibas-Lassalle to examine *Irénikon* with a view to suppressing it, the latter, along with Delpuch, offered only one criticism: Amay was too occupied with Anglicans and Protestants, but there were no errors in *Irénikon*.

6. See St. Paulinus of Nola (403 AD), *P.L.* 61, 327; Sulpicius Severus (405 AD), *P.L.* 20, 108, etc.

7. His tomb was recently discovered. For Beauduin's account of this trip, see his "La vie monastique dans le désert de Judée," *Irénikon* 6 (1929), pp. 633–642.

8. Edouard Beauduin to OR, quoting LB, Rome, 12/21/29.

9. LB, "L'Union des Eglises—une conférence de dom Lambert Beauduin à Constantinople," *Irénikon* 7 (1930), pp. 10–13.

10. Pierre Dumont (1901–1970), ordained for the diocese of Tournai in 1925, joined the Monks of Unity in 1926. In 1930, as a result of the trip in the Near East, Beauduin oriented him toward a projected foundation at Constantinople, which was never realized due to the restrictions subsequently imposed on Amay. Dumont, director of Eastern affairs in Belgium from 1941–1956, was succeeded by Beauduin's nephew, Edouard. Dumont was then named rector of the Greek College in Rome, worked on a pre-conciliar commission, and was associated with the Secretariat for Unity until 1967.

11. He confided this to the nuns at Chatou, where he spent a number of years of his exile, in an interview with Sr. Bruyas in the summer of 1966.

CHAPTER 10

TRIAL AND EXILE

1. Cappuyns, *op. cit.*, p. 769. See p. 776 where Capelle's letter is quoted: "Beauduin's ideas on authority and monastic obedience are incompatible with mine which are those of the congregation": 3/2/31. Capelle had been named co-adjutor to the abbot of Mont César in January 1928 and delegated abbot for Amay, October 1928. In 1931 he resigned as delegated abbot and Etcheverry took over.

2. It is interesting to note that faced with further accentuation of the Russian character of Amay, Capelle had gone to Rome. Recounting his audience of December 17, 1929 in a letter to LB (1/10/30), he stated that Pius agreed that the majority should stay Latin and seemed to indicate that he knew d'Herbigny and Sincero held the opposite view: Cappuyns, *ibid.*, pp. 769–770.

3. LB to Reynders, Constantinople, 2/3/30.

4. LB, "Les Patriarches," *Irénikon* 1 (1926), pp. 239–244, 267–274; Mercier's letter, *Irénikon* 3 (1927), pp. 150–151.

5. Bouyer, *op. cit.*, p. 154.

6. Letter of Capelle to Reynders, 10/5/30, quoted in Cappuyns, *op. cit.*, p. 723.

7. Bouyer, *op. cit.*, p. 155.

8. According to the *Annuaire Pontifical Catholique* (Battandier, 1931) p. 876, the Pontifical Commission for Russia was composed of d'Herbigny as president and Msgr. Giobbe as secretary, and among the members, Msgr. Pizzardo (the same Giuseppe Pizzardo who had figured in the episode concerning Mercier's Pastoral on the Malines Conversations). There was also a Russian priest, Fr. Bratko, who acted as recorder; Beauduin always thought it was he who told the members of the special commission that the suppression of Amay would be disastrous from the point of view of Orthodox relations. Whether or not Bratko assisted at the deliberations of the special commission is unknown. He is now dead.

9. Cappuyns, *op. cit.*, p. 447.

10. LB to MC, Rome, 3/29/31. Cf. Cappuyns, *op. cit.*, pp. 780–781.

11. D'Herbigny's own lightning-like fall is attributed to, among other things, the pope's discovery of just such abuses of the papal name. The author is indebted for some clarifications on the procedure (and violations of procedure) in this trial to Rousseau (letter of 2/27/72) and Becquet (notes to author, May 1971, pp. 11–12, and letters of 3/6/72 [p. 2] and 3/17/72).

12. Cappuyns, *op. cit.*, p. 778. Cappuyns claims that this was the work of d'Herbigny and that Etcheverry announced the suppression of Amay. Rousseau (who was there) denies the latter point, although he admits that the decree might have been among Etcheverry's papers.

13. From various reliable sources, including notes sent to the author by Reynders and Rousseau in the summer of 1967, and letters from Rousseau (2/27/72) and Becquet (3/6/72). Stoelen had already returned to Mont César in 1929, de Wyels in 1930 to Affligem. In 1928 Gillet (a Studite monk, never a monk of Amay) and in 1929 van der Mensbrugge went over to Orthodoxy.

14. Cappuyns, *op. cit.*, pp. 776–782, for a fairly detailed description of these events to which the author is deeply indebted.

15. LB to JJ, Rome, 4/21/31 and 5/3/31.

16. LB to OR, Amay, 8/14/31.

17. LB to MC, Paris, 7/1/31.

18. LB to Reynders, 7/17/31.

19. LB to JJ, Mont César, 9/4/31.

20. Cappuyns, *op. cit.*, letter dated 2/8/32, p. 785. D'Herbigny's letter of 2/8/32, sent under the signature of the commission, was a veritable decree. It stated that for serious reasons Beauduin had been excluded from all involvement in Amay since 1930. The evidence of financial mismanagement in 1931 only reinforced the validity of this decision. (This referred to the Boland

affair, first handled in 1927–1928 and used in various ways in 1929, 1930, and 1931. It entered the picture once again in 1932.) See Chapter 5 for details of d'Herbigny's fall.

21. *Ibid.*, p. 786.

22. Notes of Msgr. E. Beauduin from a conversation with LB on 7/20–24/58, at Chalivoy.

23. LB to IVH, En Calcat, 4/20/32.

24. Bouyer, *op. cit.*, p. 160.

25. *Ibid.*, p. 160. According to Becquet, the monks are especially active in the printed apostolate: publishing a missal, retreats, and the like.

26. LB to MC, En Calcat, 5/29/32.

27. LB to Canon Gillet, En Calcat, 8/8/32.

28. LB to MC, En Calcat, 8/17/32.

29. LB to MC, En Calcat, 3/31/33.

30. LB to JJ, En Calcat, 7/9/32.

31. LB to JJ, En Calcat, 12/14/33.

32. Bouyer, *op. cit.*, pp. 163–165.

33. This last detail was recounted by Rousseau in an interview, 1966.

34. Balfour left in September 1932, Laporta in 1934. Reynders has a large dossier of documents on Amay, especially of the "conversations by mail" with which Laporta was particularly involved.

35. LB to PD, En Calcat, 11/21/33.

36. See Chapter 5.

37. Bouyer, *op. cit.*, p. 159.

38. Cappuyns, *op. cit.* pp. 793–803. This entire section is drawn almost exclusively from Cappuyns heavily documented treatment of Beauduin's defense, which charge Beauduin had given him, and which Cappuyns attempted to discharge in this article in 1966.

39. In the legal publication of the *Moniteur* (the official Belgian bulletin for the constitution of non-profit organizations *associations sans but lucratif* or ASBL), all of Beauduin's brothers' names were listed along with his.

40. Cappuyns, *op. cit.*, pp. 805–806, letter dated 2/15/34.

41. *Ibid.*, p. 786.

CHAPTER 11

THE PARISIAN EXILE BEGINS

1. The ad read: "Prêtre religieux cherche aumônerie région parisienne." (A religious priest seeks a chaplaincy in the Paris region.)

2. Cf. "L'Union des Eglises," *Cahiers Ste. Françoise* (October 1937), pp. 10–14, signed XXX. This article gives LB's reflections on these ecumenical conferences.

3. Letter of Mother Marie Pascal Dickson to the author, 7/29/71.

4. Fr. Paul Grammont, now abbot of the famous monastery of Bec-

Hellouin in Normandy, to which the two communities moved in 1949. The intention of their prayer is for the unity of the Church, and, because of their historical links with England, especially for the Anglicans.

5. These quotes are taken from Mother Paschal's notes.

6. Cf. *Bullétin de Notre Dame de la Ste. Espérance*, 1935–1936.

7. Bouyer eventually became an Oratorian priest and first biographer of Beauduin.

8. This and some of the following incidents are cited from *Amicale des Anciennes*, No. 10, 1961, Bon Saveur de Chatou.

9. Sr. Bruyas, in an interview during the summer of 1966. Sr. Bruyas, a member of the community at Chatou, had known Beauduin as a pupil, postulant and young professed.

10. Now Fr. Charles Mercier, chaplain to some nuns in Vernon. Basile Mercier was a novice of Beauduin's in 1927 and sent from Amay in 1935 to teach at the Institut.

11. Beauduin in fact did inherit some of those papers—for instance, the letters from Msgr. Van Ballaer, friend and counselor of the cardinal since the time before his nomination as archbishop of Malines; this correspondence is still in Chevetogne.

12. The author is indebted to Marc de Vivie for much of the material in the preceding section on Beauduin's life at Chatou. It was taken from extracts of a letter from de Vivie to Becquet, 8/11/71, communicated by Becquet to the author in August 1971.

13. "Lambert, come! Come!" Recounted in Bouyer, *op. cit.*, p. 180; supplementary details of this relationship furnished by Rousseau, May 1971, and Becquet.

14. M. Villain, "Un pionnier de l'Unité Chrétienne," *L'Union* (May 1960), p. 12.

15. "Les noces d'or sacerdotales de dom Lambert Beauduin au Mont César," *Libre Belgique*, April 24, 1947, in "Chronique religieuse."

16. A.-G. Martimort, "Dom Lambert Beauduin et le C.P.L.," *QLP* 40 (1959), p. 244. Martimort points out that so deep was the bishop's devotion to the monk that he frequently proclaimed that he owed everything to Beauduin. Cf. R. Harscouet, *Horizons liturgiques* (Tournai, 1942), p. 24. Harscouet died in 1954.

17. LB to MC, En Calcat, 4/3/33.

18. These details were gathered by A. Bugnini from conversations held in France in the fall of 1946 and subsequently published in his article "L'odierno movimento liturgico," in *Illustrazione Vaticana* (1948), p. 86. The CPL has been replaced by the CNPL—National Pastoral and Liturgical Center, an organization completely different in structure and spirit from the CPL.

19. A.-G. Martimort, *loc. cit.*

20. H. de Lubac, *Catholicisme* (Paris: Editions du Cerf, 1938).

21. Father Roguet in an interview admitted that this book had influenced him in his vocation as a liturgist.

22. Testimony of Canon A. Müller, Institut Catholique of Paris, in a letter

dated 9/20/66. On February 16, 1947, Beauduin gave a conference at Vanves on Marmion and Destrée (Beauduin's former novice master).

23. A.-G. Martimort, *op. cit.*, p. 242.

24. A condensation of Beauduin's article "Normes pratiques pour les reformes liturgiques," *MD* 1 (1945), pp. 11–15.

25. *Ibid.*, pp. 16–20 and 22. A summary of Cardinal Gennari's views.

26. Details furnished by A.-G. Martimort in a letter to the author, 3/16/72. See his criticism of the para-liturgies of Colombes in *MD* (1946).

27. In 1945 he presented a paper at the Vanves session on "Baptême et eucharistie" which appeared in *MD*, No. 6 (1946), pp. 56–75; at the 1946 session, "La messe sacrifice de louange," printed in *La Messe et sa catéchèse*, (*Lex Orandi*, No. 7, 1947), pp. 138–153; at the 1948 session, "Le Viatique," printed in *MD*, No. 7 (1948), pp. 117–129; and in 1949, "Ciel et resurrection," *Le mystère de la mort et sa célébration* (*Lex Orandi*, No. 12), pp. 253–272.

28. LB. "La messe, sacrifice de louange," pp. 138–153. The report on this meeting was given by Fr. Roguet in an interview in September, 1966.

29. LB, "Le Viatique," *La Maison-Dieu* 15 (1948), pp. 117–129.

30. *Mediator Dei*, *AAS* 39 (1947), pp. 587, 591–595.

31. In an interview with Father Roguet in 1966.

32. *Mélanges Liturgiques* (Centre Liturgique: Louvain, 1954).

33. "La Lettre de S. Em. le Cardinal Tardini à S. Em. le Cardinal van Roey," *QLP* 40 (1959), pp. 197, 198.

34. Cf. R. Aubert, *op. cit.*, p. 248.

35. Father Roguet in an interview, September 1966.

36. Msgr. E. Beauduin in an interview, September 1966.

37. O. Rousseau, op. cit. (*l'Oriente cristiano*, 1965), p. 79. Cf. Rousseau, *The Progress of the Liturgy;* articles by Roguet and Martimort in *Maison-Dieu* 62.

38. Cf. *Informations Catholiques Internationales*, January 15, 1964, pp. 30–31. (The date of the visit should be corrected to 1928, and Montini's friend's name to Gazioli.)

CHAPTER 12
THE EXILE ENDS

1. Bouyer, *op. cit.*, p. 181.

2. *Ibid.*, p. 176.

3. Clement Lialine, a monk of Amay, to OR, citing a conversation with Beauduin on 2/21/40.

4. Notes dated 1945, pp. 7, 2, 2bis.

5. Father de Féligonde became prior of the community of St. Gregoire, l'Hayles-Roses. Cf. an article which appeared in *La Cité qui chante*, February, 1960, cited in *In Memoriam*, p. 42.

6. An exempt order had certain privileges which made it almost entirely

independent of the bishop in whose diocese it was located; cf. Canon 488, Code of Canon Law. This privilege applied primarily to monasteries, but in some instances even parishes (an almost non-existent situation in the United States) enjoyed this immunity from episcopal interference. Obedience in such instances was to a hierarchy within the order rather than to the bishop, which occasionally created a conflict of interest. Beauduin would opt for diocesan interests first. Cf. Canon 492, Nos. 1 and 2, and Canon 496.

7. Quotes are taken from a copy of the project made available through the kindness of Fr. Charles (Basile) Mercier, Beauduin's associate at Chatou at this time. This document appears in its entirety in my *Ecumenical Ecclesiology of Dom Lambert Beauduin (1873–1960)* (Washington, D.C.: The Catholic University of America, 1967), pp. 294–298.

8. If anything, the condition worsened in the post-war years. During a stay in France, 1959–1961, the author met one priest who was the pastor of thirteen churches. It was not only a question of vocation shortage but the fact of religious indifference that made it impractical to appoint one man as pastor per church when each church could only claim a handful of practicing Catholics out of a sizable formerly Catholic population.

9. Vatican II re-established the role of the priest-worker and suggested that the idea of the Mission de France be used elsewhere, and even that it be made into a special prelature, an interdiocesan clergy dependent on the whole episcopacy. Cf. *Declaration on Priests*, nn. 8 and 10.

10. A Dominican seminary originally established in Lille in 1923 at the request of the Holy See to prepare Russian missionaries for the Orient. When the Jesuits started Russicum at Rome in 1928, Istina was transformed into a center of studies. The seminary was officially suppressed in 1932, and in 1936 Istina moved to Paris with the authorization of the Holy See. (From an interview with Monsignor Dumont, O.P.—founder of Istina—and Father le Guillou, O.P.)

11. Bouyer, *op. cit.*, p. 9.

12. Many of these details were provided by Etienne Fouilloux, professor of history at Paris, who is preparing a doctoral dissertation on Catholicism and ecumensim in Western Europe (1914–1952).

13. According to Father le Guillou, O.P., who was present at the meeting— from an interview in September 1966.

14. Cited in *In Memoriam*, p. 22. The archimandrite died shortly afterward on February 11, 1960. Unfortunately none of the letters from Beauduin were saved.

15. Begun in 1908 by Spencer Jones (1857–1943) and James Paul Wattson (1863–1940), who converted to Roman Catholicism toward the end of 1908 and is better known in America as the Fr. Paul who founded the Atonement Fathers, this time of prayer for unity has received the encouragement of every pope since Pius X.

16. *A la Memoire de L'Abbé Paul Couturier, 1881–1953* (Lyon: Vitte, 1954); G. Curtis, *Paul Couturier and Unity in Christ* (Westminster: Eckenrode, 1964).

17. Regarding the stay at Amay in 1932, cf. Maurice Villain, "La Vie et l'oeuvre de l'Abbé Paul Couturier," in *A la Memoire* . . . , p. 17, and G. Curtis, *op. cit.*, p. 50.

18. The actual profession of Couturier as oblate took place in the mountain country of Isère. On August 17, 1933, he wrote to Belpaire the Prior of Amay: "I write to you as a son, since now I belong to the priory of Amay as its oblate. . . . I had hoped to make my profession as external oblate on the day of the Assumption. This has not been possible. It was on Sunday the 13th that I came down far from our village in the woods to Saint-Ours. After shriving me, the aged curé received me as oblate in his lovely church, empty at the moment. I seemed to feel the great Benedictine peace. Here am I henceforth associated very closely to your joys, sufferings, prayers, merits, and labors. Here I will pray far away from you all, for all of you, and I will endeavor, inspired by the spirit of Amay, to be a sort of small, very small advance post in the jungle of France and of Lyons." Quoted by G. Curtis, *op. cit.*, p. 49.

19. G. H. Tavard, *Two Centuries of Ecumenism—The Search for Unity* (New York: New American Library, 1962), pp. 122f.

20. The author is indebted to Sr. Marguerite de Beaumont of the community of Grandchamp for the details and letters quoted in this section.

21. Becquet to the author in an interview, July 1969; supplementary details added in a letter of 7/23/71.

22. TB to author, July 1, 1972. One of the major obstacles prior to Becquet's taking office was that previous priors apparently either did not favor or did not press for Beauduin's return.

23. LB to JJ, Cormeilles-en-Parisis, 12/3/24. Cf. LB, "Etude de la théologie," *BMOS* (May 1935), pp. 367–370, a review of Denys Gorce, *Le Laic Théologien* (1934).

24. "Vue prophétique de l'église," especially the second point developed which treats of the role of the laity specifically.

25. This document first appeared in the author's doctoral dissertation "The Ecumenical Ecclesiology of Dom Lambert Beauduin (1873–1960)" (Washington, D.C.: The Catholic University of America, 1967), pp. 299–303. It was subsequently reprinted in *Irénikon* 3 (1969), pp. 390–395.

26. Becquet to the author, July 1969.

27. Cf. *Irénikon*, 1957, p. 425 or *In Memoriam, L.B.*, p. 49.

28. Interviews with Theodore Strotmann, Nicolas Egender, Bruno Reynders and Olivier Rousseau, August 1966. Also Bouyer, *op. cit.*, p. 181.

29. Notes taken by OR in conversation with LB in 1960, on occasion of a questionnaire from the diocese of Namur. Cf. Martimort, *Maison-Dieu* No. 66 (1961), p. 2.

30. R. Aubert, "L'ecclésiologie au concile du Vatican," *Le Concile et Les Conciles*, p. 266. It is interesting to note that the Eastern bishops especially objected, long used to patriarchal powers and greater independence from Rome.

31. Canon Willem Van der Elst, acting chaplain for the seminarians in the army.

32. Victor Dechamps, *Oeuvres complètes de S.E. le Cardinal Dechamps* (12 vols.: Malines).

33. O. Rousseau, "La Vraie Valeur de l'Episcopat dans l'Eglise," *Irénikon* 29 (1956), p. 131. The Belgian translation of these documents first appeared in *La Revue Générale* 1 (1875), pp. 354–356: Bismarck's letter and the episcopal response. Pius IX's response to the bishops appeared on pp. 477–478.

34. The letter of the bishops was published in *Irénikon* 5 (1928), pp. 231f. in Beauduin's article, "l'Infallibilité du pape et l'union," pp. 231–238.

35. J. E. van Roey, "L'Episcopat et la Papauté," *Collectanea*, February 1929, pp. 141f.

36. O. Rousseau, "La Constitution *Lumen Gentium* dans le cadre des mouvements renovateurs de théologie et de pastorale des dernières décades," *L'Eglise de Vatican II* (Paris: Editions du Cerf, 1966), p. 43, where Rousseau makes reference to R. Aubert's *La théologie catholique au milieu de XX siècle*, (Cahiers de l'actualité religieuse; Tournai, 1954) and S. Jaki's, *Les tendances nouvelles de l'ecclésiologie* (Rome, 1957).

37. LB to Charles Dumont (editor of *Collectanea*, of the Cistercian Abbey of Chimay, Belgium), written at Chatou, 1/3/45.

38. Rousseau in "La vraie valeur . . . ," *op. cit.*, p. 8, cites from J. Beyer's conference given at the *Congrès des dirigéants de la Croisade eucharistique* at Nivelles, 1955. The talk, entitled "Le Souvérain Pontife, centre vital et l'unité de l'Eglise," included the following comments: "We shouldn't be astonished that little by little what the bishops were formerly in their dioceses will today be fulfilled by the pope who will take this mission in hand. . . . If the Church wants to stay in the world which is becoming unified, the papacy must speak; it must speak often and direct everything. . . . As states will disappear, bishoprics will lose their sovereignty, leaving to Peter and to his successors the general direction of every Catholic movement, of all Catholic action, of every apostolate."

39. *Ibid.* Canon law states: *Episcopus definitur: Ille . . . qui recepit sacerdotii plenitudinem. . . .* Cited by D. Craisson in his *Manuale totius juris canonici* (Parish, 1863), Vol. I, p. 473, from Bouix, *De Episcopo*, Vol. I, p. 93. Congar concludes from a study by Monsignor Andrieu on the papal career from liturgical documents of the Middle Ages (*Rev. Sc. Rel.*, 1947, pp. 90f), that "the episcopacy *is* the sacrament of orders itself in its state of fullness": *MD*, No. 14 (1948), p. 128.

40. Cardinal J. G. Saliège as quoted by G. Martimort, *De l'évêque* (*La Clarté-Dieu* 19: Paris, 1946), p. 5.

41. Bishop Emile Guerry, *L'Evêque* (Bibl. Ecclesia 5: Paris, 1954). Cf. pp. 126f. where he cites J. Beyer's *Les Instituts séculiers* (Bruges, 1954).

42. The letter and papal brief were republished in *Irénikon* 29 (1956), pp. 121f., in the original as well as in translation.

43. O. Rousseau, "Pioneri dell 'apostolato unionistico: Dom Lambert Beauduin," *Oriente Christiano* (Palermo, 1965), pp. 77–79. Cf. Küng, *Structures of the Church*, for a contemporary discussion of this question, pp. 207f.

44. L. Beauduin, "L'Union des Eglises et le Concile du Vatican," *RCIF*, Vol. 5, No. 31 (1925), p. 12. Beauduin is quoting some words of Dr. Beresford Kidd cited by Msgr. Battifol in *Catholicisme et Papauté* (Paris, 1925), pp. 9-10.

45. *Episcopalis consecrationis*, *AAS* 37 (May 21, 1945), pp. 131-132.

46. L. Beauduin, "Les directives de l'Eglise," *MD*, No. 5 (1946), p. 110.

47. L. Beauduin, "L'Infallibilité du Pape et l'Union," *Irénikon* 3 (1927), p. 451.

48. L Beauduin, *Liturgy: The Life of the Church*, p. 2.

49. L. Beauduin, "L'Unité de l'église et le concile du Vatican," *Eglise et Unité* (1948), pp. 43-44.

50. A. M. Charue, "L'évêque dans l'Eglise," *Revue diocésaine de Namur* (January–February, 1957), pp. 1f. He also published in *Le Clergé diocésain* (Tournai) two excellent studies on the episcopacy: Chapter 6, "Les évêques et leur mission universelle," and Chapter 7, "Le caractère sacrementel de l'Episcopat."

51. Archives de Chevetogne–cf. *Au Service de la Parole de Dieu Mélanges offerts à Monseigneur André-Marie Charue Evêque de Namur* (Gembloux: Editions J. Duculot, 1968), p. 485, footnote 45.

52. Archives of Chevetogne.

53. *Ibid.*

54. *Ibid.*

55. OR to the author as recounted to OR by Capovilla.

56. Bouyer, *op. cit.*, p. 183.

57. Aubert, *op. cit.*, p. 248.

58. M. J. Grootaers, *In Memoriam*, p. 44, an extract from an article in *De Standaard* (January 15, 1960), translated from the Flemish.

59. LB to Idesbald van Houtryve, Rome, 12/18/22.

60. Rousseau, *op. cit.*, p. 3. With regard to the word "collegiality" itself, Rousseau gives Congar credit for having suggested it as a translation of "sobornost" in 1951; cf. *L'Eglise de Vatican II*, p. 44. Three years earlier in *Eglise et Unité*, Beauduin had translated it as conciliarity, and his understanding and explanation of the term seems a close approximation of collegiality, although in context it is limited to the question of infallibility. Cf. discussion of infallibility and sobornost in Chapter 14.

61. Cf. *RCIF*, No. 31, 5 (1925), p. 13. "Let us pray that it will soon resume its work and give us a *Constitutio dogmatica secunda* on the powers of the teaching Church and of the bishops."

62. "He who says 'Amen' on dying is eternally living."

CHAPTER 13
BEAUDUIN'S THEOLOGICAL LEGACY

1. Cf. especially O. Rousseau, "Dom Lambert Beauduin, pioniero dell' ecumenismo" in *Oriente cristiano* (Palermo), April 1965, pp. 77f.; also by

the same author, "Le monastère de Chevetogne," in *Unitas* (French edition) 1968, pp. 152–153.

2. M. Cappuyns, *op. cit.*, p. 426.

3. LB to CM, Chatou, 5/4/48.

4. O. Rousseau, "Autour du jubilé du mouvement liturgique, 1909–1959," *QLP* 40 (1959), p. 215.

5. LB, "Notre travail pour l'union," *Irénikon* 7 (1930), p. 399.

6. Much of the following sections appeared in "Les idées fondamentales de l'ecclésiologie de dom Lambert Beauduin", by Sonya A. Quitslund, *Nouvelle Revue Théologica* 91 (1969), pp. 1073–1096.

7. Dionysius Petavius, *Dogmata Theologica*, Paris, 1644.

8. T. de Régnon, *Etudes de Théologie positive sur la Sainte Trinité*, Paris, 1882–1889.

9. J. C. Murray, "Our Response to the Ecumenical Revolution," *Religious Education* 62 (March–April, 1967), p. 91.

10. See, for example, "L'Occident à l'école de l'Orient," *Irénikon* 1 (1926), pp. 10–20, 65–73.

11. See, for example, "La Liturgie eucharistique au concile de Trente," *QL* 1 (1911), pp. 132–145.

12. See "L'Union des Eglises et le Concile du Vatican," *RCIF*, Vol. 5, No. 31 (1925), p. 12, where Beauduin quotes the words of Kidd.

13. *Ibid.*, p. 13. Cf. H. Küng, *Structures of the Church* (Nelson, 1963), for a contemporary treatment, especially p. 360, note 22.

14. L. Beauduin, "Jubilé du Monastère de l'Union, (1925–1950)," *Irénikon* 23 (1950), pp. 372–373.

15. Letter dated Amay, June 1926. The dissertation was never written, but Reynders later published in *QLP* (1935), pp. 72–87, an article entitled "L'humanité du Christ notre chef", which Beauduin could not praise enough.

16. One can find in the contents of Mersch confirmation of the appropriateness of his fundamental intuition. Only the mention of the Council of Florence may seem strange. From the Council of Florence itself, only several allusions, hardly useful, are to be found in the *Decree ad Armenos*. Mersch does not even refer to it.

17. LB, "A propos de la définition de l'assomption," *Irénikon* 24 (1951), p. 397, quoting notably this remark of Canon Mature: "Monophysitism is the ordinary temptation of pious but ignorant persons. The Christ whom they adore, to whom they pray, is, as they say, the 'good God,' and they understand by that a God appearing to be more or less a man in order to make himself accessible to us."

18. In a letter to Charles Moeller (C.M.) from Chatou, 4/20/51, Beauduin referred to the ultimate in Marian excesses which had appeared in an unfortunate work by R. Laurentin, *Marie, L'Eglise et le Sacerdoce*. This book met with strong opposition in theological circles (cf. Bouyer's review in *Dieu Vivant*, No. 26, 1954, p. 151). Beauduin, commenting on Laurentin's untenable position, wrote to Moeller, "Never again will anyone dare to treat the subject

of Marian priesthood seriously (already condemned, moreover, by Rome). It's a real atomic bomb": Chevetogne, 6/21/54. Undoubtedly he alludes to what is said in footnote 19.

19. Here is how this idea was subtly enunciated by J. Lebon, at the moment when devotion to Mary as mediatrix was going strong in milieux close to Cardinal Mercier, with whom Beauduin was not at all in agreement on this point: "In consenting to the death of Jesus, in associating herself with him in order to offer his precious life *to the Father*, Mary, let us say it again, sacrifices a victim which is indeed hers, which belongs to her" ("La Bienheureuse Vièrge Marie, médiatrice de toutes les grâces," in *La vie diocésaine du diocèse de Malines*, 1921, p. 259). Moreover, several months before the appearance of this sentence, Rome had sent at the request of Cardinal Mercier the Mass of Mary Mediatrix approved for the dioceses of Belgium. Although in the minds of some Malinois theologians this was the first step toward a dogmatic definition (cf. *ibid.*, p. 96), Rome had very clearly stated her position in the collect: "*Domine Jesu Christe, noster apud Patrem mediator*" (our Lord Jesus Christ, who with the Father is our mediator) which, according to the recollection of several, was a correction of the original formula submitted, the latter having been judged imprecise.

20. LB to CM, Chatou, 4/9/51. Beauduin is referring especially to Cardinal Suenen's book on the Legion of Mary.

21. This article, "Le Sacré-Coeur de Jesus dans la Liturgie," *QLP* 8 (1923), pp. 95–103, was to have been followed by a second in which John Eudes would not receive Beauduin's complete approbation. A visit from the general of the Eudists who came to thank him profusely for his first *mise au point* halted the continuation of this article. Beauduin no longer dared to engage in the critique he wanted to make and the article remained "to be continued."

22. LB, "Le Cycle de Noel," *QLP* 7 (1922) pp. 241–250. L. Billot, *De Verbo incarnato* (Rome: S.C. de Propagande Fide, 1900), is quoted elsewhere in Beauduin's notes on the incarnation.

23. From notes taken by M. Cappuyns at a retreat given by LB in 1920.

24. *Cahier brun*, an undated retreat in one of Beauduin's notebooks, p. 26.

25. Cited in a letter from E. Beauduin to Rousseau, 12/21/29.

26. C. Moeller, "Le Chalcédonisme et le néo-chalcédonisme," in *Das Konzil von Chalkedon* (Wurtzburg, 1951), Vol. 1, pp. 637–720. The statement with which Beauduin takes exception is found in footnote 86, p. 717. It is interesting to note that Moeller himself repeats this warning against Monophysitism in a later article: "Jesus Christ in the Minds of the Moderns," *Lumen Vitae* 7 (1952), pp. 509–527.

27. LB to CM, Chevetogne, 7/3/51.

28. LB to CM, Chevetogne, 3/18/53. His condemnation of Denys is doubly interesting because Bouyer accuses Beauduin of being Dionysian. Cf. Bouyer, *op. cit.*, p. 57, a charge which this letter shows to be ungrounded, or at most a gross exaggeration of Beauduin's actual position.

29. LB to JJ, Strasbourg, 9/26/31.

30. LB, "Notes et Documents—sur le sens des mots 'présence sacre-mentelle'," *QLP* 27 (1946), p. 152. Résumé of several key ideas found in his response to a Benedictine prioress some fifteen years earlier.

31. LB *Notre Piété Pendant L'Avent* (Louvain: Mont César, 1919), pp. 45-46.

32. LB to Roger Debar (RD), a monk of Ligugé, Chatou, 12/21/42.

33. LB to CM, Chevetogne, 3/30/53.

34. L. Beauduin, "Les Fêtes de Pâques," *RCIF* 12 (1932), pp. 3-5.

35. LB to JJ, Pepinster, 10/27/30.

36. LB to JJ, Amay, 11/10/30.

37. Cf. *Cahier Brun* (one of Beauduin's notebooks from the late 1930's and early 1940's), p. 46, where Beauduin refers specifically to the *Sentences*.

38. LB to RD, Chatou, 4/7/43.

39. L. Beauduin, "La Liturgie Pascale," *QL* 2 (1912), p. 293.

40. LB, *Cahier Brun*, p. 24.

41. Beauduin himself was guilty of an occasional trinitarian ambiguity. In "La Pentecôte-L'Esprit qui fait les vivants," *QL* 3 (1913), p. 241, he speaks of Christ as Father of the new humanity and of his rights to this paternity. He was trying to express Christ's rule as the new Adam. Fortunately, later writings give ample proof that Christ is our mediator and brother, not our father.

42. LB to JJ, 7/9/32. Copious extracts of this letter are given by L. Bouyer, *op. cit.*, pp. 172f.

43. These are the prayers originally said at the altar: collect, offertory prayers, canon, communion prayers and post-communion. While this trini-tarian element may seem to have been lost in the shortened conclusions to the orations, perhaps the liturgists feel that its presence is safeguarded by the new eucharistic prayers.

44. L. Beauduin, "Essai de manuel . . .", *QL* 4 (1914), 355.

45. *Ibid.*, p. 356.

46. *Ibid.*, p. 357.

47. De Régnon, *op. cit.* I, p. 365.

48. Notes taken during a retreat by Beauduin at Vanves, 1946. Archives of the Benedictine Convent at Vanves, pp. 10-11.

49. LB to RD, Chatou, 12/21/42; also see LB, "Notes de la liturgie," *Cours et Conférences de la Semaine Liturgique de Maredsous* 1 (August 19-24, 1912), pp. 128-130.

50. See H. Lamiroy (future bishop of Bruges), *De Essentia Sanctissimi Missae Sacrificii* (Louvain, 1919). This more than 500-page compilation of all the known opinions and systems failed to inspire Beauduin.

51. LB, "Essai . . . ," *QLP* 6 (1921), pp. 45-46, 192-206; see "Cainte Messe et Sainte Communion," *QLP* 6 (1921), pp. 148-150; "Le Saint Sacrifice de la Messe," *QLP* 7 (1922), pp. 196-205, which is a review of de la Taille's *Mysterium Fidei*. Beauduin was much impressed with the author's bold and sure originality. A final synthesis appears in *La Messe et sa catéchèse* (Collection Lex Orandi: Paris, 1947), pp. 138-153: "La Messe sacrifice de louange." See Chapter 11 for his debate with Capelle.

52. LB, *op. cit.*, p. 51.

53. LB, "La liturgie source de vie spirituelle," *VS* 71 (1944), p. 343.

54. LB, "Essai . . ." *QLP* 6 (1921), p. 194.

55. L. Beauduin, "Jubilé du Monastère de l'Union (1925–1959)," *Irénikon* 23 (1950), pp. 375–376.

56. L. Beauduin, "Prière pour l'unité," *Cahiers de Sainte Françoise Romaine*, No. 3 (December 1937), pp. 80–82.

57. L. Beauduin, "Essai . . ." *QL* 3 (1913), pp. 143–144.

58. L. Beauduin, "La Vie liturgique, son but," *VLsm*, No. 1 (1909), pp. 1–8.

59. L. Beauduin, "La Concélébration eucharistique," *QLP* 8 (1923), p. 34.

60. LB, "La Concélébration eucharistique," *QLP* 7 (1922), pp. 275–285; 8 (1923), pp. 23–34; *Gedenboek XXVII Internationaal eucharistisch Congres* (Amsterdam, 1924), pp. 518–534; *MD* (1946), pp. 7–26.

61. This topic was pursued especially in the early issues of *VLsm* and *QL*. The battle was soon won but not before a few seemingly impregnable citadels fell. See especially L. Beauduin, "La Communion des Fidèles au moment liturgique," *QL* 2 (1911), pp. 119f., where he presents objections to communion during Mass, given in response to a questionnaire sent to schools and institutions.

62. *Ibid.*, p. 117.

63. LB to JJ, Rome, 5/3/31.

64. LB to PL, Amay, 5/31/30 (PL-Paul Leyniers).

65. LB to PL, Strasbourg, 7/3/32.

66. LB to PL, Chatou, 4/21/42.

67. LB to PL, En Calcat, 2/6/33.

CHAPTER 14
TOWARD A REFORMED CHURCH

1. LB to OR, Rome, 2/13/24.

2. LB to JJ, En Calcat, 6/2/33.

3. LB, "Vue Prophétique . . ." reprinted in *Irénikon* 3 (1969), pp. 390–395.

4. Notes taken on a conversation of LB with JJ, Brussels, 2/9/32.

5. Haquin, *op. cit.*, note 30, p. 137, a quotation from Beauduin's course of 1911.

6. LB, "La vraie prière de l'Eglise, Rapport au congrès de Malines de 1909," *QLP* 40 (1959), pp. 218–220.

7. *Cahier Brun* (one of Beauduin's notebooks probably dating from the late 1930's and early 1940's), p. 23.

8. The following section on Schrader's schema is heavily indebted to R. Aubert's "L'ecclésiologie au concile du Vatican," in *Le Concile et les Conciles* (Paris-Chevetogne, 1960), pp. 245–284 (Proceedings from the Chevetogne ecumenical week of 1959). The revision drawn up by another Jesuit, Kleutgen, also had serious weaknesses, giving little space to the role of the Holy Spirit and overlooking Scripture as a primary source for developing

the idea of the nature of the Church. As a result, the mystery of the mystical body was all but ignored. Cf. Mansi, *op. cit.*, Vol. 53, pp. 308–317. Two additional sources could be added: Adrien-Etienne Gréa, *L'Eglise et sa divine Constitution* (Paris: Société Générale de librairie catholique, 1885) and Humbert Clérissac, *le Mystère de l'Eglise* (5th edition; Paris: Editions du Cerf, 1917), which contain parts of Vatican I's schema on the Church. Clérissac's book is also available in English (New York: Sheed and Ward, 1937).

9.   I   Definition of the Church: the Church is the mystical body of Christ.

      II   The religion of Christ could only live in a society instituted by him; hence it only lives in the Church instituted by him.

      III The Church receives her existence and constitution from Christ; it is the true, perfect, spiritual and supernatural society. Role of the Holy Spirit.

      IV   There is a visible magisterium, priesthood and government.

      V   There is the unity of one body.

      VI   This unity is necessary for salvation.

      VII Concerning those outside the Church through their own fault (VI and VII and especially directed against the problem of indifferentism).

      VIII The properties of the Church.

      IX   The infallibility of the Church.

      X   The hierarchy of threefold power (the word "bishop" is not used at all and only alluded to in seven lines).

      XI   The primacy of the pope (initially this was only with regard to his jurisdiction; the matter of infallibility was a later addition).

      XII The temporal sovereignty of the Church.

      XIII The separation of Church and State is rejected.

      XIV The necessity of states to respect the precepts of the Church.

      XV   Special questions (especially for canonists).

                                        Aubert, *op. cit.*, pp. 248–259.

Although never promulgated *in toto*, the schema finally appeared in Mansi-Petit, 1899–1927, a new printing and continuation in sixty volumes of Mansi's thirty-one volumes (1757–1798).

10. The author is indebted to O. Rousseau for pointing out this and several other details discussed in the following section. Cf. his "L'Evolution Théologique de dom Lambert-Beauduin dans les perspectives des deux conciles du Vatican," in *Mélanges Liturgiques*, dedicated to Dom Bernard Botte, to appear in December 1972.

11. G. Morin, "Le Pallium," *Le Messager des Fidèles* (*Rev. Béné*, 1889), p. 258, citing the thesis of Thierry Ruinart, O.S.B.

12. O. Rousseau, "Divina autem Providentia . . . Histoire d'une texte conciliare," *Ecclesia a Spiritu Sancto edocta* (*Mélanges G. Philips*), Louvain, 1970, pp. 281f.

13. LB, "Vue Prophétique . . ."

14. LB, "La Vie liturgique à Rome jadis et aujourd'hui," *Irénikon* 1 (1926), pp. 329–338. The educational campaign launched by this and subsequent

articles undoubtedly helped to restore the pontifical liturgy at Rome. Recent popes such as John XXIII and Paul VI have done much to eliminate this once valid criticism, going far beyond Beauduin's proposals by adding, to a restored pontifical liturgy, pastoral visits to factories, prisons, peasants, etc.

15. LB, "Rapprochement anglo-oriental," *Irénikon* 1 (1926), p. 173.

16. LB, "L'Unité de l'église et le concile du Vatican," *Eglise et Unité* (Lille: Collection "Catholicité," 1948), p. 44.

17. *Ibid.; cf.* pp. 16–17 for historical precedence in rewording a definition.

18. *Ibid.*, p. 38.

19. LB, "L'Infallibilité du Pape et l'union," *Irénikon* 5 (1928), pp. 95–96.

20. L. Beauduin, "La centralisation romaine," *Irénikon* 6 (1929), pp. 146–148.

21. *Ibid.*, pp. 152–153; also "Consultations inopportunes," *QLP* 8 (1923), pp. 37–45.

22. L. Beauduin, "L'Union des Eglises et le Concile du Vatican," *RCIF*, No. 31, 5 (1925), p. 12.

23. D. J. Wolf and J. V. Schall (eds.), *Current Trends in Theology* (Garden City: Doubleday, 1965), pp. 250f.

24. LB, "L'Unité de l'église . . ." *loc cit.*, p. 42.

25. H. Küng, *op. cit.*, p. 315. Since Innocent III, the title "vicar of Christ" has been reserved exclusively to the pope; previously it was peculiar to bishops, priests and princes.

26. L. Beauduin, "L'Union des Eglises . . ." *op. cit.*, p. 11.

27. LB, "Vue prophétique de l'Eglise."

28. 1970.

29. LB, "L'esprit paroissial—autrefois et aujourd'hui," *QL* 2 (1912), p. 309. This topic is discussed in a series of articles in *QL* 2 (1911–1912), pp. 16–26, 80–90, 305–311.

30. LB, "L'esprit paroissial . . ." *op. cit.*, p. 305. Trent tried to restore a sense of parish life, and as late as 1624 the Council of Bordeaux decreed that to miss Mass more than three times in your parish was cause for excommunication. Cf. p. 311 of this same article.

31. LB, "La Famille et la liturgie," *Revue Liturgique et Bénédictine* 1 (1911), pp. 552–560.

32. LB, *Notre Piété Pendant l'Avent* (1919), pp. 16–17.

33. LB, "La Fête de Noël," *QL* 5 (1919), p. 5.

34. LB, *Liturgy: The Life of the Church*, p. 20.

35. *Ibid.*, p. 21.

36. LB to CM, Chatou, 3/9/51.

37. LB, "L'Encyclique *Mediator Dei*," *MD*, No. 13 (1948), p. 17; *AAS* 39 (1947), pp. 521–595.

38. LB, "La Liturgie: Définition-Hiérarchie-Tradition," *QLP* 29 (1948), pp. 131–132.
39 (1947), pp. 521–595.

40. Y. Congar, *Lay People in the Church*, tr. D. Attwater (Paramus: Newman Press, 1956), pp. 14–15.

41. *Ibid.*, p. 9.

42. *Cahier Brun*, p. 42. These notes seem to form part of a retreat dated July 6, 1942.

43. *Ibid.*

44. LB, "La liturgie, source de vie spirituelle," *VS* 71 (1944), pp. 339–340 (emphasis added).

45. From notes taken by M. Cappuyns, O.S.B., at a retreat given by LB, September 12–19, 1920.

46. LB, "Notes sur l'Ascèse," *RCIF*, No. 51 (March 11, 1932), p. 1.

47. *Ibid.*, p. 2.

48. *Idem.*

49. *Idem.*

50. LB, *Liturgy the Life of the Church*, p. 51.

51. *Ibid.*, p. 52.

52. LB, "Notes sur l'Ascèse," p. 4.

53. LB to JJ, Cormeilles-en Parisis, 12/3/34.

54. These notes were made available to us through the kindness of Dr. Clottens' widow.

55. Aubert, *op. cit.*, p. 247.

56. "He who says 'Amen' on dying is eternally alive": words of Beauduin cited in *Dom Lambert Beauduin In Memoriam.*

Introduction to the Bibliography
of Beauduin's Works

Although Beauduin's most productive years were between 1909 and 1930, his works span a period of fifty years. (A complete list follows this introduction). His writings fall into three general categories: one book, some pamphlets more than 200 articles, and countless letters. The letters remain in private collections or in the archives of Chevetogne. A number of the articles are to be found in the older liturgical centers such as Saint John's Abbey, Collegeville, Minnesota, which helped familiarize an American elite with Beauduin's ideas in 1926 when it published the translation of his *La Piété de l'Eglise* (1914) as *Liturgy, the Life of the Church*. This short but provocative book, discussed in Chapter Two, presented the fundamental principles which inspired the leaders of the Belgian liturgical movement of 1909. Beauduin produced only one other major piece of writing which unfortunately remained unfinished—the doctrinally rich "Essai de manuel fondamental de liturgie" which appeared in installments in *Questions Liturgiques* between 1912 and 1921.

Most of the periodicals which published Beauduin's works are probably unfamiliar to readers in the United States. Four to which he contributed with some regularity were closely linked to his career. In each case he was either the originator or one of the co-originators: *La Vie Liturgique, supplément mensuel* (Louvain, Mont César), *Les Questions Liturgiques* (Louvain, Mont César), *Irénikon* (Amay, then Chevetogne), *La Maison-Dieu* (Paris).

La Vie Liturgique had a brief career: 1909–1919. Originally, it addressed itself primarily to the clergy, sought to orient them into the particular liturgical season, and served as a clearinghouse for pastoral problems concerning the liturgy. *La Vie Liturgique* lasted one liturgical year. It did not die but in Advent of 1910 it was expanded into a more serious attempt at broader scholarship: *Les Questions liturgiques*.

The latter's publication, interrupted only by the two World Wars, has endured down to the present with only a slight change. In 1919 it became *Les Questions liturgiques et paroissiales*, acknowledging publicly what had been its orientation from the very beginning. The articles dealt not only with current liturgical problems and questions but also with future liturgical possibilities. For this reason, many articles were of an historical nature, tracing the development, significance and symbolism of different rites and customs, in the Eastern as well as Western Church.

Among these four periodicals, *Irénikon* has achieved international renown. First published in 1926, it continues to address itself to the ecumenical question. One of the final results of Beauduin's liturgical interests is *La Maison-Dieu*, an outgrowth of his activities in the Paris region during the Second World War. Since the appearance of its first issue in 1945, *La Maison-Dieu* has become in the eyes of many the most outstanding liturgical periodical of its kind.

In addition to the above, Beauduin also published a number of articles in some relatively unknown monthlies: *Bulletin mensuel des oblates séculières et de l'union spirituelle des veuves de France* (Cormeilles-en-Parisis) (which became in 1937 *Cahiers de Sainte Françoise Romaine*) and *Bulletin de Notre Dame de la Sainte Espérance*. These were periodicals of a limited circulation, published by the community of Benedictines for whom he was chaplain at one time.

Mélanges Liturgiques, a collection of two hundred sixty-eight pages assembled on the occasion of his eightieth birthday by the monks of Mont César, contains some of the best of Beauduin. The contents include his major work, *La Piété de l'Eglise*, important selections from his "Essai . . . ," and an excellent selection of articles on various topics of enduring liturgical interest.

The letters of Beauduin to his friends provide another rich source of theological thought. A prolific letter writer, he sometimes wrote as often as two or three times a month to the same person. The majority of the letters cited in this work are in the archives of Chevetogne. These extracts are printed with the kind permission of the addressees: Jean Jadot, today bishop and nuncio to Thailand (JJ), Paul Leyniers, chaplain at Brussels (PL), Monsignor Charles Moeller, today under-secretary of the Congregation of the Faith (CM), and Olivier Rousseau of Chevetogne (OR). The first two correspondents were promising young seminarians when Beauduin first wrote. An article by Monsignor Charles Moeller, a noted scholar and disciple of Beauduin, gave rise to a series of letters which centered on the humanity of Christ and give us some insight into Beauduin's Christological concerns. The numerous letters to Rousseau are especially rich in details about the foundation of Amay and the founder's ideas on the Church.

Beauduin's straightforward style is always very readable. While the earlier theological writing is, perhaps, sometimes overly schematic and scholastic for a modern reader, he generally adapts his style to his audience and the subject matter.

At least three other works, not by Beauduin, but by those who knew him, should be given special mention: *Dom Lambert Beauduin—in memoriam*, a testimony to their founder by the monks of Chevetogne in which several excellent articles about his life and work are collected, as well as excerpts from obituary notices and recollections written by churchmen of all Faiths; Louis Bouyer's book, *Dom Lambert Beauduin un homme d'Eglise* (Paris, Casterman, 1964), the first attempt at a biography but which the author prefers to call by a more modest name, a testimonial or witness to the man; and the doctoral dissertation of André Haquin, *Histoire du renouveau liturgique belge* (1882–1914), submitted to the Faculté de Théologie at Louvain University (1966) and recently published in the collection "Recherches et Synthèses de Sciences Religieuses" under the title *dom 1. beauduin et le renouveau liturgique au tournant du xxe siècle* (1969).

In a class by itself is *L'Eglise et les églises*, 1054–1954, a masterful two volume work by such scholarly friends as Yves Congar, O.P., the late Lucien Cerfaux, Jean Daniélou, S.J., Charles Moeller, François Dvornik, Oscar Halecki, Jean-Jacques von Allmen, Olivier Rousseau, etc., presented to Beauduin in honor of his eightieth birthday. Commemorating the ninth centenary of the separation between East and West, this book consists of studies which pertain to Christian unity, and discuss such topics as the schism, the history of the Eastern churches, and the Catholic Church's efforts toward reunion. While neither volume is directly concerned with the life of Beauduin nor the history of Amay, they represent a tribute to the scholarship and concern for the East inspired both by Beauduin and his monks of Amay.

Bibliography

BIBLIOGRAPHY OF LAMBERT BEAUDUIN
CHRONOLOGICALLY ARRANGED

1909

La Vie liturgique, son but, *VL, sm,* No. 1, 1–10.
L'année ecclésiastique, *VL, sm,* No. 1, 11–19.
Liturgie: Questions générales. Ecueils à éviter, *VL, sm,* No. 2, 1–8.
Chronique de l'oeuvre, *VL, sm,* No. 2, 23–27, 56–60.
La vraie prière de l'Eglise. *Rapport au Congrès de Malines de 1909.* Vol. 5.
    Bruxelles: Société Anonyme, 1–6.
Rapport de Promovenda sacra liturgia (July), in A. Haquin, *Dom Lambert*
    Beauduin et le renouveau liturgique, Gembloux: Duculot, 1970, 234–237.

1910

Explication de la messe, *VL, sm,* No. 3, 29–34.
Messe des catéchumènes, *VL, sm,* No. 5, 105–111; No. 6, 125–135.
Correspondance échangée, *VL, sm,* No. 6, 148–153.
Messe des catéchumènes, *VL, sm,* No. 7, 159–173.
Correspondance échangée, *VL, sm,* No. 7, 183–188.
Correspondance échangée, *VL, sm,* No. 8, 214–218.
Compte rendu de la réunion liturgique, juin 1910, *VL, sm,* Nos. 9, 10, 11, 222–
    320.
Journée liturgique à Chèvremont, *VL, sm,* No. 12, 4–32.
Trilogie de l'Avent, *QL,* 1 (1910)), 12–21.
Epîtres, évangiles et oraisons des dimanches de l'Avent, *QL,* 1 (1910), 22–31.
Le Projet d'École liturgique (June), in A. Haquin, *op. cit.,* 242–244.

1911

Le cycle de Noël, *QL*, 1 (1911), 58–59, 61–72.
Le cycle pascal, la Septuagésime, *QL*, 1 (1911), 109–118.
La Liturgie eucharistique au concile de Trente, *QL*, 1 (1911), 132–145.
Le Carême, *QL*, 1 (1911), 171–180.
La Liturgie eucharistique au concile de Trente (suite), *QL*, 1 (1911), 192–213.
Le Temps pascal, *QL*, 1 (1911), 239–252.
Les Fêtes de Pâques à Hippone, *QL*, 1 (1911), 253–260.
La Croix de l'autel, *QL*, 1 (1911), 279–285.
La Pentecôte, *QL*, 1 (1911), 319–326.
Le Ciborium, *QL*, 1 (1911), 391–399.
L'Esprit paroissial autrefois et aujourd'hui, *QL*, 2 (1911), 16–26.
L'Esprit paroissial autrefois et aujourd'hui (suite), *QL*, 2 (1911), 80–90.
La Communion des fidèles au moment liturgique, *QL*, 2 (1911), 115–125.
La Famille et la liturgie, *RLB*, 1 (1911), 552–560.

1912

La Bulle *"Divino afflatu,"* *QL*, 2 (1912), 167–200.
Préparation au Baptême, *QL*, 2 (1912), 213–217.
La Liturgie pascale, *QL*, 2 (1912), 293–304.
L'Esprit paroissial autrefois et aujourd'hui (suite), *QL*, 2 (1912), 305–311.
La Future Réforme liturgique, *QL*, 2 (1912), 338–351.
Le Temps de la Pentecôte, *QL*, 2 (1912), 372–383.
L'Autel liturgique, *QL*, 2 (1912), 384–392.
L'Idéal monastique et la vie chrétienne des premiers jours, *QL*, 2 (1912), 460–463.
Méditations pour l'octave de la Toussaint, *QL*, 2 (1912), 521–528.
Griefs contre le Mouvement liturgique, *QL*, 2 (1912), 529–536.
Note sur le *Ritus servandus in celebratione missae*, *QL*, 3 (1912), 17–24.
La Communion dans les deux rites, *QL*, 3 (1912), 25–30.
Un plus grand Noël, *QL*, 3 (1912), 49–55.
Essai de manuel fondamental de liturgie, *QL*, 3 (1912), 56–66.
L'Ordre des acolytes, *QL*, 3 (1912), 67–79.
Notes et informations, *QL*, 3 (1912), 80–85.
Les Origines de la messe, *QL*, 3 (1912), 85–95.
La Rénovation liturgique, son importance, sa réalisation. *La section belge au XXVIII Congrès eucharistique de Vienne, 11–15 septembre 1912.* (Gand: 1913), 167–173.

1913

L'Expulsion des pénitents, *QL*, 3 (1913), 121–128.
Essai de manuel fondamental de liturgie (suite), *QL*, 3 (1913), 143–148.
Le Canon de la messe, *QL*, 3 (1913), 149–159.

Quelles sont les principales rubriques des acolytes? *QL*, 3 (1913), 163–166.
Quelle est l'origine de l'huméral? *QL*, 3 (1913), 179–182.
Quelques modèles de ciborium, *QL*, 3 (1913), 166–167.
Questions posées, *QL*, 3 (1913), 183–184.
Le Christ trimphant, *QL*, 3 (1913), 189–196.
Essai de manuel fondamental de liturgie (suite), *QL*, 3 (1913), 201–209.
La Pentecôte. L'Esprit qui fait les vivants, *QL* (1913), 241–253.
Essai de manuel fondamental de liturgie (suite), *QL*, 3 (1913), 271–280.
Donnez-nous sans tarder le cérémonial des acolytes, *QL*, 3 (1913), 302–310.
Retraite liturgique, *QL*, 3 (1913), 313–316.
Retraite liturgique "Ut unum sint," Louvain: Mont César, 120 p.
L'Initiation à Rome au VIIᵉ siècle, *QL*, 3 (1913), 338–345; (also in *CCSL* 2: 325–336.)
Fête de la Toussaint, *QL*, 3 (1913), 365–371.
Dédicace des églises, *QL*, 3 (1913), 372–376.
Algemeene Liturgie Bezwaren tegen de liturgische beweging, *Lit. Tijd.*, 3 (1913), 81–90.
"Liturgie catholique" par Dom M.F. Festugière (recension), *QL*, 3 (1913), 391–394.
L'Ordre des acolytes (suite), *QL*, 3 (1913), 423–429.
Nouveau *Motu proprio "Abhinc duos annos,"* *QL*, 4 (1913), 3–26.
Le Culte de l'église cathédrale, *QL*, 4 (1913), 27–30.
Les Textes de l'Avent (Les hymnes), *QL*, 4 (1913), 31–41.
Mise au point nécessaire. Réponse au R.P. Navatel, *QL*, 4 (1913), 83–104.
Le Cérémonial des acolytes, *QL*, 4 (1913), 164–167.
Notes de la liturgie, I. (Maredsous, août 1912), *CCSL*, 1 (1913), 124–142.

1914

La Septuagésime, *QL*, 4 (1914), 171–178.
Le Carême au XVᵉ siècle, *QL*, 4 (1914), 271–275.
Les Stations du Carême, *QL*, 4 (1914), 276–280.
Notre Pâque, *QL*, 4 (1914), 327–336.
Essai de manuel fondamental de liturgie (suite), *QL*, 4 (1914), 350–361.
Heure da la Messe et Jeûne eucharistique, *QL*, 4 (1914), 362–373.
Méditations pour la première semaine d'août, *QL*, 4 (1914), 412–425.
L'Initiation chrétienne au VIIᵉ siècle dans *CCSL*, Vol. 2, août, 1913. Louvain: Mont César, 325–336.
La Piété de l'Eglise. Louvain: Mont César.

1915

La pieta della Chiesa. Vicenza: Société Anonyme.

1919

La Fête de Noël, *QLP*, 5 (1919), 1–13.
Quelques particularités liturgiques, *QLP*, 5 (1919), 14–18.
Les Nouvelles Préfaces, *QLP*, 5 (1919), 19–25.
Notre Piété pendant l'Avent. Louvain: Mont César.

1920

La Portée ascétique des stations de Carême, *QLP*, 5 (1920), 65–72.
Essai de manuel fondamental de liturgie (suite), *QLP*, 5 (1920), 83–90.
Messe basse ou Messe solennelle? *QLP*, 5 (1920), 90–97.
L'Initiation chrétienne et la Semaine pascale à Rome, *QLP*, 5 (1920), 137–150.
Les additions successives à la messe, *QLP*, 5 (1920), 158–166.
Essai de manuel fondamental de liturgie (suite) *QLP*, 5 (1920), 217–228.
L'Heure de la messe, *QLP*, 5 (1920), 245–257.
Le temps de l'Avent. Bruxelles: Collection, "Société d'Etudes religieuses."
L'Avent. Liège: Collection, "Etudes religieuses."
De Godsvrucht der heilige Kerk. Louvain: Mont César.

1921

Le Carême ancien. A propos d'un livre récent, *QLP*, 6 (1921), 14–23.
L'Offertoire jadis et aujourd'hui, *QLP*, 6 (1921), 30–45.
Essai de manuel fondamental de liturgie (suite), *QLP*, 6 (1921), 45–56.
Les Prières après la messe basse et *l'editio typica* du missel, *QLP*, 6 (1921), 62–64.
Renseignements sur *l'instrumentum pacis*, *QLP*, 6 (1921), 66–67.
La Fête-Dieu, *QLP*, 6 (1921), 81–95.
Sainte Messe et sainte communion, *QLP*, 6 (1921), 148–150.
Décret du St. Office à propos de certaines peintures d'Eglises, *QLP*, 6 (1921), 159–160.
Le Concile de Vaison, *QLP*, 6 (1921), 177–185.
Essai de manuel fondamental de liturgie (suite), *QLP*, 6 (1921), 192–206.
Messes dialoguées, *QLP*, 6 (1921), 235–240.
La Messe dialoguée, *QLP*, 6 (1921), 263–278.
Le Carême. Bruxelles: Collection, "Société d'Etudes religieuses."
Le Carême. Liège: Collection, "Etudes religieuses."
La Pentecôte. Bruxelles: Collection, "Etudes religieuses."

1922

Le Genie du rite romain. A propos d'un livre récent (E. Bishop), *QLP*, 7 (1922), 35–41.
Le Culte de saint Michel, *QLP*, 7 (1922), 161–166.
La Toussaint et l'adoration de l'Agneau, *QLP*, 7 (1922), 166–173.

Les Fêtes de la dédicace de l'Eglise, *QLP*, 7 (1922), 173–178.

Les Honoraires de messe, *QLP*, 7 (1922), 179–195.

Le Saint Sacrifice de la messe. A propos d'un livre récent (M. de la Taille, S.J.), *QLP*, 7 (1922), 196–205.

Encore la messe dialoguée, *QLP*, 7 (1922), 223–226.

Le Trentain et les messes des 3ᵉ, 7ᵉ, et 30ᵉ jours après le décès, *QLP*, 7 (1922), 231–234.

Le Cycle de Noël, *QLP*, 7 (1922), 241–250.

La Concélébration eucharistique, *QLP*, 7 (1922), 275–285.

Données sur les origines du culte de Notre-Dame, dans *Textes et rapports du congrès marial tenu à Bruxelles en septembre, 1921*. Vol. 1, 216–230.

1923

La Concélébration eucharistique (suite), *QLP*, 8 (1923), 23–34.

Consultations inopportunes, *QLP*, 8 (1923), 37–45.

Le Sacré-Coeur de Jésus dans la liturgie, *QLP*, 8 (1923), 95–103.

Liturgie *pro sponso et sponsa*, *QLP*, 8 (1923), 109–120.

Le Décret *Optime novit* sur le jeune eucharistique avant la messe, *QLP*, 8 (1923), 143–145.

1924

Le Mystère pascal vécu. *La Vie et les Artes liturgiques*, 10 (1923–1924), 241–249.

"*Omnium ecclesiarum mater et caput*," *QLP*, 9 (1924), 169–173.

1925

L'Enseignement religieux jadis et aujourd'hui. *CCSL, août, 1924*. Vol. 3, Malines. Louvain: Mont César, 3–22.

La Concélébration eucharistique. *Gedenkboek XXVIIᵉ internationaal eucharistisch Congres*. Amsterdam, 1924, 518–534.

Une oeuvre monastique pour l'Union des Eglises. Louvain: Mont César.

L'Union des Eglises et le Concile du Vatican, *RCIF*, 5, No. 31, (Oct. 23), 10–13.

1926

L'Esprit paroissial dans la tradition. *CCSL, août 1925*. Vol. 4. Louvain: Mont César, 11–42.

De quoi s'agit-il? *Irén.*, 1 (1926), 4–10.

L'Occident à l'école de l'Orient I. Le Mystère pascal, *Irén.*, 1 (1926), 10–20.

L'Occident à l'école de l'Orient II. La Fête-Dieu, *Irén.*, 1 (1926), 65–73.

Preface to M. A. Dieux, *Croisade pour l'unité du monde chrétien*. Paris, 1926.

Dans quel esprit nous voudrions travailler, *Irén.*, 1 (1926), 117–119.

Rapprochement anglo-oriental, *Irén.*, 1 (1926), 165–173.
Les Patriarches, *Irén.*, 1 (1926), 239–244.
Les Patriarches (suite), *Irén.*, 1 (1926), 267–274.
La Vie liturgique à Rome jadis et aujourd'hui, *Irén.*, 1 (1926), 329–338.
L'Esprit paroissial dans la tradition. Louvain: Mont César.
Liturgy, the Life of the Church. Trans. V. Michel. Collegeville: Liturgical Library.

1927

Le vrai travail pour l'union, *Irén.*, 3 (1927), 5–10.
Documents. Autour des conversations de Malines, *Irén.*, 3 (1927), 150–151.
L'Infaillibilité du pape et l'union, *Irén.*, 3 (1927), 449–453.
Le Cardinal Mercier et la réunion des Eglises. Les Eglises d'Orient, *Le Cardinal Mercier (1851–1926).* Bruxelles, Louis Desmet-Verteneuil, 151–156.

1928

Une visite à la laure orthodoxe de Potchaiev. *Pages de Gloire*, 6ᵉ sér. Bruges: Desclée de Brouwer, 1927–1928, 48–56.
L'Encyclique *'Mortalium animos'* du janvier, 1928, *Irén.*, 5 (1928), 81–91.
L'Infaillibilité du pape et l'union (suite), *Irén.*, 5 (1928), 91–98.
Le Cardinal Mercier et la reunion des Eglises d'Orient, *Irén.*, 5 (1928), 225–230.
L'Infaillibilité du pape et l'union (suite), *Irén.*, 5 (1928), 231–238.
Union et conversions, *Irén.*, 5 (1928), 481–492.

1929

Restauration liturgique à Rome, *RCIF*, 9, No. 5 (26 avril), 2–4.
La "centralisation romaine," *Irén.*, 6 (1929), 145–153.
La Liturgie et la séparation des Eglises, *Irén.*, 6 (1929), 321–331.
La vie monastique dans le désert de Judée, *Irén.*, 6 (1929), 633–642.

1930

L'Eglise anglicane unie non absorbée. *The Conversations at Malines*, ed. Lord Halifax. Londres: Phillip Allan, 241–261.
L'Union des Eglises, *Irén.*, 7 (1930), 10–13.
Notre travail pour l'union, *Irén.*, 7 (1930), 385–401.
Liturgie et catéchisme en Orient et en Occident, *Irén.*, 7 (1930), 649–658.
Recension de *Topic of the Month, Malines once more: Dom Beauduin's ballon d'essai*, *Irén.*, 7 (1930), 471–473.
Utilitas Scientiae de antiqua ecclesiae disciplina. Acta Conventus Pragensis pro studiis orientalibus anno 1929 celebrati. Olomuc, 1930, 96–102.

1931

La Liturgie et les conciles d'Ephèse et de Chalcédoine, *QLP*, 16 (1931), 190–198.

Notre piété pendant l'Avent. Collection, "La Liturgie catholique," Louvain: Mont César.

1932

La sainte Quarantaine, *RCIF*, 11 No. 46 (5 fevrier), 4–6.
Notes sur l'ascèse, *RCIF*, 11 No. 51 (11 mars), 1–4.
Les Fêtes de Pâques, *RCIF*, 12, No. 1 (25 mars), 3–5.

1934

La Vie Catholique- Les Conversations de Malines. *La Revue du Siècle*, 13 mai 1934, 84–87 (signed XXX).
La Vie de l'oblate et l'Apostolat. *BMOS*, novembre 1934, 57–64.

1935

La Septuagésime. *BNDSE*, Jan. 1935, 4–7.
La Vie de l'Eglise. *BMOS*, janvier-fevrier 1935, 144–154.
Etude de la théologie. *BMOS*, mai 1935, 367–370.
Notes Liturgiques de voyage. *BNDSE* 59, novembre-décembre 1935, 89–92.
Vers Pâques. *BNDSE* March 1935, 17–21.
Temps de la Pentecôte. *BNDSE* May 1935, 33–36.
La Messe dialoguée. *BNDSE* Sept.-Oct. 1935, 68–71.

1936

Messe dialoguée. *BMOS*, mai 1936, 288–291 (reprinted from *BNDSE* 1935).
Notes liturgiques de voyage. *BNDSE* 59, janvier-fevrier 1936, 107–110; mai-juin 1936, 137–140; juillet-août 1936, 153–156; novembre-décembre 1936, 186–189.
Diurnal latin-francais. *BNDSE* March 1936, 121–125.

1937

L'Union des Eglises. *CSFR*, septembre 1937, 348–360.
L'Union des Eglises. *CSFR*, octobre 1937, 10–14 (signed XXX).
Une mise au point. *CSFR* octobre 1937, 15–16.
Prière pour l'Unité. *CSFR* décembre 1937, 78–83.

1938

La Liturgie commune. *CSFR* janvier 1938, 115–123.
Vita liturgica. Rio de Janeiro: Mosteiro de S. Bento.

Ste. Françoise Romaine et le concile de Florence. *CSFR* avril 1938, 213–217.

1939
Dom Vonier. *CSFR* March 1939, 193–195.

1940
L'Année 1939 et l'union des Eglises. *CSFR* Feb.-Mar. 1940, 124–126 (signed D. Sidé but by Beauduin).

1941
Les Pères de l'Eglise. Collection, "Pages catholiques," Paris: Albin Michel.

1944
La Liturgie, source de vie spirituelle. *VS*, 71 (1944), octobre, 333–351.

1945
Normes pratiques pour les reformes liturgiques, *MD*, No. 1, 9–22.
La Messe chantée, sommet de la vie paroissiale, *MD*, No. 4, 104–123.
La Prière de l'Eglise. *VS, juillet,* 41–47.

1946
Constitution Apostolique sur le rôle des évêques co-consécrateurs, *MD*, No. 5, 107–110.
La Septuagésime. *SE*, No. 13, mars 1946, 8–11. (reprinted from *BNDSE* 1935).
Vers Pâques. *SE*, avril 1946, 76–80. (reprinted from *BNDSE* 1935).
Baptême et Eucharistie, *MD*, No. 6, 56–75.
La Concélébration, *MD*, No. 7, 7–26.
Sur le sens des mots "présence sacramentelle," *QLP*, 27 (1946), 150–154.
Les directives de l'Eglise- Le Commun des Souverain Pontifes, *MD*, No. 5, 110–113.

1947
Le Sacrement de confirmation, *MD*, No. 9, 96–100.
La Messe, sacrifice de louange, Dans *La Messe et sa catéchèse*. Paris: Collection Lex Orandi, 138–153.

1948
L'Encyclique *Mediator Dei*, *MD*, No. 13, 7–25.
Le Viatique, *MD*, No. 15, 117–129.

La Liturgie: définition, hiérarchie, tradition, *QLP*, 29 (1948), 123–144.
L'Unité de l'Eglise et le concile du Vatican. *Eglise et Unité*. Lille: Collection, "Catholicité," 11–56.
Alleluia. Collection, "Bible et Missel," Paris: Ed. du Cerf.
Dom Marmion et la Liturgie, *VS*, 78 (1948), 33–45.

1949

La Communion en dehors de la messe, *MD*, No. 17, 127–129.
Les Messes "en noir," *MD*, No. 17, 129–130.

1950

Jubilé du monastère de l'Union, *Irén.*, 23 (1950), 369–376.
Des Saints dans la liturgie, *MD*, No. 21, 71–81.
Preface to E. Froidure, *La perle du bagne: Suzanne Van Durme*. Brussels, 1950.

1951

Jubilé du monastère de l'union (suite), *Irén.*, 24 (1951), 28–36.
A propos de la définition de l'Assomption, *Irén.*, 24 (1951), 390–398.
Autour de la Lettre *Patriotisme et Endurance*. *Revue Cardinal Mercier*, avril, 33–44.
La Nouvelle Messe pour la fête de l'Assomption, *MD*, No. 25, 140–144.
Le Cierge pascal, *MD*, No. 26, 23–27.
Le Décret du 9 février 1951 et les espoirs qu'il suscite, *MD*, No. 26, 110–111.
Ciel et Resurrection. Dans *Le Mystère de la mort et sa célébration*. Paris: Collection Lex Orandi, 253–272.

1952

Le Schisme de Photius, *MD*, No. 29, 151–152.
Preface to R. Aubert, *Problèmes de l'unité chrétienne, initiation*. Chevetogne-Paris, 1952.

1953

Le Triomphe par la Croix. *Le Messager des Oblats*, No. 130, 6–13.
Le Cardinal Mercier et ses suffragants en 1914. *RGB* Juillet.
Pie X et le renouveau liturgique. *Actas del XXXV Congresso Eucharistico Internacional*, Barcelona, 1952. Sesiones de Estudio, Vol. 1, 760–763.

1954

Thirty Years After. *Pax*, No. 269, 21–26.
Mélanges liturgiques. Louvain: Mont César.

1956

Pour la restauration de la semaine sainte, *MD*, No. 45, 5–8.

1959

Message (à l'occasion du cinquantenaire du mouvement liturgique), *QLP*, 40 (1959), 200–201.
La Vraie prière de l'Eglise. Rapport au congrès de Malines de 1909, *QLP*, 40 (1959), 218–221.

1969

Letters to Paul Halflants, May 7 and June 28, 1893. *ETL*, vol 4, no. 3 (1969), 456–466.
Vue prophétique de Dom Lambert Beauduin sur la situation actuelle de l'Eglise, *Irén.*, 42 (1969), 390–395.

UNPUBLISHED MATERIALS: LETTERS

Letters to Roger Debar, monk of Ligugé
    written at Chatou, 12/21/42
    written at Chatou, 4/7/43
Letter to Pierre Dumont
    written at En Calcat, 11/21/33
Letter to Charles Dumont
    written at Chatou, 1/3/45
Letter to Chanoine Gillet
    written at En Calcat, 8/8/32
Letters to Idesbald Van Houtryve
    written at Mont César, undated
    written at Rome, 12/18/22
    written at Rome, 5/2/23
    written at En Calcat, 4/2?/32
Letters to Jean Jadot
    written at Pepinster, 10/27/30
    written at Amay, 11/10/30
    written at Rome, 4/21/31
    written at Rome, 5/3/31
    written at Mont César, 9/4/31
    written at Strasbourg, 9/26/31
    written at Brussels, 2/11/32
    written at Strasbourg, 5/28/32
    written at En Calcat, 7/9/32
    written at En Calcat, 1/23/33
    written at En Calcat, 6/2/33

written at En Calcat, 12/14/33
written at Cormeilles-en-Parisis, 12/3/34
Letters to Paul Leyniers
written at Amay, 5/31/30
written at Strasbourg, 7/3/32
written at En Calcat, 2/6/33
written at Chatou, 4/21/42
Letter to Cardinal Mercier
written at Mont César, 7/6/09
Letters to Bruno Reynders
written at Amay, 6/4/26
written at Constantinople, 2/3/30
written, 7/17/31
Letters to Msgr. Charles Moeller
written at Chalivoy, 4/1/39
written at Chatou, 5/12/47
written at Telertat, 8/23/47
written at Chatou, 5/4/48
written at Chatou, 11/2/49
written at Chatou, 3/9/51
written at Chatou, 3/22/51
written at Chatou, 4/9/51
written at Chatou, 4/20/51
written at Chevetogne, 7/3/51
written at Chevetogne, 3/18/53
written at Chevetogne, 3/30/53
written at Chevetogne, 6/21/54
Letters to Olivier Rousseau
written at Mont César, 8/16/22
written at Mont César, 9/29/23
written at Rome, 12/7/23
written at Rome, 2/13/24
written at Rome, 2/14/24
written at Rome, 3/16/24
written at Rome, 4/25/24
written at Rome, 5/25/24
written at Rome, 5/29/24
written at Rome, 12/31/24
written at Rome, 5/12/25
written at Rome, 6/13/25
written at Belgium, 8/20/25
written at Amay, 10/ /26
written at Amay, 1/7/27
written at Amay, 8/19/27
written at Amay, 9/ /27
written at Amay, 8/21/28

written at Rome, 2/1/29
written at Amay, Easter, 1930
written at Amay, 8/14/31
written at Strasbourg, 1/16/32
written at Chatou, 2/9/43
Letter to Gommaire Laporta
  written at Amay, 10/4/25
Letter of Edouard Beauduin to Olivier Rousseau, citing Lambert Beauduin
  written at Rome, 12/21/29

UNPUBLISHED NOTES

"Projet d'érection d'un institut monastique en vue de l'apostolat de l'Union des Eglises" written in 1924, sent to Mercier who forwarded it to Pius XI.
"Suppression d'*Irénkon*," February, 1928.
"L'Union des Eglises—Fondation d'Amay. Apostolat unioniste" written at En Calcat in 1932.
"Cahier Brun"—a collection of notes for three different retreats, the first, undated, the second, 1941, and the third, July 6, 1942.
"Note sur Amay" dated September 1942.
Notes on Diocesan spirituality, dated 1945.
"Projet d'érection" Paris, circa 1945.
"Note sur les circonstances historiques d'Amay" sent to Nicolas Egender 1950.
"Rough draft of a letter to Bishop Charue" circa 1957.
"Trois griefs contre l'Eglise" rough draft 1959.

NOTES TAKEN DURING RETREATS,
CONVERSATIONS, AND COURSES GIVEN BY BEAUDUIN

Retreat of September 12–19, 1920, notes taken by M. Cappuyns.
Retreat at Cormeilles, 1940; Archives of Olivétans at Bec—notes by Mère Pascal.
Retreat at Cormeilles, December, 1943: Archives of Olivétans at Bec—notes by Mère Pascal.
Retreat at Vanves, 1946; Archives of Vanves F-6.
De Ecclesiae, notes taken during class lectures, 1911–1912, by Dom Duesberg.
Conversation, Brussels, 2/9/32, notes taken by Jean Jadot.
Conversation, 2/21/40, as recounted by Clement Lialine in a letter to Rousseau.
Conversation, July 20–24, 1958, at Chalivoy.
Conversation, c. 1959, notes taken by Rousseau.

SECONDARY SOURCES
BOOKS

Beauduin, Edouard. *La Vie du Cardinal Mercier.* Tournai: Casterman, 1966.
Becquet, Thomas. *L'Union des Eglises, Le Mouvement Actuel.* Liège: Saint Jean, undated.

Les Bénédictins d'Amay à Chevetogne. Gembloux: J. Duculot, 1939.

Bouyer, Louis. *Dom Lambert Beauduin, un homme d'Eglise.* Tournai: Casterman, 1964.

————. *Liturgical Piety.* Notre Dame: University of Notre Dame Press, 1954.

————. *The Liturgy Revived.* Indiana: University of Notre Dame Press, 1964.

Congar, Yves. *Chrétiens en Dialogue.* (Unam Sanctam 50). Paris: Editions du Cerf, 1964.

Gratieux, Albert. *L'Amitié au Service de l'Union.* Paris: Bonne Presse, 1950.

Halifax, Charles. *Reunion and the Roman Primacy, An Appeal to the Members of the English Church Union.* London: A. R. Mowbray Ltd. and Co., 1925.

————. *The Conversations at Malines.* London: Philip Allan, 1930.

Halifax et al. *Conversations at Malines.* London: Oxford University Press, 1927.

Haquin, André. "Histoire du renouveau liturgique belge (1882–1914)." Unpublished Ph.D. dissertation, University of Louvain, 1966.

————. *Dom Lambert Beauduin et le renouveau liturgique au tournant du XX*e *siècle.* Paris: Editions J. Duculot, 1969.

In Memoriam Dom Lambert Beauduin. Chevetogne, 1960.

Koenker, Ernest. *Liturgical Renaissance in the Roman Catholic Church.* St. Louis: Concordia Publishing House, 1954.

Korpusinski, Tadeusz, "L'importance pastorale de la liturgie d'après Dom Lambert Beauduin." Unpublished thesis. Louvain, 1971.

Lambeth Conference 1930. London: 1930.

Le Monastère de Chevetogne. 2d. ed. Chevetogne, 1960.

Marx, Paul. "*The Life and Work of Virgil Michel.*" Unpublished Ph.D. dissertation, The Catholic University of America, 1953.

Oldmeadow, Ernest James. *Francis Cardinal Bourne.* 2 vols. London: Burns, Oates & Co., 1940–1944.

ARTICLES

Aubert, Roger. "L'ecclésiologie au concile du Vatican," in *Le Concile et Les Conciles.* Chevetogne: Editions du Chevetogne, 1960, 245–284.

————. "Un homme d'Eglise, Dom Lambert Beauduin," *La Revue Nouvelle* Vol. 31, no. 3, (1960), 225–249.

Becquet, Thomas. "La figure et l'oeuvre de Dom Lambert Beauduin," *RGB*, (avril, 1960), 1–9. Reprinted as an extract by Ad. Goemaere Editeur, Imprimeur du Roi, Bruxelles.

————. "Jean XXIII et l'Oecumenisme," *Foi Vivante*, No. 9 (1961), 177–181.

Bugnini, Annibale. "L'odierno movimento liturgico," *Illustrazione Vaticana* (1948), 86.

Buysse, Paul. "Hommage à Dom Lambert Beauduin," *QLP*, XL (1959), 225–242.

Cappuyns, Maieul. "Dom Lambert Beauduin (1873–1960). Quelques documents et souvenirs," *RHE* LXI (1966), 424–454, 761–806.

———. "Liturgie et Théologie," *QLP*, XL (1959), 249–272.

Coppens, J. "Quelques lettres de Dom Lambert Beauduin, étudiant en philosophie au petit séminaire de St. Trond," *ETL* (1969), 456–466.

Delforge, Thomas. "L'influence de Dom Marmion," *Lumière du Christ*, No. 159 (1960), 66–67.

Eldarov, Giorgio. "Chevetogne Polo Ecumenico," *Città di Vita*, XX (1965), 95–102.

Harscouet, Raoul. "Le mouvement liturgique et la spiritualité," *QLP*, XL (1959), 213–221.

Martimort, Aimé. "Dom L. Beauduin et le Centre de Pastorale Liturgique," *QLP*, XL (1959), 243–252.

———. "Le renouveau liturgique et l'unité chrétienne," *Eleona*, No. 42 (1962), 7–21.

Moeller, Charles. "Un homme d'Eglise," *La Libre Belgique* (15 juillet 1965), 8.

Pinsk, Johannes. "Quelques fruits du mouvement liturgique," *QLP*, XL (1959), 243–248.

Quitslund, Sonya. "Les idées fondamentales de l'ecclésiologie de dom Lambert Beauduin," *NRT*, 91 (1969), 1073–1096.

———. " 'United not Absorbed': Does it Still Make Sense?" *JES* vol. 8, no. 2 (1971), 255–285.

Roguet, A. M. "Notre Père Dom Lambert Beauduin," *MD* LXII (1960), 7–9.

Rousseau, Olivier. "Après dix ans: le semaine unioniste de Bruxelles en 1925," *Irén*, XII (1935), 599–611.

———. "Autour du jubilé du mouvement liturgique 1909–1959," *QLP*, XL (1959), 202–217.

———. "La Constitution 'Lumen Gentium' dans le cadre des mouvements renovateurs de theologie et de pastorale des dernières décades," in *L'Eglise de Vatican II*. Paris: Editions du cerf, 1966, 35–56.

———. "Dom Lambert Beauduin, apôtre de la liturgie et de l'Unité chrétienne," *MD*, XL (1955), 128–132.

———. "Dom Lambert Beauduin et la vie monastique (1873–1960)," *Revue Mabillon*, L (1961), 265–278.

———. "Un homme d'Eglise, Dom L. Beauduin initiateur monastique," *VS*, CIV (1961), 45–64.

———. "In Memoriam: Don Clément Lialine (1901–1958)," *Irén*, XXXI (1958), 165–182.

———. "In Memoriam: Dom Lambert Beauduin (1873–1960)," *Irén*, 1 (1960), reprinted in *Dom Lambert Beauduin in Memoriam*, p. 50.

———. "Un pionnier de l'unité chrétienne: Dom Lambert Beauduin," *La Croix*, (janvier 1960), 5.

———. "Pioneri dell'apostolato unionistico: Dom Lambert Beauduin," *Oriente Christiano*, (1965), 77–79.

———. "Le Monastère de Chevetogne," *Unitas* (French edition 1968, 152–153.

————. "Le Prochain Concile et l'unité de l'Eglise," *Irén*, XXXII (1959), 309–333.

————. "La Revalorisation du Dimanche dan l'Eglise Catholique depuis 50 ans," *Estratto da miscellanea Liturgica onore di sua Eminenza il Cardinale Giacomo Lercaro.* Desclée: Editori Pontifici, 1966, p. 525f.

————. "La Vraie Valeur de l'Episcopat dans l'Eglise," *Irén*, XXIX (1956), 121–142.

Suenens, Leon Joseph. "Toward Unity and Freedom in the Church," *National Catholic Reporter*, May 28, 1969, 7.

Tardini, Domenico. "Hommage à Dom Lambert Beauduin," *Irén*, XXXII (1959), 367–368.

Tissérant, Eugène. "Une lettre de Son Eminence le Cardinal Tissérant à Dom Lambert Beauduin," *Irén*, XXX (1957), 448–449.

"United Not Absorbed," *The Tablet*, January 31, 1970, p. 98.

Vandenbroucke, François. "Dom Lambert Beauduin," *Lumière du Christ*, No. 158 (1960), 31–36.

————. "Un Portrait de Dom Lambert Beauduin," *QLP*, LV (1964), 201–205.

Villain, M. "Un pionnier de l'Unité Chrétienne," *L'Union* (May, 1960), 12.

Wagner, Johannes. "La Reforme de la liturgie de Pie X à la vielle du concile," *QLP*, XLV (1964), 41–54.

Woodlock, F. "The Malines Conversations Report," *The Month* 155 (1930), 238–246.

————. "Topics of the Month: Malines once more; Dom Beauduin's *ballon d'essai*," *The Month*, 155 (1930), 267–279.

GENERAL WORKS
BOOKS

Abbott, Walter, ed. *The Documents of Vatican II.* New York: America Press, 1966.

Acta Apostolicae Sedis. Rome: Typis Polyglottis Vaticanis.

A la Memoire de l'Abbé Paul Couturier 1881–1953. Lyon: Vitté, 1954.

Aubert, Roger. *La Théologie catholique au milieu de XXe siècle.* (Cahiers de l'actualité religieuse). Tournai: Casterman, 1954.

————. *Le Saint Siège et l'Union des Eglises.* Bruxelles: Editions Universitaires, 1947.

Au Service de la Parole de Dieu, Mélanges offerts à Monseigneur André-Marie Charue évêque de Namur. Gembloux: Editions J. Duculot, 1968.

Battifol, P. *Catholicisme et Papauté.* Paris: 1925.

Beyer, Jean Baptiste. *Les Institute séculiers.* Bruges: Desclée de Brouwer, 1954.

Billot, Louis. *De Verbo incarnato.* Rome: S. C. de Propagande Fide, 1900.

Billuart, Charles. *Summa Sancti Thomae.* Paris: Le Coffre, 1874–1886.

Birkenhead, Earl of. *The Life of Lord Halifax.* London, 1964.

Borschak, Elie. *Un Prélat Ukrainien le Métroplite Cheptickyj (1865–1944).* Paris: Editions franco-Ukrainiennes, 1946.

Bouix, Dominique. *De Episcopo.* Paris: J. Lecoffre et socios, 1859.

Busch, William. *The Mass Drama.* 2d. ed. Collegeville, Minn.: Liturgical Press, 1933.

Callahan, Daniel. *The Mind of the Catholic Layman.* New York: Scribner's Sons, 1963.

Caprile, G. *Il concilio Vaticano II.* Rome: La civiltà cattolica, 1969.

Cardolle, Canon J. *Un Précurseur, un docteur, un pionnier social-Monseigneur Pottier (1849-1923).* Bruxelles: Edition du mouvement ouvrier chrétien, 1951.

Cardwell, Ann. *Poland and Russia: The Last Quarter Century.* New York: Sheed and Ward, 1944.

Clérissac, Humbert. *Le Mystère de l'Eglise.* 5th ed. Paris: Editions du Cerf, 1917.

Congar, Yves. *After Nine Hundred Years.* Translated by Fordham University Staff. New York: Fordham University Press, 1959.

————. *Lay People in the Church.* Translated by Attwater. Westminster: Newman Press, 1956.

Craisson, D. *Manuale totius juris canonici.* Paris: V. Palmé, 1863.

Curtis, Geoffrey. *Paul Couturier and the Unity in Christ.* Westminster: J. William Eckenrode, 1964.

De Bivort de la Saudée, Jacques. *Anglicans et catholiques. Le problème de l'Union Anglo-romaine, 1833-1933.* Paris-Bruxelles: Librairie Plon, 1949.

Dechamps, Victor. *Oeuvres complètes de Son Eminence le Cardinal Dechamps.* 12 vols. Malines: H. Dessain (no Date).

De Lubac, Henri. *Catholicisme.* Paris. Editions Du Cerf, 1938.

De la Taille, Maurice. *Mysterium Fidei.* Paris: Beauchesne, 1931.

De Moreau, H. *Dom Hildebrand de Hemptinne.* Maredsous: Editions de Maredsous, 1930.

De Régnon, Théodore. *Etudes de théologie positive sur la Sainte Trinité.* 4 vols. Paris: Victor Retaux et Fils, Editeurs, 1892-1898.

De T'Serclaes, Charles. *Le Pape Léon XIII.* 3 vols. Paris: Desclée, 1894.

D'Herbigny, Michel. *Les "Sans Dieu" militants et la propagande mondiale du communisme.* Paris: Fédération nationale catholique, 193-.

————. *L'âme religieuse des Russes d'après leurs plus récentes publications* (1925).

————. *La Tyrannie soviétique et le malheur russe* (1923).

————. *Theologica de ecclesia.* Paris: Beauchesne, 1920-1921.

————. *Un Newman russe, Vladimir Soloviev.* Paris, 1911.

Duchesne, Louis. *The Churches Separated from Rome.* Translated by Arnold Matthew. London: K. Paul, Tranch, Trubner & Co., Ltd., 1907.

Dvornik, François. *Byzance et la Primauté Romaine.* (Unam Sanctam 49) Paris: Editions du Cerf, 1964.

Engelmann, Ursmar. *Beuron.* Munich-Zurich: K. Zink, 1957.

Frere, W. H. *Recollections of Malines.* London: Centenary Press, 1935.

Gennari, Casimiro. *Questioni Canoniche.* 2d. ed. Rome: P. Veratti, 1908.

Gorce, Denys. *Le Laïc Théologien.* Paris: A. Picard, 1934.

Gréa, Adrien-Etienne. *L'Eglise et sa divine Constitution.* Paris: Société Générale de Librairie catholique, 1885.

Guéranger, Prosper. *Année liturgique.* 7 vols. Paris: Henri Oudin, 1878–1901.

——. *Essai historique sur l'Abbaye de Solesmes.* Le Mans: Fleuriot, 1846.

Guerry, Emile. *L'Evêque.* (Bible. Ecclesia, 5). Paris: A. Fayard, 1954.

Halecki, Oscar. *From Florence to Brest 1439–1596.* Printed as manuscript in connection with Vol. 5 *Sacrum Poloniae Millenium.* Rome: Via delle Bottegne Oscure 15, 1958. Stamped inside: Fordham University Press.

——. *Poland and Christendom.* Houston: University of St. Thomas, 1964.

Harscouet, Raoul. *Horizons Liturgiques.* Tournai: Casterman, 1942.

Hemmer, Hippolyte, et al. *Monsieur Portal, Prêtre de la mission 1855–1926.* Paris, 1947.

Hilpisch, Stephanus. *Benedictinism in the Changing Centuries.* Collegeville, Minn.: Liturgical Press, 1958.

Hughes, J. J. *Absolutely Null and Utterly Void.* Washington: Corpus Books, 1968.

Jaki, Stanislas. *Les tendances nouvelles de l'ecclésiologie.* Rome: Herder, 1957.

Jugie, Martin. *Le Schisme byzantin. Aperçu historique et doctrinal.* Paris: P. Lethiellaux, 1941.

Jungmann, Josef. *Pastoral Liturgy.* Translated by Challoner Publications, Ltd. London: George Berridge & Co., Ltd., 1962.

Kennan, George. *Russia and the West under Lenin and Stalin.* Boston: Little, Brown & Co., 1961.

——. *Russia Leaves the War.* (*Soviet-American Relations, 1917–1920*). Princeton: Princeton University Press, 1956.

Knowles, David. *Christian Monasticism.* New York: McGraw-Hill Book Co., 1969.

Korolevsky, Cyril. *Histoire des patriarcats melkites depuis le schisme monophysite du 6ème siècle, jusqu'à nos jours.* 2 vols. Paris: Picard, 1911.

——. *Le Métropolite André Szepticky.* Grotta Ferrata: "S. Nilo," 1920.

——. *L'Uniatisme.* (*Irénikon* collection, Nos. 5–6). Gembloux, 1927.

Kostuik, Hryhory. *Stalinist Rule in the Ukraine. A Study of the Decade of Mass Terror 1929–1939.* New York: Frederick A. Praeger, Pub., 1960.

Küng, Hans. *Structures of the Church.* New York: Nelson, 1963.

Kurth, Godefroid. *Les Origines de la civilisation moderne.* 6th ed. Paris: P. Tegui, 1912.

——. *The Church at the Turning Points of History.* Translated by V. Day. Helena: Naegele Printing Co., 1918.

Lamiroy, Henri. "De Essentia Sanctissimi Missae Sacrificii." Unpublished Ph.D. dissertation, University of Louvain, 1919.

Laurentin, René. *Marie, L'Eglise et le Sacerdoce.* Paris: Nouvelles Editions latines, 1953.

Leclercq, Henri. *Histoire des conciles d'après les documents originaux.* 9 vols. Paris: LeTouzey, 1907f.

L'Eglise et les Eglises 1054–1954. 2 vols. Chevetogne: Editions de Chevetogne, 1954.

Leib, Bernard. *Rome, Kiev et Byzance à la fin du XIe siècle.* Paris: Auguste Picard, 1924.

Le Monastère St. Pierre de Solesmes. Solesmes: Editions de Solesmes, 1955.

Le Mont César 1899–1949. Louvain: Editions de l'Abbaye du Mont César, 1949.

Lockhart, John Gilbert. *Charles Lindley Viscount Halifax.* 2 vols. London: 1961.

Macmillan, Arthur. *Fernand Portal 1855–1926, Apostle of unity.* London: 1961.

Manning, Clarence. *Ukraine under the Soviets.* New York: Bookman Associates, 1953.

Mansi, Giovanni. *Sacrorum conciliorum nova et amplissima collectio.* 31 vols. Florence and Venice: 1757–1798, new printing and continuation published by L. Petit & J. B. Martin in 60 vols., Paris, 1899–1927.

Marmion, Columba. *Christ in His Mysteries.* Translated by a nun of Tyburn Convent. St. Louis: B. Herder Book Co., 1923.

———. *Christ the Ideal of the Monk.* Translated by a nun of Tyburn Convent. 8th ed. St. Louis: B. Herder Book Co., 1934.

———. *Le Christ vie de l'âme.* Maredsous: Editions de Maredsous, 1949.

Martimort, Aimé. *De l'évêque.* (La Clarté-Dieu, 19). Paris: Editions du Cerf, 1946.

Mayer, Heinrich. *Benediktinisches Ordensrecht in der Beuroner Kongregation.* 4 vols. Beuron: 1929–1936.

Mercier, Désiré. *Oeuvres Pastorales.* 3 vols. Brussels—Paris, 1913.

———. *Oeuvres Pastorales.* vol. 7 (1929).

Mersch, Emile. *The Theology of the Mystical Body.* St. Louis: B. Herder Book Co., 1952.

Meyendorff, Jean. *Orthodoxy and Catholicity.* New York: Sheed & Ward, 1966.

———. *The Orthodox Church.* Translated by J. Chapin. London: Darton, Longman & Todd, 1962.

O'Brien, Elmer. (ed.) *Convergence of Traditions—Orthodox, Catholic and Protestant.* New York: Herder & Herder, 1967.

Petavius, Dionysius. *Dogmata Theologica.* Paris: 1644.

Petri, Barbara. "The Ukrainian Situation at the End of World War I." Unpublished Master's thesis, The Catholic University of America, 1955.

Pire, A. F. *Histoire de la congrégation des Aumôniers du Travail.* Charleroi, 1942.

———. *Retraites Mensuelles à l'Usage des Aumôniers du Travail.* Anvers: St. Norbert, 1937.

Pitra, Jean Baptiste. *Analecta Novissima.* Paris: Roger et Chernowitz, 1885–1888.

———. *Analecta sacra Spicilegio Solesmensi parata.* Paris: Jouby et Roger, 1876–1884.

———. *Spicilegium Solesmense.* Paris: Didot fratres, 1852–1858.

Prat, Ferdinand. *The Theology of St. Paul.* 2 vols. Westminster: Newman Press, 1946.

Ramsey, A. M. *The Gospel of the Catholic Church.* London: Longman & Green, 1956.

Religion in the USSR. Edited by Boris Iwanow. Translated by James Larkin. Munich: Carl Gerber Grafische Betriebe KG, 1960.

Rome and the Study of Scripture. 7th ed. St. Meinrad: Grail Publications, 1962.

Rousseau, Olivier. *The Progress of the Liturgy.* Translated by the Benedictines of Westminster Priory. Westminster: Newman Press, 1951.

Scheeben, Matthias. *The Mysteries of Christianity.* St. Louis: B. Herder Book Co., 1946.

Schmemann, Alexander. *The Historical Road to Eastern Orthodoxy.* Translated by Lydia Kesich. New York: Holt, Reinhart and Winston, 1963.

Sherwood, Polycarp, ed. *Unity of the Churches of God.* Baltimore: Helicon Press, 1963.

The Sovietization of Culture in Poland. Newtown, England: The Montgomeryshire Printing Co., Ltd., 1953.

Suarez, Francisco. *Opera Omnia,* Paris: Vives, 1886.

Swidler, Leonard J. *The Ecumenical Vanguard.* Pittsburgh: Duquesne University Press, 1966.

Tavard, G. H. *Two Centuries of Ecumenism—the Search for Unity.* New York: New American Library, 1962.

Van de Pol, W. H. *Anglicanism in Ecumenical Perspective.* Pittsburgh, 1965.

Von Hefele, Karl. *Conciliengeschichte.* 9 vols. (8 and 9 by Hergenrother). Freiburg i. Br.: 1855 ff. 1873 ff. Revised by H. Leclerq 1907.

Wolf, D. J. and Schall, J. V. (eds.) *Current Trends in Theology.* Garden City: Doubleday, 1965.

Zernov, Nicholas. *The Russians and Their Church.* London: SPCK, 1964.

———. *The Russian Religious Renaissance of the Twentieth Century.* New York: Harper and Row, 1963.

ARTICLES

Attwater, Donald. "Andrew Szepticky," *Blackfriars,* XXIX (1948), 53–59.

Aubert, Roger. "L'histoire des Conversations de Malines," *Col M,* LII (1967), 43–54.

———. "Les conversations de Malines Le Cardinal Mercier et le Saint Siège," *Bulletin de la Classe des Lettres et des Sciences Morales et Politiques.* 5th series, vol. 53 (1967), 87–159.

———. "Quelques mots sur l'Eglise Anglicane," *Col M,* LII (1967), 3–6.

Beyda, Francis. "Szepticky Museum," *ECQ,* IX (1952), 401–408.

Bouyer, Louis. "Marie, L'Eglise et le Sacerdoce, recension," *Dieu Vivant,* XXVI (1954), 151.

Brown, Geoffrey and Dessain, Joseph. "La célébration du 40ᵉ anniversaire des 'Conversations de Malines,'" *Col M*, LII (1967), 7–12.

Butler, Christopher. "United Not Absorbed," *The Tablet*, March 7, 1970, 220–221.

——. "Bishop Christopher Butler proposes a model for the reunion of the Roman Catholic and Anglican Churches," *The Listener*, April 2, 1970, 441–442.

Callahan, D. "Liturgie en langue vivante'—a review," *TS*, XVI (1955), 625f.

Charue, André, "L'évêque dans l'Eglise," *Revue diocésaine de Namur*, (janvier-février, 1957), 1f.

Congar, Y. "Do the New Problems of Our Secular World Make Ecumenism Irrelevant?" *Concilium*, vol. 4. no. 6 (April 1970), 11–21.

D'Herbigny, Michel. "Seize jours à Moscou, October 4–20, 1925," *Etudes* 185 (1925), 513–540, 658–676.

——. "Pâques 1926 en Russie," *Etudes* 188 (1926), 257–282, 421–447.

——. "L'Eglise vivante de Russie ou le clergé rouge," *Etudes*, 174 (1923), 257–275.

——. "Les préludes de la révolution russe d'après les memoires du Comte Witte," *Etudes* 180 (1924), 5–29.

Korolevsky, Cyril. "Les premiers temps de l'histoire du Collège grec de Rome," *Stoudion*, III (1929), 3–39, 80–84.

——. "Sources de l'histoire du collège grec," *Stoudion*, III (1929), 85–89.

"Cyril Korolevsky," (obituary notice) *ECQ* 13 (1959), 88–89.

Lebon, J. "La Bienheureuse Vièrge Marie, médiatrice de toutes les grâces," *La vie diocésaine de Malines* (1921), 259.

Leo XIII. "Lettre de Léon XIII au Cardinal Dusmet, le 4 janvier 1887," *Stoudion*, I (1924), 103.

Lilienfeld, André. "L'anniversaire," *Irén*, III (1927), 1–3.

Mercenier, F. "Le Métropolite André Szeptycki, *Irén*, 19 (1946), 49–65.

Mercier, D. J. "Les Conversations de Malines," *Oeuvres* Pastorales 7 (1929).

Miller, M. "The Confiscation and Destruction of Church Property in the Ukraine," *Religion in the USSR*, (ed. by B. Iwanow). Munich: Carl Gerber Grafische Betriebe K. G., 1960.

Moeller, Charles. "Le Chalcédonisme et le néo-chalcédonisme," Vol. 1 of *Das Konzil von Chalkedon*. Wurtzburg: Echter Verlag, 1951, 637–720.

——. "Jesus Christ in the Minds of the Moderns," *Lumen Vitae*, VII (1952), 509–527.

Morin, G. "Le Pallium," *Le Messager des Fidèles (Rev. Béné)* (1889), p. 258.

Murray, J. "Living languages in Catholic Worship—a review," *TS*, XIX (1958), 123.

Murray, John C. "Our Response to the Ecumenical Revolution," *Religious Education*, LXII (March-April, 1967), 91–92, 119.

Navatel, J. J. "L'Apostolat liturgique et la Piété personnelle," *Etudes* (Nov. 20, 1913), 449–478.

Ostoya, A. "Poland and the Ukraine," *Catholic World*, CLXXIV (1951), 104–107.

Ostoyan, H. "Pope Pius X and the Metropolitan Szepticky," *ECQ* IX, (1952), 409–412.

Reynders, Bruno. "L'Humanité du Christ notre Chef," *QLP*, XIX (1935), 72–87.

Rousseau, Olivier. "La Question des rites entre Grecs et Latins des premiers siècles au concile de Florence," *Irén*, XXII (1949), 233–269.

———. "Divina autem Providentia . . . Histoire d'une texte conciliare," *Ecclesia a Spiritu Sancto edocta* (*Mélanges G. Philips*) Louvain, 1970, p. 281f.

———. "In Memoriam: Dom Clément Lialine (1901–1958)," *Irén* XXXI (1958), 166–167.

Schmemann, A. "Orthodox Tradition, The Church" *Convergence of Traditions—Orthodox, Catholic and Protestant*. Edited by E. O'Brien, New York: Herder & Herder, 1967.

Szepticky, Andrew. "Eastern and Western Mentality," *ECQ* IX (1952), 393–401, (originally printed in *Pax*, Jan. and April, 1933).

———. "Le rôle des occidentaux dans l'oeuvre de l'union des Églises," *Stoudion*, III (1929), 153–169.

———. "La Restauration du monachisme slave," *Les Questiones Missionaires*, Abbey of St. André.

———. "Monasticisme et L'Union," (conference of Feb. 18, 1921) *Stoudion* (1923) 10–12, 33–40.

Suenens, Léon Joseph. "Address of His Eminence Cardinal Suenens Concluding the Academic Session at the Lecture Hall of the Seminary of Malines," *Col M*, LII (1967), 16–25.

Testis. "The Metropolitan Andrew Sheptitsky," *ECQ*, V (1944), 343–348.

Vancik, Vladimir. "The Death of Metropolitan Sheptitsky," *Catholic Mind*, XLIII (1945), 142–147; (reprinted from *Narod*, Chicago, Dec. 10, 1944).

Van Caloen, Gerard, "La Question Religieuse chez les Grecs," *RB*, VIII (1891), 117–129.

Van Roey, J. E. "L'Episcopat et la Papauté," *Col M*, February, (1929), 141f.

Visser't Hooft, W. H. "Nathan Soederblom, figure de prophète du mouvement Oecuménique," *Oecumenica* 2 (1967), 145.

Willebrands, Jan. "Ecumenical Significance of the Visit of the Archbishop of Canterbury to the Holy Father," *Unitas* 19 (1967), 8–17.

Index

359